GO!
with

the Internet

Volume 1

Shelley Gaskin and Rebecca Lawson

PEARSON

Prentice
Hall

Upper Saddle River, New Jersey

This book is dedicated to my students, who inspire me every day, and to my husband, Fred Gaskin.
—Shelley Gaskin

*This book is dedicated to my children, Rachel and Katy. May
they never forget to keep reaching for their dreams.*
—Rebecca Lawson

Library of Congress Cataloging-in-Publication Data

Gaskin, Shelley.
  Go! with. Internet explorer 7.0 / Shelley Gaskin and Rebecca Lawson.
    p. cm.
  ISBN-13: 978-0-13-230002-5
  ISBN-10: 0-13-230002-8
  1. Microsoft Internet explorer. 2. Browsers (Computer programs) 3. Internet. I. Lawson, Rebecca.
II. Title.
  TK5105.883.M53G393 2007
  005.7'1376--dc22

                                                                                    2007021030

Vice President and Publisher: Natalie E. Anderson
**Associate VP/Executive Acquisitions Editor,
  Print:** Stephanie Wall
Executive Acquisitions Editor, Media: Richard Keaveny
Product Development Manager: Eileen Bien Calabro
Editorial Project Manager: Sarah Parker McCabe
Development Editor: Ginny Munroe
Editorial Assistants: Becky Knauer
Executive Producer: Lisa Strite
Content Development Manager: Cathi Profitko
Media Project Manager: Alana Meyers
Production Media Project Manager: Lorena Cerisano
Director of Marketing: Margaret Waples
Senior Marketing Manager: Jason Sakos
Marketing Assistants: Angela Frey, Kathryn Ferranti
Senior Sales Associate: Rebecca Scott

Managing Editor: Lynda J. Castillo
Production Project Manager:
  Wanda Rockwell
Production Editor: GGS Book Services
Photo Researcher: GGS Book Services
Manufacturing Buyer: Natacha Moore
Production/Editorial Assistant: Sandra K. Bernales
Design Director: Maria Lange
Art Director/Interior Design: Blair Brown
Cover Photo: Courtesy of Getty Images, Inc./Marvin
  Mattelson
Composition: GGS Book Services
Project Management: GGS Book Services
Cover Printer: Phoenix Color
Printer/Binder: RR Donnelley/Willard

Microsoft, Windows, Vista, Word, PowerPoint, Outlook, FrontPage, Visual Basic, MSN, The Microsoft Network, and/or other Microsoft products referenced herein are either trademarks or registered trademarks of Microsoft Corporation in the U.S.A. and other countries. Screen shots and icons reprinted with permission from the Microsoft Corporation. This book is not sponsored or endorsed by or affiliated with Microsoft Corporation.

Credits and acknowledgments borrowed from other sources and reproduced, with permission, in this textbook are as follows or on the appropriate page within the text.

Pages 2, 62, and 206: Getty Images, Inc.; page 3: Pearson Education/PH College; pages 7-13: Jupitermedia Corporations; pages 20 and 22: Librarians' Internet Index; pages 34 and 207: Getty Images, Inc. - Stone Allstock; page 39: AP Wide World Photos; page 63: Dorling Kindersley Media Library; pages 79–89, 91, 92, 97, 99, 101, 103, and 105: Government Information Technology Agency; page 95: National Park Service; page 124: Federal Trade Commission; pages 144 and 338: PhotoEdit, Inc.; pages 145, 273, 276, 283–289, 292, 295–299, 301, 343, 344, and 357–360: Google; pages 149, 171, 211, 213, 215, 217–220, 224, 226–229, 231, 233, 234, 250, 341, 353–356, and 376: Yahoo! Inc.; pages 154 and 156: Microsoft Corporation; page 158: refdesk.com; page 162: LIBWEB; page 164: The Library of Congress; page 167: The WWW Virtual Library; page 175: Bright Planet Corporation; page 177: HighBeam; page 182: Visisimo, Inc.; page 184: Gigablast Inc.; page 272: Omni-Photo Communications, Inc.; pages 278 and 279: Technorati; page 303: Davis Wiki; page 306: National Gardening Association; page 339: Earth Observatory, NASA; page 349: National Oceanic and Atmospheric Administration; pages 352 and 354: The Weather Channel; pages 362 and 371: Travelocity; page 372: The New York Times; and page 374: Jagex Ltd.

10 9 8 7 6 5 4 3 2 1
ISBN 10: 0-13-230002-8
ISBN 13: 978-0-13-230002-5

Contents in Brief

Chapter 1   **Introducing the Internet** 1

Chapter 2   **Browsing the World Wide Web** 61

Chapter 3   **Searching the World Wide Web** 143

Chapter 4   **Communication Using E-mail** 205

Chapter 5   **Collaborating on the World Wide Web** 271

Chapter 6   **Locating Resources on the World Wide Web** 337

Glossary G-1

Index I-1

Table of Contents

Internet Explorer 7.0

Chapter 1 Introducing the Internet.........................1

PROJECT 1A Locating a Local ISP   **3**

Objective 1 Consult a Web Site to Locate an ISP that Offers Service in a Specific Area   **4**
Activity 1.1   Searching for ISPs in Your Local Area   4

Objective 2 Refine Searches to Distinguish Among the Features of Each ISP   **9**
Activity 1.2   Refining Your Search Results   9

Objective 3 Compare Information You Find on the Web   **15**
Activity 1.3   Creating a Document that Compares ISPs   15

PROJECT 1B Researching Internet History   **18**

Objective 4 Browse a Directory for Information   **18**
Activity 1.4   Searching for Internet History at the Librarians' Internet Index   18

Objective 5 Describe Events and Technologies that Affected the Development of the Internet   **23**
Activity 1.5   Creating a Timeline of Historical Events Affecting the Internet   23

PROJECT 1C Connecting to the Internet   **25**

Objective 6 Define Common Internet Terms   **25**

Objective 7 Analyze URLs, DNS, and Server Structure   **27**

Objective 8 Identify Hardware and Software Needed for Internet Connections   **32**

Objective 9 Explain Internet Connection Methods   **33**

Objective 10 Describe Wireless Connection Options   **34**

PROJECT 1D Exploring Internet History   **36**

Objective 11 Summarize the Early History of the Internet   **36**

Objective 12 Name Early Key Developers of the Internet   **37**

Objective 13 Describe the Unique Features of Hypertext   **38**

Objective 14 Describe Popular Uses of the Internet Today   **40**
Summary   44
Key Terms   44
Matching   46
Fill in the Blank   47
Rubric   48
Mastering the Internet   49
GO! Search   59

Chapter 2 Browsing the World Wide Web ...61

PROJECT 2A Browsing the World Wide Web   **63**

Objective 1 Perform Commands with Internet Explorer   **64**
Activity 2.1   Exploring the Menu Bar   64
Activity 2.2   Showing and Hiding Toolbars   68
Activity 2.3   Customizing Text Size   69
Activity 2.4   Locating Favorites and Tools on the Menu Bar   71

Objective 2 Perform Commands with the Toolbar   **74**
Activity 2.5   Exploring the Toolbar   74
Activity 2.6   Using Tabs in Your Browser Window   79

Objective 3 Specify a Default Home Page   **83**
Activity 2.7   Specifying a Default Home Page   83

Objective 4 Browse the World Wide Web Using Links, the Address Bar, History, and Favorites Center   **86**
Activity 2.8   Browsing the World Wide Web Using Links   86
Activity 2.9   Browsing the World Wide Web Using the Address Bar   87
Activity 2.10   Browsing the World Wide Web Using the History Feature   88
Activity 2.11   Browsing the World Wide Web with the Favorites Center   90

PROJECT 2B Managing Web Content with Internet Explorer   **94**

Objective 5 Print, Save, and E-mail a Web Page   **94**
Activity 2.12   Printing Text and Graphics Found on Web Pages   94

Activity 2.13 Saving Web Pages and Graphics 96
Activity 2.14 E-mailing Web Pages and Links
to Web Pages 98

**Objective 6 Create a Desktop Shortcut to
a Web Page 100**
Activity 2.15 Creating a Desktop Shortcut 100

**Objective 7 Clear the Cache, Cookies, and
History 101**
Activity 2.16 Clearing the Cache and Cookies 102
Activity 2.17 Managing the History 104

PROJECT 2C Identifying How Browsers Work 107

Objective 8 Describe How Plug-ins Work 107

**Objective 9 Identify and Compare Several
Popular Web Browsers 108**

**PROJECT 2D Examining Privacy Risks and
Security Issues of Browsing 116**

**Objective 10 Determine the Risks of
Using the World Wide Web 116**

**Objective 11 Identify Safe Browsing
Strategies 121**

Summary 126

Key Terms 126

Matching 128

Fill in the Blank 129

Rubric 131

Mastering the Internet 132

GO! Search 142

Chapter 3 Searching the World Wide Web 143

**PROJECT 3A Implementing Basic Search
Technique 145**

**Objective 1 Formulate a Keyword Query to
Implement a Search 146**
Activity 3.1 Developing Queries for a Search 146
Activity 3.2 Identifying Search Engines and Their
Characteristics 147
Activity 3.3 Creating a Document to Compare
Search Engines 151

Objective 2 Search with the Address Bar 152
Activity 3.4 Searching with the Address Bar 152

**Objective 3 Search with the Instant Search
Feature 155**
Activity 3.5 Searching with the Instant Search
Feature 155

Objective 4 Locate Expert Resources 157
Activity 3.6 Exploring Expert Resources 157
Activity 3.7 Creating a Document to Compare
Expert Resources 160

**Objective 5 Find Online Library Catalogs
and Scholarly Resources 161**
Activity 3.8 Finding Online Library Catalogs
and Other Scholarly Resources 161
Activity 3.9 Creating a Document to Compare
Library Resources 165

PROJECT 3B Performing Advanced Searches 166

Objective 6 Search with Boolean Operators 166
Activity 3.10 Searching with Boolean Operators
and Advanced Search Features 166

**Objective 7 Locate News and Opinion
Resources 169**
Activity 3.11 Finding News at Google 169
Activity 3.12 Searching for News Using
Advanced Search Features 170
Activity 3.13 Searching for Business News
Resources 172
Activity 3.14 Creating a Document to Compare
News and Opinion Resources 173

**Objective 8 Find Invisible Web Resources
and Specialized Databases 173**
Activity 3.15 Locating the Invisible Web and
Specialized Databases 174
Activity 3.16 Creating a Document to Compare
Invisible Web Resources 178

PROJECT 3C Exploring Search Tools 180

**Objective 9 Implement a Search Using a
Directory Search Site 180**

**Objective 10 Implement a Search Using a
Meta-Search Engine 181**

**PROJECT 3D Developing Search Strategy
Guidelines 183**

**Objective 11 Explore How a Search
Engine Works 183**

Objective 12 Evaluate Search Results 185

Summary 189

Key Terms 189

Matching 190

Fill in the Blank 191

Rubric 192

Mastering the Internet 193

GO! Search 203

Chapter 4 Communication Using E-mail 205

PROJECT 4A Signing Up for a Web-Based
E-mail Account **207**

Objective 1 Locate and Set Up a
Web-Based E-mail Account **208**
Activity 4.1 Setting Up a Web-Based E-mail
Account 208

Objective 2 Compose and Send a Basic
E-mail Message **214**
Activity 4.2 Creating a Basic E-mail Message 214
Activity 4.3 Creating a Signature File and
Signing Out of Your Account 218

PROJECT 4B Managing Web-Based E-mail
Programs **222**

Objective 3 Receive and Reply to an E-mail
Message with an Attachment **222**
Activity 4.4 Checking for E-mail and Opening
E-mail with an Attachment 223
Activity 4.5 Using the Reply and Forward
Features 225

Objective 4 Print an E-mail Message **228**
Activity 4.6 Printing an E-mail Message 228

Objective 5 Create Folders and Filters **230**
Activity 4.7 Creating a Folder and Moving
E-mail into It 230
Activity 4.8 Creating a Filter 232

Objective 6 Delete E-mail from
Your Account **235**
Activity 4.9 Deleting E-mail and Signing Out 235

PROJECT 4C Exploring E-mail Systems,
Protocols, Netiquette, and
Nuisances **237**

Objective 7 Compare E-mail Systems **237**

Objective 8 Identify Appropriate E-mail
Netiquette **242**

Objective 9 Minimize Nuisances Associated
with E-mail **244**

PROJECT 4D Exploring Mailing Lists and
Newsletters **247**

Objective 10 Explore Mailing Lists **247**

Objective 11 Find Special Interest
Newsletters **252**

Summary 254
Key Terms 254
Matching 256
Fill in the Blank 257

Rubric 258
Mastering the Internet 259
GO! Search 269

Chapter 5 Collaborating on the World Wide Web 271

PROJECT 5A Creating Your Own Blog **273**

Objective 1 Locate Existing Blogs **274**
Activity 5.1 Locating Blogs with a Search
Engine 274
Activity 5.2 Comparing Blog Search Tools 279

Objective 2 Set Up an Account at a
Blogging Web Site **281**
Activity 5.3 Signing Up for a Blogging
Account 281

Objective 3 Publish Posts to
Your Blog **284**
Activity 5.4 Posting to a Blog 284

PROJECT 5B Locating Newsgroups **291**

Objective 4 Search for USENET Newsgroups **291**
Activity 5.5 Locating a USENET Newsgroup 291

Objective 5 Locate a Web-Based Newsgroup **294**
Activity 5.6 Locating a Web-Based Newsgroup 295

Objective 6 Read and Reply to Threads at a
Web-Based Newsgroup **296**
Activity 5.7 Reading Threads at a Web-Based
Newsgroup 296
Activity 5.8 Joining a Newsgroup and
Posting a Reply 299

PROJECT 5C Exploring Other Web-Based
Communication Tools **302**

Objective 7 Discover Wikis and Vlogs **302**

Objective 8 Identify Message Boards,
Web-Based Forums, and
Bulletin Boards **305**

Objective 9 Explore Instant Messaging and
Compare Instant Messengers **307**

PROJECT 5D Comparing Synchronous
Communication Tools **311**

Objective 10 Identify Types of IRC
and Chat **311**

Objective 11 Define Internet Telephony
and VoIP **314**

Objective 12 Describe Video Conferencing **316**

Summary   318

Key Terms   318

Matching   320

Fill in the Blank   321

Rubric   323

Mastering the Internet   324

GO! Search   334

Chapter 6 Locating Resources on the World Wide Web..........337

PROJECT 6A   Accessing a Special-Interest Web Site for Health Information   **339**

Objective 1   Perform a Directory Search and Evaluate a Special Interest Web Site   **340**

Activity 6.1   Locating Health Information Using a Directory   340

Objective 2   Perform a Search for Special-Interest Web Sites Using a Search Engine and an Advanced Search   **342**

Activity 6.2   Locating Health Information Online Using a Search Engine   343

Activity 6.3   Locating Health Information Online Using an Advanced Search   344

Objective 3   Compare Types of Special-Interest Web Sites   **346**

Activity 6.4   Comparing Health Information Web Sites   346

PROJECT 6B   Comparing Push and Pull Content on the Web   **348**

Objective 4   Access Weather Information Online   **348**

Activity 6.5   Locating Weather Information Online   348

Objective 5   Install a Feed on Your Computer   **350**

Activity 6.6   Installing and Using a RSS Feed   351

Objective 6   Manage Travel Arrangements Online   **356**

Activity 6.7   Searching for Maps and Travel Directions to Businesses   357

Activity 6.8   Exploring Travel Arrangement Sites   361

PROJECT 6C   Finding Informational Resources on the Web   **364**

Objective 7   Find People Using Online Resources   **364**

Objective 8   Locate Legal Information and Educational Opportunities   **366**

PROJECT 6D   Locating Entertainment Sites   **371**

Objective 9   Identify Award-Winning Web Sites and Portals   **371**

Objective 10   Compare Gaming Sites   **373**

Objective 11   Explore Multimedia Resources   **376**

Summary   380

Key Terms   380

Matching   381

Fill in the Blank   383

Rubric   384

Mastering the Internet   385

GO! Search   394

Glossary G-1

Index..I-1

Letter from the Editor

Dear Instructors and Students,

The primary goal of the *GO!* Series is two-fold. The first goal is to help instructors teach the course they want in less time. The second goal is to provide students with the skills to solve business problems using the computer as a tool, for both themselves and the organization for which they might be employed.

The *GO!* Series was originally created by Series Editor Shelley Gaskin and published with the release of Microsoft Office 2003. Her ideas came from years of using textbooks that didn't meet all the needs of today's diverse classroom and that were too confusing for students. Shelley continues to enhance the series by ensuring we stay true to our vision of developing quality instruction and useful classroom tools.

But we also need your input and ideas.

Over time, the *GO!* Series has evolved based on direct feedback from instructors and students using the series. *We are the publisher that listens.* To publish a textbook that works for you, it's critical that we continue to listen to this feedback. It's important to me to talk with you and hear your stories about using *GO!* Your voice can make a difference.

My hope is that this letter will inspire you to write me an e-mail and share your thoughts on using the *GO!* Series.

Stephanie Wall
Executive Editor, *GO!* Series
stephanie_wall@prenhall.com

GO! System Contributors

We thank the following people for their hard work and support in making the GO! System all that it is!

Super Reviewers

Donham, Marilyn	Washtenaw Community College
Flores, Karl	Grossmont-Cuyamaca Community College District
Ganjalizadeh, Saiid	The Catholic University of America
Goodson, Jennifer	University of Oklahoma
Hock, Margaret	City College of San Francisco
Maack, Mary	University of California, Los Angeles
MacVie, Andrew	University at Buffalo
Madesn, Donna	Kirkwood Community College
McCaskill, Matt	Brevard Community College
Morgan, Brian	Marshall University
Paul, Sunil	University of South Dakota
Rossi, Deb	Montana Tech of The University of Montana
Sibley, Dorothy	Florida Community College at Jacksonville
Swisher, Bob	University of Oklahoma
Wilcox, Gary	University at Buffalo

Technical Editors

Lynn Bowen
Jane Perschbach

Series Reviewers

Abraham, Reni	Houston Community College
Agatston, Ann	Agatston Consulting Technical College
Alexander, Melody	Ball Sate University
Alejandro, Manuel	Southwest Texas Junior College
Ali, Farha	Lander University
Amici, Penny	Harrisburg Area Community College
Anderson, Patty A.	Lake City Community College
Andrews, Wilma	Virginia Commonwealth College, Nebraska University
Anik, Mazhar	Tiffin University
Armstrong, Gary	Shippensburg University
Atkins, Bonnie	Delaware Technical Community College
Bachand, LaDonna	Santa Rosa Community College
Bagui, Sikha	University of West Florida
Beecroft, Anita	Kwantlen University College
Bell, Paula	Lock Haven College
Belton, Linda	Springfield Tech. Community College
Bennett, Judith	Sam Houston State University
Bhatia, Sai	Riverside Community College
Bishop, Frances	DeVry Institute—Alpharetta (ATL)
Blaszkiewicz, Holly	Ivy Tech Community College/Region 1
Branigan, Dave	DeVry University
Bray, Patricia	Allegany College of Maryland
Brotherton, Cathy	Riverside Community College
Buehler, Lesley	Ohlone College
Buell, C	Central Oregon Community College
Byars, Pat	Brookhaven College
Byrd, Lynn	Delta State University, Cleveland, Mississippi
Cacace, Richard N.	Pensacola Junior College
Cadenhead, Charles	Brookhaven College
Calhoun, Ric	Gordon College
Cameron, Eric	Passaic Community College
Carriker, Sandra	North Shore Community College
Cannamore, Madie	Kennedy King
Carreon, Cleda	Indiana University—Purdue University, Indianapolis
Chaffin, Catherine	Shawnee State University
Chauvin, Marg	Palm Beach Community College, Boca Raton
Challa, Chandrashekar	Virginia State University
Chamlou, Afsaneh	NOVA Alexandria
Chapman, Pam	Wabaunsee Community College
Christensen, Dan	Iowa Western Community College
Clay, Betty	Southeastern Oklahoma State University
Collins, Linda D.	Mesa Community College
Conroy-Link, Janet	Holy Family College
Cosgrove, Janet	Northwestern CT Community
Courtney, Kevin	Hillsborough Community College
Cox, Rollie	Madison Area Technical College
Crawford, Hiram	Olive Harvey College
Crawford, Thomasina	Miami-Dade College, Kendall Campus
Credico, Grace	Lethbridge Community College
Crenshaw, Richard	Miami Dade Community College, North
Crespo, Beverly	Mt. San Antonio College
Crossley, Connie	Cincinnati State Technical Community College
Curik, Mary	Central New Mexico Community College
De Arazoza, Ralph	Miami Dade Community College
Danno, John	DeVry University/Keller Graduate School
Davis, Phillip	Del Mar College
DeHerrera, Laurie	Pikes Peak Community College
Delk, Dr. K. Kay	Seminole Community College
Doroshow, Mike	Eastfield College
Douglas, Gretchen	SUNYCortland
Dove, Carol	Community College of Allegheny
Driskel, Loretta	Niagara Community College
Duckwiler, Carol	Wabaunsee Community College
Duncan, Mimi	University of Missouri-St. Louis
Duthie, Judy	Green River Community College
Duvall, Annette	Central New Mexico Community College
Ecklund, Paula	Duke University
Eng, Bernice	Brookdale Community College
Evans, Billie	Vance-Granville Community College
Feuerbach, Lisa	Ivy Tech East Chicago
Fisher, Fred	Florida State University
Foster, Penny L.	Anne Arundel Community College
Foszcz, Russ	McHenry County College
Fry, Susan	Boise State University
Fustos, Janos	Metro State
Gallup, Jeanette	Blinn College
Gelb, Janet	Grossmont College
Gentry, Barb	Parkland College
Gerace, Karin	St. Angela Merici School
Gerace, Tom	Tulane University
Ghajar, Homa	Oklahoma State University
Gifford, Steve	Northwest Iowa Community College

Glazer, Ellen	Broward Community College	Laspina, Kathy	Vance-Granville Community College
Gordon, Robert	Hofstra University	Le Grand, Dr. Kate	Broward Community College
Gramlich, Steven	Pasco-Hernando Community College	Lenhart, Sheryl	Terra Community College
Graviett, Nancy M.	St. Charles Community College, St. Peters, Missouri	Letavec, Chris	University of Cincinnati
		Liefert, Jane	Everett Community College
Greene, Rich	Community College of Allegheny County	Lindaman, Linda	Black Hawk Community College
		Lindberg, Martha	Minnesota State University
Gregoryk, Kerry	Virginia Commonwealth State	Lightner, Renee	Broward Community College
Griggs, Debra	Bellevue Community College	Lindberg, Martha	Minnesota State University
Grimm, Carol	Palm Beach Community College	Linge, Richard	Arizona Western College
Hahn, Norm	Thomas Nelson Community College	Logan, Mary G.	Delgado Community College
Hammerschlag, Dr. Bill	Brookhaven College	Loizeaux, Barbara	Westchester Community College
Hansen, Michelle	Davenport University	Lopez, Don	Clovis-State Center Community College District
Hayden, Nancy	Indiana University—Purdue University, Indianapolis		
		Lord, Alexandria	Asheville Buncombe Tech
Hayes, Theresa	Broward Community College	Lowe, Rita	Harold Washington College
Helfand, Terri	Chaffey College	Low, Willy Hui	Joliet Junior College
Helms, Liz	Columbus State Community College	Lucas, Vickie	Broward Community College
Hernandez, Leticia	TCI College of Technology	Lynam, Linda	Central Missouri State University
Hibbert, Marilyn	Salt Lake Community College	Lyon, Lynne	Durham College
Hoffman, Joan	Milwaukee Area Technical College	Lyon, Pat Rajski	Tomball College
Hogan, Pat	Cape Fear Community College	MacKinnon, Ruth	Georgia Southern University
Holland, Susan	Southeast Community College	Macon, Lisa	Valencia Community College, West Campus
Hopson, Bonnie	Athens Technical College		
Horvath, Carrie	Albertus Magnus College	Machuca, Wayne	College of the Sequoias
Horwitz, Steve	Community College of Philadelphia	Madison, Dana	Clarion University
Hotta, Barbara	Leeward Community College	Maguire, Trish	Eastern New Mexico University
Howard, Bunny	St. Johns River Community	Malkan, Rajiv	Montgomery College
Howard, Chris	DeVry University	Manning, David	Northern Kentucky University
Huckabay, Jamie	Austin Community College	Marcus, Jacquie	Niagara Community College
Hudgins, Susan	East Central University	Marghitu, Daniela	Auburn University
Hulett, Michelle J.	Missouri State University	Marks, Suzanne	Bellevue Community College
Hunt, Darla A.	Morehead State University, Morehead, Kentucky	Marquez, Juanita	El Centro College
		Marquez, Juan	Mesa Community College
Hunt, Laura	Tulsa Community College	Martyn, Margie	Baldwin-Wallace College
Jacob, Sherry	Jefferson Community College	Marucco, Toni	Lincoln Land Community College
Jacobs, Duane	Salt Lake Community College	Mason, Lynn	Lubbock Christian University
Jauken, Barb	Southeastern Community	Matutis, Audrone	Houston Community College
Johnson, Kathy	Wright College	Matkin, Marie	University of Lethbridge
Johnson, Mary	Kingwood College	McCain, Evelynn	Boise State University
Johnson, Mary	Mt. San Antonio College	McCannon, Melinda	Gordon College
Jones, Stacey	Benedict College	McCarthy, Marguerite	Northwestern Business College
Jones, Warren	University of Alabama, Birmingham	McCaskill, Matt L.	Brevard Community College
Jordan, Cheryl	San Juan College	McClellan, Carolyn	Tidewater Community College
Kapoor, Bhushan	California State University, Fullerton	McClure, Darlean	College of Sequoias
Kasai, Susumu	Salt Lake Community College	McCrory, Sue A.	Missouri State University
Kates, Hazel	Miami Dade Community College, Kendall	McCue, Stacy	Harrisburg Area Community College
		McEntire-Orbach, Teresa	Middlesex County College
Keen, Debby	University of Kentucky	McLeod, Todd	Fresno City College
Keeter, Sandy	Seminole Community College	McManus, Illyana	Grossmont College
Kern-Blystone, Dorothy Jean	Bowling Green State	McPherson, Dori	Schoolcraft College
		Meiklejohn, Nancy	Pikes Peak Community College
Keskin, Ilknur	The University of South Dakota	Menking, Rick	Hardin-Simmons University
Kirk, Colleen	Mercy College	Meredith, Mary	University of Louisiana at Lafayette
Kleckner, Michelle	Elon University	Mermelstein, Lisa	Baruch College
Kliston, Linda	Broward Community College, North Campus	Metos, Linda	Salt Lake Community College
		Meurer, Daniel	University of Cincinnati
Kochis, Dennis	Suffolk County Community College	Meyer, Marian	Central New Mexico Community College
Kramer, Ed	Northern Virginia Community College		
		Miller, Cindy	Ivy Tech Community College, Lafayette, Indiana
Laird, Jeff	Northeast State Community College		
Lamoureaux, Jackie	Central New Mexico Community College	Mitchell, Susan	Davenport University
		Mohle, Dennis	Fresno Community College
Lange, David	Grand Valley State	Monk, Ellen	University of Delaware
LaPointe, Deb	Central New Mexico Community College	Moore, Rodney	Holland College
		Morris, Mike	Southeastern Oklahoma State University
Larson, Donna	Louisville Technical Institute		

Morris, Nancy	Hudson Valley Community College
Moseler, Dan	Harrisburg Area Community College
Nabors, Brent	Reedley College, Clovis Center
Nadas, Erika	Wright College
Nadelman, Cindi	New England College
Nademlynsky, Lisa	Johnson & Wales University
Ncube, Cathy	University of West Florida
Nagengast, Joseph	Florida Career College
Newsome, Eloise	Northern Virginia Community College Woodbridge
Nicholls, Doreen	Mohawk Valley Community College
Nunan, Karen	Northeast State Technical Community College
Odegard, Teri	Edmonds Community College
Ogle, Gregory	North Community College
Orr, Dr. Claudia	Northern Michigan University South
Otieno, Derek	DeVry University
Otton, Diana Hill	Chesapeake College
Oxendale, Lucia	West Virginia Institute of Technology
Paiano, Frank	Southwestern College
Patrick, Tanya	Clackamas Community College
Peairs, Deb	Clark State Community College
Prince, Lisa	Missouri State University-Springfield Campus
Proietti, Kathleen	Northern Essex Community College
Pusins, Delores	HCCC
Raghuraman, Ram	Joliet Junior College
Reasoner, Ted Allen	Indiana University—Purdue
Reeves, Karen	High Point University
Remillard, Debbie	New Hampshire Technical Institute
Rhue, Shelly	DeVry University
Richards, Karen	Maplewoods Community College
Richardson, Mary	Albany Technical College
Rodgers, Gwen	Southern Nazarene University
Roselli, Diane	Harrisburg Area Community College
Ross, Dianne	University of Louisiana in Lafayette
Rousseau, Mary	Broward Community College, South
Samson, Dolly	Hawaii Pacific University
Sams, Todd	University of Cincinnati
Sandoval, Everett	Reedley College
Sardone, Nancy	Seton Hall University
Scafide, Jean	Mississippi Gulf Coast Community College
Scheeren, Judy	Westmoreland County Community College
Schneider, Sol	Sam Houston State University
Scroggins, Michael	Southwest Missouri State University
Sever, Suzanne	Northwest Arkansas Community College
Sheridan, Rick	California State University-Chico
Silvers, Pamela	Asheville Buncombe Tech
Singer, Steven A.	University of Hawai'i, Kapi'olani Community College
Sinha, Atin	Albany State University
Skolnick, Martin	Florida Atlantic University
Smith, T. Michael	Austin Community College
Smith, Tammy	Tompkins Cortland Community Collge
Smolenski, Bob	Delaware County Community College
Spangler, Candice	Columbus State
Stedham, Vicki	St. Petersburg College, Clearwater
Stefanelli, Greg	Carroll Community College
Steiner, Ester	New Mexico State University
Stenlund, Neal	Northern Virginia Community College, Alexandria
St. John, Steve	Tulsa Community College
Sterling, Janet	Houston Community College
Stoughton, Catherine	Laramie County Community College
Sullivan, Angela	Joliet Junior College
Szurek, Joseph	University of Pittsburgh at Greensburg
Tarver, Mary Beth	Northwestern State University
Taylor, Michael	Seattle Central Community College
Thangiah, Sam	Slippery Rock University
Thompson-Sellers, Ingrid	Georgia Perimeter College
Tomasi, Erik	Baruch College
Toreson, Karen	Shoreline Community College
Trifiletti, John J.	Florida Community College at Jacksonville
Trivedi, Charulata	Quinsigamond Community College, Woodbridge
Tucker, William	Austin Community College
Turgeon, Cheryl	Asnuntuck Community College
Turpen, Linda	Central New Mexico Community College
Upshaw, Susan	Del Mar College
Unruh, Angela	Central Washington University
Vanderhoof, Dr. Glenna	Missouri State University-Springfield Campus
Vargas, Tony	El Paso Community College
Vicars, Mitzi	Hampton University
Villarreal, Kathleen	Fresno
Vitrano, Mary Ellen	Palm Beach Community College
Volker, Bonita	Tidewater Community College
Wahila, Lori (Mindy)	Tompkins Cortland Community College
Waswick, Kim	Southeast Community College, Nebraska
Wavle, Sharon	Tompkins Cortland Community College
Webb, Nancy	City College of San Francisco
Wells, Barbara E.	Central Carolina Technical College
Wells, Lorna	Salt Lake Community College
Welsh, Jean	Lansing Community College Nebraska
White, Bruce	Quinnipiac University
Willer, Ann	Solano Community College
Williams, Mark	Lane Community College
Wilson, Kit	Red River College
Wilson, Roger	Fairmont State University
Wimberly, Leanne	International Academy of Design and Technology
Worthington, Paula	Northern Virginia Community College
Yauney, Annette	Herkimer County Community College
Yip, Thomas	Passaic Community College
Zavala, Ben	Webster Tech
Zlotow, Mary Ann	College of DuPage
Zudeck, Steve	Broward Community College, North

About the Authors

Shelley Gaskin, Series Editor, is a professor of business and computer technology at Pasadena City College in Pasadena, California. She holds a master's degree in business education from Northern Illinois University and a doctorate in adult and community education from Ball State University. Dr. Gaskin has 15 years of experience in the computer industry with several Fortune 500 companies and has developed and written training materials for custom systems applications in both the public and private sector. She is also the author of books on Microsoft Outlook and word processing.

Rebecca Lawson is a faculty member at Lansing Community College where she coordinates the curriculum for the Internet program by developing instructional materials, teaching online and face-to-face courses, and mentoring adjunct faculty. She holds a master's degree in educational technology from Michigan State University. Her major areas of interest include the assessment of computer literacy skill levels to facilitate student retention and the use of social networking tools to support learning in blended and online environments.

chapterone

Introducing the Internet

OBJECTIVES

At the end of this chapter, you will be able to:

OUTCOMES

Mastering these objectives will enable you to:

1. Consult a Web Site to Locate an ISP that Offers Service in a Specific Area
2. Refine Searches to Distinguish Among the Features of Each ISP
3. Compare Information You Find on the Web

Project 1A
Locate a Local ISP

4. Browse a Directory for Information
5. Describe Events and Technologies that Affected the Development of the Internet

Project 1B
Research Internet History

6. Define Common Internet Terms
7. Analyze URLs, DNS, and Server Structure
8. Identify Hardware and Software Needed for Internet Connections
9. Explain Internet Connection Methods
10. Describe Wireless Connection Options

Project 1C
Connect to the Internet

11. Summarize Early History of the Internet
12. Name Early Key Developers of the Internet
13. Describe the Unique Features of Hypertext
14. Describe Popular Uses of the Internet Today

Project 1D
Explore Internet History

Lake Michigan City College

Lake Michigan City College is located along the lakefront of Chicago—one of the country's most exciting cities. The college serves its large and diverse student body and makes positive contributions to the community through relevant curricula, partnerships with businesses and nonprofit organizations, and learning experiences that allow students to be full participants in the global community. The college offers three associate degrees in 20 academic areas, adult education programs, and continuing education offerings on campus, at satellite locations, and online.

Introducing the Internet

Using the Internet, you are able to locate former classmates, communicate with friends using e-mail or chat, and find people, phone numbers, and directions to almost any place in the world. You can explore the museums of the world or shop for items that are unavailable at your local mall—all with the click of the mouse button. You can manage your finances, gain knowledge of educational opportunities, or conduct research about your family heritage. You can do these things any time of day and from any location. The Internet connects you to the world.

Project 1A **Locating a Local ISP**

Lake Michigan City College is seeking the most cost-efficient method to connect to the Internet. In Activities 1.1 through 1.3, you will assist the Resource Development director by searching for ISPs that serve the local area, and then you will evaluate various ISPs based on features and costs. You will create a comparison report of ISPs.

For Project 1A, you will need the following file:

New blank Notepad document

You will save your file as
1A_Local_ISP_Firstname_Lastname

Figure 1.1

Objective 1
Consult a Web Site to Locate an ISP that Offers Service in a Specific Area

Every computer that connects to the Internet must be covered by an agreement made with a company or organization that provides access to the Internet. This type of organization is called an **Internet Service Provider**, or **ISP**. For your home computer, your ISP might be your local telephone or cable company, a local ISP, or a national service such as America Online (AOL) or Microsoft Network (MSN).

To connect to the Internet from your home computer, you must first determine which ISP serves your geographic area, and then contact one to arrange for service. ISPs vary in terms of location served, the Internet connection methods provided, and the costs. Costs are usually based on a per-month fee, and it is common to purchase service for a specified period of time. This is referred to as a **subscription fee**. After you locate an ISP that serves your geographic area, you must evaluate the connection method, services provided, and costs, and then determine if you want to use the ISP as your provider.

Alert!

Assessing Project 1A and Project 1B

For Projects 1A and 1B of this chapter, you and your instructor can evaluate your approach to the problem and your result by consulting the scoring rubric located in the end-of-chapter material. For these hands-on projects, there is no online quiz.

Activity 1.1 Searching for ISPs in Your Local Area

In this activity, you will research ISPs available in your local area code.

1 On the left side of the Windows taskbar, click the **Start** button [start], and then point to **All Programs**. Compare your screen with Figure 1.2.

The **Start menu** displays. The **Start button** is found in the lower left corner of your screen. Clicking the Start button causes the Start menu to display. The Start menu provides access to all the programs and helpful features on your Windows computer through a series of commands.

The **taskbar** is part of the Windows operating system that displays buttons for all open programs and files, so that you can toggle—move—between them. The taskbar is found at the bottom of your screen.

Organizations, school computer labs, and individuals often customize the arrangement of programs on the Start menu. If **Internet Explorer** is used as the standard **browser** program on your computer, it typically displays at the top of the Start menu along with the standard e-mail program. A **Web browser**, or browser, is a software program that enables you to view HTML documents and access files related to those documents. Internet Explorer, also referred to as **IE**, is a browser developed by Microsoft and is designed to work with the Windows operating system.

In other cases, IE may display at the top of the Start menu. If the Internet Explorer logo displays as a desktop icon, double-click the desktop icon to start the program.

Internet Explorer as a desktop icon

Internet Explorer listed as a program

Figure 1.2

Internet Explorer at the top of the Start menu

All Programs

Taskbar

Start button

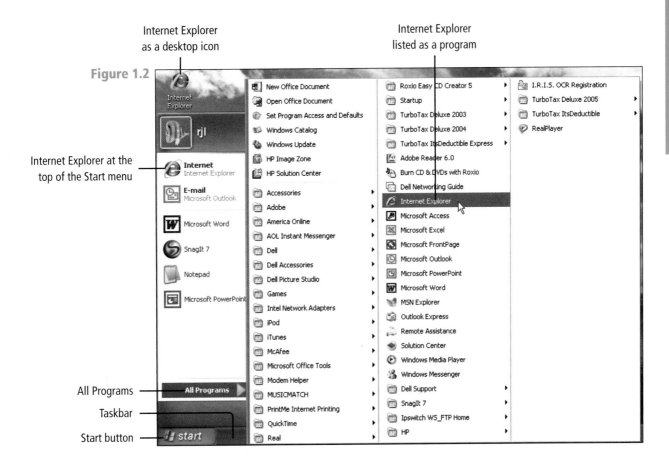

2 From the **Start** menu, click **Internet** to start the Internet Explorer program. If necessary, in the upper right corner of the Internet Explorer window, click the **Maximize button** to enlarge the window to fill the computer screen completely. Notice that after you

click the **Maximize** button, the **Restore Down button** displays. Clicking the **Restore Down** button will make the window smaller and enable you to move the **Internet Explorer** window.

Each time you start Internet Explorer when you are connected to the Internet, the **default home page** that has been set up on your computer opens and displays in the browser window. A default home page is the first page that displays when a Web browser, such as Internet Explorer, is started. Because the default home page can be customized, many organizations, schools, and individuals set it to a frequently used Web page. For example, at your college, the default home page is probably set to the first page of the college's Web site.

The individual documents on the Web are called **Web pages** or **pages**. A collection of related Web pages that resides on an organization's host computer is referred to as a **Web site**. The starting point or the first page of each Web site is called the **home page**. For example, your college likely has a Web site with many different Web pages containing information about a wide variety of topics including the courses, people, and events at your college. This entire collection of pages is your college's Web site.

The organization's **host computer** is a computer that has access to all other computers on a network and provides services for those computers, such as the storage of Web pages. A **Web server** is the software that controls access to the HTML documents that comprise a Web site.

3 Near the top of the **Internet Explorer** screen that displays, locate the **Address bar**. Compare your screen with Figure 1.3—note that your screen may differ from Figure 1.3 depending on the settings for your Internet Explorer program.

To navigate to a specific Web site that you want to view, use the **Address bar** of your Web browser. The Address bar is the toolbar in Internet Explorer into which you type the address of the Web site that you want to display. The address you type is called a **Uniform Resource Locator**, most commonly known as a **URL**. The URL is the text-based address of a Web site with which your Web browser software locates the Web resources associated with the Web site.

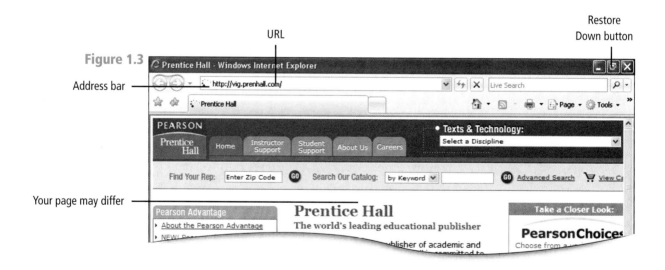

Figure 1.3

4 In the **Address bar**, click one time to select the existing text, type **http://www.thelist.com** and then press Enter. Locate the **Search By Location/Area Code** link. Compare your screen with Figure 1.4.

The home page of The List of ISPs Web site displays. The List of ISPs Web site provides *The Definitive ISP Buyer's Guide.* Here you can conduct a search for an ISP by location/area code, country code, U.S. nationwide, and Canada nationwide.

Companies and organizations change their Web sites' page layouts and organizational structures periodically. Your version of The List of ISPs home page might look different from what is shown in Figure 1.4.

Search By Location/Area Code link

Figure 1.4

The List of ISPs home page

5 Click the **Search By Location/Area Code** link. If you live outside of the United States, click the **Search By Country Code** link.

A page listing area codes served by ISPs in the United States and Canada displays.

6 On the right of your screen, locate the scroll bar, and then at the bottom of the scroll bar, click the **down scroll arrow,** ▼ so that you can view the lower portions of the screen, which are not currently in view. Web pages that are too long to fit on the screen will display the scroll box so that you can view the lower portion of the screen. Drag the scroll box or click the down scroll arrow until you your state and area code displays on the screen. Compare your screen with Figure 1.5.

Figure 1.5

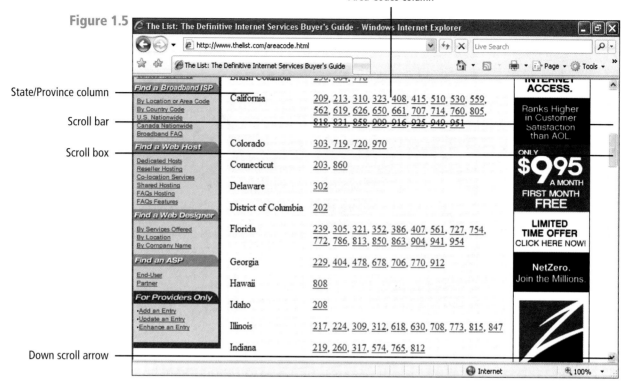

Area Codes column

State/Province column

Scroll bar

Scroll box

Down scroll arrow

7 Locate your state and click the link for your area code. Then, scroll down the page that displays to review the company names of ISPs in your area. Note if the ISPs offer dial-up services, dedicated services, or both. You may need to click links at the bottom of the page to view more of the alphabetical listing. Compare your screen with Figure 1.6. Notice that your screen may differ if you searched for a different area code. Keep your browser open for the next activity.

Dial-up connections are connections that are made over standard telephone wires by using a modem. A ***modulator/demodulator***, or ***modem***, is a hardware device that converts data packets from digital to analog so that they can travel along analog lines. The modem in your computer translates the request for a Web page from a digital form to an analog form so that the request can be sent along analog telephone lines. When the requested data returns to your computer, the modem then translates the data back from an analog form to a digital form so that your browser can display the data. A dial-up connection is a slow data transmission method but is inexpensive and easily available in most locations.

A ***dedicated service*** is a communication service that is provided to a single specific user, typically a business or organization. With dedicated service, only the single user—the business or organization—has access to the server, which ensures that the single user will receive the fastest connection speeds.

Figure 1.6

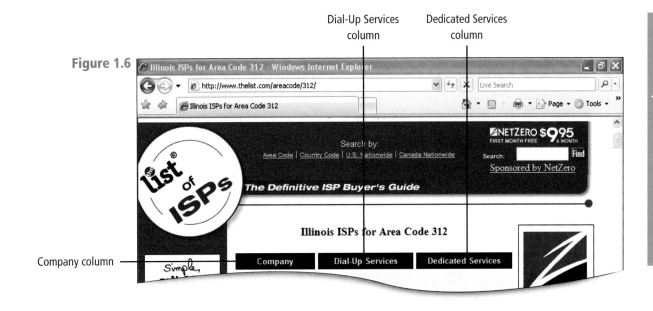

Dial-Up Services column

Dedicated Services column

Company column

Objective 2
Refine Searches to Distinguish Among the Features of Each ISP

Most ISPs offer a specific connection method in return for a monthly subscription fee. A few ISPs are available free of charge but support themselves through persistent advertisements that display at the top, in the center, or on the side of every Web site you view. Often, ISPs provide additional services such as free, limited-space e-mail accounts and Web server storage space. A quality ISP should provide technical support 24 hours a day, 7 days a week.

When choosing an ISP, you should consider the cost of the monthly subscription, the connection methods provided, and the connection speed. National ISPs generally provide more services for less cost than local ISPs.

Selecting an ISP depends on the match between an organization's or person's needs and the services offered by the ISP. Based on those needs, you can refine your search to narrow the list of ISPs in your area. Selecting the best ISP may be influenced by recommendations from friends, family, or a colleague.

Activity 1.2 Refining Your Search Results

In this activity, you will refine your search results to determine which ISP is the best one for the Resources Development director to recommend to Lake Michigan City College.

1 Near the middle of the page, locate the **Refine Your Search** box. Locate the **Dial-up** link. Compare your screen with Figure 1.7.

The List of ISPs Web site offers options to help you locate ISPs that offer only the type of service that you are interested in using. The

Web site categorizes ISPs by connection method, such as dial-up, business and dedicated services, DSL/cable, and fixed wireless.

Refine Your Search box

Figure 1.7

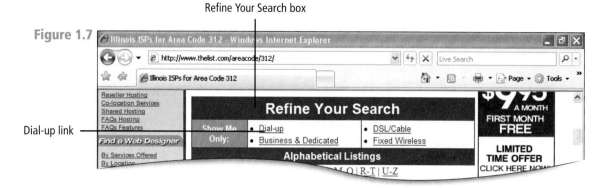

Dial-up link

2 Click the **Dial-up** link to display a list of ISPs that offer dial-up services in your area, and then scroll the page to review the company names, the type of dial-up service, and bandwidth options offered. In large metropolitan areas, you may need to click links at the bottom of the page to view more of the alphabetical listing.

3 Click the **company name** of the first ISP in the alphabetical listing to display details about that ISP. Write down the name of the ISP and the amounts of the setup fee and subscription fee. Figure 1.8 shows results that are typical of what displays when you use the Refine Your Search feature.

Details about the selected ISP, such as Web site address, telephone number, area codes or country codes served, services offered, fees, and the date when last revised display. These types of details are important to consider before signing up with an ISP.

ISP detail page

Figure 1.8

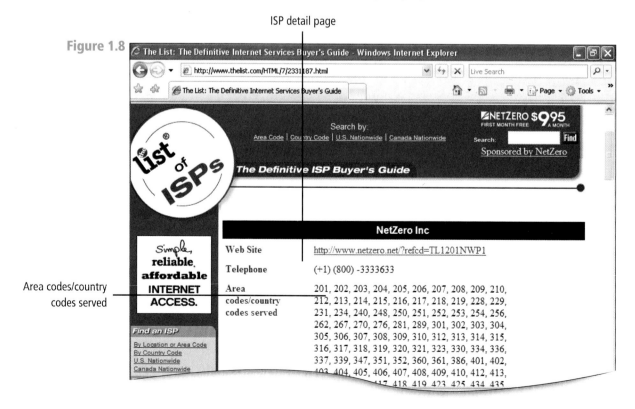

Area codes/country
codes served

4 In the upper left corner of your screen, click the Web browser's **Back** button to return to the page that displays ISPs offering dial-up service in your area code or country code. Click the **company** link of the second or third ISP in the alphabetical listing, and then review its services and fees. Write down the name of the ISP and the amounts of the setup fee and subscription fee. Figure 1.9 shows the location of the **Back** button and **Forward** button in the Web browser.

The Web browser's Back and Forward buttons allow you to move between Web sites that you have visited during your browsing session. The **Back button** moves you to the last Web page that you visited. The **Forward button** moves you to the Web page you were viewing before you clicked the Back button. The *Recent Pages arrow* to the immediate right of the Forward button provides access to a list of recently viewed Web pages.

Forward button

Figure 1.9

Back button

Recent Pages arrow

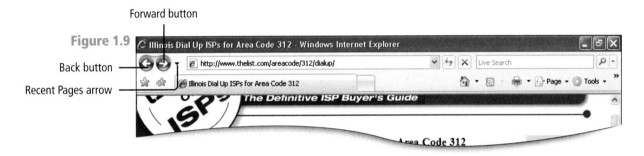

5 Click the **Back** button to return to the page that displays ISPs offering dial-up service in your area. Scroll to view the **Refine Your Search** box, and then click the **Business & Dedicated** link.

A list of ISPs that offer dedicated service for your area displays. Both columns, *Dial-Up Services* and *Dedicated Services*, are fully populated with options. **Bandwidth** is an important consideration for supporting business transactions. Bandwidth is the transmission speed or transfer capacity of data on a network. Dedicated service offers much faster transmission speeds. Most business customers prefer to use ISPs that offer dedicated services instead of dial-up service because a dedicated service offers faster transmission speeds. Dial-up services are not fast enough for business use.

6 On the page that displays ISPs that offer dedicated services, scroll down to review the company names of ISPs and the type of dedicated services and connection services offered. You may need to click links at the bottom of the page to view more of the alphabetical listing.

7 Click the **company name** of the first ISP in the alphabetical listing. Write down the name of the ISP, the setup fee, and subscription fee amounts.

8 Click the **Back** button to return to the page that displays ISPs that offer dedicated services. Click the **company name** of the second ISP in the alphabetical list. Write down the name of the ISP, the setup fee, and subscription fee amounts.

⑨ Click the **Back** button 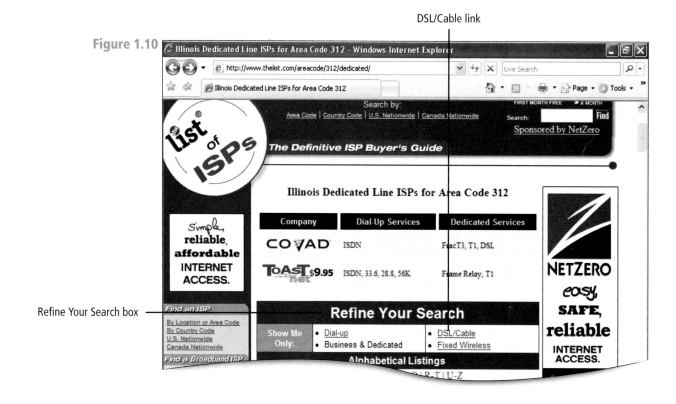, and then scroll as necessary to locate the **Refine Your Search** box. Compare your screen with Figure 1.10. Then, click the **DSL/Cable** link.

ISPs that offer DSL and cable service for your area display. Notice that both columns, *Dial-Up Services* and *Dedicated Services*, are fully populated with options. ISPs that offer DSL and cable services often offer dial-up services, too.

Digital Subscriber Lines (DSL) are available in some areas; availability is based on your geographic proximity to the telephone company equipment. DSL is a digital communications technology that uses standard telephone lines to transmit data but at a higher rate of speed than a standard dial-up connection. Both telephone use and an Internet connection can occur at the same time.

Cable connections are made over the same cables as those used for cable television transmission. Both Internet and cable television connections can occur at the same time. The connection speed will vary depending on how many people use the connection at the same time.

DSL/Cable link

Figure 1.10

Refine Your Search box

⑩ Scroll down the page, review the company names of ISPs, and then verify that the term *DSL* is found in the *Dedicated Services* column. You may need to click links at the bottom of the page to view more of the alphabetical listing.

⑪ Click the **company name** of the first ISP in the alphabetical listing. Write down the name of the ISP, the setup fee, and subscription fee costs.

12 Click the **Back** button ⬅ to return to the page that displays ISPs offering DSL and cable service in your area. Select the link of the second ISP in the alphabetical listing. Write down the name of the ISP, the setup fee, and subscription fee costs.

13 Using the techniques you have practiced, navigate to the **Refine Your Search** box. Compare your screen with Figure 1.11, and then click the **Fixed Wireless** link.

A Web page displays with a listing of the ISPs that offer wireless service for your area code or country code. Notice that both columns, *Dial-Up Services* and *Dedicated Services*, are fully populated with options but that none of them indicate wireless. This is because wireless services display under the category *Broadband Services Offered* found at each individual ISP page. **Broadband** refers to high-speed transmission media that can carry voice, data, and video at the same time.

Direct satellite system (DSS), such as DISH Network and DIRECTV, uses a satellite dish and television cables to connect to the Internet. Data flows between your computer and satellite dish, the provider's receiving satellite dish, and a satellite orbiting the Earth. The quality of a satellite connection can vary depending on environmental conditions. Figure 1.12 shows how a satellite connection works.

Wireless fidelity connection, or **Wi-Fi**, permits connection to the Internet based on radio waves in a manner similar to walkie-talkie communication—but at a much higher rate of speed. A Wi-Fi connection enables mobility because the computer does not need to use any wires for connection. Wi-Fi connection points are called **hotspots** or **access points**. A hotspot consists of a small box that is hardwired to the Internet. Hotspots are now commonly found in airports, coffee shops, hotels, and libraries, where they typically transmit data to people who are using laptops.

Fixed Wireless link

Figure 1.11

Refine Your Search box

Figure 1.12
(1) Your request to view a Web page is sent from a satellite dish to an orbiting satellite. (2) The request moves from an orbiting satellite to the satellite server. (3) The satellite server retrieves the Web page data from the Internet and (4) the Web page data is returned back to the satellite server. (5) The Web page data moves to the orbiting satellite. (6) The Web page data is then moved back to your satellite dish.

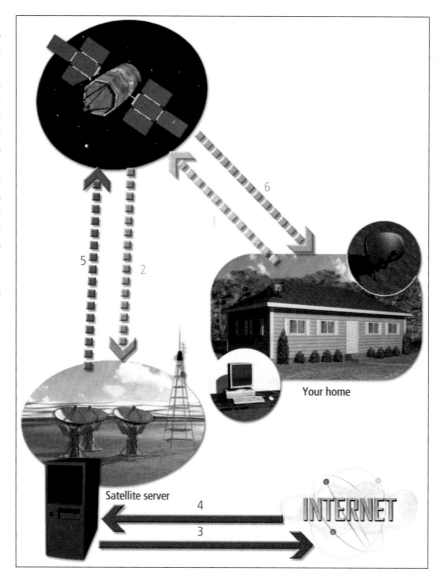

Your home

Satellite server

INTERNET

14 Click the **company name** of the first ISP in the alphabetical list. Scroll as necessary, and then in the **Broadband Services Offered** category, verify that *Wireless* is an option. Write down the name of the ISP, the setup fee, and subscription fee costs.

15 Click the **Back** button to return to the page that displays ISPs offering wireless service in your area code or country code. Click the **company** link of the second ISP in the alphabetical list. Write down the name of the ISP, the setup fee, and subscription fee costs.

16 Click the **Back** button as many times as necessary to return to the page displaying the alphabetical list of ISPs in your area code. Keep your browser open for the next activity.

Objective 3
Compare Information You Find on the Web

Doing research on the Web enables you to compare products or services, so that you can decide which product to buy or what service to recommend to a friend, boss, or colleague. The wealth of information at your fingertips makes it easy to do comparisons.

Activity 1.3 Creating a Document that Compares ISPs

Now that you have gathered information about ISPs and the setup and subscription fees for your area, you will create a document to summarize your findings. You can create a simple comparison document that summarizes this information using Notepad. **Notepad** is a plain text editor that is part of the Windows operating system. In this activity, you will use Notepad to create and save a simple document that compares the ISPs you researched.

1 Decide on a location where you can store the Notepad document—either in a folder on your computer's hard drive or a folder on a removable storage device such as a USB flash drive.

2 Click the **Start** button ![start], and then click **My Computer**. Navigate to the location you have decided on for storing your document. On the left side of your screen, under the File and Folder Tasks, click **Make a new folder**. In the text box labeled *New Folder* that displays, using your own first and last names, type **Chapter_1_Internet** Be sure to use the underscore key, which is ⟨⇧ Shift⟩ + ⟨ - ⟩. Then press ⟨Enter⟩. **Close** ![X] the **My Computer** window when you are finished.

3 On the Windows taskbar, click the **Start** button ![start]. Point to **All Programs**, point to **Accessories**, and then point to **Notepad**. Compare your screen with Figure 1.13. Click **Notepad** to open a blank Notepad document.

The Notepad program opens. The Windows operating system enables you to open multiple software programs at the same time. You can move between Notepad and Internet Explorer by using the taskbar to move back and forth between the open Web site and the open Notepad document. The Notepad document displays when you click the Notepad button on the taskbar. When you click the Internet Explorer button on the taskbar, Internet Explorer displays.

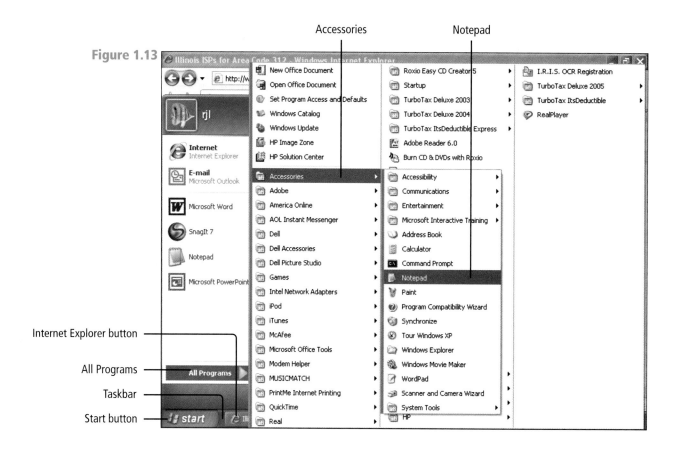

Figure 1.13

Accessories

Notepad

Internet Explorer button

All Programs

Taskbar

Start button

4 In the upper right corner of the **Notepad** window, click the
Maximize button [image] to enlarge the window to fill the computer
screen completely. At the blinking insertion point in the **Notepad**
window, type **1A_Local_ISP_Firstname_Lastname** Be sure to substitute
your own name for *Firstname Lastname*.

5 Press Enter two times to create a blank line, and then start a new
paragraph. Type a short paragraph for each of the four connection
methods you researched in the previous activity. In each paragraph,
include the name of the two ISPs you explored for each connection
method. Then, document the setup fee and the subscription fee for
each ISP.

As you create your comparison document, you can refer back to
The List of ISPs Web site by clicking the Internet Explorer button
on the taskbar.

6 In the final paragraph, type a paragraph that states which ISP you
recommend based on connection method and fees.

7 At the top of the **Notepad** window, on the menu bar, click **File**,
and then from the displayed **File** menu, click **Page Setup**. In the
displayed **Page Setup** dialog box, click in the **Header** box. Select and
then delete any existing text. Click in the **Footer** box, and then
select and delete any existing text. Then, using the underscore character as indicated and your own first and last names, type
1A_Local_ISP_Firstname_Lastname Compare your screen with
Figure 1.14.

Page Setup dialog box   Footer

Figure 1.14

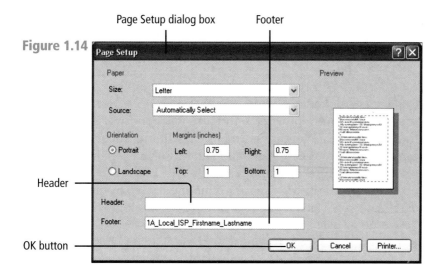

Header

OK button

8 Click **OK** to close the **Page Setup** dialog box.

9 At the top of the **Notepad** window, on the menu bar, click **File**, and then from the displayed **File** menu, click **Save As** to display the **Save As** dialog box. Click the **Save in arrow**, and then navigate to the storage location—the **Chapter_1_Internet** folder—where you are storing your documents for this course. Click in the **File name** box, and then type **1A_Local_ISP_Firstname_Lastname**

Your document is saved as 1A_Local_ISP_Firstname_Lastname to the folder where you are storing your files. By default, Notepad saves the file as a text file with the **extension** *.txt*. An extension is a three-letter set of characters added to the end of the file name that indicates the file type.

10 Check your *Chapter Assignment Sheet* or *Course Syllabus* or consult your instructor to determine whether you are to submit your assignments by printing on paper or electronically, using your college's course information management system. Electronically, you can submit the *.txt* file created in Notepad. To submit the document electronically, follow the instructions provided by your instructor. To print on paper from Notepad, under the **File** menu, click **Print**, and then print accordingly.

11 **Close** ☒ the **Notepad** window to **Exit** Notepad. **Close** ☒ the **Internet Explorer** window to **Exit** Internet Explorer.

End **You have completed Project 1A** ——————————

Project 1B Researching Internet History

An instructor for the Computer Literacy course at Lake Michigan City College has asked students to create a project that involves researching the history of the Internet. Students will conduct research on the Internet and then create a timeline outlining important events. In Activities 1.4 and 1.5, you will locate information on the technologies used in early Internet history. To do this research, you will use a virtual library. Then, you will create a timeline to depict technologies and key events of world history that affected the development of the Internet.

For Project 1B, you will need the following file:

New blank Notepad document

You will save your file as
1B_Internet_Timeline_Firstname_Lastname

Objective 4
Browse a Directory for Information

There are various resources for locating information on the World Wide Web. **Search engines**, such as Google, and directories, such as the Open Directory Project, are used to find information. A search engine is a computer program used to locate files, documents, and Web pages containing specific **keywords**. A keyword is a word or phrase that represents the subject you want to find out about and is used to begin a search. You find search engines at Web sites developed specifically for this service or as part of other Web sites as a value-added service. To use a search engine, you type a keyword representing the topic of interest into a text box, and then click a button on the Web page to start the search. A list of hyperlinks to new Web sites that are related to your topic displays on screen. You can visit any of the Web sites in the list to try to locate more information about your topic.

A **directory**, on the other hand, is compiled by human beings and consists of an alphabetical list of subject categories arranged in a hierarchy leading from a set of broad subject areas to more detailed subcategories for individual Web sites or Web resources. A **virtual library** is a specialized type of directory in which the resources are organized by information professionals, such as librarians. Typically virtual libraries contain excellent, reliable resources that have been analyzed and rated in the same way that books and materials in public libraries are analyzed and rated.

Activity 1.4 Searching for Internet History at the Librarians' Internet Index

Many scientific, historical, political, and technological events of the latter half of the twentieth century contributed to the development of the Internet. In this activity, you will use a virtual library to locate information on these events. The Librarians' Internet Index is a virtual library that enables you to perform directory searches to locate information on many topics. You will visit the Librarians' Internet Index to locate five key events, people, and technologies that were important to the development of the Internet.

1 On the left side of the Windows taskbar, point to, and then click the

Start button ![start]. From the **Start** menu that displays, click **Internet** to start the Internet Explorer program. If necessary, in the upper right corner of the **Internet Explorer** window, click the **Maximize**

button ![maximize] to enlarge the window to fill the computer screen completely.

As an alternative, click the Start button, point to All Programs, and then locate and then click Internet Explorer; or on the desktop, double-click the Internet Explorer icon.

2 In the **Address bar**, click one time to select the existing text, type **http://lii.org** and then press Enter. Compare your screen with Figure 1.15.

The home page of the Librarians' Internet Index (LII) Web site displays on screen. Several subject categories are displayed.

In the URL for the Librarians' Internet Index, the protocol *http*, comes first, followed by punctuation, *://*, to separate it from the rest of the URL. Notice that there is no *www* as is commonly found in other URLs. The server for this Web site is simply named *lii*. The **top-level domain**, or **TLD**, *.org*, indicates that a nonprofit organization owns this Web site. The TLD is the highest level in the Domain Name System expressed as the last part of the domain name and is represented by a period and three letters.

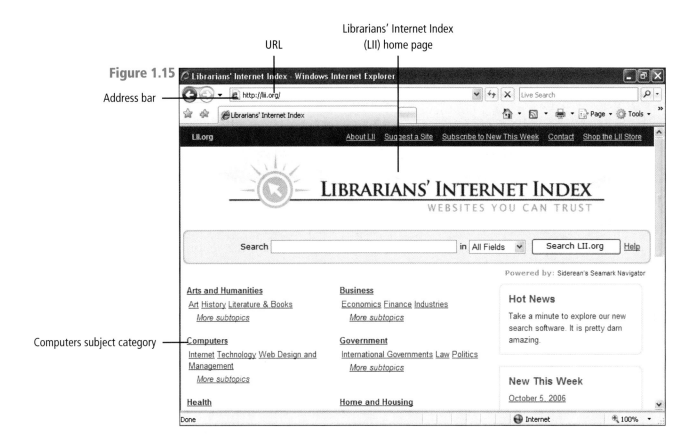

Figure 1.15

Address bar

URL

Librarians' Internet Index
(LII) home page

Computers subject category

Typing the URL into the Address bar of a browser and then pressing [Enter] causes the Web site with that address to display within the browser window. The URL provides the information about the server and the exact files you want to view. The URL indicates the protocol and a path for finding the Web site you want to view.

The protocol used on the Web is typed as *http*, which stands for the HyperText Transfer Protocol. However, you need not type the protocol because the browser assumes the protocol used is HTTP. If you want to use a different protocol, then you must specify it as part of the URL.

The **path** is the sequential description of the storage location of the HTML documents and files making up the Web page and stored in the hierarchy of directories and folders on the Web server. In this case, a directory is an organizational unit used to group data and files on a server or computer. Specific punctuation—:// and /—is used to separate the various parts of the URL. Figure 1.16 shows the specific **syntax**—order of writing—for the URL that must be followed so that your browser software can interpret your request.

The URL provides the following information to the Web browser:

• The protocol—usually *http*—to use for the transfer of the file from the server to the browser. This may or may not be written when expressing the URL in the Address bar.

- The domain name made up of the name of the host computer and the top-level domain.

The URL may also include:

- The path specifying the directories and folders containing the desired file. If a directory or folder is not specified, the browser requests the default directory or folder on the server.

- The name and extension of the file. If a file name is not specified, the browser requests the default file, which is named index.htm or default.htm.

Figure 1.16

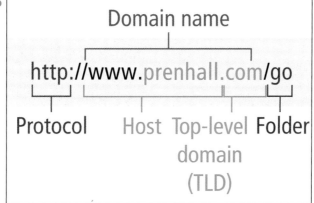

In the first column, locate the **Computers** subject category, and then just beneath it, locate and click the **Internet** link. Compare your screen with Figure 1.17.

The Internet page, with many categories of Internet-related topics, displays. Web sites change their page layout and organization periodically. Your version of the LII Internet Web page may differ from the one shown in Figure 1.17.

Figure 1.17

URL

Address bar

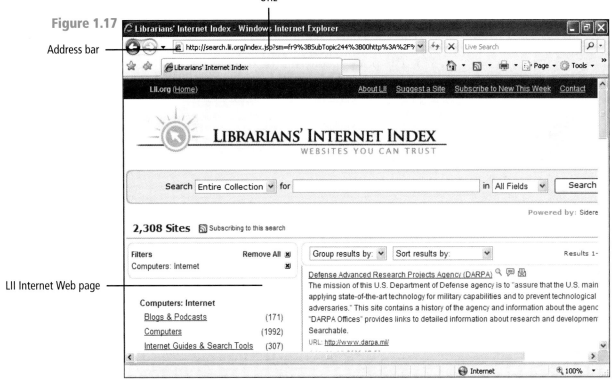

LII Internet Web page

4 Scroll down the page as necessary, and then under the **Computers: Internet** section, click the **More Subtopics** link. On the new page that displays, locate and click the **History** link.

A Web page displays the links to several Internet history resources. Among the links, you will find a variety of articles, historical resources, and timelines.

5 On the right side of the screen, right-click a link of one of the Internet history resources that you find interesting. From the sub-menu that displays, click **Open in New Tab**.

A new tab opens within your browser displaying the Web site that you selected. Internet Explorer has the capability to support multiple open tabs at the same time.

Tabbed browsing is a feature that enables you to open multiple Web pages within the same browser window. This capability enables you to see the information at the new Web site without losing the original Web site. You move between the Web sites by clicking each Web site's tab at the top of the browser window, just below the toolbars. If the link did not open in a new tab, click the Back button to return to the Internet History Web page.

6 Click the new tab, and then read the information about Internet history on the new Web page that displays. After you complete your exploration of the new site, click the **Librarians' Internet Index tab** to return to the **LII Internet History** Web page.

7 Using the tab technique you just practiced, open two more links to other resources that have information on the history of the Internet; specifically, look for dates, names, and events. After reviewing each site, click the **Librarians' Internet Index tab** to return to that Web page.

8 Using any of the sites you reviewed—you can visit them again by clicking the appropriate tab—write down on a sheet of paper any combination of five key events, people, or technologies that affected Internet development. Be sure to note the approximate date of the entries. Then, close the open tabs for the three Web sites you used for research and return to the **Librarians' Internet Index Internet History** Web page.

The list of items you write down will form the basis for the creation of your own Internet history timeline.

9 Keep your browser open for the next activity.

Objective 5
Describe Events and Technologies that Affected the Development of the Internet

Simple searches on the Internet enables you to perform a variety of tasks, from writing a report to finding a vacation destination. As you develop more skill with searching, you will be empowered to learn more about science, history, politics, art, business, technology, and the world around you.

Activity 1.5 Creating a Timeline of Historical Events Affecting the Internet

In this activity, you use the five key events, people, and technologies that you chose in the preceding activity to develop your own Internet history timeline. You will organize these items from oldest to most recent so that you can easily create a timeline using Notepad.

1 On the Windows taskbar, click the **Start** button ![start]. Point to **All Programs**, point to **Accessories**, and then click **Notepad** to open a blank Notepad document. If necessary, Maximize the Notepad window. If Notepad is already open, you can start a new document. To do this, from the File menu, click New.

2 At the blinking insertion point in the **Notepad** window, type **1B_Internet_Timeline_Firstname_Lastname** Press Enter two times to create a blank line. Type the date of the earliest Internet event, person, or technology you researched in the previous activity, and then type - Next, type the name of the actual event, person, or technology and using your own words, type one sentence that describes the importance of the event, person, or technology. Press Enter two times.

3 Using the same technique you used in Step 2, type the next oldest date, and then write about another event, person, or technology you researched. Using your own words, describe its importance. Then, press Enter two times.

4 Using the technique you in Steps 2 and 3, complete the remaining timeline by typing the dates, names, and summary items until all of the information has been placed in this document.

5 At the top of the **Notepad** window, on the menu bar, click **File**, and then from the displayed **File** menu, click **Page Setup**. In the displayed **Page Setup** dialog box, click in the **Header** box, and then select and delete any existing text. Click in the **Footer** box, and then select and delete any existing text. Type **1B_Internet_Timeline_ Firstname_Lastname** Click **OK** to close the **Page Setup** dialog box.

6 At the top of the **Notepad** window, on the menu bar, click **File**, and then click **Save As**. In the displayed **Save As** dialog box, click the **Save in arrow**, and navigate to the **Chapter_1_Internet** folder where you are storing your documents for this course. Click in the **File name** box to select the existing text, and then type **1B_Internet_Timeline_Firstname_Lastname** Click the **Save** button.

Your document is saved to your Chapter_1_Internet folder as 1B_Internet_Timeline_Firstname_Lastname.

7 Check your *Chapter Assignment Sheet* or *Course Syllabus* or consult your instructor to determine whether you are to submit your assignments by printing on paper or electronically, using your college's course information management system. To print on paper from Notepad, under the **File** menu, click **Print**, and then print accordingly. Electronically, you can submit the *.txt* file created in Notepad. To submit the document electronically, follow the instructions provided by your instructor.

8 Close ☒ the **Notepad** window. **Close** ☒ the **Internet Explorer** window.

End You have completed Project 1B ————————————

Project 1C **Connecting to the Internet**

In Objectives 6 through 10, you will use basic Internet terminology to analyze the framework of the Internet. You will determine the appropriate hardware and software required for enabling an Internet connection. You will classify connection methods and define wireless connection options.

Objective 6
Define Common Internet Terms

What is the Internet?   The *Internet*, also referred to as *the Net*, is a worldwide system of networked computers that uses a common set of rules that enable collaboration, communication, and commerce. The *World Wide Web*, which is abbreviated *WWW* and is also referred to as *the Web*, is part of the larger Internet—the part with which you are probably most familiar.

The World Wide Web displays interconnected *hypertext* documents called Web pages. These Web page documents contain text, graphics, and multimedia. Hypertext is text that is linked together in a way that lets you browse through related topics in a nonlinear web of associations.

Think of the Internet as a network of interconnected computers and the World Wide Web as a network of interconnected pages of information. The Web pages contain *hypertext links*, also called *hyperlinks* or *links*, that link to other Web pages that reside on computers located anywhere in the world. A hypertext link is a connection, often represented by blue underlined text or blue bordered images in a Web page, that, when clicked, transfers visitors to another location on the Web page, another page of the Web site, or to a different Web site altogether.

What is hypertext?   Recall that hypertext is text that is linked together in a way that lets you browse through related topics in a nonlinear web of associations. For example, in a Web page containing the word *French*, links might take you to information about the people of France or to a style of cooking.

Because hypertext is nonlinear, you link to related documents in any order. In contrast, books—like this one—are linear, which means they are meant to be read from beginning to end. Figure 1.18 helps to explain how hypertext links documents together.

Figure 1.18

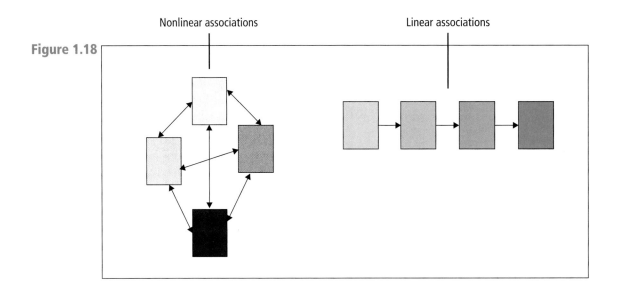

Nonlinear associations   Linear associations

How does my computer view the Web pages? Documents that can be viewed as Web pages are created using a markup language called **HyperText Markup Language**, usually referred to as **HTML**. HTML uses tags to mark a Web page's text and graphics. The tags indicate to a Web browser how it should display the elements of the Web page.

To view HTML documents or Web pages on your computer, you must use software called a Web browser. The most common Web browser is Microsoft Internet Explorer, also referred to as IE. Other browsers, such as Netscape Browser, Firefox, Opera, and Safari are available free of charge; you **download** them at the browser developers' Web site. To download means to receive a file over a network. Internet Explorer is included with your Windows operating system, and you do not need to do anything special to install or use it.

To move—**browse**—from one Web site to another, or among pages on a Web site, click any displayed hyperlink, and your browser software will display the associated Web page. Browsing is sometimes referred to as **surfing**. When you point to a hyperlink—either text or an image—the Link Select pointer ⬚ displays, as shown in Figure 1.19. Clicking a hyperlink makes your browser display the Web page to which the text or image is linked.

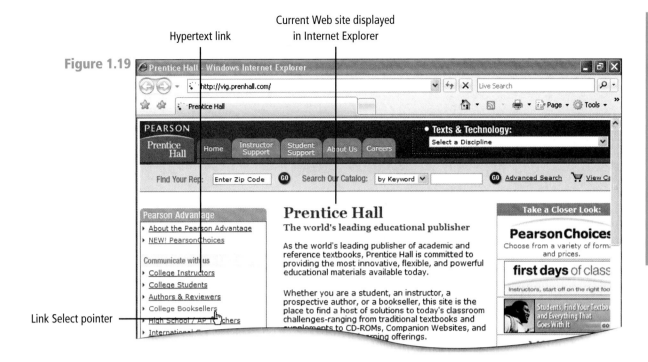

Figure 1.19

Hypertext link

Current Web site displayed in Internet Explorer

Link Select pointer

Objective 7
Analyze URLs, DNS, and Server Structure

What happens when I request a Web site by typing a URL? When you type a URL into the Address bar or click a link to browse to another Web site, you are requesting to view a Web site. This request initiates what is known in computing as *client-server architecture*. Client-server architecture is the interaction between a client computer and a server computer. The computer you are working on is referred to as the *client*, and the computer on which the information is stored—often an organization's host computer—is referred to as the *server*.

A client is a network-connected computer that is used to make requests to view files and other resources provided by another computer. A server is a network-connected computer that stores files and has administrative software to control access to network resources. When you request a Web site, the Web server part of the server will respond to the request. Using client-server architecture, the URL that you type directs the browser on your computer to make a request of the Web server at the location where the Web site is stored to retrieve, transfer, and then display on your screen a copy of the requested Web pages, also referred to as *files*. A file is a complete, named collection of information that serves as a basic unit of storage and by which a computer can distinguish one set of information from another. Figure 1.20 illustrates client-server architecture.

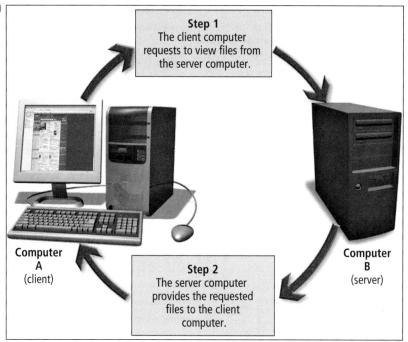

Figure 1.20

Step 1
The client computer requests to view files from the server computer.

Computer A (client)

Computer B (server)

Step 2
The server computer provides the requested files to the client computer.

How do the client and server computers communicate with each other to complete the display of information on my computer? For your computer to communicate with another computer and to have copies of the files transfer with as little error as possible, both computers must follow various sets of rules. These sets of rules are referred to as *protocols*. A protocol describes a common set of rules for how computers communicate and exchange information.

What protocols are used for the transfer and display of files on the Internet? Computers connected to the Internet use *Transmission Control Protocol/Internet Protocol (TCP/IP)*. TCP/IP is the set of rules or protocols for data transmission and communications over the Internet. TCP/IP governs the breakup of data into packets, the routing of the packets, and the subsequent reassembly of packets back into data.

During the request to display a Web page, another protocol is used. *HyperText Transfer Protocol*, also referred to as *HTTP*, is the protocol used to carry the request from the Web browser on the client computer to the server computer, and then to transport copies of files from the server computer back to your client computer in order to display the Web page in the browser.

After the server receives the request for a Web site, the server computer locates the files that make up the Web site. Copies of the requested files are broken down into small packets of data and routed back to the client computer, where the packets are reassembled into the files that display on your screen. Recall that TCP/IP governs the breakup and reassembly of these data packets.

What makes up a Web page? Web pages are formatted using HTML and transmitted under the rules of HTTP. HTML is a tag-based markup language that uses tags to mark Web pages in a manner that can be interpreted by browser software and indicate how screen elements such as text and graphics should be displayed.

A Web page viewed on your computer screen often displays both text and images. What you may not realize is that each image is stored as a separate file, and the text is stored in the HTML document. The HTML document includes not only the text, but also the file names of the pictures, links to other pages, and formatting codes—tags—to control the colors, position, and size of all the elements. Each browser may interpret the formatting in a slightly different manner. It was the development of HTML that made the easy transmission of text and graphics on the same screen possible, and thus made the World Wide Web portion of the Internet possible.

Popular software programs used to create Web pages include Microsoft **FrontPage** and **Dreamweaver**. Dreamweaver was developed by Macromedia and is now owned by Adobe. Both FrontPage and Dreamweaver automatically enter the necessary HTML tags necessary as a Web page is being created in either program. Other Microsoft programs used to develop Web pages include SharePoint Designer and Expression Web.

Notepad, a plain text editor, can also be used as a program to create Web pages. With Notepad, you type the HTML tags, page content, and file names of the screen elements, and then save the document as an HTML file. When saving an HTML file, you can use either *.htm* or *.html* as the extension. The three-letter extension *.htm* is the older form and comes from a time when only three letters could be used as an extension. Now, either form of the extension is accepted. Figure 1.21 shows a Web page as it is being created in Notepad.

HTML
file name   Notepad title bar

Figure 1.21

HTML tags

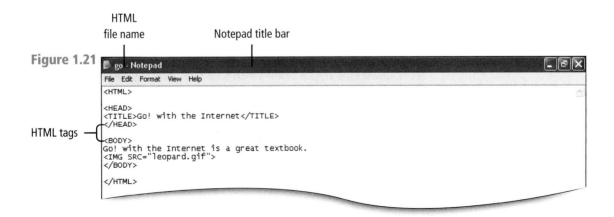

Web pages are made up of various file types, all of which are stored on the server computer—the Web server. The Web server is organized into a hierarchy of directories. Directories are used to organize files and information so the person using the directories is not overwhelmed by the number of directories. Directories are further divided into subdirectories and then folders. Files are stored within the folders. The file types are primarily HTML files but may also include graphic files such as JPG or GIF files, animation files such as GIF or FLASH files, music files such as MP3 or WAV, or video files such as AVI or WMV files. When displaying a Web site, the browser software requests, receives, and properly displays the Web pages and any associated files on your computer.

What is an IP address?   Regardless of its physical location, each server computer connected to the Internet has a unique address called its *IP address*. IP stands for *Internet Protocol*. An IP address is a number that uniquely identifies each computer connected to the Internet to other computers connected to the Internet, for the purpose of communication and the transfer of data packets.

IP addresses are grouped as a series of four sets of numbers separated by dots, such as *66.249.71.56*. Because of this, an IP address is also known as a *dotted quad*. IP addresses range from 0.0.0.0 to 255.255.255.255 and they are organized into classes that help to identify the type of network and the *node*—a specific point of location—for each computer or server.

IP addresses are based on the *IPv4 standard*—the current standard of the Internet Protocol. The mathematical possibilities for IP addresses using the IPv4 standard have almost been reached due to the explosive growth of the Internet. To allow for the future growth of the Internet, a new standard named *IPv6* has been proposed and is gradually being brought into use. IPv6 is sometimes referred to as *IPng*, which stands for *Internet Protocol next generation.*

Are IP addresses and a URLs the same things?   Because a Web server is identified by a numerical IP address, you can view a Web site stored on a server by typing its IP address into a Web browser's Address bar. For example, you could type **http://64.142.8.101** to view a specific Web site. However, most people find it easier to remember a text-based name—the URL—rather than a numerical IP address. When you type **http://lii.org** into the Address bar, the Librarians' Internet Index Web site displays.

How does the URLs that I type in the Address bar find the numerical IP address of the site that I want to access?   The *Domain Name System*, also referred to as the *DNS*, is a hierarchical system under which host computers on the Internet have both a text-based URL and a numeric IP address. When you type a text-based URL, the DNS performs a translation to the numerical IP address. This translation process is called *name resolution*. Figure 1.22 shows how the name resolution occurs.

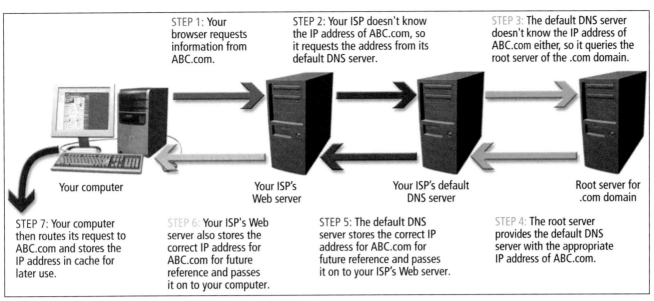

STEP 1: Your browser requests information from ABC.com.

STEP 2: Your ISP doesn't know the IP address of ABC.com, so it requests the address from its default DNS server.

STEP 3: The default DNS server doesn't know the IP address of ABC.com either, so it queries the root server of the .com domain.

Your computer

Your ISP's Web server

Your ISP's default DNS server

Root server for .com domain

STEP 7: Your computer then routes its request to ABC.com and stores the IP address in cache for later use.

STEP 6: Your ISP's Web server also stores the correct IP address for ABC.com for future reference and passes it on to your computer.

STEP 5: The default DNS server stores the correct IP address for ABC.com for future reference and passes it on to your ISP's Web server.

STEP 4: The root server provides the default DNS server with the appropriate IP address of ABC.com.

Figure 1.22

A **domain name** is the part of the text-based URL that identifies the company or organization that owns the Web site. Recall that the top-level domain, also referred to as the TLD, is the highest level in the Domain Name System and is expressed as the last part of the domain name. Within the Domain Name System, the top-level domain is one of several broad categories into which all domain names fall. For example, in the URL **http://lii.org**, the top-level domain is *.org.*

Because there are so many existing domain names and many new requests for domain names, an organization called the **Internet Corporation for Assigned Names and Numbers (ICANN)** oversees the registration of new domain names and administers IP addresses. ICANN proposes new top-level domains and holds public forums for the discussion of new TLD creation. There are a number of top-level domains available for use. Early TLDs included *.com* , *.gov*, *.org*, and *.net*. Additional TLDs have been added to the original list. Two-letter country code TLDs are reserved for use by Web sites located in specific countries. The table shown in Figure 1.23 lists some of the top-level domains used for identifying Web sites belonging to organizations.

Established Top-Level Domains and Who Uses Them

.aero for aviation sites	*.int* for international organizations
.biz for commercial sites only	*.mil* for military sites
.com for commercial or personal sites	*.museum* for museum sites
.coop for cooperative sites	*.name* for personal sites
.edu for educational institution sites	*.net* for Internet infrastructure sites
.gov for government sites	*.org* for nonprofit organization sites
.info for commercial or personal sites	*.pro* for licensed professionals

Figure 1.23

Why are domain names important to organizations? A well-chosen domain name is important to the marketing efforts of many organizations. For example, an easy-to-remember URL becomes part of an organization's brand in the same manner as a logo or trademark. Organizations with an established brand name usually try to purchase all the domain name variations for their brand and purchase all similarly spelled domain names. Using this strategy, even if someone mistypes the URL, the organization's Web site is still displayed.

More Knowledge

ICANN and Registering Domain Names

There are several ICANN-accredited registrars and resellers, such as Network Solutions and Register.com. An important step in obtaining a domain name is to check for the availability of the name by using **WHOIS**. WHOIS is a specialized search tool that searches multiple domain name registration databases for registry information. It determines if a domain name is taken, who currently owns the domain name, and when it may become available. You will find a link to WHOIS at every ICANN-accredited registrar's Web site.

Objective 8
Identify Hardware and Software Needed for
Internet Connections

Do I need special software for my computer to communicate with the Internet?   Your computer must have appropriate software—a Web browser—to communicate with the Internet. Web browsers make it easy for you to make a request for a specific Web site to be displayed on your computer screen. The requests can be made by clicking a hypertext link or by typing the URL directly into the Address bar of the Web browser and then pressing Enter.

What kind of hardware do I need to connect to the Internet?
Specific hardware, usually inside the computer, is required to make a connection to the Internet. Your request to view a specific Web site is broken down into small data packets before the transmission of your request takes place. These data packets are in digital format while stored inside the computer.

If the transmission of data packets takes place over cable, analog telephone, or DSL lines, a conversion from digital to analog must take place. Recall that a modulator/demodulator, or modem, is a hardware device that converts data packets from digital to analog so that they can travel along analog lines. When the analog packets arrive at the other computer, the modem then converts the packets from analog back to digital format. Transmission on a digital transmission line does not require this type of conversion and so is faster.

What ISP does my college or workplace use?   At your workplace or college, it is likely that the computers are connected in a **local area network**, or **LAN**. A LAN is a group of computers and devices forming a network and located in a limited area connected so that any computer or device can communicate with any other computer or device on that network. For example, at work or in your classroom, you may share a printer on the network with other individuals. For an Internet connection, it is likely that your company or college has a direct Internet connection, or gets a connection from some ISP. Sometimes a county government will have a direct Internet connection, and then acts as the ISP for schools and government agencies within the county. Thus, your company or college functions as an ISP for the individual computers in its local network.

Objective 9
Explain Internet Connection Methods

What are some common Internet connection methods? Connection methods vary by the speed and *transmission media* of the connection. Transmission media refers to the physical structure of the network that carries the data packets. The transmission media can be telephone wires, the cable over which cable TV is transmitted, or types of radio frequencies. Connection methods include dial-up, DSL, cable, direct satellite system, and Wi-Fi.

How is connection speed measured? Connection speed is measured in bandwidth and expressed as *bits per second* or *bps*. A *bit* is the smallest unit of data that can be used in computing or sent along a network. Any given character, letter, or number is made up of 8 bits and is called a *byte*.

Transmission rates can range from a thousand bps (kilobits per second or Kbps) to a million bps (megabits per second or Mbps) or a billion bps (gigabits per second or Gbps). Dial-up is the slowest connection method, ranging from 28.8 Kbps to 56 Kbps. Wi-Fi offers the fastest potential connection method with ratings ranging from 11 Mbps up to a maximum of 54 Mbps. The table in Figure 1.24 compares transmission media, speed, and advantages and disadvantages among connection methods.

Internet Connection Methods

Media	Speed	Advantages	Disadvantages
Dial-up	Up to 56 Kbps	Inexpensive and easily available.	Slow data transmission.
DSL	Up to 1.5 Mbps	Uses same lines as telephone but at a much faster speed.	Works best when you are located near the telephone company equipment. Available in levels of service and speed from the ISP.
Cable	Up to 1.5 Mbps	Uses same lines as cable TV but enables simultaneous TV and Internet use.	Available only where cable TV is available—transmission rate speeds vary based on number of people using the connection. Available in levels of service and speed from the ISP.
Direct satellite system (DSS)	500 Kbps	Available in remote areas.	The quality of connection can vary.
Wireless Fidelity (Wi-Fi)	Typically up to 11 Mbps. Newer devices enable up to 54 Mbps.	Does not require hard wires and so allows for mobility.	Requires you to be near a hotspot or access point.

Figure 1.24

Why are Wi-Fi connections so popular?   A wireless connection enables greater flexibility in how, when, and where you can do school work or conduct business transactions. There are no wires or cables that hold you to a desk, but you must be near a hotspot. Wi-Fi connections are becoming more popular due to the growth in the number of available hotspots in public places, such as local coffee shops or cyber cafes, such as the one shown in Figure 1.25, and in homes.

Increased speed makes Wi-Fi use appealing. In addition, there has been an increase in the development of the types of equipment that support Wi-Fi. You can connect with Wi-Fi using a laptop, personal digital assistant (PDA), or a cell phone. Until recently, it was hard to imagine how easily you could use so many devices to connect the Internet.

Figure 1.25

How does Wi-Fi work?   To connect to the Internet using a wireless connection, you must have a Wi-Fi card and special software installed on your desktop computer or laptop computer. The software will try to detect a hotspot. If a hotspot is detected, then you are able to access the Internet using a Web browser. To maintain a connection, you must remain within range of the hotspot. The range can vary depending on physical limitations such as walls or proximity to other appliances using the same radio frequency.

Because wireless development is still new, there are many providers and multiple standards. Additionally, many schools and businesses are in the process of creating their own wireless LANs—local area networks—for use by their own organizations. To accomplish this, multiple hotspots are installed within each building. Wi-Fi standards vary in range, number of connections available per access point, and data transmission speeds. At this point in time, not all organizations use Wi-Fi or have access to the same wireless standard, and interacting with other organizations using wireless connection can be difficult. For the foreseeable future, many organizations are likely to provide both wired and Wi-Fi connections.

End You have completed Project 1C ————————————————

Online Quiz

Project 1C

Take the online self-study quiz for this chapter:

1. Go to **www.prenhall.com/go** and select the textbook *GO!* **with the Internet**.

2. Select **chapter 1**.

3. Select Self-Study Quiz Project 1C.

Project 1D **Exploring Internet History**

In Objectives 11 through 14, you will explore the history of the Internet and examine early government use, scholarly use, and key developers of the Internet. You will describe the origins of hypertext and define the relationship between hypertext and linking. You will examine today's popular uses of the Internet.

Objective 11
Summarize the Early History of the Internet

How did the Internet begin?   The Internet began as a network developed for collaboration and communication among governmental agencies and scientists. The United States Department of Defense developed the **Advanced Research Projects Agency**, known as **ARPA**, to promote scientific research and technological development in order to help the United States gain a leading edge in the race in science and technology among the world's developed nations. In the mid-1960s, U.S. scientists worked with government agencies to develop a large network— **ARPANET**—that would enable communication in the event of a catastrophe. Not only would the network allow for sensitive governmental communications, but also the exchange of academic and scientific research. Around the same time, research was conducted in the technology of breaking information into small data packets that could be passed along a network over various routes and end up at the same destination. This technology became know as **packet switching**. These two technologies were put together to form what eventually became the Internet.

Was the Internet only for military use?   Initially, ARPANET was created for governmental communications. However, this network also proved to be valuable to scientists for collaboration on projects in the early years of ARPANET. Scientists were able to perform research and share their findings with other scientists at four universities across a limited geographic region in the United States. They were able to pass large text files containing their research findings along the network so that other scientists could test the research. This was the forerunner of today's e-mail and e-mail attachments.

Around this same time, **USENET** developed as an electronic bulletin board for research discussion among researchers and scientists. People who were using USENET could read, post, or reply to a specific topic of interest by using a system of threaded discussion boards.

Other scientists worked together to develop network protocols that made the network faster and refined the techniques for sharing information. More advances in hardware and cabling components led to increased data transmission rates, and eventually more groups wanted to use ARPANET. So, the government split the network and renamed a portion of it **MILNET**. MILNET was used for military communications and support while ARPANET remained focused on scientific research and exchange of ideas by scientists. By the late 1980s, ARPANET seemed slow and antiquated by advances made in technology. It was disbanded by the government and replaced with **NSFNET**. NSFNET linked educational and scientific researchers for several years. Eventually NSFNET was disbanded and most universities began using ISPs for their Internet connections.

These remarkable developments in the early history of the Internet took place over a short time period. Figure 1.26 summarizes these developments. ARPANET began as a text-based network requiring such great skill and knowledge to use that only scientists who knew and understood the commands and keystrokes could make it function. In more recent years, the Internet has become one of the most widely used communication venues invented and one of the major societal influences of the late twentieth century history.

Early Government and Scholarly Uses of the Internet

Development	Impact
ARPA	Promoted scientific research and technological development.
ARPANET	Provided a communication network for sensitive governmental, academic, and scientific use.
MILNET	Enabled military communication and support after being split off from ARPANET.
NSFNET	Replaced ARPANET and linked educational and scientific researchers in the late 1980s.
Packet switching	Enabled information to be broken down into small packets and routed over various routes to end up at the same destination.
USENET	Permitted threaded discussions by researchers and scientists in an electronic bulletin board system.

Figure 1.26

Objective 12
Name Early Key Developers of the Internet

Who originated the term hypertext?   Hypertext enables the organization, storage, and retrieval of many types of documents over the Internet. Recall that hypertext is text linked together in a way that lets you browse through related topics in a nonlinear web of associations.

This nonlinear organization and retrieval of documents has not always been named hypertext; the idea has actually been around since 1945. Although several people have worked to develop this concept, Dr. Vannevar Bush is credited with being the originator of the idea.

How did Dr. Vannevar Bush develop the idea of hypertext?
Vannevar Bush served as President Roosevelt's science advisor during World War II. In July of 1945, he published an article entitled "As We May Think" in the magazine *The Atlantic Monthly*. The article described a machine called *Memex*. The machine could store text and graphics enabling what Bush termed *associative indexing* of information. At that time, systems for information retrieval worked in a strictly linear manner beginning with a heading, main classes, then subclasses, and so on.

Dr. Bush proposed that the retrieval process should use associations so that it mimicked the way the human mind was thought to work. The human mind was thought to move through information in various patterns, starting with an idea and then whatever the mind has associated with that idea. Memex enabled two pieces of information to be linked to each other. Any pattern of linking could be called up again at a later time.

Did Bush ever develop his Memex machine? Memex never came into existence. Because Bush worked in isolation, he was limited in how to develop the technology to make Memex a reality. However, the article and the idea were highly respected by many. Fifteen years later, the idea surfaced again. In the 1960s, Ted Nelson began working on a literary software project called *Xanadu*, which was inspired by Bush's idea of associative indexing. Nelson published his project ideas in a book called *Literary Machines* where the term *hypertext* was first used.

Xanadu was a centralized document database consisting of all of the written information of all time. Nelson envisioned a reference system using hypertext to support the ability to link between documents and to enable the editing of the documents within the reference system. The Xanadu project continued for many years generating much discussion and debate among followers. However, the idea was never fully implemented.

What other individuals were important to the development of the Internet? During the late 1960s, several other people became interested in hypertext. While at Brown University, Dr. Andries van Dam developed a *Hypertext Editing System* that ran on an IBM/360 mainframe. This is noted as the first actual use of hypertext. The system was later used to document data in the Apollo space program. Doug Englebert created the *oNLine System*, known as *NLS*, at the Stanford Research Institute. NLS enabled sharing and cross-referencing of more than 100,000 papers and reports. This idea was very similar to Ted Nelson's Xanadu project.

Around the same time, the National Science Foundation and the RAND Corporation worked to develop the communications network called ARPANET that could be used by the federal government in case of nuclear attack. As previously discussed, this network was made up of several nodes—locations on a network—that could originate, store, and pass information to any other node as small packets of data. Using packet switching, these packets could take several routes and still arrive at the intended destination as an entire message. This project evolved into the Internet.

Objective 13
Describe the Unique Features of Hypertext

Who finally made the idea of hypertext a reality? The idea of hypertext did not fully catch on until Sir **Tim Berners-Lee** proposed the World Wide Web in 1989. Berners-Lee was a scientist working at **CERN**, or

European Organization for Nuclear Research, at the time. CERN is the world-renowned particle physics laboratory on the border between Switzerland and France; the name was derived from the French name French Conseil Européen pour la Recherche Nucléaire.

Berners-Lee proposed combining the use of the Internet with hypertext to create a tool for collaboration and data sharing among scientists engaged in engineering and physics research projects. Berners-Lee, Robert Cailliau, and others worked together to make an interactive web of documents accessible by anyone on the network from any point on the network. Berners-Lee is also credited with the development of HTML, HTTP, and the first Web browser, called *WorldWideWeb*. Figure 1.27 shows Sir Tim Berners-Lee.

Figure 1.27

Berners-Lee had the foresight to realize this system could overcome issues of limited travel budgets and a lack of time for travel. He planned for everyone on the network to use the Web as a notebook, a calendaring system, and a mail service.

Eventually these combined technologies developed to the point where a system of hypertext documents could be reached not only by the scientists but also the general population. During a symposium held at the Massachusetts Institute of Technology, Berners-Lee shared his idea of the World Wide Web with the public at the first **World Wide Web Consortium** meeting. From there, the WWW continued to develop into the widely used hypertext-based Internet medium for collaboration and commerce that exists today. The World Wide Web Consortium, commonly referred to as the **W3C**, continues its mission to create standards and guidelines for the Web. Figure 1.28 summarizes the important contributions made by early key developers.

Developers and Their Contributions

Key Developer	Contribution
Tim Berners-Lee	WorldWideWeb browser
Vannevar Bush	Associative indexing
Doug Englebert	oNLine System
Ted Nelson	Xanadu
Andries van Dam	Hypertext Editing System

Figure 1.28

Objective 14
Describe Popular Uses of the Internet Today

How is the Internet used?   The Internet has grown from a text-based tool for research and national defense projects to an integral part of global commerce and communication. Using the Internet, you can communicate with others by sending e-mail or talking in a chat room, regardless of how far they may be from you; find new sources of information in newspapers; check weather reports; or take classes online. You can conduct business transactions online with other businesses. And you can be entertained as you shop, play games, or listen to or download music. Figure 1.29 shows some of the more popular uses of the Internet.

Figure 1.29

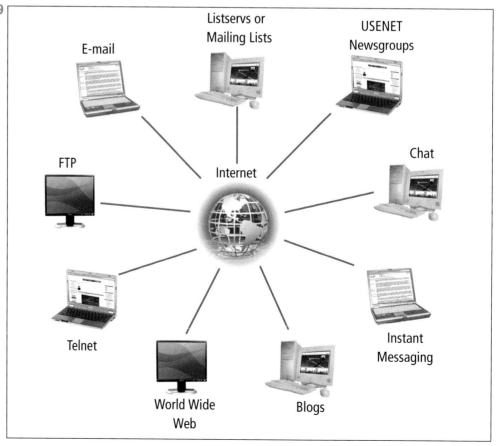

Communication

What is e-mail? *E-mail* is the most popular use of the Internet. E-mail is a service that provides for the exchange of messages and documents over the Internet or over an organization's network. E-mail is a form of *asynchronous communication*; that is, the participants do not need to be online at the same time, and all participants can view the communication when they want to do so. On the other hand, *synchronous communication* takes place when two or more participants are online at the same time communicating with each other. This is also referred to as *real-time communication*.

Listservs or *mailing lists* are subscription-based lists of several names and e-mail addresses combined under one e-mail address. Listservs are managed by software that enables a single e-mail message to reach many people at one time to facilitate the discussion of a specific topic area. Listserv members can send e-mail to and receive e-mail from everyone else who is a member of the listserv; all members see and read the same e-mails. Because the participants need not be online at the same time, this is an asynchronous form of communication.

What is a newsgroup? A *newsgroup* is a networked system of threaded discussion boards where individuals can read, post, or reply on a specific topic of interest. Groups of participants are organized within topic areas. You must subscribe to a newsgroup before you can participate. Participation takes place in asynchronously; you read the main discussion item and then reply to any item that interests you. In this way, a threaded discussion develops over time with many comments from newsgroup members.

You can access newsgroups by using a *newsreader* or by using a Web site to read the archived messages. A newsreader is a software program that enables the subscription to and participation within a newsgroup. Many of the archives of the older USENET newsgroups are now available at the Google Groups Web site and can be easily read by using your browser. You also can start your own newsgroup at Google Groups.

What is chat? *Chat* is interactive, text-based synchronous discussions among two or more participants performed by using an Internet-connected computer and specialized software. Chat takes place in *chat rooms*, which can be found at specific Web sites or by downloading special software on your computer. Several people can use the same chat room. Everyone can post and read what everyone else is typing. Unlike USENET newsgroups, the discussions are not threaded but instead display on the screen in a chronological format in the order that they are typed. This can make it difficult for participants to follow the same train of thought.

Although chat is primarily a text-based communication tool, some chat rooms are now enhanced with audio and video capability. Public chat rooms let you chat with people you may or may not know, raising concerns about personal safety. Always use common sense when participating in chat rooms. For example, you may not want to use your name or give other identifying information in a chat room.

What is instant messaging? *Instant messaging*, or *IM*, is an interactive, text-based synchronous discussion similar to chat. IM clients alert you when someone from your contact list is online so participants can communicate in real time. You must download special software to your computer and then create a user ID to participate in instant messaging. Typically you create a contact list with the names and the user IDs of your friends or colleagues. Usually only two people participate within one IM window, but you can instant message more people if you want.

Improvements to IM software enable sharing of files, audio, and links. To speed the typing of the conversations, *emoticons* and *acronyms* are used as abbreviations within the discussion. Emoticons are a series of keyboard characters, text, or inline images that create a face displaying an emotion. Typically, the faces become visible by tilting your head to the left. Acronyms are a series of letters that stand for the first letter of words in a phrase. Instant messaging is growing in popularity and may soon become as commonly used as e-mail.

What is a blog? *Blog* is short for *Web log*. A Web log is a Web site in the form of a journal or news site that is frequently updated and represents the personality of the author of the Web site. Growing in popularity as an Internet-based communication tool, blogs enable readers to leave comments. Some blogs include video and other forms of multimedia.

Remote Communication

What other Internet uses are there? *Telnet* is a protocol that enables you to access a remote computer to complete tasks as if you were sitting at the keyboard of that computer. Telnet is a text-based synchronous communication. Telnet relies on the use of the letters and arrow keys of the keyboard for operation. Telnet is used by some companies to enable employees to access their benefit records for updating their records on large corporate mainframe computers. Telnet is also used by some libraries for accessing their card catalogs, although it has now largely been replaced by a Web-based catalog system.

Transferring Files

What is FTP? *File Transfer Protocol*, or *FTP*, is a protocol that enables you to copy files from one computer to another on a network. FTP is commonly used to share large files or for uploading HTML documents to a Web server. To use FTP, you need a software program called an *FTP client*. FTP clients let you make a connection to an FTP site and then copy files to and from that site. Some FTP clients are a separate software program that you must install before use. Other FTP clients can be a built-in part of the computer's browser. To use an FTP client to copy files, you may need a password and user ID to log in and create a connection to another computer. However, some computers may be set up to accept anonymous or guest FTP log-ins where no user ID or password is needed.

What exactly defines the World Wide Web? Recall that the World Wide Web (WWW) is the part of the Internet that displays interconnected hypertext documents containing HTML, text, graphics, and multimedia. The World Wide Web contains the total set of interlinked hypertext documents that reside on Web servers all over the world. By using a Web browser, you can locate and display these HTML documents synchronously. The World Wide Web can be used in many ways. The table shown in Figure 1.30 summarizes the categories of Internet use.

Categories of Popular Internet Uses

Use	Sending Mode	Type of Information	Number of Users
Blog	Asynchronous	Text, graphics, multimedia	Multiple
Chat	Synchronous	Text, graphics, multimedia	Multiple
E-mail	Asynchronous	Text, graphics, multimedia	One to one or multiple
FTP	Synchronous	Text, graphics, multimedia	One to one
Instant messaging	Synchronous	Text, graphics, multimedia	One to one or multiple
Listserv	Asynchronous	Text, graphics, multimedia	Multiple
Telnet	Synchronous	Text	One to one
USENET Newsgroup	Asynchronous	Text	Multiple
World Wide Web	Synchronous	Text, graphics, multimedia	Multiple

Figure 1.30

 End **You have completed Project 1D** ———————————

Online Quiz

Project 1D

Take the online self-study quiz for this chapter:

1. Go to **www.prenhall.com/go** and select the textbook *GO!* **with the Internet.**

2. Select **chapter 1.**

3. Select Self-Study Quiz Project 1D.

Assessments

Summary

In this chapter, you were introduced to the Internet. You consulted a Web site to locate local ISPs offering service for your area and created a written comparison of the ISPs. You searched a virtual library to locate information and create a timeline of early technologies and events that affected the Internet's development. You explored connecting to the Internet and defined basic Internet terms. You analyzed URLs, DNS, and server structure, and you identified the hardware and software needed for connecting to the Internet. In addition, you explained connection methods and described wireless connection options. You summarized the early history of the Internet, named early key developers, and described the unique features of hypertext. You described the categories of today's popular Internet uses.

Key Terms

Access point 13

Acronym 42

Address bar 6

Advanced Research
    Projects Agency
    (ARPA)................36

ARPANET 36

Asynchronous
    communication 41

Back button..............11

Bandwidth 11

Berners-Lee, Tim.......38

Bit 33

Bits per
    second (bps) 33

Blog 42

Broadband 13

Browse 26

Browser 4

Byte 33

Cable connection........12

CERN 38

Chat.......................41

Chat room 41

Client.....................27

Client-server
    architecture 27

Dedicated service 8

Default home page 5

Dial-up connection 8

Digital Subscriber Line
    (DSL).................12

Direct satellite system
    (DSS).................13

Directory 18

Domain name 31

Domain Name System
    (DNS)................30

Dotted quad.............30

Download 26

Dreamweaver 29

E-mail 41

Emoticon 42

Extension 17

File 27

File Transfer Protocol
    (FTP)................42

Forward button 11

FrontPage 29

FTP client 42

Home page.................6

Host computer 6

Hotspot 13

Hyperlink.................25

Hypertext 25

Hypertext link
    (Hyperlink
    or Link)...............25

HyperText Markup
    Language (HTML) 26

HyperText Transfer
    Protocol (HTTP) 28

Instant messaging
    (IM).................42

Internet
    (or the Net)..........25

Internet Corporation for
    Assigned Names and
    Numbers (ICANN) 31

Internet Explorer
    (IE) 4

Internet Protocol (IP)
    address 30

Internet Service
    Provider (ISP) 4

IPv4 standard 30

(Continued)

Assessments

Key Terms

IPv6 (or IPng) 30

Keyword 18

Link 25

Listserv 41

Local area
    network (LAN) 32

Mailing list 41

Maximize button 5

MILNET 36

Modulator/demodulator
    (or Modem) 8

Name resolution 30

Newsgroup 41

Newsreader 41

Node 30

Notepad 15

NSFNET 37

Packet switching 36

Page 6

Path 20

Protocol 28

Real-time
    communication 41

Restore Down button 5

Search engine 18

Server 27

Start button 4

Start menu 4

Subscription fee 4

Surf 26

Synchronous
    communication 41

Syntax 20

Tabbed browsing 22

Taskbar 4

Telnet 42

Top-level
    domain (TLD) 19

Transmission Control
    Protocol/Internet
    Protocol (TCP/IP) 28

Transmission media ..33

Uniform Resource
    Locator (URL) 6

USENET 36

Virtual library 18

Web browser 4

Web log 42

Web page 6

Web server 6

Web site 6

WHOIS 32

Wireless fidelity
    (Wi-Fi) 13

World Wide Web
    (WWW or the Web) 25

World Wide Web
    Consortium (W3C) 39

Matching

Match each term in the second column with its correct definition in the first column by writing the letter of the term on the blank line in front of the correct definition.

_____ **1.** A part of the Internet that displays interconnected hypertext documents containing text, graphics, and multimedia.

_____ **2.** The text-based address of a Web site with which the Web browser software locates the Web resources associated with the Web site.

_____ **3.** The set of rules or protocols for data transmission and communications over the Internet governing the breakup of data into packets, the routing of the packets, and the subsequent reassembly of packets back into data.

_____ **4.** The protocol used to carry the request from the Web browser on the client computer to the server computer, and then to transport copies of files from the server computer back to the client computer for display by the browser.

_____ **5.** A hierarchical system under which host computers on the Internet have both a text-based URL and a numeric IP address.

_____ **6.** The organization that oversees the registration of new domain names and administers IP addresses on the Internet.

_____ **7.** A company or organization that provides access to the Internet.

_____ **8.** A digital communications technology that uses standard telephone lines to transmit data but at a higher rate of speed than a standard dial-up connection.

_____ **9.** A unit of measure for bandwidth—the transmission speed or transfer capacity of data on a network.

_____ **10.** A group of computers and devices forming a network and located in a limited area connected so that any computer or device can communicate with any other computer or device on that network.

_____ **11.** Text linked in a way that lets individuals browse through related topics in a nonlinear web of associations.

_____ **12.** A large network developed by ARPA in the 1960s that would enable sensitive governmental communications and the exchange of academic and scientific research without interruption in the event of a catastrophe.

A ARPANET

B Bits per second (bps)

C Digital Subscriber Line (DSL)

D Domain Name System (DNS)

E E-mail

F File Transfer Protocol (FTP)

G Hypertext

H HyperText Transfer Protocol (HTTP)

I Internet Corporation for Assigned Names and Numbers (ICANN)

J Internet Service Provider (ISP)

K Local Area Network (LAN)

L Transmission Control Protocol/Internet Protocol (TCP/IP)

M Uniform Resource Locator (URL)

N Newsgroup

O World Wide Web (WWW)

_____ **13.** A networked system of threaded discussion boards for discussion where individuals can read, post, or reply on a specific topic of interest.

_____ **14.** A service that provides for the exchange of messages and documents over the Internet or over an organization's network.

_____ **15.** A protocol that enables individuals to copy files from one computer to another on a network.

Fill in the Blank

Write the correct answer in the space provided.

1. The software program that enables individuals to view HTML documents and access files related to those documents is called a(n) _____.

2. A network-connected computer that is used to make requests to view files and other resources provided by another computer is called the _____.

3. The part of the text-based URL that identifies the company or organization that owns the Web site is the _____.

4. A high-speed, wireless Internet connection made over radio frequencies is called _____.

5. Wi-Fi connection points are called _____.

6. The transmission speed or transfer capacity of data on a network measured in bits per second is called _____.

7. Computer hardware that converts data packets from digital format to analog format so that they can travel along analog lines is called a(n) _____.

8. A number that uniquely identifies each computer connected to the Internet to other computers connected to the Internet for the purpose of communication and the transfer of data packets is called the _____.

9. The highest level in the Domain Name System expressed as the last part of the domain name is called a(n) _____.

10. A subscription-based list of several names and e-mail addresses combined under one e-mail address generally managed by software and used for the discussion of specific topic areas is called a(n) _____.

11. A software program that enables the subscription to and participation within a newsgroup is called a(n) _____.

12. Interactive, text-based synchronous discussions among two or more participants performed using an Internet-connected computer and specialized software is called _____.

13. Interactive, text-based synchronous discussions between two people participating within one window are called _____.

14. A protocol that enables you to access a remote computer to complete tasks as if you were sitting at the keyboard of that computer is called _____.

15. The first Web page displayed after starting a Web browser, such as Internet Explorer, is referred to as the _____.

Assessments

Rubric

Projects 1A and 1B in the front portion of this chapter, and Projects 1E through 1J that follow have no specific correct result; your result will depend on your approach to the information provided. Make Professional Quality your goal. Use the following scoring rubric to guide you in how to approach the search problem, and then to evaluate how well your approach solves the search problem.

The *criteria*—Internet Mastery, Content, Format and Layout of Search Results, and Process—represent the knowledge and skills you have gained that you can apply to solving the search problem. The *levels of performance*—Professional Quality, Approaching Professional Quality, or Needs Quality Improvements—help you and your instructor evaluate your result.

	Your completed project is of Professional Quality if you:	**Your completed project is Approaching Professional Quality if you:**	**Your completed project needs Quality Improvements if you:**
1–Internet Mastery	Choose and apply the most appropriate search skills, tools, and features and identify efficient methods to conduct the search and locate valid results.	Choose and apply some appropriate search skills, tools, and features, but not in the most efficient manner.	Choose inappropriate search skills, tools, or features, or are inefficient in locating valid results.
2–Content	Conduct a search that is clear and well organized, contains results that are accurate, appropriate to the audience and purpose, and are complete.	Conduct a search in which some results are unclear, poorly organized, inconsistent, or incomplete. Misjudge the needs of the audience.	Conduct a search that is unclear, incomplete, or poorly organized, containing some inaccurate or inappropriate content.
3–Format and Layout of Search Results	Format and arrange all search results to communicate information and ideas, clarify function, illustrate relationships, and indicate relative importance.	Apply appropriate format and layout features to some search results, but not others. Overuse search techniques, causing minor distraction.	Apply format and layout that does not communicate the search results clearly. Do not use format and layout features to clarify function, illustrate relationships, or indicate relative importance. Use available search techniques excessively, causing distraction.
4–Process	Use an organized approach that integrates planning, development, self-assessment, revision, and reflection.	Demonstrate an organized approach in some areas, but not others; or, use an insufficient process of organization throughout.	Do not use an organized approach to solve the problem.

Assessments

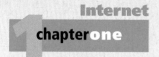
Project 1E—Registering a Domain Name

Objectives: 4. *Browse a Directory for Information;* **7.** *Analyze URLs, DNS, and Server Structure.*

In this Assessment, you will look for an available domain name for the history club at Lake Michigan City College. You will gather information by browsing the dmoz Open Directory Project, a directory, to locate a free domain name registration tool. Then, you will use the domain name registration tool to locate a domain name for your history club. After gathering the information, you will use Notepad to summarize your findings.

For Project 1E, you will need the following file:

New blank Notepad document

You will save your file as
1E_Domain_Firstname_Lastname

1. On the left side of the Windows taskbar, point to and then click the **Start** button. On the **Start** menu that displays, click **Internet** to start the Internet Explorer program. In the upper right corner of the **Internet Explorer** window, click the **Maximize** button to enlarge the window to fill the computer screen completely.

2. In the **Address bar**, click one time to select the existing text, type **http://dmoz.org** and then press Enter. The **dmoz Open Directory Project** home page displays. The dmoz Open Directory Project is a directory of Internet resources and Web sites that is edited and updated by human volunteers. The dmoz Open Directory Project is organized into broad categories. You browse for specific topics by clicking terms that interest you to filter down through the choices and narrow down the topic areas. It also enables you to search for specific terms by using a search form.

3. Locate the **Computers** heading, and then click the **Internet** link to display a subdirectory of links associated with the Internet. Drag the scroll box or click the down scroll arrow to scroll down the page, if necessary, and then locate the **Domain Names** link and click it. At the top of the resulting Web page, several categories of information about domain names are displayed.

4. Locate and click the **Name Search** link. On the resulting Web page, scroll down, and then review the list of registration tools. Click the **Better-Whois.com** link to display the **Better-Whois.com** home page. Better-Whois.com searches shared databases of registered domain names.

(Project 1E–Registering a Domain Name continues on the next page)

Assessments

(Project 1E–Registering a Domain Name continued)

5. In the **Search** text box, type a name that you would like to use as the club name. Click the **Search** button. Take a moment to review the resulting Web page. If the name is reserved, try another TLD or another name. If the club name is available, note the name of a registration provider, and the price of registering the club's name as a domain name. Repeat the search using the club name with two different top-level domains—do not complete the actual registration process.

6. On the Windows taskbar, click the **Start** button. Point to **All Programs**, point to **Accessories**, and then click **Notepad** to open a blank Notepad document. If necessary, **Maximize** the **Notepad** window. Type a title, press [Enter] two times, and then in your own words write a brief paragraph summarizing what you learned. Specify the URL of the Web site where you gathered your information, the three domain names that you tried, the status of their availability, the name of a registration provider, and the fee for registering each domain name.

7. At the top of the **Notepad** window, on the menu bar, click **File**, and then from the displayed **File** menu, click **Page Setup**. In the displayed **Page Setup** dialog box, click in the **Header** box, and then select and delete any existing text. Click in the

Footer box, and then select and delete any existing text. Then, using the underscore character as indicated, and using your own first and last names, type **1E_Domain_Firstname_Lastname** Click **OK** to close the dialog box.

8. At the top of the **Notepad** window, on the menu bar, click **File**, and then from the displayed **File** menu, click **Save As**. In the displayed **Save As** dialog box, click the **Save in arrow,** and navigate to the disk and **Chapter_1_Internet** folder where you are storing your documents for this course. In the **File name** box, type **1E_Domain_Firstname_Lastname**

9. Check your *Chapter Assignment Sheet* or *Course Syllabus* or consult your instructor to determine whether you are to submit your assignments by printing on paper or electronically, using your college's course information management system. To print on paper from Notepad, under the **File** menu, click **Print** and print accordingly. Electronically, you can submit the *.txt* file created in Notepad. To submit the document electronically, follow the instructions provided by your instructor.

10. **Close** the **Notepad** window to **Exit** Notepad. **Close** the **Internet Explorer** window, closing all tabs if prompted to do so, to **Exit** Internet Explorer.

End   **You have completed Project 1E** ——————————

Assessments

Project 1F—Creating a Dictionary of Internet Terminology

Objective: 6. *Define Common Internet Terms.*

Darron Jacobsen, Vice President of Administrative Affairs at Lake Michigan City College, would like to prepare a dictionary of commonly used Internet terminology to help his staff communicate more clearly about the Internet. You will visit the TechEncyclopedia Web site and get the definitions for ten Internet terms. After gathering the definitions, you will create a dictionary of the terms and their meaning.

For Project 1F, you will need the following file:

New blank Notepad document

You will save your file as
1F_Dictionary_Firstname_Lastname

1. On the left side of the Windows taskbar, point to and then click the **Start** button. From the **Start** menu that displays, click **Internet** to start the Internet Explorer program. In the upper right corner of the **Internet Explorer** window, click the **Maximize** button, if necessary, to enlarge the window to fill the computer screen completely.

2. In the **Address bar**, click one time to select the existing text, type **http://www.techweb.com/encyclopedia** and then press Enter. The **TechEncyclopedia** home page displays. TechEncyclopedia is part of the TechWeb Web site and provides the definition for more than 20,000 IT terms. To use TechEncyclopedia, you may fill in a form to get a definition for a specific term or click a link to read random definitions. You may also browse links for the Top 10 Terms.

3. Near the top of the **TechEncyclopedia** Web page, in the **DEFINE THIS IT TERM** text box, type one of the key terms from this chapter, and then click the **Define** button. The word, its definition, and a brief article of explanation display. Make notes for the word and a short definition.

4. Scroll down to locate the **DEFINE THIS IT TERM** link. Type another key term, and then click the **Define** link to display the definition for another term.

5. Using the technique you have just practice, continue this process until you are able to gather the definitions for ten Internet terms.

6. Organize the terms in alphabetical order.

7. **Start** Notepad, and if necessary, **Maximize** the **Notepad** window. Type the first term in the list, press Spacebar, type -, and then press

(Project 1F—Creating a Dictionary of Internet Terminology continues on the next page)

Assessments

Mastering the Internet

(Project 1E–Creating a Dictionary of Internet Terminology continued)

the Spacebar again. Type the short definition for the term. Press Enter two times. Repeat this process to create an alphabetical listing of the ten terms and their definitions.

8. At the top of the **Notepad** window, on the menu bar, click **File**, and then from the displayed **File** menu, click **Page Setup**. In the displayed **Page Setup** dialog box, click the **Header** box, and then delete any existing text. Click in the **Footer** box, delete any existing text, and then using the underscore character as indicated, and substituting your own first and last names, type **1F_Dictionary_Firstname_ Lastname** Click **OK** to close the dialog box.

9. At the top of the **Notepad** window, click **File**, and then click **Save As**. In the displayed **Save As** dialog box, click the **Save in arrow**, and then navigate to the disk

and the **Chapter_1_Internet** folder where you are storing your documents for this course. In the **File name** box, type **1F_Dictionary_Firstname_Lastname** and then click **Save** to save your file.

10. Check your *Chapter Assignment Sheet* or *Course Syllabus* or consult your instructor to determine whether you are to submit your assignments by printing on paper or electronically, using your college's course information management system. To print on paper from Notepad, under the **File** menu, click **Print** and print accordingly. Electronically, you can submit the *.txt* file created in Notepad. To submit the document electronically, follow the instructions provided by your instructor.

11. **Close** the **Notepad** window. **Close** the **Internet Explorer** window.

End **You have completed Project 1F** ———————————————

Assessments

Project 1G—Finding a Local Wireless Hotspot

Objectives: 1. *Consult a Web Site to Locate an ISP that Offers Service in a Specific Area;* **2.** *Refine Searches to Distinguish Among the Features of Each ISP;* **3.** *Compare Information You Find on the Web;* **9.** *Explain Internet Connection Methods;* **10.** *Describe Wireless Connection Options.*

The Associate Dean for Adult Basic Education, Lisa Huelsman, is interested in providing more support for adult learners. She feels that adult learners would be able to study and do research more often if they knew more places where they could connect to the Internet. In the following Assessment, you will visit the Wi-FiHotspotList.com Web site to locate hotspots in your geographic area. After conducting the search, you will create a comparison document stating which method you prefer for conducting the search and then list the names and addresses of hotspots in your geographic area.

For Project 1G, you will need the following file:

New blank Notepad document

You will save your file as
1G_Hotspots_Firstname_Lastname

1. On the Windows taskbar, click the **Start** button. From the **Start** menu that displays, click **Internet** to start the Internet Explorer program, and then **Maximize** the window if necessary.

2. In the **Address bar**, click one time to select the existing text, type **http://www.wi-fihotspotlist.com** and press Enter. The **Wi-FiHotspotList.com** home page displays. Wi-FiHotspotList.com functions as a search engine or as a directory for locating hotspots, or wireless access points, around the world. You can locate hotspots by providing either a whole or partial street address or by browsing a directory of regions.

3. In the middle of the home page, type a full or partial address. Click the **Find a Hotspot** button to bring up the name and address where you can find a hotspot. Click the name of the location to display location details and a map of the location.

4. Click the **Search Again** link to begin a new search. Scroll down, and then click the **Browse by Region** link to reveal a list of countries. Click the **United States** link. Then, click your state. Click your city, or continue clicking the categories until you are able to locate the hotspot nearest to where you live or your school.

(Project 1G–Finding a Local Wireless Hotspot continues on the next page)

Assessments

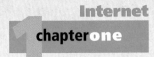

chapter one **Internet**

Mastering the Internet

(Project 1G–Finding a Local Wireless Hotspot continued)

5. **Start** Notepad, and if necessary, **Maximize** the **Notepad** window. Add the file name and your name to the **footer** of the document: **1G_Hotspots_Firstname_Lastname** At the beginning of the document, add a title, and then insert a blank line. In your own words, write a brief comparison to summarize which method you prefer for conducting the search. Then, list the names and addresses of hotspots in your area. Include a statement of whether you will use one of the hotspots.

6. At the top of the **Notepad** window, click **File**, and then click **Save As**. In the displayed **Save As** dialog box, click the **Save in arrow**, and then navigate to the disk and **Chapter_1_Internet** folder where you are storing your documents for this

course. In the **File name** box, type **1G_Hotspots_Firstname_Lastname** and then **Save** the document.

7. Check your *Chapter Assignment Sheet* or *Course Syllabus* or consult your instructor to determine whether you are to submit your assignments by printing on paper or electronically, using your college's course information management system. To print on paper from Notepad, under the **File** menu, click **Print** and print accordingly. Electronically, you can submit the *.txt* file created in Notepad. To submit the document electronically, follow the instructions provided by your instructor.

8. **Close** the **Notepad** window. **Close** the **Internet Explorer** window.

End **You have completed Project 1G**

Assessments

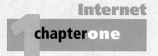
Mastering the Internet

Project 1H–Identifying an Early Internet Developer

Objectives: 4. *Browse a Directory for Information;* **5.** *Describe Events and Technologies that Affected the Development of the Internet;* **12.** *Name Early Key Developers of the Internet.*

James Smith, Vice President of Student Affairs at Lake Michigan City College has asked you to make a presentation to incoming freshmen during their orientation. In the following Assessment, you will visit the Living Internet Web site to search for information on one of the early developers of the Internet. After conducting your search, you will write a short biography that includes the name of the developer you chose and a description about his or her impact on the development of the Internet.

For Project 1H, you will need the following file:

New blank Notepad document

You will save your file as
1H_Developer_Firstname_Lastname

1. On the Windows taskbar, click the **Start** button. From the **Start** menu, click **Internet** to start the Internet Explorer program. **Maximize** the **Internet Explorer** window, if necessary.

2. In the **Address bar**, click one time to select the existing text, type **http://www.livinginternet.com** and then press Enter. The **Living Internet** home page displays. The Living Internet Web site is a directory that offers an extensive amount of information about Internet history, its design, use, and other related topics. The information is uniquely organized into an easily navigated grid of topics or may be searched as a directory.

3. Scroll down the Web page to locate the directory portion of the Web page, and then click the **People** link. A Web page displays that lists many people who helped develop the Internet. Click the link for one person who was not mentioned in this chapter. Make note of the person's name, what he or she contributed to the development of the Internet, and the dates of that person's contribution.

4. **Start** Notepad, and if necessary, **Maximize** the **Notepad** window. Add the file name and your name to the **footer** of the document: **1H_Developer_Firstname_Lastname** In your own words, write a brief paragraph summarizing your research. Specify the person's name, what he or she contributed to the development of the Internet, and the dates when the contribution was made.

(Project 1H–Identifying an Early Internet Developer continues on the next page)

Assessments

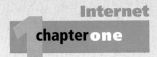

 Mastering the Internet

(Project 1H–Identifying an Early Internet Developer continued)

5. At the top of the **Notepad** window, click **File**, and then click **Save As**. In the displayed **Save As** dialog box, click the **Save in arrow**, and navigate to the disk and **Chapter_1_Internet** folder where you are storing your documents for this course. In the **File name** box, type **1H_Developer_ Firstname_Lastname** and then **Save** the document.

6. Check your *Chapter Assignment Sheet* or *Course Syllabus* or consult your instructor to determine whether you are to submit

your assignments by printing on paper or electronically, using your college's course information management system. To print on paper from Notepad, under the **File** menu, click **Print** and print accordingly. Electronically, you can submit the *.txt* file created in Notepad. To submit the document electronically, follow the instructions provided by your instructor.

7. **Close** the **Notepad** window. **Close** the **Internet Explorer** window.

End **You have completed Project 1H** ————————————————————————

Assessments

Mastering the Internet

Project 1I—Learning About Popular Internet Activities

Objective: 14. *Describe Popular Uses of the Internet Today.*

Dr. James Smith, Vice President of Student Affairs, is preparing a presentation for freshman orientation. He would like you to research the current uses of the Internet and how it has impacted society and the educational system. In the following Assessment, you will visit the Pew Internet & American Life Project Web site to learn more about popular Internet activities. You will create a brief document describing the impact of the Internet on an aspect of American life that you feel is relevant to the freshman orientation presentation.

For Project 1I, you will need the following file:

New blank Notepad document

You will save your file as
1I_Internet_Activity_Firstname_Lastname

1. On the Windows taskbar, click the **Start** button. Click **Internet** to start the Internet Explorer program, and then **Maximize** the browser window if necessary.

2. In the **Address bar**, click one time to select the existing text, type **http://www.pewinternet.org** and then press `Enter`. The home page of the **Pew Internet & American Life Project** Web site displays. The Pew Internet & American Life Project studies the effects of the Internet on American society. This site provides data, presentations, and articles on the latest trends for Internet usage.

3. In the upper left corner, click the **Reports** link to display recent reports and memos. In the column, labeled *Report Topics*, click the **Online Activities and Pursuits** link. In the *Recent Reports and Memos* area, locate an article that you find interesting.

4. Click the **Learn More** link to read a summary of the report or memo. Note the name of the report, the date of the report, and a summary of the important ideas presented in the report. You can read the entire report by clicking the **View PDF of Report** link. A **PDF file** is a file that was created by using the Adobe Acrobat program. Typically, you can read a *.pdf* file but you cannot modify it unless you have been given rights to do so by the document's creator. To read a PDF file, you must have Adobe Reader software installed on your computer. You can download Adobe Reader from **http://www.adobe.com/products/acrobat/readstep2.html**.

(Project 1I—Learning About Popular Internet Activities continues on the next page)

Assessments

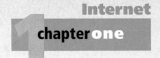
(Project 1I–Learning About Popular Internet Activities continued)

5. **Start** Notepad and if necessary, **Maximize** the **Notepad** window. Add the file name and your name to the **footer** of the document: **1I_Internet_Activity_Firstname_ Lastname** In your own words, write a brief paragraph stating the name and date of the Pew Internet & American Life Project report, and a summary of what you feel are the most important ideas you found in the report.

6. At the top of the **Notepad** window, click **File**, and then click **Save As**. In the displayed **Save As** dialog box, click the **Save in arrow,** and navigate to the disk and **Chapter_1_Internet** folder where you are storing your documents for this course. In the **File name** box, type **1I_Internet_ Activity_Firstname_Lastname** and then **Save** the document.

7. Check your *Chapter Assignment Sheet* or *Course Syllabus* or consult your instructor to determine whether you are to submit your assignments by printing on paper or electronically, using your college's course information management system. To print on paper from Notepad, under the **File** menu, click **Print** and print accordingly. Electronically, you can submit the *.txt* file created in Notepad. To submit the document electronically, follow the instructions provided by your instructor.

8. **Close** the **Notepad** window. **Close** the **Internet Explorer** window.

End **You have completed Project 1I** ————————————————————

Assessments

Project 1J—Locating WWW Training Resources

Objective: 3. *Compare Information You Find on the Web;* **4.** *Browse a Directory for Information.*

For Project 1J, you will need the following file:

New blank Notepad document

You will save your file as
1J_Training_Firstname_Lastname

Clarence Krasnow, Director of Resource Development, needs to compile a list of four Web sites to use as training resources for Lake Michigan Community College faculty and staff. Dr. Krasnow wants one site that provides computer definitions, one site that provides general resources about computing, one site that explains file formats, and one site that explains how to get connected to the Internet using a modem or other connection method. Using the concepts presented in this chapter and the Librarians' Internet Index Web site, locate four Web sites that meet Clarence's needs. In Notepad, create a summary document listing each Web site by name, its URL, and the type of information the Web site provides. Save your document as **1J_Training_Firstname_Lastname** and then submit it to your instructor as directed.

End **You have completed Project 1J** ──────────────

chaptertwo

Browsing the World Wide Web

OBJECTIVES

At the end of this chapter, you will be able to:

1. Perform Commands with Internet Explorer
2. Perform Commands with the Toolbar
3. Specify a Default Home Page
4. Browse the World Wide Web Using Links, the Address Bar, History, and Favorites Center

5. Print, Save, and E-mail a Web Page
6. Create a Desktop Shortcut to a Web Page
7. Clear the Cache, Cookies, and History

8. Describe How Plug-ins Work
9. Identify and Compare Several Popular Web Browsers

10. Determine the Risks of Using the World Wide Web
11. Identify Safe Browsing Strategies

OUTCOMES

Mastering these objectives will enable you to:

Project 2A
Browse the World Wide Web

Project 2B
Manage Web Content with Internet Explorer

Project 2C
Identify How Browsers Work

Project 2D
Examine Privacy Risks and Security Issues of Browsing

City of Desert Park

The City of Desert Park, Arizona, is a thriving city with a population of just under 1 million. Desert Park's temperate year-round climate attracts both visitors and businesses. Desert Park is in the middle of the fastest-growing region in the country, serving all the major markets in the western United States. The location of this southwest city is ideal because of its proximity to southern California and the international markets of the Pacific Basin and Mexico.

Desert Park has plenty of room for long-term growth. Only 50 percent of the land in the city has been developed. Most of the undeveloped land already has a modern infrastructure and assured water supply in place. Additionally, voters recently approved a plan for a light rail system connecting the city.

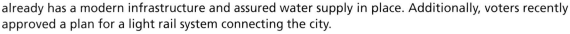

Desert Park is one of the most popular vacation destinations in the world, with its sunny climate and easy driving to the scenic wonders of Arizona such as the Grand Canyon and the Sonoran Desert Museum.

Browsing the World Wide Web

The World Wide Web (WWW) is an important part of society. Originally the Internet was used only by scientific researchers and government workers. With the development of the WWW, it now serves as a repository of information and resources that can be used in everyday lives. You can easily locate resources for personal, educational, or professional uses. To access this information, use any computer with an Internet connection that has a Web browser installed on it.

Project 2A Browsing the World Wide Web

Shane Washington, Director of Office Operations, has started a training initiative. He would like everyone in the office to use Internet Explorer for their work with the World Wide Web. In Activities 2.1 through 2.11, you and the office staff for the City of Desert Park, Arizona will use Internet Explorer to browse the Web. You will participate in the training initiative by identifying and performing commands on the menu bar and on the toolbar. You will specify a default home page, and browse the World Wide Web using links and the Address bar. You will use the History and the Favorites Center features to locate Web sites.

For Project 2A, you will need the following file:

Web page printout

**You will print your file with the footer
2A_Firstname_Lastname**

Figure 2.1

Objective 1
Perform Commands with Internet Explorer

Browsers offer many features that enable you to perform commands as you browse the Web. Although each browser may use unique names when referring to some of these features, the tasks that you perform with any browser are similar and are found on **toolbars**. A toolbar is an area of a software program's interface that provides text or buttons, which when clicked, enable you to perform certain commands and tasks within that software program.

Typically, many of the most important commands and tasks are contained in a **menu bar**. A menu bar is a horizontal bar near the top of the browser window that contains expandable menu-style headings for performing important commands and tasks. Because a browser window is limited in size, a menu bar can be hidden when you prefer to have more of the screen available for viewing Web pages.

Activity 2.1 Exploring the Menu Bar

In this activity, you begin your training by starting Internet Explorer 7 and identifying parts of the Internet Explorer window. You will gain familiarity with the Tools button and perform several commands with the menu bar. You will print an entire Web page.

1 **Start** Internet Explorer and if necessary, click the **Maximize** button to enlarge the window to fill the screen completely. In the **Address bar**, click one time to select the existing text, and then type **http://www.prenhall.com** Press the Enter key.

The Prentice Hall home page displays.

2 At the top of the screen, locate the blue area called the **title bar**. On the left side, notice the Web browser's logo, the title of the Web page, and the Web browser name. On the right side, notice the **Minimize** , **Restore Down** , and **Close** buttons.

The title bar is a blue, horizontal bar at the top of the browser window that identifies the program and displays the name of the active Web page. The **Minimize, Restore Down, and Close buttons** enable you to customize the screen's size.

Note — Maximize or Restore Down?

The *Maximize* button enables the customization of the screen by enlarging the browser window to take up the entire computer screen. If the window is already maximized, the button is called the *Restore Down* button because when clicked, it will restore the window back to its original size.

3 On the right side of the screen, under the **Minimize**, **Restore Down**, and **Close** buttons, locate the **Tools** button. On the right side of the **Tools** button, click the **down arrow**. In the submenu that displays, scroll down and point to the **Menu Bar** command. Compare your screen with Figure 2.2. Click the **Menu Bar** command to display the menu bar near the top of the browser window.

The *Tools button* enables you to perform several commands that are frequently used while browsing the Web, such as safe browsing strategies, displaying toolbars within the browser interface, and setting browsing preferences. Just as with other buttons and commands, the Tools button can expand and collapse to display a *submenu*. A submenu is a detailed list of commands that displays after clicking a command that enables you to perform several tasks to enhance your browsing experience.

One of the submenu commands found under Tools is the Menu Bar command. Previous versions of Internet Explorer included the menu bar as a fixed feature of the Web browser window. Current versions of Internet Explorer enable you to control the amount of space available in the Web browser screen by displaying or hiding the menu bar. When the menu bar is displayed, it displays as a horizontal bar near the top of the browser window that contains several expandable menu-style headings for performing important commands and tasks. You may have used a similar menu bar in other software programs, such as a word processing program.

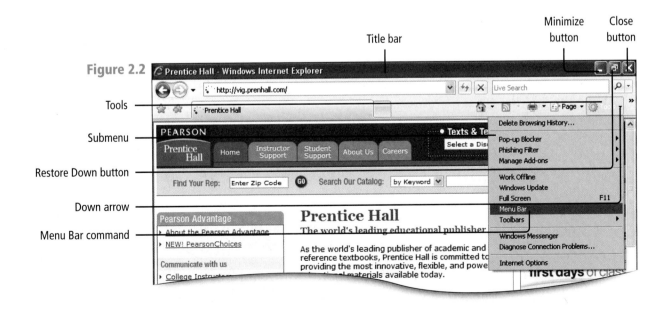

Figure 2.2

Title bar

Minimize button

Close button

Tools

Submenu

Restore Down button

Down arrow

Menu Bar command

4 On the menu bar, notice the commands for working with Web pages. The table in Figure 2.3 summarizes the menu bar commands and their functions. Click the **File** command. On the submenu, notice several more commands display. Compare your screen with Figure 2.4.

You save Web pages by clicking the Save As command. You click Close Tab to close the currently displayed Internet Explorer screen. You print Web pages by clicking Print. You send a Web page or the link to a Web page via e-mail by clicking Send.

Another Way

To Hide the Menu Bar

To maximize the browser window, you can hide the menu bar. You can still perform the commands and tasks found on the menu bar. The most commonly used commands and tasks are available by using other commands and buttons visible on the toolbar. For example, to print a Web page, you can use the Print command under the File menu or on the toolbar, click the Print button.

Menu Bar Commands and Their Functions

Command	Key Functions
File	Save, print, or send a Web page.
Edit	Select, cut, copy, and paste information.
View	Control display of toolbars and screen.
Favorites	Organize and view favorite Web sites.
Tools	Set privacy and security options.
Help	Locate helpful tips and support.

Figure 2.3

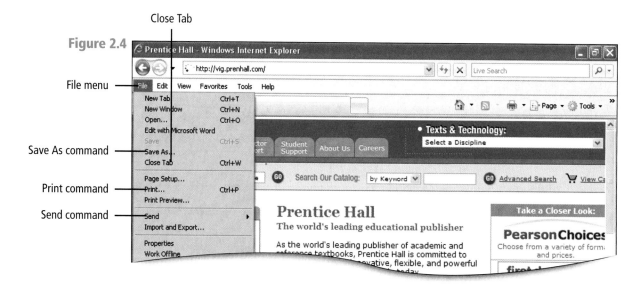

Close Tab

Figure 2.4

File menu

Save As command

Print command

Send command

5 On the menu bar, click **File**, and then click **Page Setup** to open the **Page Setup** dialog box.

The Page Setup dialog box is divided into four sections: Paper, Headers and Footers, Orientation, and Margins (inches). The options in each of these sections control the quality of the Web page you print. In the section labeled *Paper*, you choose the paper size and paper source. In the section labeled *Headers and Footers*, you type information into the text boxes to annotate the top or the bottom of the printed Web page.

The section labeled *Orientation* enables you to choose between Portrait, which sets up the layout of the Web page vertically on the paper, and Landscape, which sets up the Web page horizontally on the paper. These options are helpful when printing Web pages with content that is designed to display wider than Letter-size paper. Adjustments can also be made in the Margins section to modify the printed Web page by making it fit better with the size of the paper used.

6 In the **Page Setup** dialog box under the **Header** section, click in the **Header** box, and delete any existing text. Under the **Footer** section, click in the **Footer** box, and delete any existing text. Then, using the underscore character as indicated and your own first and last names, type **2A_Firstname_Lastname** Click **OK** to add your name as the footer to the Web page and to close the **Page Setup** dialog box. On the menu bar, click **File**, and then click **Print Preview** to display the **Print Preview** dialog box.

The Print Preview dialog box shows what the Web page will look like when it prints, including the footer you typed. You can print directly from this dialog box. Other commands at the top of the Print Preview dialog box enable you to make adjustments to the printed page's width percentage and orientation.

7 In the **Print Preview** dialog box, click the **Close** button to close the dialog box. On the menu bar, click **File**, and then click **Print** to display the **Print** dialog box.

8 In the **Page Range** section, click the **All** option. Click the **Print** button to print out the entire Web page.

The Print dialog box closes and the entire Web page is printed. Your printed Web page may be composed of several sheets of paper to print all of the vertical content of the Web page. In addition, many Web pages have content that is too wide to print completely within the dimensions of typical printer paper. Many Web sites offer printer-friendly versions of their Web pages that are formatted to fit perfectly on an 8.5-by-11 sheet of paper. Internet Explorer automatically tries to modify the size of any Web page in order to make it fit the width of the paper but you can also adjust for size before printing.

9 On the menu bar, click **Edit**. The Edit menu displays a submenu of commands.

The Edit menu commands enable you to select, cut, copy, and paste text in the same way you can in a word processing program.

10 From the **Edit** menu, click **Select All**. Notice that all of the text and images on the Web page in your browser are selected. Click anywhere in the browser window to unselect the text and images.

11 On the menu bar, click **Edit**, and then click **Find on this Page**. Compare your screen with Figure 2.5.

The Find dialog box displays. It enables you to specify a word or phrase to locate on the current Web page. You can match whole words, match the case of the letters in the word, or search up or down within the document.

Find dialog box

Figure 2.5

Edit

12 In the **Find** box, type the word **college** and then click the **Next** button.

The Find dialog box remains open and on top of the current Web page. The first instance of the word *college* on the Web page will display as selected text. You can continue searching for the word by clicking the Next button until all instances of the word have been found.

13 In the **Find** dialog box, click the **Close** button ⊠. Keep your browser open for the next activity.

Activity 2.2 Showing and Hiding Toolbars

Some of the Web sites you visit contain a lot of content. By hiding some of the toolbars, your screen gains space to display more content. By showing some of the toolbars, you gain easier access to several key features and commands. In this activity, you will practice showing and hiding several of the toolbars that are part of your browser's window as you continue the training initiative.

1 On the menu bar, click **View**, and then click **Toolbars**. Notice that the Toolbars command has a small arrow to the right of it to indicate that there will be additional commands on a submenu.

The submenu has options for showing or hiding several toolbars within the Web browser window. Check marks to the left of the submenu commands indicate which toolbars display in the browser window. Clicking any checked toolbar command removes the check mark and the toolbar no longer displays in the browser window. Clicking an unchecked command makes the toolbar display in the browser window.

2 On the **View** menu, point to **Status Bar.**

A description of the Status Bar function displays on the ***status bar*** in the lower left of your browser's window. A status bar is a horizontal bar near the bottom of the browser window that provides information about the security of a site, about a link's destination as you position the mouse pointer over a link, or information about any submenu command.

3 On the **View** menu, click **Status Bar** to remove the check mark next to it and to remove the status bar from your browser window.

The View menu closes and the status bar is no longer displayed. You can see more of the content on the Web page in the browser window.

4 On the menu bar, click **View**, point to **Status Bar**, and notice that although the Status Bar command is listed, there is no longer a check mark next to it. Click the **Status Bar** command.

The View menu closes and the status bar is again displayed in the browser window.

5 On the menu bar, click **View** and then point to **Status Bar**. Notice the Status Bar command now has a check mark next to it and the status bar displays in the browser window.

6 Keep your browser open for the next activity.

Activity 2.3 Customizing Text Size

Accessibility compliance is an initiative to provide features that accommodate people with visual or physical disabilities so that they can access the Internet. These features enable modifications to be made to the browser and the display of Web sites. For example, the Text Size command provides control of the font size displayed on a Web page so that the content is more easily read. Not only is this is an important feature for visually impaired people, it is also useful when making a presentation or when text must be displayed, using a projector. You continue your training in Activity 2.3 by changing the text size in your browser.

1 On the menu bar, click **View** and then point to **Text Size**. Notice that the Text Size command has a small arrow to the right of it to indicate that there will be additional commands on a submenu. Compare your screen with Figure 2.6.

The submenu has options for selecting the text size displayed within the Web browser window. A dot to the left of the submenu commands indicates which text size is currently used to display text in the browser window.

Current text size

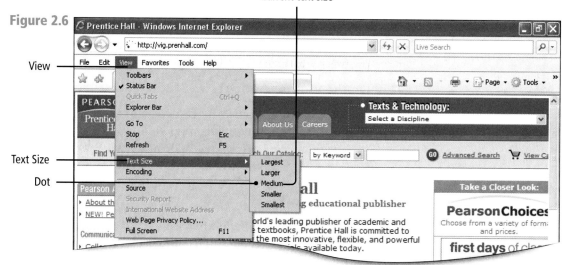

Figure 2.6

View

Text Size

Dot

■2■ In the **Text Size** submenu, notice which submenu command has a dot next to it. You will return the computer to its initial setting after this activity. Click **Largest**. As an alternative, if the Largest command is already selected, click another size that does not have a dot next to it.

The View menu closes and the text on the Web page displays in a larger font size.

Alert

Does your text not display correctly?

If the Web designer has set the text to a specific size, the text may not respond to the Text Size commands unless you alter the accessibility settings for the browser. You can do so by using the Tools menu and the Internet Options submenu.

■3■ On the menu bar, click **View**, then click **Text Size**. In the submenu, click **Smallest.**

The View menu closes and the text on the Web page displays in a small size.

■4■ On the menu bar, click **View**, then click **Text Size**. In the submenu, click **Medium.** Alternatively, click the setting that was the original setting.

The text size returns to the default size for your browsing preferences.

Another Way

To Modify Text Size

The text size can also be modified without the use of the menu bar. To do this, click the Page button down arrow, and then click Text Size to display the same size options you access with the Text Size command on the menu bar.

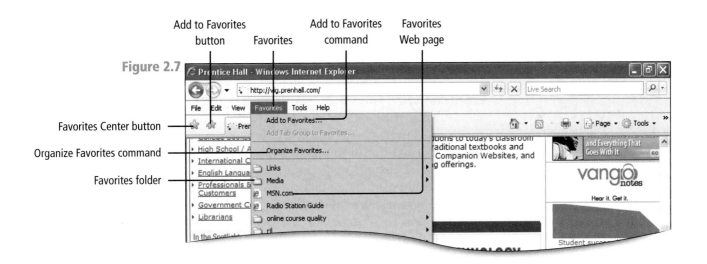

5 Keep your browser open for the next activity.

Activity 2.4 Locating Favorites and Tools on the Menu Bar

In this activity, you and the office staff of the City of Desert Park continue your training with Internet Explorer by locating more commands on the menu bar.

1 On the menu bar, click **Favorites**. Alternatively, you can also click the **Favorites Center** button [icon] or the **Add to Favorites** button [icon]. Compare your screen with Figure 2.7. Your **Favorites** list may display slightly differently.

A submenu with the commands Add to Favorites and Organize Favorites displays. The **Favorites Center** is a feature of Internet Explorer that contains a list of Web sites you have visited before and that you have added to a Favorites list, so that you can easily return to the sites again.

Although a few folders and Web sites are provided by default, more folders and Web sites can be added by using either the Add to Favorites command or the Organize Favorites command.

Figure 2.7

2 On the menu bar, click the **Tools** button to display the Tools menu commands. Alternatively, you can click the **Tools** button. Compare your screen with Figure 2.8. Click anywhere to close the Tools menu.

The Tools menu provides many commands such as Delete Browsing History, Pop-up Blocker, Phishing Filter, Manage Add-ons, Windows Update, Window Messenger, Diagnose Connection Problems, and Internet Options. All of these commands are used to optimize your Web browser and to control *privacy* settings. These settings enable you to determine how much privacy you require for personal information, such as your e-mail messages and stored files.

One commonly used command on the Tools menu is the Pop-up Blocker command. A **pop-up** is a new instance of a browser window that displays on top of the current browser window to display ads or other information. Many Web users prefer to block pop-ups to speed up the load time for quicker viewing of a Web site or because the advertisements become annoying.

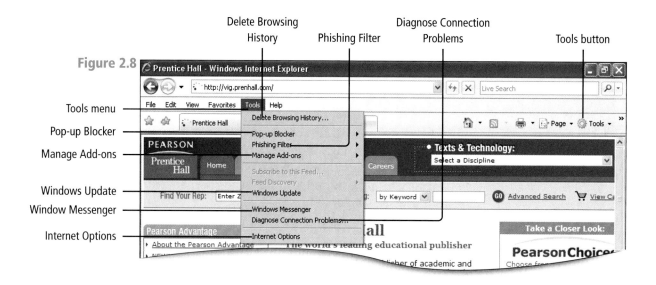

Figure 2.8

In addition to advertisements, pop-ups are sometimes used to direct Web users to go to a fraudulent Web site. In this type of use, some of these pop-ups may display legitimate alert messages or new Web pages. However, unless you observe the pop-ups carefully and close them carefully, you may unwittingly be directed to a fraudulent Web site. Always read each pop-up carefully. If you do not understand the message, simply close the pop-up by clicking the Close button in the upper right corner of the pop-up. Be careful when selecting the correct button because some pop-ups contain multiple Close buttons in an additional attempt to confuse you. If you are ever in doubt about the correct technique to close a pop-up or Web site, simply right-click the pop-up's button on the taskbar and click the Close command in the context-sensitive menu that displays. Figure 2.9 shows what this menu looks like.

A **context-sensitive menu** is a Windows feature that displays a small pop-up window containing a menu of commands relating to the object that has been right-clicked.

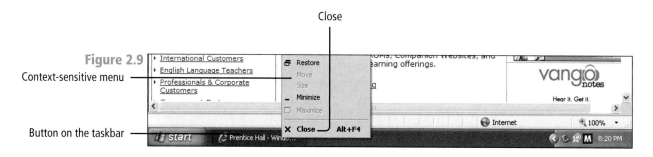

Figure 2.9

3 On the menu bar, click the **Tools** button, and then click **Internet Options**.

The Internet Options dialog box displays. Internet Options has several commands to control general settings presented in a series of separate tabs.

- The General tab enables you to delete your browsing history by deleting *temporary Internet files*, *cookies*, *history*, form data, or passwords. Temporary Internet files are copies of Web pages, images, and media that are saved for faster viewing.

Cookies are small text files sent from a Web server and stored on the client computer that transmits data back to the Web server. Cookies are considered a privacy concern because they collect and store personal data such as your browser versions and IP address. Cookies can be used to identify the users, provide a customized browsing experience, or are commonly used to pre-fill checkout forms at e-commerce Web sites. In addition, cookies can be used to keep track of what you are ordering or to help build sales by suggesting items similar to those you may have purchased in the past. Most browsers enable you to set how long to keep a cookie or to alert you when a cookie is being sent to your computer, so that you can refuse to accept it if you want. You can disable the acceptance of cookies by configuring your browser settings, but some sites will not function if you do so.

The history is a browser feature where a list is automatically generated for Web sites that have been visited during a browsing session.

- The Privacy tab enables you to block cookies and pop-ups.

- The Security tab enables you to view and customize settings for Web content. *Security* includes the technologies involved with features keeping your data and computer free from unauthorized access.

- The Content tab enables you to specify settings to control content ratings, security certificates, and your personal information.

Other tabs in the Internet Options include the *Connections* tab where you can set up an Internet connection and the *Programs* tab where you set specific programs as the default to perform tasks such as the program to use for e-mail or newsgroups. The *Advanced* tab enables you to set default settings for accessibility, browsing, printing, multimedia, and security.

4 In the **Internet Options** dialog box, click **OK** to close it. Then on the menu bar, click **Help**. Compare your screen with Figure 2.10.

Help is one of the most important commands on the menu bar because you can find out how to do something or provide feedback to Microsoft using this tab. Contents and Index is a command that enables you to perform a search to find help with any task or topic associated with Internet Explorer. You can also take the Internet Explorer Tour, get Online Support, use the Customer Feedback Option, Send Feedback, or find out About Internet Explorer.

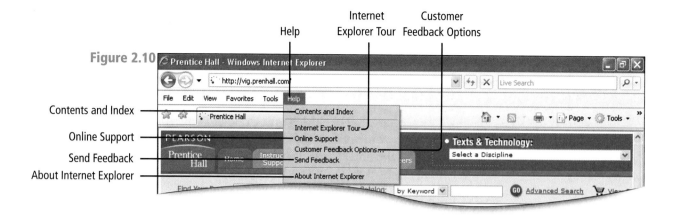

Figure 2.10

Help

Internet Explorer Tour

Customer Feedback Options

Contents and Index
Online Support
Send Feedback
About Internet Explorer

5 On the menu bar, click **Help** to collapse the menu. On the right side of your screen, click the **Tools button down arrow**, and then click **Menu Bar** to remove the check mark. The menu bar is hidden. Keep your browser open for the next activity.

Objective 2
Perform Commands with the Toolbar

The toolbar area, near the top of the Internet Explorer window, contains buttons that trigger the most commonly performed commands during Web browsing. It is often more convenient to click a button on the toolbar than it is to make the menu bar visible so that you can locate the command. Using the toolbar you can search for Web pages, add pages to your Favorites Center, or view your History. The toolbar enables you to navigate back and forth between Web pages by using tabs, and you can return to your default home page.

Activity 2.5 Exploring the Toolbar

In this activity, you will explore several features of the toolbar.

1 At the top of the browser window, directly below the title bar, locate the toolbar.

The toolbar consists of several buttons representing shortcuts to commonly performed tasks. The toolbar has been designed to be compact and still provide easy access to the most commonly performed tasks.

2 On the top row of the toolbar, locate the buttons and text boxes that perform navigational tasks: the **Back** button ⊙, the **Forward** button ⊙, the **Refresh** button ⊡, and the **Stop** button ⊠. Hold your mouse over each of the buttons, and notice the ScreenTip that displays. On the right side of the **Forward** button, click the

down arrow ⌄. Compare your screen with Figure 2.11. Your screen may differ slightly. Table 2.12 summarizes the buttons and their functions.

A **ScreenTip** is a Windows feature that temporarily displays a small box providing information about, or the name of, a screen element as you hold the mouse pointer over buttons or images in Internet Explorer or other Web browsers.

After you click the down arrow, a list of recently visited Web pages displays. You can click any of the Web pages in the list to return to that Web page.

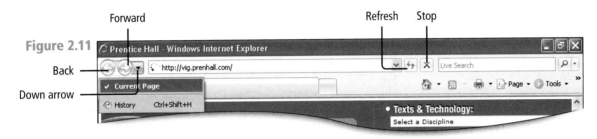

Figure 2.11

Forward · Back · Down arrow · Refresh · Stop

Toolbar Buttons and Their Functions

Button	Function
Back	Moves you to the previous Web page that you visited immediately before the Web page you are currently viewing.
Forward	Moves you to the Web page you were on before clicking the Back button.
Refresh	Enables the current Web page to reload the most recent version of the Web page into the same browser window.
Stop	Ends the retrieval of a requested Web page.

Figure 2.12

3 Near the middle of the top row of the toolbar, locate the **Address bar**.

Recall that the Address bar is a toolbar in Internet Explorer into which you type the address—Uniform Resource Locator or URL—of a specific Web site that you want to display in the browser window. You type directly into the Address bar and press `Enter` to move to a new Web page. As you browse and click a hyperlink to move to a new Web page, the URL in the Address bar automatically changes to the new URL.

When you request to view a Web page, the Web browser sends the request for the files that make up the Web page by using the URL to specify the address, or **path**, to the Web page. The path is the sequential description of the storage location of the HTML documents and files making up the Web page and stored in the hierarchy of directories and folders on the Web server. The Web server locates each file that makes up the Web page by using the path named in the URL. The Web server retrieves the requested file and sends it back to the Web browser for you to view. The sending and receiving process takes place in just a few seconds depending on your Internet connection method and speed.

4 Near the right side of the top row of the toolbar, locate the **Instant Search** text box and the **Search** button.

Instant Search is a search tool that enables you to locate Web sites, images, and maps on the Internet. Internet Explorer includes this feature as part of its browser interface.

5 In the **Instant Search** text box, click one time to select the existing text, and then type **What hotels are near the Grand Canyon?** Click the **Search** button.

The Search button begins the searching process. When the search is complete, several links to Web sites about this topic display. By clicking the Search down arrow, you can perform other search functions such as Find on this Page. Find on this Page enables you to search for your search question on the currently displayed Web page.

Alert

Do you have a different search engine?

Live Search is the default search engine for Internet Explorer. However, you can change the default search engine by clicking the down arrow immediately to the right of the Search button and then clicking Find More Providers or Change Search Defaults.

6 In the top left corner of the browser window, click the **Back** button .

The Web page that you visited immediately before this Web page displays.

7 In the second row of the toolbar, locate the next set of buttons: **Favorites Center** and **Add to Favorites**. These buttons help you locate or return to Web pages that have already been viewed. On the right side of the second row, locate several more buttons: **Home** , **Feeds** , **Print** , **Page**, and **Tools**. On the far right of the second row, notice a set of **double arrows** that lead to the **Help** command. Compare your screen with Figure 2.13.

The *Feeds button* is a feature that detects if a Web page uses *Really Simple Syndication*, or *RSS*. Really Simple Syndication—RSS—is a system developed to automatically alert subscribers of updates made to sites such as blogs, news, weather, or sports Web sites.

The *Home button* is a button that always returns you to the default home page that is set for the computer you are working on.

The *Print button* enables you to quickly print the current Web page without opening the Print dialog box.

The **Page button** contains a submenu of commands to perform many common tasks related to the current Web page such as opening a new browser window, saving the Web page, or sending either a link to the page or the entire page itself to someone, using e-mail. Recall that the Tools button enables you to perform several commands that are frequently used while browsing the Web.

You can access the **Help** feature by clicking the double arrows at the right end of the row. Help provides access to an index of answers to questions about using Internet Explorer, a tour of Internet Explorer, online support, and feedback options.

Figure 2.13

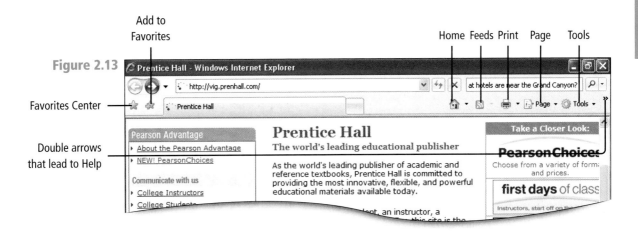

On the toolbar, click the **Favorites Center** button. Locate the three categories: *Favorites*, *Feeds*, and *History*. Click the **Favorites** category to display the default folders. In the upper right corner of the **Favorites Center**, point to the **green arrow** to pin the **Favorites Center** to the Web page. Compare your screen to Figure 2.14. Then click the green arrow.

The Favorites Center displays on the left side of the browser window as a panel **pinned**—remain stationary—to the browser window. The Web page now displays in the right side of browser window.

The Feeds category is a feature that detects whether a Web page uses Really Simple Syndication (RSS). Recall that the Feeds button is also available in the browser window.

Favorites   Feeds   Green arrow

Figure 2.14

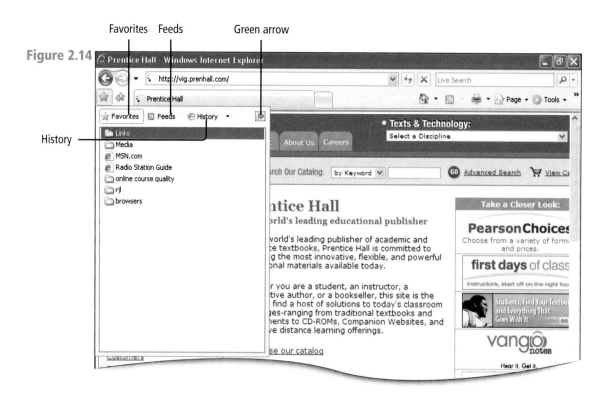

History

---

9. On the toolbar, click the **Add to Favorites** button ⬆ to display a submenu of commands. Locate the **Add to Favorites** command, the **Import and Export** command, and the **Organize Favorites** command.

The Add to Favorites command enables you to add a Web site to an existing folder or to create new folder and add a Web site to the new folder. The Organize Favorites command enables you to create a new folder, rename, delete, or move a favorite Web site or folder within the Favorites Center. The Import and Export command launches a wizard that enables you to share—import or export—favorites, feeds, or cookies from Internet Explorer with other programs or files.

10. In the **Favorites Center**, locate and click the **History** button. Notice several units of time display ranging from *3 Weeks Ago* to *Today*.

The History feature contains a list of the Web sites you have visited over a set number of days. You do not have to manually add in the Web sites to this list because it is automatically created by the browser. You can set the number of days to keep the list. You can sort through the list by specifying the day or week that you are interested in viewing or by searching.

11. In the **Favorites Center**, click the **Today** link to display the Web sites you have visited today. In the upper right corner of the **Favorites Center**, to the right of **History**, click the **down arrow** to display a submenu of criteria for displaying the History list including By Date, By Site, By Most Visited, By Order Visited Today, or Search History.

12 In the upper right corner of the **Favorites Center** panel, click the **Close** button $\boxed{\times}$.

The Favorites Center closes and the Web page returns to full screen.

13 On the right side of the toolbar, click the **Home** button $\boxed{}$.

The default home page displays. Regardless of how many Web pages you view or Web sites you visit, clicking the Home button always returns you to the default home page that is set for the computer you are working on.

14 On the right side of the toolbar, locate the **Feeds** button $\boxed{}$. Next, locate the **Print** button $\boxed{}$. Locate and click the **Page button down arrow**, and then locate and click the **Tools button down arrow**.

The *Tools* button contains a submenu of commands that control security tasks associated with the control of your screen and several options associated with the use of the Internet. All of the tasks are also available under Tools in the menu bar.

15 Keep your browser open for the next activity.

Activity 2.6 Using Tabs in Your Browser Window

The remaining features of the browser window help you navigate the World Wide Web. In this activity, you will explore these features.

1 Near the top part of the browser window, in the second row of the toolbar, locate the **tab**. Notice the text in the tab matches the text in the title bar. Compare your screen with Figure 2.15.

Tabs provide convenient browsing by speeding up your browsing experience and reducing the number of buttons visible on the taskbar. A *tab* is an area of the browser window that displays the name of the Web site and also enables navigation between Web sites. *Tabbed browsing* permits multiple Web sites to be open within a single browser window. An additional Web page can load on a new tab while you read the original page. You can then quickly and easily navigate between each Web page by clicking each tab within the open browser window.

Figure 2.15

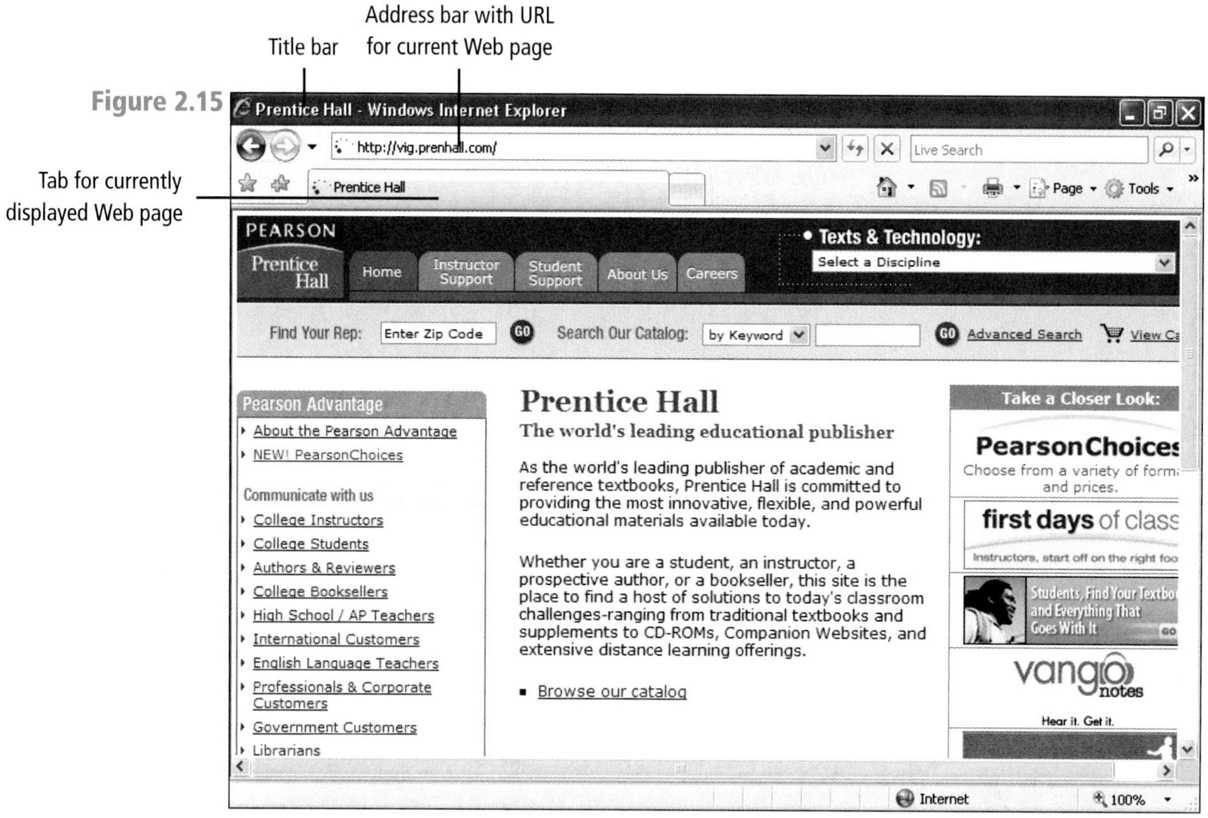

Title bar

Address bar with URL
for current Web page

Tab for currently
displayed Web page

2 In the tabbed area, to the right of the tab displaying the current Web page, click the **New Tab**. Notice the new tab moves in front of the other tab and displays an overview of how to work with tabs. Compare your screen with Figure 2.16.

The new tab is located to the right of the original tab at the top of the Web page. You can choose the **Learn more about tabs** link to see how tabs work. You have the option to not view this overview again by clicking the **Don't show this page again** check box. You can close the currently displayed tab by using the Close button in the upper right corner of that tab.

A third tab—the *Quick Tabs* button—displays on the left of the original tab. Quick Tabs is a feature that displays only when multiple tabs are open and permits navigation among open tabs. Quick Tabs provide a *thumbnail*, which is a graphic depicting a miniature version of each open Web page that can be used for navigation.

Figure 2.16

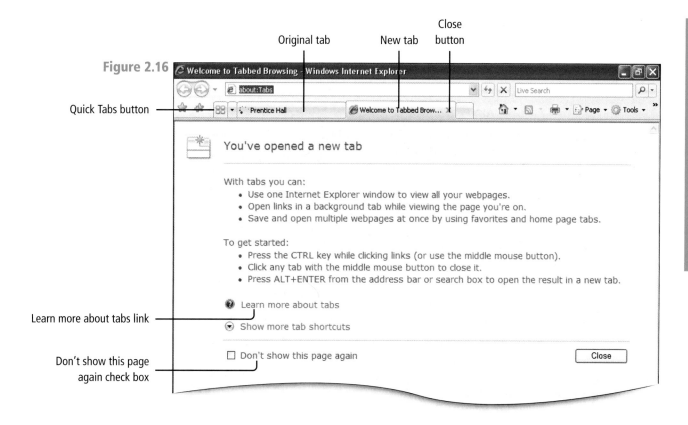

Original tab   New tab   Close button

Quick Tabs button

Learn more about tabs link

Don't show this page again check box

3 On the left side of the screen, point to the **Quick Tabs** button 🔲.

To the immediate right of the **Quick Tabs** button, click the **Tab list down arrow** 🔲.

The Tab list displays a list of open Web sites. A check mark displays on the left of the current tab, but you can navigate to any of the Web pages by clicking it in the list.

4 Click the **Tab list down arrow** 🔲 again to collapse the list. Point to, and then click the **Quick Tabs** button 🔲. Notice several thumbnails of open Web pages display. Hold your mouse over the first thumbnail. On the right of each thumbnail, notice the **Close** button 🔲.

A page showing thumbnails of each open Web page displays. Each thumbnail is labeled with the name of the Web site. A ScreenTip showing the name of the Web page displays when you hold your mouse over each thumbnail. You can close each Web page by clicking the Close button.

5 Click the **first thumbnail** to return to that Web page. Click the **second tab** to return to the overview Web page. On the right side of the **second tab**, click the **Close** button 🔲 to return to the original Web page.

6 Take a moment to study the table in Figure 2.17 to review the features of the browser window.

7 In the upper right corner of the browser window, click the **Close** button ☒ to close Internet Explorer.

Internet Explorer Features

Feature	Description
Address bar	A toolbar in Internet Explorer into which you type the address—Uniform Resource Locator or URL—of a specific Web site that you want to display in the browser window.
Back	A button that moves you to the last Web page that you visited immediately before the Web page you are currently viewing.
Favorites Center	A feature of Internet Explorer that contains a list of Web sites you have added there because you like the Web sites and may want to return there easily again.
Feeds	A feature of Internet Explorer that detects whether a Web page uses Really Simple Syndication, or RSS, for updates made to the content of a Web page.
Forward	A button that moves you to the Web page you were on before clicking the Back button.
Home	A button that always returns you to the default home page that is set for the computer you are working on.
Instant Search	A search tool that enables you to locate Web sites, images, and maps on the Internet and is included as part of the Internet Explorer interface.
Menu bar	A horizontal bar near the top of the browser window that contains expandable menu-style headings for performing important commands and tasks. Display of the menu bar is optional.
Minimize, Restore Down, and Close buttons	Enables customization of the screen for size and availability.
Page	A button that contains a submenu of commands to perform many common tasks related to the current Web page such as opening a new browser window, saving the Web page, or sending either a link to the page or the entire page itself to someone by using e-mail.
Print	A button that enables you to quickly print the current Web page without opening a Print dialog box.
Refresh	A button that enables the current Web page to reload the most recent version of the Web page into the same browser window.
Status bar	A horizontal bar near the bottom of the browser window that provides information about the security of a site and information about a link's destination as you roll over a link.
Stop	A button that ends the retrieval of a Web page.
Tab	An area of the browser window that displays the name of the Web site and also enables navigation between Web sites.
Taskbar	A part of the Windows operating system that displays the Start button, the notification area, and buttons for all open programs and files while enabling you to toggle between programs and files.
Title bar	A blue, horizontal bar at the top of the browser window that identifies the program and displays the name of the active Web page.
Tools	A button that enables you to perform several commands that are frequently used while browsing the Web.

Figure 2.17

Objective 3
Specify a Default Home Page

After you start Internet Explorer on your Internet-connected computer, the default home page displays. The default home page is also displayed whenever the Home button is clicked on the toolbar. You can specify the default home page on your computer and set it to any Web page you choose. Schools often set the default home page of all campus and lab computers to the main Web page of the school's own Web site to make it easy to access frequently used resources, such as their e-mail system. A *portal* is also commonly used as a default home page. A portal is a Web page that contains interesting content, frequently used links, and services, such as current and breaking news, e-mail access, and search capabilities.

Activity 2.7 Specifying a Default Home Page

In this activity, you will change the default home page on the office computers to the official State of Arizona Web site—Arizona @ Your Service.

1 **Start** Internet Explorer and click the **Maximize** button ▣ to enlarge the window to fill the computer screen completely.

Internet Explorer starts and displays the default home page that has been set for your computer.

Alert

Do you need to change your settings?
Certain security software and pop-up blockers may prevent you from modifying your system's settings. In addition, some schools prevent computer lab or classroom computers from being modified from their default setting or may prevent certain activities from being performed. You may need to change the system's settings back to the default home page for your school's or business's preferred home page after completing this chapter's activities. Check with your instructor for additional instructions before completing this chapter.

2 In the **Address bar**, click one time to select the existing text, then type **http://www.az.gov** and press Enter. Alternatively, click the **Go** button → located to the right of the **Address bar**.

The *Go button* → is shown as a green arrow at the right end of the Address bar. It displays as you type and temporarily replaces the Refresh button. The Go button takes you to the URL that is typed in the Address bar.

Arizona @ Your Service, the official Web site of the state of Arizona, displays. The Web site is a portal containing links leading to several interesting and important categories for the citizens of Arizona or people who want to find out more about Arizona.

3 On the right side of the toolbar, click the **Tools** button. On the submenu, point to **Internet Options**. Compare your screen with Figure 2.18, and then click **Internet Options**.

The Internet Options dialog box displays with several tabs across the top of the dialog box. These tabs include: General, Security, Privacy, Content, Connections, Programs, and Advanced. You can perform several important tasks by using the commands in each tab of the dialog box.

Arizona @ Your Service Web page   Internet Options   Tools button

Figure 2.18

4 Click the **General tab** if it does not display by default.

The General tab is divided into five main sections: Home page, Browsing history, Search, Tabs, and Appearance.

5 Under the **Home page** section, locate the **Address** box. The **Address** box contains the default home page address. Below the **Address** box are three buttons: *Use current*, *Use default*, and *Use blank*. Compare your screen with Figure 2.19.

The **Use current** button sets the default home page to the Web page that you are currently viewing. The **Use default** button sets the default home page to the Web page that was selected as default when Internet Explorer was first installed on the computer. The **Use blank** Web page sets a blank Web page as the default home page.

Internet Options dialog box

Figure 2.19

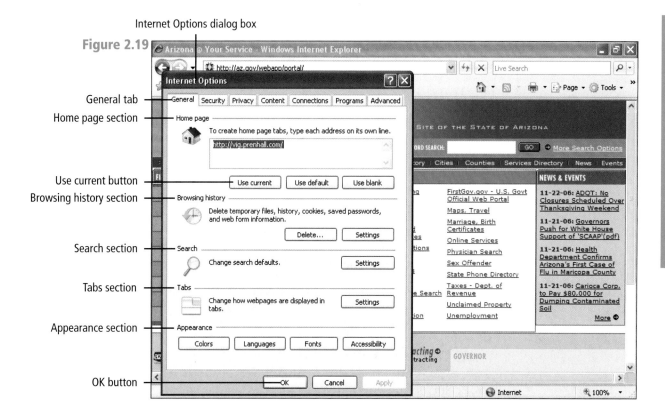

General tab

Home page section

Use current button

Browsing history section

Search section

Tabs section

Appearance section

OK button

6 Click the **Use current** button. Notice that the URL in the **Address** box changes to the URL that displays the **Arizona @ Your Service** Web site. Click **OK**.

The Internet Options dialog box closes and you are returned to Internet Explorer. The new default home page is now set to the Web page being currently displayed—**Arizona @ Your Service**.

7 Click the **Back** button 🔙 to go to a previously viewed Web page. On the toolbar, click the **Home** button 🏠 to move to the new default home page.

Because the Arizona @ Your Service Web page has been set as the default home page, it will display whenever the Home button is clicked on the toolbar or whenever you start Internet Explorer.

8 Click the **Close** ❎ button to close the browser window.

9 **Start** Internet Explorer and click the **Maximize** button ⬜ to enlarge the window to fill the computer screen completely.

The Arizona @ Your Service Web page displays. If your school or business does not enable you to change the default home page, repeat these steps to return the computer setting to its original default home page.

10 Keep your browser open for the next activity.

Objective 4
Browse the World Wide Web Using Links, the Address Bar, History, and Favorites Center

To locate and display—browse—Web pages, you can use several techniques. Typically, you click hyperlinks to move from one Web page to another. You can also use the Address bar to reach any Web page by typing the URL and then pressing ⌷Enter⌷ on the keyboard. While you are browsing, Internet Explorer automatically keeps a list of each Web site that you visit—the History. Using History enables you to easily return to any of these Web sites. With Favorites Center, you can create your own list of Web sites that you may want to visit again.

Activity 2.8 Browsing the World Wide Web Using Links

The City of Desert Park office staff does a lot of research on the World Wide Web. In this activity, you will browse the World Wide Web using links.

1 On the Arizona @ Your Service Web page, read and review the content of the page. In the main area of the **Internet Explorer** window, locate the current Web page that is displayed. Notice the links that are visible throughout the content of the Web pages.

2 In the left column, locate the hyperlink labeled **Government Employees**. Point to the hyperlink with your mouse pointer until it turns into the **Link Select pointer** 🖑, and then click the first hyperlink on the submenu to move to another Web page.

You can easily move to another Web page by clicking any of the hyperlinks displayed on the current Web page. A link may lead to another Web page that is part of the same Web site or it may lead to another Web site.

Clicking a link makes new content display in the screen. As you point to a link, the mouse pointer changes into the *Link Select pointer*, which is the mouse pointer view that displays as a pointing hand as you point to a link. Each destination URL displays in the lower left corner of the screen in the status bar. This information is helpful because one of the most common ways to scam Web users is to redirect them to a fraudulent Web site. In this type of scam, the correct URL may be listed on the Web page as the link text but the destination URL may lead to a different, fraudulent Web site.

At times the content of the Web page is larger than can be viewed in one screen. *Scroll bars* display vertically on the right side of the current Web page or horizontally on the edge of the current Web page to enable you to move the content so that the hidden parts of the Web page come into view.

3 On the toolbar, click the **Back** button 🔙 to return to the Arizona @ Your Service Web page. Near the middle of the page, locate and click the **FirstGov.gov** link.

The FirstGov.gov home page displays. FirstGov is the U.S. Government's official Web portal.

4 Click the **Back** button 🔙 to return to the **Arizona @ Your Service** Web page. Compare your screen with Figure 2.20.

5 Keep your browser open for the next activity.

Link Select pointer   FirstGov.gov link   Scroll bar

Figure 2.20

Back button

Government Employees link

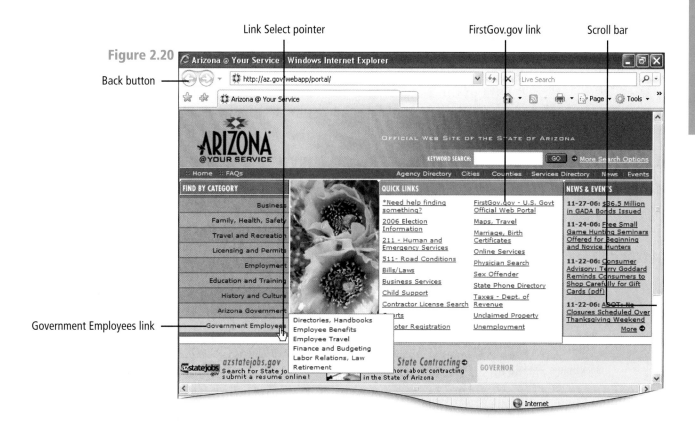

Activity 2.9 Browsing the World Wide Web Using the Address Bar

Many businesses, schools, and organizations advertise their Web sites by providing their URL in marketing materials, such as magazine advertisements, television and radio commercials, on billboards, or other advertisements. Individuals may promote their personal Web site on business cards. In this activity, you will use the Address bar to locate Web pages related to Arizona tourist attractions.

1 In the **Address bar**, click one time to select the existing text, and then type **http://www.desertmuseum.org** and press Enter.

The Arizona-Sonora Desert Museum Web site is displayed in the browser window.

If you know the URL, you can visit Web sites by typing the URL into the Address bar found near the top of the browser window, and then pressing Enter on the keyboard. As you type, the Refresh button 🔁 temporarily turns into the Go button →. You can click to the Go button → to go to that Web site as an alternative to pressing Enter on the keyboard.

In addition, as you type a new URL in the Address bar, a list of URLs displays directly beneath the Address bar. Internet Explorer remembers the last 25 Web addresses you entered and displays a list containing Web site addresses that start with the characters you type. When you type the *www*, Internet Explorer displays a list of all the sites you have accessed recently that begin with www. The list gets shorter with each character you type. If you see the address of the site you want to visit displayed in the drop-down list, click the item in the list so that you don't have to type the complete address.

2 On the toolbar, click the **Back** button 🔙 to return to the previously viewed Web page.

3 In the **Address bar**, click one time to select the existing text, and then type **http://www.nps.gov/grca** and press ⌅.

The National Park Service U.S. Department of Interior Grand Canyon home page displays in the browser window.

4 On the toolbar, click the **Back** button 🔙 to return to the previously viewed Web page. Click the **Forward** button 🔜 to return to the **Grand Canyon** Web site again. Click the **Back** button 🔙 one more time to return to the previously viewed Web page. Compare your screen with Figure 2.21.

Forward button   Address bar

Figure 2.21

Back button

Activity 2.10 Browsing the World Wide Web Using the History Feature

As you visit Web sites, Internet Explorer creates a history of what you visited through the History feature. This feature creates a list of the Web sites you have visited and enables you to go back to any Web site that you have visited in the past. This is helpful if you do not remember the Web site's URL. In this activity, you will view Web sites that you have visited in the past and do a search for your college's Web site.

1 On the toolbar, click the **Favorites Center** button ⭐. On the right side of the **Favorites Center** panel, click the **green arrow** button to pin the **Favorites Center** to the Web page. In the **Favorites Center**, click the **History** button. Compare your screen with Figure 2.22.

The History panel displays on the left side of the browser window. The default listing displays the several options for viewing previously visited Web sites by date, beginning with *3 Weeks Ago*. By default, the *Today* option is highlighted.

If you click the History button down arrow, you will also find an option to perform a search for a Web site. Close the History panel at any time by clicking the Close button ☒ in the upper right corner of the panel.

Figure 2.22

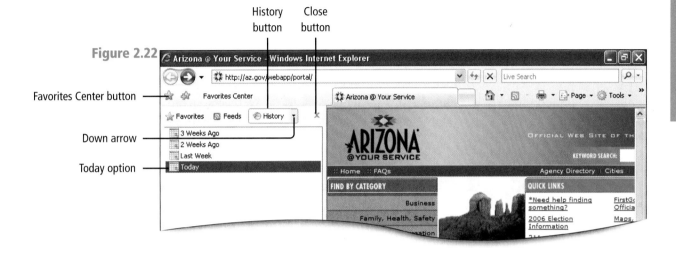

2 In the **History** panel, click the **Today** option to display the names and URLs of Web pages that you have visited today. Click the first Web site listed.

The list expands to display any pages you have visited within that Web site.

3 In the **History** panel, click the name of the previous day to display a new list of Web site folders in the **History** panel. These are the Web sites visited on that day. Click one of the Web site folders and then click the first Web page name listed to navigate to that Web page.

Alert

What if you can't see yesterday's Web sites?

You may not be able to see any folders for days other than today in your History panel. Your computer may be set to keep the History list for only one day, so the Today folder may be the only one that displays.

4 On the toolbar, click the **Home** button ⌂ to return to your default home page.

5 In the **History** panel, click the **down arrow**, and then click the **Search History** link.

The Search for text box displays. The flashing insertion point indicates where you type in a name or URL of a Web site you want to locate again. As you type into the text box, the Search Now button becomes available to begin the search.

6 In the **Search for** text box, type your college's Web site URL. Notice that as you type the URL, the **Search Now** button becomes active. Click the **Search Now** button.

Links to any Web sites meeting the search criteria—pages within your college's Web site—display in the History panel. If you have not been to your college's Web site recently, then no search results will be returned.

7 In the **History** panel, click the first Web page returned as a result of the Search—your college's URL—to display it on the right panel of the screen. Then in the upper right corner of the **Favorites Center**, click the **Close** button ⊠.

The History panel closes and a Web page from your college's Web site takes up the full screen of the browser window.

8 Keep your browser open for the next activity.

Activity 2.11 Browsing the World Wide Web with the Favorites Center

In this activity, you will view the Favorites Center and its default list of Web sites. You will use the Add to Favorites feature to add a new folder and a new Web site to the Favorites Center list. You will use the Organize Favorites feature to delete a folder and a Favorites Center listing.

1 On the toolbar, click the **Favorites Center** button ⭐ to display the **Favorites Center** panel. On the right side of the **Favorites Center** panel, click the **green arrow** button to pin the **Favorites Center** to the Web page. Then click the **Favorites** button, if necessary, to display Favorites instead of the History list.

2 On the toolbar, double-click the **Add to Favorites** button ⭐. In the submenu that displays, notice the **Add to Favorites** and **Organize Favorites** commands.

You can easily organize these sites into a folder in the Favorites Center. You can delete any of the folders and addresses, add new listings, and organize addresses for your favorite sites into new folders.

3 On the toolbar, double-click the **Favorites Center** button ⭐, click the **Links** folder. Several names of Web sites display. Notice the mouse pointer turns into the **Link Select pointer** 🖑 as you point to each one. Compare your screen with Figure 2.23.

Add to
Favorites button

Links
folder

Figure 2.23

Favorites Center button —

Favorites button —

List of Web sites —

Link Select pointer —

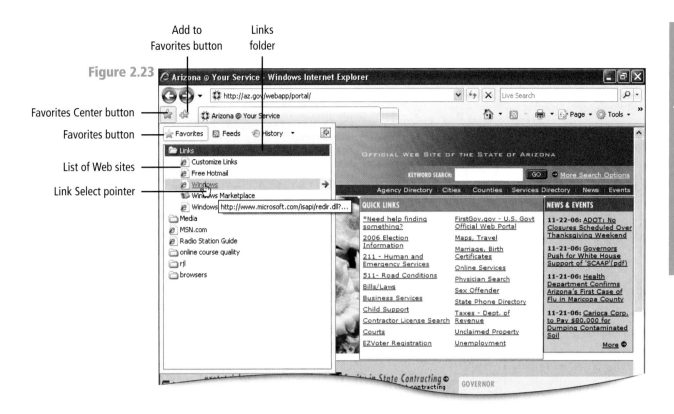

4 In the **Favorites Center** panel, in the **Links** folder, click the first link.

The Web site displays in the browser window.

5 In the **Favorites Center** panel, click the **Links** folder to close it.

On the toolbar, click the **Home** button 🏠 to return to the default home page.

6 In the **Address bar**, click one time to select the existing text, then type **http://www.nps.gov/grca** and press the Enter key.

The National Parks Service U.S Department of Interior Grand Canyon Web page displays in the browser window.

7 On the toolbar, click the **Add to Favorites** button 🌟. In the sub-menu that displays, click the **Add to Favorites** command. In the **Add a Favorite** dialog box that displays, click the **New Folder** button. The **Create a Folder** dialog box displays. Compare your screen with Figure 2.24.

The Create a Folder dialog box enables you to type a folder name and create the folder in a location that you choose.

Folder   Create a Folder   Add a Favorite   New Folder
Name   dialog box   dialog box   button

Figure 2.24

Add to Favorites button ──

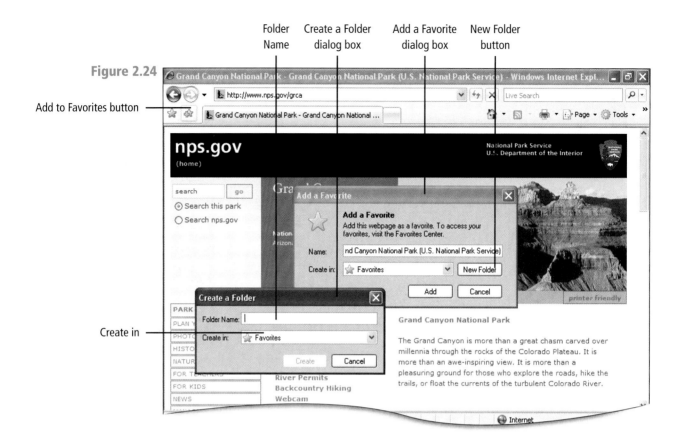

Create in ──

8 In the **Create a Folder** dialog box, in the **Folder Name** box, type **Firstname_Lastname** substituting your first and last names. In the **Create in** menu, click **Favorites**. If necessary, use the down arrow to locate the Favorites folder. Click **Create**.

The Create a Folder dialog box closes and the new folder displays in the Create in text box of the Add a Favorite dialog box. By default the name of the Web page automatically displays in the Name text box of the Add a Favorite dialog box.

9 In the **Add a Favorite** dialog box, click the **Add** button.

The displayed Web site is added to the new folder that you created. You can check this by clicking the new folder in the Favorites Center. You may need to scroll down the list of folders to locate the new folder.

10 On the toolbar, click the **Add to Favorites** button . In the sub-menu, click the **Organize Favorites** command. In the **Organize Favorites** dialog box that displays notice that the list of Favorites folders and Web sites displays in the top of the dialog box. Locate the five buttons at the bottom of the dialog box: *New Folder, Move, Rename, Delete,* and *Close.*

Each button performs tasks to help you organize your Favorites.

11 At the top of the **Organize Favorites** dialog box, scroll down if necessary to find the **Firstname_Lastname** folder, and then click it. Then click the **Delete** button. In the **Confirm Folder Delete** dialog box that displays, click **Yes**. In the **Organized Favorites** dialog box, click **Close**.

The Firstname_Lastname folder is deleted from the Favorites list.

12 In the **Favorites Center** panel, click the **Close** button ⊠. On the toolbar, click the **Home** button 🏠 to return to your default home page. In the upper right corner of the browser window, click the **Close** button ⊠ to close Internet Explorer.

End **You have completed Project 2A** ——————————

Project 2B Managing Web Content with Internet Explorer

In Activities 2.12 through 2.17, you and the office staff for the City of Desert Park, Arizona use Internet Explorer to manage Web content as part of the recent training initiative. Shane Washington, Director of Office Operations, would like everyone in the office to manage Web content by printing, saving, and sharing Web pages. You will create a desktop short-cut to a Web page. You and the staff will also maintain the browser for efficiency and security by clearing the cache, cookies, and History.

For Project 2B, you will need the following file:

Web page printouts

You will save your files as
2B_Print_Text_Firstname_Lastname
2B_Save_Web_Page_Firstname_Lastname
2B_Save_Graphic_Firstname_Lastname

Objective 5
Print, Save, and E-mail a Web Page

Using the Web to research, gather information, save, and share information can quickly become unmanageable if you aren't able to organize the information. Managing Web content enables you to work efficiently as you explore the Web and use information that you find there. For example, you can print or save parts of a Web page or entire Web pages so that you can view them again when you are *offline*. This means you can use your Web browser to see the Web page without being connected to the Internet. The Web browser will display the files directly from the storage disk or device. You can e-mail a Web page or links to a Web page when you want to share Web content with others.

Activity 2.12 Printing Text and Graphics Found on Web Pages

Internet Explorer enables you to print or save both text and graphics found on Web pages. In this activity, you will share information about the Arizona-Sonora Desert Museum Web site with the staff in the City of Desert Park office by printing text from the Web page and a graphic found on the Web page.

1 **Start** Internet Explorer and click the **Maximize** button to enlarge the window to fill the computer screen completely. Alternatively, click the Address bar to select the existing text, type **http://www.az.gov** and then press the Enter key if your default home page is set to another site.

The Internet Explorer window displays the Arizona @ Your Service Web page that was set as your default home page in the previous activity.

2 On the right side of the **Arizona @ Your Service** Web page, locate the **News & Events** section. At the beginning of the section, click and drag your mouse over the links to select the text.

The selected text displays with a blue highlight over it.

3 On the toolbar, click the **Print button down arrow** ⬛ to display a submenu of commands. Click **Page Setup**.

The Page Setup dialog box displays.

4 In the **Page Setup** dialog box, locate the **Header** and **Footer** boxes. Click in the **Header** box, and then delete any existing text. Click in the **Footer** box, and then delete any existing text. Then, using the underscore character as indicated and your own first and last names, type **2B_Print_Text_Firstname_Lastname** Click **OK** to add the **footer** and to close the **Page Setup** dialog box.

5 On the toolbar, click the **Print button down arrow** ⬛, and then click **Print** to open the **Print** dialog box.

6 In the **Page Range** section, click the **Selection** option. Compare your screen with Figure 2.25.

Selected links on
Web page

Figure 2.25

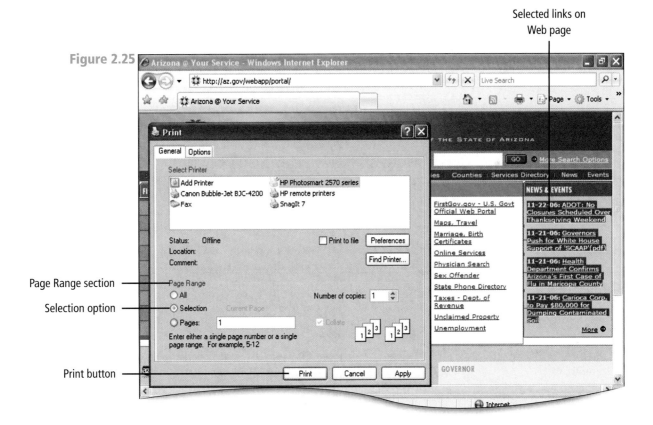

Page Range section

Selection option

Print button

7 Click the **Print** button to print out the selected text.

The Print dialog box closes and the selected text prints out. The footer displays at the bottom of the printout.

8 On the **Arizona @ Your Service** Web page, locate a graphic and right-click it with your mouse to display a context-sensitive menu.

Recall that a context-sensitive menu is a Windows feature that displays a small pop-up window containing a menu of commands relating to the object that has been right-clicked. In this case, the context-sensitive menu will show several commands that you can perform with the graphic.

9 From the context-sensitive menu, click **Print Picture** to display the **Print** dialog box. In the **Page Range** section, click the **All** option.

Click the **Print** button to print the picture.

The Print dialog box closes and only the graphic from the Web page is printed.

10 Keep your browser open for the next activity.

Activity 2.13 Saving Web Pages and Graphics

Saving a Web page or graphics from a Web page enables you to view or share either the entire Web page or the graphics anytime you want. In this activity, you will share information with the Desert Park office staff by first saving an entire Web page. You will save one of the graphics located on the Web page by using the context-sensitive menu.

1 Decide on a location where you can store a document—either in a folder on your computer's hard drive or a folder on a removable storage device such as a USB flash drive. Click the **Start** button and then click **My Computer**. Navigate to the desired location, and if necessary, create a folder for this course into which you can store documents. Name the folder **Chapter_2_Browsing**. Close **My Computer** when you are finished.

2 From the **Arizona @ Your Service** Web page displayed in the browser window, on the toolbar, click the **Page button down arrow** to display a submenu of commands. Click **Save As** to open the **Save Webpage** dialog box.

3 In the upper part of the **Save Webpage** dialog box, on the right side of the **Save in** text box, click the **down arrow** to display the locations for saving the Web page.

A hierarchy of drives and folders displays. You can choose where to save your Web page. If you click Desktop, the Web page will save on the desktop of the computer you are currently using. If you choose a storage disk or drive such as your Flash drive, 3½ inch Floppy, or CD-RW, the Web page will be saved to that device and you will be able to open it at different computer.

4 Navigate to the **Chapter_2_Browsing** folder that you created for this chapter.

5 In the lower part of the **Save Webpage** dialog box, on the right side of the **Save as type** text box, click the **down arrow** to display the options for saving the Web page. Click the **Web Page, complete** option to save the entire Web page as an HTML file. Notice that the **File name** text box contains the name of the Web site by default.

6 In the **File name** text box, click one time to select the existing text, and then type **2B_Save_Web_Page_Firstname_Lastname** Compare your screen with Figure 2.26, and then click the **Save** button.

The Save Webpage dialog box closes and the Web page is saved onto your storage disk or device. The graphics on the Web page are saved with the Web page text when you use this option. You will be able to view the Web page offline.

Save Webpage   File name
dialog box   text box   Save button

Figure 2.26

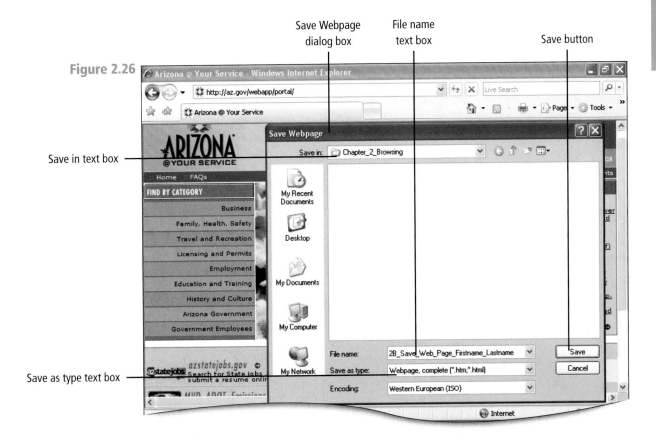

7 On the **Arizona @ Your Service** Web page displayed in the browser, locate a graphic, move your mouse over the graphic and right-click the graphic to display a context-sensitive menu.

The context-sensitive menu shows several commands that you can perform with the graphic such as saving or printing the picture.

8 From the context-sensitive menu, click **Save Picture As** to display the **Save Picture** dialog box.

9 In the upper part of the **Save Picture** dialog box, on the right side of the **Save in** text box, click the **down arrow** ⌄ to display the locations for saving the Web page. Click **Chapter_2_Browsing**.

10 In the lower part of the **Save Picture** dialog box, on the right side of the **Save as type** text box, click the **down arrow** [▾] to display the options for saving the graphic. Do not make a selection—leave the default file type in place. Take a moment to study the table in Figure 2.27, which shows the most commonly used Web graphics file types and the three-letter extension used for each type.

Several files types for graphics are used on the Web. The correct file type displays by default. You cannot modify the graphic file types as you save a graphic file. You can change file types only using a special graphics software program.

Web Graphic File Types

File Type	Three-Letter Extension
Bitmap	.bmp
Graphics Interchange Format	.gif
Joint Photographic Experts Group	.jpg or .jpeg
Portable Network Graphics	.png

Figure 2.27

11 In the **File name** text box, type **2B_Save_Graphic_Firstname_Lastname** Click the **Save** button.

The Save Picture As dialog box closes. The graphic is saved in the folder you have set up for your course work.

12 Keep your browser open for the next activity.

Activity 2.14 E-mailing Web Pages and Links to Web Pages

In this activity, you will propose to Shane Washington, Director of Office Operations for the City of Desert Park, that the office staff should use the Arizona @ Your Service Web site as the default home page. In this activity, you will send the entire Web page and a link to the Web page to Shane using e-mail.

1 On the toolbar, click the **Home** button [ ] to display the **Arizona @ Your Service** Web site. Alternatively, you may need to click the Address bar to select the existing text, type **http://www.az.gov** and then press the [Enter] key if your default home page is set to another site.

2 On the toolbar, click the **Page** button and then click **Send Page by E-mail** to open your e-mail client.

The command Send Page by E-mail enables you to send the entire page to someone's e-mail account. If your computer has been configured to use a default e-mail client, that e-mail client will open and display a blank e-mail message on top of the browser window. If you do not have a default e-mail client configured on your computer, you will be asked to create a new profile in Microsoft Outlook Express before the blank e-mail message displays. Internet Explorer uses Microsoft Outlook Express as its default e-mail client.

3 In the blank e-mail message, locate the text box labeled **To** and type in your own e-mail address so you can receive the Web page. Then click the **Send** button.

An e-mail message with a copy of the Arizona @ Your Service Web page in the body of the message is sent to your e-mail address.

4 On the toolbar, click **Page**, and then point to **Send Link by E-mail** to open your e-mail client. Compare your screen with Figure 2.28. Then click the **Send Link by E-mail** command.

The Send Link by E-mail command sends just a link to the Web page, not the entire Web page, to someone's e-mail account. Your default e-mail client or Microsoft Outlook Express opens and displays a blank e-mail message.

Send Page by E-mail   Page button

Figure 2.28

Send Link by E-mail

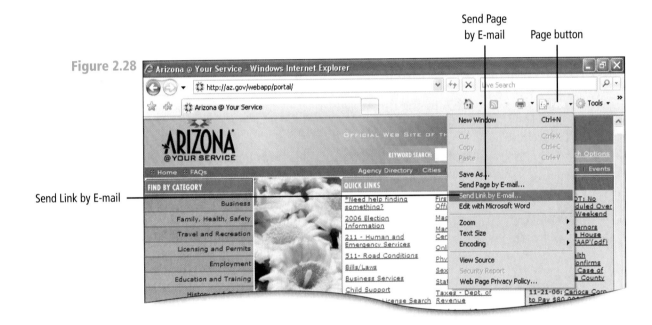

5 In the blank e-mail message, locate the text box labeled **To** and type in your own e-mail address so you can receive a link to the Web page. Then click the **Send** button.

An e-mail message is sent to your e-mail address with an attachment containing a link to the Arizona @ Your Service Web page.

6 Keep your browser open for the next activity.

Objective 6
Create a Desktop Shortcut to a Web Page

As you browse the Web, you will likely find Web sites that you want to return to again. A ***desktop shortcut*** can be created to help you return to those pages quickly. A desktop shortcut is an icon that displays on the desktop that leads directly to a program, file, or Web page. To use a desktop shortcut, you simply double-click the icon for the desktop shortcut to start Internet Explorer and display the Web site.

Activity 2.15 Creating a Desktop Shortcut

In this activity, you will create a desktop shortcut for the University of Arizona home page.

1 In the **Address bar**, click one time to select the existing text, and then type **http://www.arizona.edu** and press Enter on the keyboard.

The University of Arizona Web site displays.

2 On the Web page, right-click anywhere except on a link or graphic to display a submenu of commands. Click **Create Shortcut** to create a desktop shortcut. In the **Internet Explorer** dialog box that displays, click the **Yes** button to confirm that you want to put a shortcut for this Web site on your desktop.

3 In the upper right part of the browser window, click the **Close** button ☒ to close the Internet Explorer program.

4 On your computer's desktop, locate the new **University of Arizona desktop shortcut** that you just created. Compare your screen with Figure 2.29.

You can identify a desktop shortcut by looking for an icon made up of a logo and the name of the Web page. A small black arrow in the lower left corner of the icon identifies it as a shortcut to the Web page.

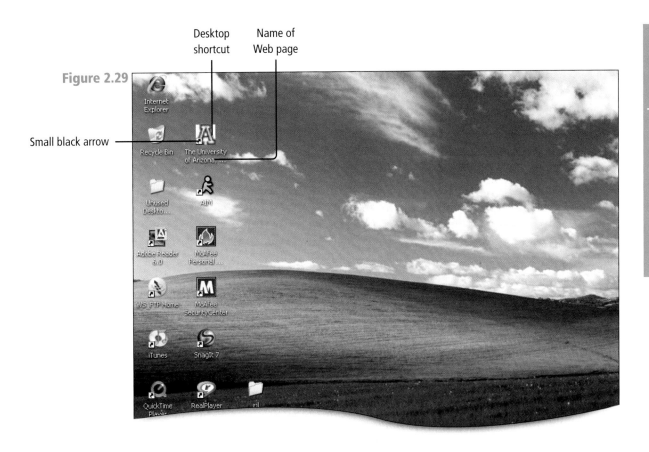

Figure 2.29

Desktop shortcut

Name of Web page

Small black arrow

5 On your computer's desktop, double-click the newly created **desktop shortcut**.

Your browser launches automatically and the University of Arizona home page displays in the browser window.

6 Click the **Maximize** button ▣ to enlarge the screen. Click the **Home** button ⌂ to return to the default home page.

7 Keep your browser open for the next activity.

Objective 7
Clear the Cache, Cookies, and History

You can work in a less risky computing environment by clearing the cookies, cache, and History from your computer's hard drive. The *cache* is a storage mechanism in the memory area of your computer's hard drive that enables the rapid retrieval of frequently used Web pages or files. Recall that cookies are small text files sent from a Web server and stored on the client computer that transmits data back to the Web server. Also recall that History is a browser feature where a list is automatically generated for Web sites that have been visited during a browsing session. Clearing these areas removes personal data from your computer's hard drive and helps to reduce your vulnerability by not revealing your browsing activities should your computer become compromised.

Activity 2.16 Clearing the Cache and Cookies

In this activity, you will delete the browsing history including temporary Internet files and cookies.

1 From the default home page displayed in the browser, on the toolbar, click the **Tools button down arrow** ⬚, and then click **Deleting Browsing History** to display the **Deleting Browsing History** dialog box.

The Deleting Browsing History dialog box is divided into five sections: Temporary Internet Files, Cookies, History, Form data, and Passwords. Each of these items can be deleted separately or you can delete all of them at once.

Form data is considered anything that you have typed into the Address bar or on Web pages during a browsing session. Deleting browsing history does not delete other areas of your hard drive such as your Favorites or feeds that you have subscribed to.

2 In the **Temporary Internet Files** section, click the **Delete files** button to display the **Delete Files** alert box. Compare your screen with Figure 2.30.

The *Delete Files* alert box displays asking you if you want to delete all temporary Internet Explorer files. Every time that you visit a Web page, the Web browser stores a copy of the Web page and the files associated with that Web page on your computer's hard drive in the cache. Internet Explorer names these files Temporary Internet files.

Whenever you want to view one of these Web pages, it is displayed from the Temporary Internet files instead of requesting it from the Web server. The use of Temporary Internet files makes it easier and faster to return to Web pages. However, because the cache eventually gets full, it can also slow down the overall performance of your computer. Deleting files will clear the disk space and may also increase the general running speed of your computer.

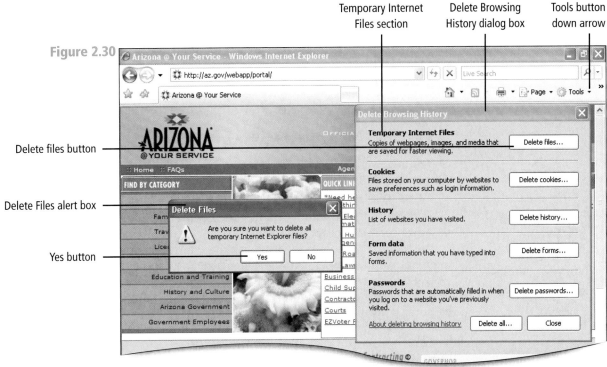

Figure 2.30

Temporary Internet Files section

Delete Browsing History dialog box

Tools button down arrow

Delete files button

Delete Files alert box

Yes button

---

3 In the **Delete Files** alert box, click **Yes**.

An hourglass displays. When it disappears, the process is complete. This process—deleting all the Temporary Internet files from the cache—may take several minutes to complete.

Another Way

To Delete All Browsing History At Once

You can delete all of your browsing history at one time by clicking Tools, Delete Browsing History, and then Delete all. In addition, you can delete your browsing history by going to Tools, Internet Options, and the General tab. In the Browsing history section, click the Delete All button to display the Delete Browsing History dialog box.

---

4 In the **Delete Browsing History** dialog box, locate the **Cookies** section. Click the **Delete cookies** button.

The Delete Cookies alert box displays and asks if you want to delete all cookies in the Temporary Internet Files folder. Cookies are used to identify the users and provide for the customization of a Web page. Many people feel storing this type of information can compromise privacy.

5 In the **Delete Cookies** alert box, click **Yes**.

An hourglass displays. When it disappears, the process is complete and you can move on the next step of this activity. It may take several minutes to complete the process. Because some cookies contain personally identifiable information used by certain Web sites to provide a customized visit to the Web site, deleting the cookies may cause you to reenter such information the next time you visit the Web site.

More Knowledge

Deleting Temporary Internet Files Each Time You Browse

You may want to delete Temporary Internet files each time you browse. This is an important privacy protection if you use kiosks, publicly available computers, or shared computers such as in a lab or classroom.

To do this, from the Tools menu, click Internet Options and then click the Advanced tab. Locate the Settings section and then scroll down and locate the Security section of the list. Click the Empty Temporary Internet Files folder when browser is closed check box. The Temporary Internet Files folder will be emptied when you close the browser. For added privacy when using publicly available computers, you should also log out or shut down the computer before leaving it.

6 When the process is complete, click **Close** to close the **Delete Browsing History** dialog box. Keep the browser open for the next activity.

Activity 2.17 Managing the History

Recall that Internet Explorer keeps track of which Web sites you have visited each time you browse the Web. You can easily return to Web pages that you have visited in recent days or weeks by using the History button in the Favorites Center. In this activity, you and the City of Desert Park office staff will clear the History folder, and then specify the number of days these Web pages will remain in the History folder.

1 From the default home page displayed in the browser, on the toolbar, click the **Tools button down arrow**, and then click **Deleting Browsing History** to display the **Deleting Browsing History** dialog box.

2 In the middle of the **Delete Browsing History** dialog box, locate the **History** section.

The History section enables you to clear the History folder. All of the Web sites in the History folder can be deleted at any time by using the Delete history button.

3 Click the **Delete history** button.

The Delete History alert box displays and asks if you want to delete your history of visited Web sites.

4 In the **Delete History** alert box, click the **Yes** button.

An hourglass displays. When it disappears, the process is complete and you can move on the next step of this activity. It may take several minutes to complete the process. All the Web sites in the History folder are removed.

5 In the **Deleting Browsing History** dialog box, click **Close** to return to the Web page.

6 On the toolbar, click the **Tools** button, then click **Internet Options**. In the **Internet Options** dialog box, click the **General tab**. In the **Browsing history** section, click the **Settings** button to display the **Temporary Internet Files and History Settings** dialog box displays.

Using this dialog box, you can control when your browser checks for updated versions of Web sites as you visit them. You can set an amount of disk space to use for storing Temporary Internet Files and a location for storage. You can also move folders, view objects, or view files.

Near the bottom of the Temporary Internet Files and History Settings dialog box, you can adjust the number of days to keep the list of Web sites you have visited—your History.

7 In the **Temporary Internet Files and History Settings** dialog box, locate the number displayed in the **Days to keep pages in history** box. Compare your screen with Figure 2.31.

Typically, the default setting for the History keeps Web pages visited in the last 20 days. Your school or business may have it set to a different default number of days.

You can click the spin button next to Days to keep pages in history to increase or decrease the number of days tracked in the History. This will reset the number of days that recently viewed Web sites will be stored in the History folder.

Figure 2.31

Temporary Internet Files and History Settings dialog box

Default setting for Days to keep pages in history

History section

Spin buttons

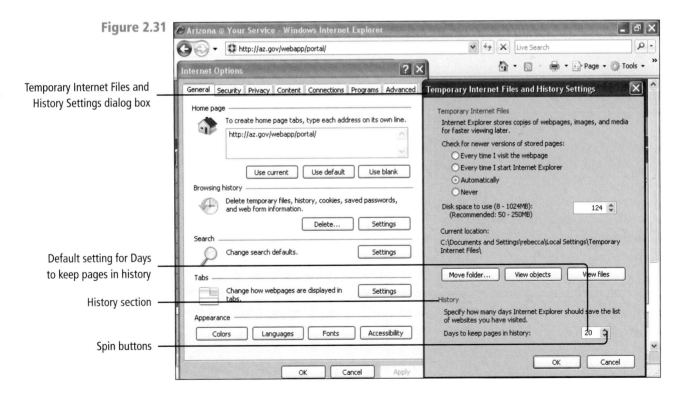

8 In the **Temporary Internet Files and History Settings** dialog box, click the **spin button** on the right side of the **Days to keep pages in history** box to set the number to **7** or a number different from what is currently set. Click **OK.**

The Temporary Internet Files and History Settings dialog box closes and you are returned to the Web page. Web pages you will visit—your History—will be kept for seven days.

If your school or business does not enable you to change settings on your computer, repeat these steps to return the computer setting to the original number of days.

9 Check your *Chapter Assignment Sheet* or *Course Syllabus* or consult your instructor to determine whether you are to submit your assignments by printing on paper, or electronically by using your college's course information management system. Electronically, you can submit the *.txt* file created in Notepad. To print on paper from Notepad, under the **File** menu, click **Print**, and then print accordingly. To submit the document electronically, follow the instructions provided by your instructor.

10 In the upper right corner of Internet Explorer, click the **Close** button ☒ to close the Internet Explorer program.

End You have completed Project 2B ─────────

Project 2C **Identifying How Browsers Work**

Using a Web browser, you can perform many activities as you browse the Web. Every Web site on the WWW is made up of HTML files and other types of files that are stored on a Web server. In Objective 8, you examine how browsers work to retrieve and display Web page multimedia content by using plug-ins. In Objective 9, you will identify several popular browsers and compare the features of each.

Objective 8
Describe How Plug-ins Work

How is the multimedia content of Web sites displayed?   Regardless of how the request to view a Web page is made—either by clicking a link or by typing the URL of a Web site into the Address bar—a copy of the requested HTML document or file is returned to your computer and displayed by the browser. The Web browser displays the Web page by reading in order each line of the HTML code that makes up the Web page and then interpreting the code into a visually appealing display. When the Web browser runs into a part of the code that embeds another file type, such as a graphic, animation, or other multimedia file, those files are also retrieved and displayed on your computer monitor.

What is a plug-in?   Using the World Wide Web, you can listen to or see many types of multimedia events, such as news broadcasts and live or recorded concerts, or you can play games. History and culture can be preserved at some Web sites that store archives of historic speeches, or old radio and television shows. Other Web sites provide audio books that can be downloaded.

In some cases, the browser is unable to support certain file types, such as animation or multimedia files that are embedded in HTML documents. Additional software—***plug-ins***—is required. Plug-ins are small software programs developed to work with a Web browser to execute proprietary files types that the browser can't interpret on its own.

How do plug-ins work?   If your computer has the correct hardware—a sound card and speakers—you can take advantage of rich multimedia resources. You also need plug-ins to help the Web browser interpret and play the multimedia files. Some plug-ins, such as Windows Media Player, are provided as part of the browser but additional plug-ins can be downloaded if necessary. Typically, new computers come with several plug-ins already installed.

When the browser runs into a line of HTML code requesting to display a file type that it doesn't support, the browser automatically launches the appropriate plug-in if it is installed on the computer. The browsing experience continues without interruption and the file is displayed nearly instantaneously, depending upon the Internet connection method you use and the speed of the connection. You are able to see video, hear sound, or view sophisticated animation all within your Web browser window.

You may be prompted at some Web sites to choose among versions of the multimedia file so that it is compatible with the plug-ins you have installed on your computer. For example, at a news site, you may be able to view video content as either RealVideo or QuickTime files.

At other Web sites, there may be only one version of the file available. In such cases, you may be prompted to ***download*** the plug-in if it is not already installed on your computer. When you download, you transfer a copy of a file or program from a site over the Internet to your computer. In this context, the site would be the plug-in developer's FTP site and the program that is copied is the plug-in.

How do you install a plug-in?   After the plug-in is downloaded to your computer, you need to install the plug-in by using a ***wizard*** before you can begin using the plug-in. A wizard is a program that helps complete a software installation process. Typically, wizards display as a pop-up that begins automatically and asks you a series of questions about your computer and your preferences as it works through the installation process. The table in Figure 2.32 lists some of the most commonly used plug-ins and the type of content they support.

Commonly Used Plug-ins

Plug-in	Content
Acrobat Reader	Enables you to view or print Adobe Portable Document Format (PDF) files.
Flash Player	Enables you to view and hear Adobe Flash content.
QuickTime	Enables you to hear, interact with, or view video, graphics, virtual reality, and audio files.
RealPlayer	Enables you to play streaming RealVideo and RealAudio files.
Shockwave	Enables you to display files created with Adobe Shockwave content.
Windows Media Player	Enables you to play streaming audio, video, and animations.

Figure 2.32

Objective 9
Identify and Compare Several Popular Web Browsers

Who was involved in the battle of the browsers?   When the World Wide Web was first introduced, there was a constant battle for the honor of being the most popular browser. At one time, the primary browser in use was Netscape Navigator, which was developed by the Netscape

Communications Corporation. But soon, improvements were made to Microsoft Internet Explorer and it was installed on all new Windows computers. America Online was another popular program because it offered the convenience of having an Internet Service Provider packaged with a Web browser.

During this time, HTML coding practices underwent many improvements. Each browser developer updated its product as new developments to HTML code occurred. Each new version of the browsers carried proprietary features that interpreted these new HTML coding practices correctly in that particular browser. However, because of the rapid development of HTML code, not every browser developer was able to keep up with every new development of code. As a result some of the updated code might be correctly interpreted by any given browser, but not in others.

Web designers began to create Web pages to display dependably in a specific browser type and version. Web sites frequently indicated which browser and version would be the best one to use in order to view the Web site as it had been designed. Eventually, HTML coding evolved to a more constant set of features and practices, Microsoft Internet Explorer gained a dominant position, and the browser battles subsided.

How do you choose a browser?   Today there are many Web browser programs available. Internet Explorer is still one of the most commonly used Web browsers. Other browsers include Netscape Browser, Firefox, Opera, and Safari. Each Web browser has similar components and screen elements with a few unique features. All browser developers provide upgrades to their products as technology improvements develop and security issues arise.

The decision to use one browser over another often depends on what you are accustomed to using, what your school or organization has decided to use as the browser, or what comes preloaded on your computer at the time of purchase. If you would like to use a different browser, simply visit the Web site of the browser developer and download the most recent version of their product. Typically, browsers are offered as *freeware*. Freeware is a software program that is made available to the user free of charge.

Internet Explorer

What features does Internet Explorer offer?   Because Internet Explorer has been around for many years, it has gained a large share of the browser market. Internet Explorer, also referred to as IE, is a Microsoft product designed to work with the Windows operating system. Microsoft has discontinued its version for the Macintosh operating system. The following list explains some of the features Internet Explorer offers. Figure 2.33 shows a Web page displayed in Internet Explorer and some of its features.

- **E-mail**—Internet Explorer provides e-mail service using the Microsoft Outlook Express program.

- **Search options**—A search option called Instant Search is integrated into the Internet Explorer browser. A search text box is provided directly on the toolbar. Although Live Search is the default, you can change the default to a different search provider.

- **Tabbed browsing**—You can quickly and easily navigate between each Web page by using small tabs within one open window.

- **Customization**—Internet Explorer provides accessibility compliance with options to customize text, colors, *style sheet* functionality, and keyboard navigation. Style sheets are a set of rules for how to format fonts, characters, and page layout within an HTML document. IE enables you to manage *add-ons*—features which enable you to personalize your browsing experience—in the areas of security, timesaving features, offline browsing, and entertainment.

- **Really Simple Syndication (RSS) feeds**—Recall that RSS is a system developed to automatically alert subscribers of updates made to sites such as blogs, news, weather, or sports sites. To get the benefits of RSS, you subscribe to a service that sends you information, such as the announcements of patches and updates. Internet Explorer supports RSS.

- **Security enhancements**—Microsoft updates Internet Explorer periodically by offering *service packs*. A service pack provides product updates and patches to solve software bugs and security issues. Service packs are available as free downloads from the Microsoft Web site or can be installed using CDs. Another security feature of IE is the ability to be configured to block content at certain Web sites through the Content Advisor feature and block pop-ups. The Phishing Filter identities Web sites that are potentially part of a phishing scam.

- **Customer Support**—The Microsoft Internet Explorer Web site offers a support center with newsgroups, Release Notes, and an area for *Frequently Asked Questions (FAQs)*. FAQs are a list of commonly asked questions and the answers to those questions. The Web site also provides links for contacting support professionals via e-mail, online, or by telephone.

Figure 2.33

Title bar with Internet Explorer logo   Tabbed browsing   Instant Search text box with the name of the default search engine displayed

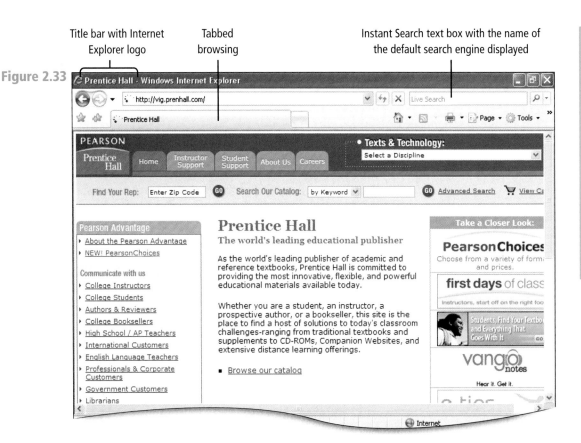

Netscape Browser

What features does Netscape Browser offer? Netscape Browser has also been available for many years. Netscape works with the Windows operating system and was developed by the Netscape Communications Corporation. It features the following:

- **E-mail**—Netscape Browser offers a built-in e-mail option, Webmail.

- **Search options**—Netscape Browser includes a Google search option as part of the toolbar.

- **Tabbed browsing**—Netscape Browser supports tabbed browsing.

- **Customization**— Netscape Browser provides similar accessibility compliance as Internet Explorer, using options to customize text, colors, style sheet functionality, and keyboard navigation. Netscape enables you to maximize the viewable screen area by combining multiple toolbars. Netscape Browser enables you to set profiles for each user that include bookmarks (known as Favorites in IE) and passwords.

- **RSS feeds**—Netscape Browser handles RSS feeds and live content such as continuously scrolling headlines across the top of the browser window. A visual indicator automatically displays when RSS feeds are available at a Web site.

- **Security enhancements**—Netscape Browser provides a Security Center where you can view a visual summary of your security settings including site ratings, pop-up blocking, ID theft protection, spyware protection, and browser updates.

- **Customer Support**—Support for Netscape users is provided at the Netscape Browser Web site through a community Web page, Browser Help page, feedback forms, or by an option to contact a technician by telephone.

Firefox

Which browser has been developed more recently?   Firefox was created by Mozilla Foundation for both Windows and Macintosh operating systems as well as Linux and other operating systems. Firefox evolved as an *open source* software program. Software is termed open source when it is available for free distribution; users provide feedback, and debug the software in cooperation with the original developers, or even modify and redistribute the programs.

Firefox is gaining in popularity for several reasons. Because it is an open source program and runs on multiple operating systems, many users work to make Firefox better. Unlike Internet Explorer and Netscape, it does not have proprietary ways of handling HTML and common scripting languages. Firefox displays Web pages more quickly than other browsers. Some of the key features include:

- **E-mail**—Firefox performs e-mail functions through its companion software program, Thunderbird.

- **Search options**—Firefox provides access to multiple search engines through the toolbar. As you search, Firefox makes suggestions for similar search terms.

- **Tabbed browsing**—Firefox uses the tabbed browsing feature so additional Web pages can load quickly on a tab while you read the original page.

- **Customization**—The interface meets federal guidelines for accessibility standards, such as keyboard navigation and DHTML support. *Dynamic HTML*, or *DHTML*, is a technology that uses HTML and scripts to generate Web pages dynamically in response to the user's input. DHTML supports visually impaired computer users enabling Web sites and programs to be read aloud instead of viewed. Firefox also enables customization of the interface by applying various add-ons.

- **RSS feeds**—Firefox handles RSS feeds through its Live Bookmarks feature.

- **Security enhancements**—Firefox provides Phishing Protection. Security updates are automatically downloaded to your computer. Firefox blocks pop-ups. Firefox enables you to delete personal data stored on your computer such as History, cookies, and saved form data, or you can clear the cache. The History is kept for a predetermined number of days as part of the browser interface. Deleting this information—History, cookies and cache—protects your privacy by not revealing your recent browsing activities.

- **Customer support**—Support is provided at the Firefox Web site with FAQs, message boards, newsgroups, guidebooks, and online chat. Third-party paid telephone support is available.

Opera

Are there other browsers that work with multiple operating systems? Opera, developed by the Norwegian firm Opera Software ASA, is another browser that was recently developed and is gaining in popularity. It was designed to work on both Windows and Macintosh operating systems. Its features include:

- **E-mail**—Opera provides its own built-in mail service, Opera Mail.

- **Search options**—A Google search option comes built in as part of the Opera toolbar. You can also add your favorite search engine instead.

- **Tabbed browsing**—Opera has tabbed browsing.

- **Customization**—Accessibility compliance is addressed by providing a customizable style sheets function. You can change text size and color as well as zoom into the content of any Web page. In addition, there is a voice feature that lets the user speak to the computer and the computer may speak to the user. Opera enables users to customize the interface style by enabling you to move features around the screen with a ***drag-and-drop*** technique. Drag-and-drop is a technique where you point to an object onscreen, then click your mouse and continue to hold down the mouse button while you move the object to another part of the screen.

- **RSS feeds**—Opera supports RSS feeds.

- **Security enhancements**—Opera provides options to accept or block cookies and pop-ups. Opera is configured to automatically clear the History and cache as you close the browser or you can delete it anytime during a browsing session.

- **Customer support**—Support for Opera users is provided at the Opera Web site with tutorials, knowledge base, and online communities. You can get paid support via e-mail.

Safari

Which browser is designed for a Macintosh? Safari is the default Web browser for computers running the Macintosh operating system. Safari was developed by Apple Computer, Inc.

- **E-mail**—Safari uses the built-in Mail program as its e-mail service and makes it easy to e-mail Web pages to friends.

- **Search options**—A Google search option comes built in as part of the Safari interface.

- **Tabbed browsing**—Safari features tabbed browsing and each page loads in quickly.

- **Customization**—Accessibility compliance is provided with a voiceover feature.

- **RSS feeds**—RSS feeds are automatically displayed at each Web site and are shown as a list in the browser window. You click any of the feeds you are interested in reading.

- **Security enhancements**—Safari provides a Private Browsing feature where your personal information and browsing sessions are not cached. Safari blocks pop-ups and provides parental controls.

- **Customer support**—The Safari Web site provides tutorials and discussion boards. There is a built-in search function and a directory search feature for help in locating information on specific topics.

Browser Summary

The table in Figure 2.34 shows a comparison of these browsers and their main features.

Feature Comparison for Popular Web Browsers

Browser	Internet Explorer	Netscape Browser	Firefox	Opera	Safari
Developer	Microsoft Corporation	Netscape Communications Corporation	Mozilla Foundation	Opera Software ASA	Apple Computer Inc.
Operating System	Windows	Windows	Windows, Macintosh, or Linux	Windows, Macintosh, or Linux	Macintosh
E-mail	Outlook Express	Webmail	Thunderbird	Opera Mail	Mail
Search Options	Integrates a Live Search text box into the toolbar	Integrates a Google search text box into the toolbar	Access to multiple search engines in toolbar	Integrates a Google search text box into the toolbar	Integrates a Google search text box into the toolbar
Tabbed Browsing	Yes	Yes	Yes	Yes	Yes
Customization	Options to customize text, color, style sheet use, keyboard navigation, add-ons	Options to customize text, color, style sheet use, keyboard navigation, combine multiple toolbars	Meets federal guidelines for accessibility standards, keyboard navigation, DHTML support, add-ons	Customizable style sheets function, voice feature, move features with drag-and-drop	Voiceover-feature
RSS feeds	Yes	Yes	Yes	Yes	Yes

(Continued)

(Continued)

Feature Comparison for Popular Web Browsers

Browser	Internet Explorer	Netscape Browser	Firefox	Opera	Safari
Security enhance-ments	Service packs, Content Advisor, Phishing Filter	Security Center	Blocks pop-ups, automatic updates, clears History, cookies, and cache, Phishing Protection	Option to accept or block cookies and pop-ups, automatic clearing of cache and History	Does not cache personal information or browsing sessions, blocks pop-ups, enables parental controls
Customer Support	How-to articles; Newsgroups; release notes; FAQs; e-mail, online, or telephone support	Community Web page, Browser Help page, feedback forms, or by telephone	FAQs, message boards, newsgroup, guidebooks, online chat, and third party paid telephone support	Online tutorials, a knowledge base, online communities and paid support via e-mail	Online tutorials, discussion boards and a directory search function

Figure 2.34

End You have completed Project 2C ——————————

Online Quiz

Project 2C

Take the online self-study quiz for this chapter:

1. Go to **www.prenhall.com/go** and select the textbook *GO!* **with the Internet**.

2. Select **chapter 2.**

3. Select Self-Study Quiz Project 2C.

Project 2D Examining Privacy Risks and Security Issues of Browsing

Browsing the Web raises issues associated with your privacy and the protection of your personal information. In Objectives 10 and 11, you will examine several risks presented when you browse the World Wide Web. You will identify browser privacy risks and explore ways to minimize your exposure. You will identify several security issues associated with browsing the Web and how to browse the Web safely.

Objective 10
Determine the Risks of Using the World Wide Web

How is my personal information collected at a Web site used?   Being aware of potential privacy risks when browsing the Web is the first step toward protecting yourself and your family against any privacy compromise. Many Web sites specifically state their *privacy policies*. Privacy policies inform you of how any information about you gathered at the Web site may be used or shared with other parties. These policies vary greatly among Web sites. Some Web sites strictly prohibit any reuse of data gathered at the Web site; other sites use all information gathered for marketing purposes or resell the information to third parties. Some Web sites collect personal data without any real need for having the information.

You should get into the habit of reading the privacy policies posted at each Web site where you conduct business to make sure you understand what information will be collected and how it will be used. Typically, a link to the privacy policy is located near the bottom of the Web page. Figure 2.35 shows a link to a privacy policy at a Web site.

Figure 2.35

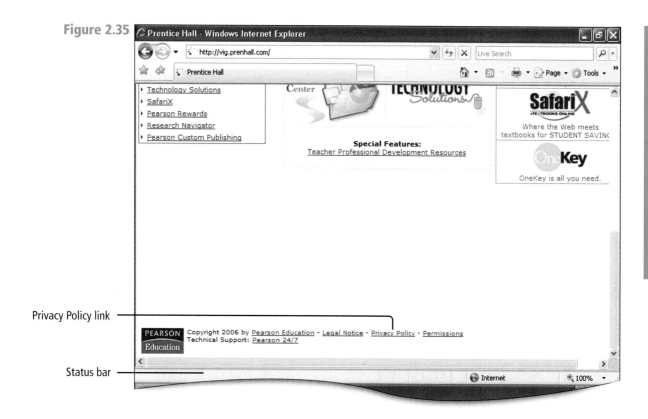

Privacy Policy link

Status bar

What is one of the most common browsing risks?   Objectionable Web content is a major concern. Because the World Wide Web is not censored or controlled, it is possible to display Web sites featuring content that you may not want to view or that you do not want your children to view. Web sites that feature strong language, graphic violence, pornographic images, or Web sites for various hate groups can be located by using search engines. You may stumble on such sites by clicking seemingly innocent links found on other Web sites or in e-mail messages.

There are several ways to help guard against objectionable content. Software programs can be installed on your computer to restrict access to Web sites that contain certain keywords. These programs are especially helpful for families with children. Many search engines enable you to filter out adult or violent content from being returned as search results. Most browsers provide settings to control the access to Web sites with certain content such as strong language, nudity, or violence. Browser settings enable the use of rating systems for Web sites or setting passwords to control access to restricted sites. Figure 2.36 shows where you configure settings to control access to certain content by using Internet Explorer as the browser.

Figure 2.36

Internet Options
dialog box

Content Advisor
dialog box

Content tab

Enable button

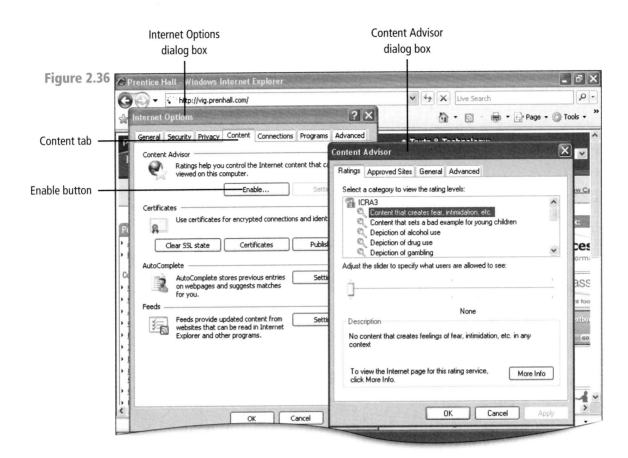

Chat Rooms and Privacy

Can chat rooms compromise your privacy? Another privacy issue involves unwanted contacts, which can arise from the use of public Web sites such as chat rooms, blogs, or Web sites used for **social networking**. Social networking Web sites provide opportunities to view personal pages; exchange e-mails, photos, and audio and videos files; and to participate in discussions or create blogs. Typically social networking sites are focused on specific interests such as music, sports, or pop culture.

The use of this type of public Web site can unknowingly invite danger into your home, posing a risk to your personal safety. Anyone can log into and create an account at social networking Web sites. Most sites have membership lists that are searchable so that it is easy to meet and interact online with many people. However, because these are public Web sites, it is difficult to be absolutely certain who is on the other side of the keyboard. Someone might say the right things making you believe a friendship is evolving from the conversations you have with that person.

Sexual predators sometimes use these sites to meet and **groom** potential victims. Grooming means to establish a level of trust and develop an increasingly exploitative relationship with a victim. Predators collect bits of information over a series of conversations and then put them together to track the identity or location of the victim. Grooming may begin as simply asking questions about a potential victim's interests to gain their confidence. From there it can escalate into favors, gifts, or money sent to the victim in exchange for specific activities. Understanding the risks associated with befriending people in public Web sites and how grooming occurs can help prevent this type of risk.

Protecting Children's Privacy

How do you protect children's privacy? Children can fall prey to online privacy risks. Families are encouraged to discuss appropriate computer use. In addition, families are urged to become familiar with the browser settings or software programs that can be configured to restrict access to social networking or other types of public Web sites. There are strategies to help educate parents and children about the potential for danger or violation of privacy when children use the Web. Some of these strategies seem obvious and yet many people, not just children, find themselves revealing more information while online than they realize. The following is a list of information to protect:

- Your name, your family's name, your mother's maiden name, and the names of your friends

- Your age, birthday, Social Security number, driver's license number, and credit card numbers

- Your address, your phone number, your school, and your school's mascot

- The date that a favorite band played in a city near you or any other information that could be put together to determine your location

Are there any laws to help to protect children? A federal law, *Children's Online Privacy Protection Act (COPPA)*, was enacted in 1998. It protects children by requiring parental consent for the collection or use of personal information gathered at Web sites from children under the age of 13.

Although parents cannot always monitor children's browsing habits, they can file complaints with the Federal Trade Commission if they feel there has been any violations of this law.

Where can I learn more about protecting my privacy and my children's privacy? The other side of keeping kids safe is giving them the information they need to help them make good decisions when faced with situations online that hold the potential for danger. Several Web sites exist that provide this kind of guidance. The National Center for Missing and Exploited Children has developed an online resource for helping everyone become more aware of the potential for dangerous situations. The Web site NetSmartz Workshop offers interactive games, videos, news, definitions, safety tips, and both online and offline activities. Kids, teens, parents, and educators can find something of value here. The table in Figure 2.37 provides several resources to help families learn more about protecting their privacy.

Web Sites Addressing Children's Online Privacy

Web Site	Purpose
Federal Trade Commission Complaint Form— *http://www.ftc.gov/ftc/complaint.htm*	This site enables you to file a COPPA violation complaint.
GetNetWise— *http://kids.getnetwise.org*	This site, created by public interest groups and Internet industrial partners, provides several tips, tools, and trouble-reporting functions.
National Center for Missing and Exploited Children— *http://www.missingkids.com*	This site provides tips for keeping kids and teens safe online.
Net Family News— *http://netfamilynews.org*	This site is an international non-profit organization that provides a forum, newsletter, podcasts, blogs, and RSS feeds that share important information about Internet safety.
NetSmartz Workshop— *http://www.netsmartz.org*	This site provides several activities for kids, teens, parents, and educators.
Privacy Rights Clearinghouse— *http://www.privacyrights.org/fs/fs21-children.htm*	This site gives good advice for protecting children's online privacy.

Figure 2.37

E-mail Privacy

What privacy risks are associated with e-mail? *Phishing* is a privacy risk that involves e-mail or Web sites or both. Phishing is the practice of sending e-mail that attempts to illegally solicit personal information by requesting information for account verification, passwords, account numbers, or other personal data. These e-mails request that you either reply to that e-mail directly with the requested information or that you click a link contained in the e-mail leading to a Web site set up to collect the personal information.

Phishing e-mails seem to come from an official entity, such as a bank or a credit card company, and they often have the appropriate logo and company name included. However, financial institutions and credit card companies do not make requests for personal information using e-mail. If you ever are in doubt about an e-mail's authenticity, you should contact the firm directly by visiting the firm in person or by calling the firm to confirm the request. Do not rely on phone numbers provided in the e-mail.

In addition to phishing, you need to be aware of **pharming**. Pharming is the practice where fraudulent Web sites are created to look like an official Web site, so that unknowing clients and customers conduct business and reveal personal information. Phishing and pharming can occur in one incident. You may be directed to the fraudulent Web site by e-mail or the Web site may turn up in as a result of a search. If you feel you have been a victim of phishing or pharming, you can report the incident. The table in Figure 2.38 provides some Web sites that explain more about the privacy risks found on the Internet.

Web Sites Addressing Consumers' Online Privacy

Web Site	Purpose
Anti-Phishing Working Group—*http://www.antiphishing.org*	This site provides a reporting service and statistics on recent trends.
Electronic Privacy Information Center—*http://www.epic.org*	This site is a public interest research center with news and resources.
Federal Consumer Information Center Consumer Action—*http://www.consumeraction.gov/caw_privacy_online.shtml*	This site provides tips on controlling online privacy.
OnGuard Online—*http://onguardonline.gov*	This site provides practical tips from the federal government and technology industry for protecting users online.
Staysafe.org—*http://lstaysafe.org*	This Web site provides a toolbox that explains how to perform tasks to keep you safe online.

Figure 2.38

Objective 11
Identify Safe Browsing Strategies

What are the security issues of using the Web?   Security is another area of concern when browsing the Web. News stories about **hackers** who gain access to servers and the personal information stored on those servers have increased in recent years. Hackers are people with sophisticated computer skills who access networks and servers to steal data, examine code, or infect computer systems with malicious programs. Hackers also read personal information as it is sent over the Internet. Data packets can be intercepted and rerouted to another server or computer. This type of security issue is hard to protect against for the typical Web user. But there are many other security issues you can protect against.

What are the most common security issues?   Many security issues associated with browsing the Web can be grouped under the heading **malware**. Malware is a software program that invades computers and networks for the purpose of disruption or destruction of the network or data. Types of malware include adware, spyware, Trojan horses, viruses, and worms.

What is adware?   **Adware** is a software program that collects information about your preferences by tracking your browsing habits, and in response, displays advertisements on your screen as pop-ups or as icons on your desktop. Pop-ups slow down browsing by causing you to respond or close the window before continuing your browsing activity. Pop-ups also slow down your computer by filling the hard drive with temporary Internet files. Adware is often concealed within freeware or other programs that you willingly download and install on your computer.

How is spyware different from adware?   Like adware, the invasion of spyware on your computer often occurs when another program is downloaded. **Spyware** is another threat to online security. Spyware is a software program that invades your computer and gathers information about you by tracking your keystrokes and collecting a list of the Web sites that you visit. Spyware can capture your IP address, your passwords, or other sensitive data. This information can then be forwarded to a third party.

What is a Trojan horse?   A **Trojan horse**, or **Trojan**, is a malware program that masquerades as a game or other program but once installed, it executes destructive code. Trojans are used to introduce other malicious programs or to set up the infected computer as a remote administrative tool that can be used for hacking into other computer systems. Trojans are often used as **dialer programs**. Dialer programs are programs used to make phone calls from your computer to international or toll numbers.

What is a virus and what does it do?   Opening files and programs that you download, opening e-mail attachments, or clicking links sent to you in e-mail messages makes your computer vulnerable for exposure to a **virus**. A virus is an unwanted program or piece of code sent to you that runs on your system causing unexpected or damaging effects. Viruses spread very quickly. Computer owners may not immediately be aware when a virus infect his or her computer.

A variety of problems occur when a computer is infected with a virus. Some are annoyances, such as the loss of control of the mouse or odd messages and images that display automatically onscreen. At other times, the damage is more severe; entire hard drives are erased, causing a loss of information and productivity in the work place.

What are worms?   A computer **worm** is a program that multiplies by itself so that it eventually fills the hard drive or a network drive, either slowing it down or making it stop altogether. Unlike some of the other malware discussed here, worms do not come hidden or attached to other programs. Worms enter your computer through unprotected communication ports such as the one used for your connection to the Internet; they then take advantage of security flaws in the operating system or the network. You can guard against worms by keeping your operating system updated with security patches and anti-virus software programs.

Do any programs help safeguard my computer?   Several software programs add additional security to your computers. **Anti-adware**, **anti-spyware**, and **anti-virus. programs** work in a similar way but focus on different forms of malware. These programs can be added separately, or you may find a program that combines all three protections into one program. After they are installed on your computer, these programs scan the hard drive or any other location you specify on your computer for known viruses and malware that may be on your computer. If a virus or other malware is located, the program will try to remove, disable, or quarantine it.

Because new viruses, adware, and spyware are always being developed, it is important to frequently update these types of software programs to keep current protection in place. The updates are often provided at the Web site of the software developers as free downloads. Most software packages have an option for automatic updates that are pushed to your computer on a schedule or whenever new threats emerge.

What is a personal firewall?   A personal *firewall* is a software program that is used to protect your computer from outside threats by blocking direct communication with the Internet. Personal firewalls are recommended for all computers especially for those using cable and wireless connection methods. There are several firewall programs available. Some of these software programs combine the functions of a firewall with anti-virus, anti-spyware and anti-adware protection.

What else can I do to reduce my vulnerability?   You have several ways to keep yourself secure while using the World Wide Web. One of the best ways protect yourself is to be an alert and informed Web user. Many kinds of security breaches can be prevented if you recognize certain visual clues as you browse. Being familiar with the browser interface and understanding dialog box messages can help you guard against intrusion on your computer.

Keeping your browser updated with all recent security patches and service packs helps to guard against several types of attacks. Most browsers automatically check for updates as you turn on your computer and access the Internet. You may also want to select a browser that does not store personal data in the History or cookies and clears the cache after each browsing session.

You can adjust your browser settings to increase security levels. Many security experts recommend setting the security levels to disable *Active X* or to prompt you when your browser encounters certain Web page elements that run on Active X. Active X is a technology that works within Web pages to display animation, multimedia, and interactive objects. Hackers can create a Web page that uses Active X to launch Trojans, or other malware.

What onscreen clues identify a secure Web site?   When using a Web site, such as for shopping or banking transactions, you want the Web site to be secure. You can identify a secure Web site by looking at the Address bar and observing the URL. A secure Web site displays the URL with an "s" after the http. In other words, the URL will begin *https://*, not *http://*.

Another onscreen clue at secure Web sites is the presence of a padlock icon as part of the browser interface. A closed padlock indicates the site is a secure Web site. An open padlock indicates an unsecure site. The padlock may display in various locations within the browser window depending on the browser you have installed. In Internet Explorer, the padlock icon displays in the upper part of the browser window to the immediate right of the Address bar. Other browsers display the padlock in the upper portion of the screen as part of a toolbar. In either case, the padlock displays as part of the browser interface and not part of the Web page itself. Hackers or someone running a phishing scam sometimes add a padlock icon to fraudulent Web sites in an attempt to fool Web users. Figure 2.39 shows a secure Web site.

URL using *https://*

Closed padlock icon

Figure 2.39

Address bar

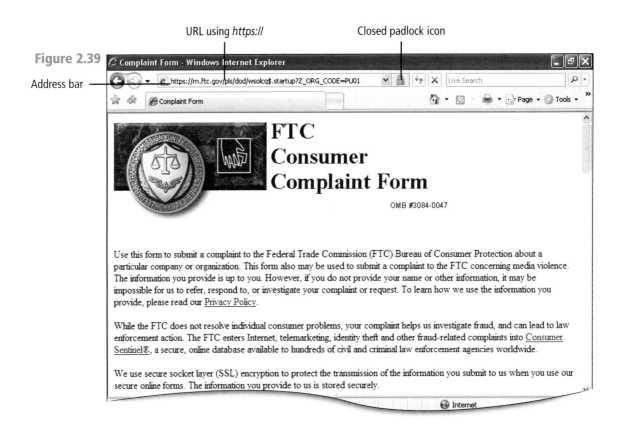

What is SSL and encryption? A closed padlock icon and the use of *https://* indicate a Web site is using **Secure Sockets Layer**, or **SSL**, to secure the transfer of data. SSL is a protocol that uses encryption during the transmission of data over the Internet. SSL is used to protect data such as credit card numbers or other personal information being sent from Web sites.

A secure Web site uses **encryption** as it passes data and personal information over the Internet. For example, encryption is used when data from Web-based forms is transmitted. Encryption is the process of scrambling or coding information as it is sent over the Internet by using a set of keys. A **public key** is an encryption tool that is used to code the data before sending it over the Internet. The file is scrambled or encrypted with a public key and then is transmitted to its destination. After it reaches the destination, the file is decoded by using a ***private key***. A private key is only available to the receiver.

End **You have completed Project 2D** ──────────────

Online Quiz

Project 2D

Take the online self-study quiz for this chapter:

1. Go to **www.prenhall.com/go** and select the textbook *GO!* **with the Internet.**

2. Select **chapter 2.**

3. Select Self-Study Quiz Project 2D.

Assessments

Summary

In this chapter, you started Internet Explorer and performed several commands commonly performed as you browse. You identified the buttons on the toolbar and performed tasks with them. You used tabs in a browser window to navigate to new Web sites. You specified a default home page. You browsed the World Wide Web by using links, the Address bar, the History button, and the Favorites feature. You managed Web content by performing such tasks as printing and saving Web page content and e-mailing a Web page. You created a desktop shortcut to a Web page. You cleared the cookies, cache, and History list from your computer's hard drive. You identified when you need a plug-in and how plug-ins work. You compared several popular Web browsers and their features. You determined the risk of browsing the Web and how to protect your privacy while online. Finally, you identified safe browsing strategies.

Key Terms

Accessibility compliance 69

Active X 123

Add-ons 110

Adware 122

Anti-adware program 122

Anti-spyware program 122

Anti-virus program 122

Cache 101

Children's Online Privacy Protection Act (COPPA) 119

Context-sensitive menu 72

Cookies 73

Desktop shortcut 100

Dialer programs 122

Download 108

Drag-and-drop 113

Dynamic HTML (DHTML) 112

Encryption 124

Favorites Center 71

Firewall 123

Feeds button 76

Form data 102

Freeware 109

Frequently Asked Questions (FAQs) 110

Go button 83

Groom 118

Hackers 121

Help 77

History 73

Home button 76

Instant Search 76

Link Select pointer 86

Malware 121

Menu bar 64

Minimize, Restore Down, and Close buttons 64

Offline 94

Open source 112

Page button 77

Path 75

Pharming 121

Phishing 120

Pinned 77

Plug-ins 107

Pop-up 72

Portal 83

Print button 76

Privacy 71

Privacy policies 116

Private key 125

Public key 124

Quick Tabs 80

Really Simple Syndication (RSS) 76

ScreenTip 75

Scroll bars 86

Secure Sockets Layer (SSL) 124

(Continued)

Assessments

Key Terms

Security 73

Service pack 110

Social
networking 118

Spyware 122

Status bar 69

Style sheet 110

Submenu 65

Tab 79

Tabbed browsing 79

Temporary Internet
files 73

Thumbnail 80

Title bar 64

Toolbar 64

Tools button 65

Trojan horse 122

Trojan 122

Virus 122

Wizard 108

Worm 122

Assessments

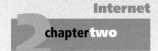
Matching

Match each term in the second column with its correct definition in the first column by writing the letter of the term on the blank line in front of the correct definition.

_____ **1.** A horizontal bar near the top of the browser window that contains expandable menu-style headings for performing important commands and tasks.

_____ **2.** Features that enable customization of the screen for size and availability.

_____ **3.** An initiative to provide features in order to accommodate people with visual or physical disabilities so that they can access the Internet with modifications to the browser or Web sites.

_____ **4.** Small text files sent from a Web server and stored on the client computer that transmits data back to the Web server.

_____ **5.** A browser feature where a list is automatically generated for Web sites that have been visited during a browsing session.

_____ **6.** The technologies involved with the features keeping your data and computer free from unauthorized access.

_____ **7.** A Windows feature that temporarily displays a small box providing information about, or the name of, a screen element as you hold the mouse pointer over buttons or images in Internet Explorer or other Web browsers.

_____ **8.** A feature of Internet Explorer that enables you to search for Web sites, images, and maps on the Internet.

_____ **9.** The mouse pointer view that displays as a pointing hand as you point to a link.

_____ **10.** A vertical and/or horizontal bar located on the edge of the browser window to enable you to move the content so that the hidden parts of the Web page come into view.

_____ **11.** A Web page that contains interesting content, frequently used links, and services such as current and breaking news, e-mail access, and search capabilities.

_____ **12.** A green arrow at the right end of the Address bar that displays as you type and will take you to the URL that is typed in the Address bar.

_____ **13.** A term that means you can use your Web browser to see a Web page without being connected to the Internet.

_____ **14.** An icon displaying on the desktop that leads directly to a program, file, or Web page.

_____ **15.** A storage mechanism in the memory area of your computer's hard drive that enables for the rapid retrieval of frequently used Web pages or files.

A Accessibility compliance

B Cache

C Cookies

D Desktop shortcut

E Go button

F History

G Instant Search

H Link Select pointer

I Menu bar

J Minimize, Restore Down, and Close buttons

K Offline

L Portal

M Scroll bars

N ScreenTip

O Security

Assessments

Fill in the Blank

Write the correct answer in the space provided for each statement.

1. A blue, horizontal bar at the top of the browser window that identifies the program and displays the name of the active Web page is called the _____.

2. A detailed list of commands, displayed after clicking a command, which enables you to perform several tasks to enhance your browsing experience, is called the _____.

3. A horizontal bar near the bottom of the browser window that provides information about the security of a site, information about a link's destination as you roll over a link, or information about any submenu command is called the _____.

4. A feature of Internet Explorer that contains a list of Web sites you have added there because you like the Web sites and may want to return there easily again is called the _____.

5. Your ability to determine which personal information, such as your e-mail messages and stored files, is shared and for what purpose is called _____.

6. A new instance of a browser window that displays on top of the current browser window to display ads or other information is called a(n) _____.

7. An area of a software program's interface that provides text or buttons which when clicked enable you to perform certain commands and tasks within that software program is called the _____.

8. A Windows feature that displays a small pop-up window containing a menu of commands relating to the object that has been right-clicked is called a(n) _____.

9. A browser feature where copies of Web pages, images, and media that are saved for faster viewing is called the _____.

10. A button that enables you to perform several commands that are frequently used while browsing the Web such as those related to safe browsing strategies, the display of toolbars within the browser interface, and setting browsing preferences is called _____.

11. An Internet Explorer feature that only displays when multiple tabs are open and permits navigation among open tabs is called _____.

(Continued)

Assessments

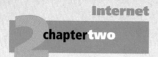
Fill in the Blank

12. A graphic depicting a miniature version of each open Web page that can be used for navigation is called _____.

13. The sequential description of the storage location of the HTML documents and files making up the Web page and stored in the hierarchy of directories and folders on the Web server is called _____.

14. A pop-up or panel that is made to remain stationary within the browser window is _____. on the screen.

15. A button that contains a submenu of commands to perform many common tasks related to the current Web page such as opening a new browser window, saving the Web page, or sending either a link to the page or the entire page itself to someone by using e-mail is called _____.

Rubric

Projects 2A and 2B in the front portion of this chapter, and Projects 2E through 2J that follow have no specific correct result; your result will depend on your approach to the information provided. Make Professional Quality your goal. Use the following scoring rubric to guide you in how to approach the search problem and then to evaluate how well your approach solves the search problem.

The criteria—Internet Mastery, Content, Format and Layout of Search Results, and Process—represent the knowledge and skills you have gained that you can apply to solving the search problem. The levels of performance—Professional Quality, Approaching Professional Quality, or Needs Quality Improvements—help you and your instructor evaluate your result.

	Your completed project is of Professional Quality if you:	Your completed project is Approaching Professional Quality if you:	Your completed project Needs Quality Improvements if you:
1–Internet Mastery	Choose and apply the most appropriate search skills, tools, and features and identify efficient methods to conduct the search and locate valid results.	Choose and apply some appropriate search skills, tools, and features, but not in the most efficient manner.	Choose inappropriate search skills, tools, or features; or are inefficient in locating valid results.
2–Content	Conduct a search that is clear and well organized, contains results that are accurate, appropriate to the audience and purpose, and are complete.	Conduct a search in which some results are unclear, poorly organized, inconsistent, or incomplete. Misjudge the needs of the audience.	Conduct a search that is unclear, incomplete, or poorly organized, containing some inaccurate or inappropriate content.
3–Format and Layout of Search Results	Format and arrange all search results to communicate information and ideas, clarify function, illustrate relationships, and indicate relative importance.	Apply appropriate format and layout features to some search results, but not others. Overuse search techniques, causing minor distraction.	Apply format and layout that does not communicate the search results clearly. Do not use format and layout features to clarify function, illustrate relationships, or indicate relative importance. Use available search techniques excessively, causing distraction.
4–Process	Use an organized approach that integrates planning, development, self-assessment, revision, and reflection.	Demonstrate an organized approach in some areas, but not others; or, use an insufficient process of organization throughout.	Do not use an organized approach to solve the problem.

Assessments

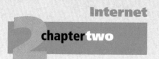
Project 2E—Creating a Browser Report

Objectives: 1. *Perform Commands with Internet Explorer;* **2.** *Perform Commands with the Toolbar;* **4.** *Browse the World Wide Web Using Links, the Address Bar, History, and Favorites Center;* **9.** *Identify and Compare Several Popular Web Browsers;* **11.** *Identify Safe Browsing Strategies.*

In this Assessment, you and the office staff for the City of Desert Park, Arizona will continue the training initiative as you use the Address bar to locate information about three recently developed Web browsers. You will visit the Web sites of three Web browsers by typing the URLs into the Address bar and reviewing each Web site. You will locate information on the key features of the browsers, such as security features and accessibility compliance for each browser. You will create a report describing the features and benefits for each browser to support your findings for Shane Washington, Director of Office Operations at City of Desert Park, Arizona.

For Project 2E, you will need the following file:

New blank Notepad document

You will save your file as
2E_Browsers_Firstname_Lastname

1. On the left side of the Windows taskbar, point to, and then click the **Start** button. From the **Start** menu that displays, click **Internet** to start the Internet Explorer program. Then in the upper right corner of the **Internet Explorer** window, click the **Maximize** button to enlarge the window to fill the computer screen completely.

2. In the **Address bar** box, click one time to select the existing text, and then type **http://www.mozilla.com** Press the Enter key. The **Mozilla** home page displays. The Mozilla Foundation developed the Firefox browser. Locate the **Products** link leading to details about the product features of Firefox. Locate the information on security features and accessibility compliance. This information will help you develop your summary report.

3. In the **Address bar** box, click one time to select the existing text, and then type **http://www.opera.com** Press the Enter key. The **Opera** home page displays. Opera Software ASA developed the Opera browser. Locate the link labeled *read more* leading to details about the product feature of Opera. Locate the information on security features and accessibility compliance. This information will help you develop your summary report.

4. In the **Address bar** box, click one time to select the existing text, and then type **http://www.apple.com/macosx/features/safari** Press the Enter

(Project 2E–Creating a Browser Report continues on the next page)

Assessments

Mastering the Internet

(Project 2E–Creating a Browser Report continued)

key. The main page of the **Safari browser information** Web page of the **Apple Computer** Web site displays. Scroll down the page to locate the details about the product features of Safari. Locate the information on security features and accessibility compliance.

5. From the Windows taskbar, click the **Start** button. Point to **All Programs**, point to **Accessories**, and then click **Notepad** to open a blank Notepad document. If necessary, **Maximize** the **Notepad** window. Type a title, and then in your own words, write a brief paragraph summarizing what you learned for each browser. Identify each browser by name and specify the URL of each Web site where you gathered your information. Give a brief description of the security features for each browser. Discuss how each browser handles accessibility compliance.

6. Write one final paragraph making your browser recommendation to Shane Washington, Director of Office Operations at City of Desert Park, Arizona.

7. At the top of the **Notepad** window, on the menu bar, click **File**, and then from the displayed **File** menu, click **Page Setup**. In the displayed **Page Setup** dialog box, click

the **Header** box, and then delete any existing text. Click in the **Footer** box, delete any existing text, and then using the underscore character as indicated, and your own first and last names, type **2E_Browsers_Firstname_Lastname** Click **OK** to close the dialog box.

8. At the top of the **Notepad** window, on the menu bar, click **File**, and then from the displayed **File** menu, click **Save As**. In the displayed **Save As** dialog box, click the **Save in arrow**, and then navigate to the folder where you are storing your documents for this course. In the **File name** box, type **2E_Browsers_Firstname_Lastname**

9. Check your *Chapter Assignment Sheet* or *Course Syllabus* or consult your instructor to determine whether you are to submit your assignments by printing on paper, or electronically by using your college's course information management system. Electronically, you can submit the *.txt* file created in Notepad. To print on paper from Notepad, under the **File** menu, click **Print**, and then print accordingly. To submit the document electronically, follow the instructions provided by your instructor.

10. **Close** the **Notepad** window. **Close** the **Internet Explorer** window.

End **You have completed Project 2E**

Assessments

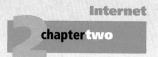

Mastering the Internet

Project 2F—Playing Music at a Multimedia Web Site

Objectives: 1. *Perform Commands with Internet Explorer;* **2.** *Perform Commands with the Toolbar;* **4.** *Browse the World Wide Web Using Links, the Address Bar, History, and Favorites;* **6.** *Create a Desktop Shortcut to a Web Page;* **8.** *Describe How Plug-ins Work.*

Ray Hamilton, Director of Fine Arts and Parks for the City of Desert Park, wants to create an official listing of preapproved online multimedia Web sites to be used in all city offices. In the following Assessment, you will use the Address bar to locate a multimedia Web site. You will add the site to your Favorites Center and create a desktop icon so you can easily return to the Web site. After exploring the Web site, you will write a brief summary of your listening experience.

For Project 2F, you will need the following file:

New blank Notepad document

You will save your file as
2F_Multimedia_Firstname_Lastname

1. On the left side of the Windows taskbar, point to, and then click the **Start** button. On the **Start** menu that displays, click **Internet** to start the **Internet Explorer** program. Then in the upper right corner of the Internet Explorer window, click the **Maximize** button to enlarge the window to fill the computer screen completely.

2. In the **Address bar**, click one time to select the existing text, and then type **http://www.npr.org** and press Enter to display the **National Public Radio (NPR)** home page. NPR uses multimedia extensively at its Web site so you can listen to news stories, programs of interest, and music. On the left side of the Web page, locate and click the **Music** link.

3. On the toolbar, click the **Add to Favorites** button. From the menu that displays, click **Add to Favorites.** In the **Add a Favorite** dialog box, click the **New Folder** button, and then create a folder in your **Favorites** list. Name it **Multimedia** and then click the **Create** button. Then click the **Add** button to add the **National Public Radio Music** Web page to the folder.

4. On the **NPR Music** Web page, right-click anywhere except on a link or graphic to display a submenu of commands. Click **Create Shortcut** to create a desktop shortcut. In the **Internet Explorer** dialog box that displays, click the **Yes** button to confirm you want to put a shortcut for this Web site on your desktop. **Close** Internet Explorer.

(Project 2F–Playing Music at a Multimedia Web Site continues on the next page)

Assessments

Mastering the Internet

(Project 2F–Playing Music at a Multimedia Web Site continued)

5. On your computer's desktop, double-click the newly created **desktop shortcut icon**. Your browser automatically launches the **National Public Radio Music** Web page. Notice that there are several kinds of music to choose from including classical, jazz, pop, or world music. Select a music genre that you want to listen to and click the link for that genre. Notice that articles for each genre display; select one of the articles. Look for the file types and the plug-ins needed to hear the music.

6. **Start** Notepad and if necessary, **Maximize** the **Notepad** window. Type a title and a brief paragraph summarizing what you liked or didn't like about the National Public Radio Web site and if you think it is appropriate to include this Web site on the list of approved sites. Include the name of the music genre that you selected and the name of the song and the artist. Name the plug-ins needed to listen to the music.

7. At the top of the **Notepad** window, on the menu bar, click **File**, and then from the displayed **File** menu, click **Page Setup**. In the displayed **Page Setup** dialog box, click the **Header** box, and then delete any existing text. Click in the **Footer** box, delete

any existing text, and then using the underscore character as indicated, and your own first and last names, type **2F_Multimedia_Firstname_Lastname** Click **OK** to close the dialog box.

8. At the top of the **Notepad** window, on the menu bar, click **File**, and then from the displayed **File** menu, click **Save As**. In the displayed **Save As** dialog box, click the **Save in arrow**, and then navigate to the folder where you are storing your documents for this course. In the **File name** box, type **2F_Multimedia_Firstname_Lastname**

9. Check your *Chapter Assignment Sheet* or *Course Syllabus* or consult your instructor to determine whether you are to submit your assignments by printing on paper, or electronically by using your college's course information management system. Electronically, you can submit the *.txt* file created in Notepad. To print on paper from Notepad, under the **File** menu, click **Print**, and then print accordingly. To submit the document electronically, follow the instructions provided by your instructor.

10. **Close** the **Notepad** window. **Close** the **Internet Explorer** window.

End You have completed Project 2F

Assessments

Project 2G—Protecting Children's Privacy

Objectives: 3. *Specify a Default Home Page;* **4.** *Browse the World Wide Web Using Links, the Address Bar, History, and Favorites;* **5.** *Print, Save, and E-mail a Web Page;* **10.** *Determine the Risks of Using the World Wide Web.*

The Deputy Mayor for Policy and Development for the City of Desert Park, Laura Chavez-Wilson, is concerned with reports of online privacy violations involving children. Laura would like to form a public schools policy regarding online safety. In the following Assessment, you will provide the City of Desert Park schools with ideas to help protect children's privacy while they are using the Web at the city's public schools. You will use the Address bar to locate information on protecting children's privacy while they are online, and you will save a Web page. You will look for tips on keeping children safe and write a list of online safety pledges for children of all ages.

For Project 2G, you will need the following files:

New blank Notepad document
Web page printout

You will save your files as
2G_Privacy_Firstname_Lastname
2G_Safety_Firstname_Lastname

1. On the left side of the Windows taskbar, point to, and then click the **Start** button. On the **Start** menu that displays, click **Internet** to start the Internet Explorer program. Then in the upper right corner of the **Internet Explorer** window, click the **Maximize** button to enlarge the window to fill the computer screen completely.

2. In the **Address bar**, click one time to select the existing text, type **http://www.netsmartz.org** and then press the Enter key to display the **Netsmartz Workshop** home page. The Netsmartz Workshop provides many educational opportunities to inform children and adults of online safety. On the toolbar, click the **Page** button and then click **Save As** to display the **Save Webpage** dialog box. In the **Save In** box, click the **down arrow** to display locations for saving the Web page. Navigate to your folder where you are storing your documents for this course. **Save** the Web page as **2G_Privacy_Firstname_Lastname**

3. Near the top of the Web page, on the right side, click the **Quick Links down arrow**. Then locate and click the **Online Risks** link. Read the **Online Risks** Web page to develop an understanding of

(Project 2G–Protecting Children's Privacy continues on the next page)

Assessments

(Project 2G–Protecting Children's Privacy continued)

types of risks for children who use the Internet. Then on the left side of the Online Risks page, locate and click the **Keep Kids & Teens Safer** link, and then click the **Safety Pledges** link. Scroll down the page and read and evaluate the pledges for each age group. Continue until you have reviewed all of the age groups.

4. **Start** Notepad and if necessary, **Maximize** the **Notepad** window. Type a title and a brief list summarizing safety practices protecting children while they are working online. Back up your list with evidence that you found on the **Netsmartz Workshop** Web site.

5. At the top of the **Notepad** window, on the menu bar, click **File**, and then from the displayed **File** menu, click **Page Setup**. In the displayed **Page Setup** dialog box, click the **Header** box, and then delete any existing text. Click in the **Footer** box, delete any existing text, and then using the underscore character as indicated, and your own first and last names, type **2G_Safety_Firstname_Lastname** Click **OK** to close the dialog box.

6. At the top of the **Notepad** window, on the menu bar, click **File**, and then from the displayed **File** menu, click **Save As**. In the displayed **Save As** dialog box, click the **Save in arrow**, and then navigate to the folder where you are storing your documents for this course. In the **File name** box, type **2G_Safety_Firstname_Lastname** For any additional Web pages you want use to support your findings, print them, using the **Print** button on the toolbar.

7. Check your *Chapter Assignment Sheet* or *Course Syllabus* or consult your instructor to determine whether you are to submit your assignments by printing on paper, or electronically by using your college's course information management system. Electronically, you can submit the .txt file created in Notepad. To print on paper from Notepad, under the **File** menu, click **Print**, and then print accordingly. To submit the document electronically, follow the instructions provided by your instructor.

8. **Close** the **Notepad** window. **Close** the **Internet Explorer** window.

End **You have completed Project 2G**

Assessments

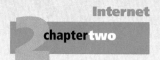
Project 2H—Guarding Against Security Risks

Objectives: 4. *Browse the World Wide Web Using Links, the Address Bar, History, and Favorites;* **5.** *Print, Save, and E-mail a Web Page;* **7.** *Clear the Cache, Cookies, and History;* **10.** *Determine the Risks of Using the World Wide Web;* **11.** *Identify Safe Browsing Strategies.*

In recent months, a dramatic increase in the number of phishing incidents has been reported to Dennis Johnson, Police Chief for the City of Desert Park, Arizona. In the following Assessment, you will use the Address bar to locate information on a securing your computer from online threats. You will review several brief online tutorials at the OnGuard Online Web site and write your recommendations about how people can secure their computers from online threats.

For Project 2H, you will need the following files:

New blank Notepad document
Web page printout

You will save your files as
2H_Security_Firstname_Lastname
2H_Security_Recommendations_Firstname_Lastname

1. On the left side of the Windows taskbar, point to, and then click the **Start** button. On the **Start** menu that displays, click **Internet** to start the Internet Explorer program. Then in the upper right corner of the **Internet Explorer** window, click the **Maximize** button to enlarge the window to fill the computer screen completely.

2. In the **Address bar**, click one time to select the existing text, and then type **http://onguardonline.gov** Press the Enter key to display the **OnGuard Online** home page. The OnGuard Online Web site provides advice from the federal government for protecting you against fraud and identity theft while online. Take a moment to review the Web site. On the toolbar, click the **Page** button, and then click **Save As** to display the **Save Webpage** dialog box. Click the **Save In down arrow** to display locations for saving the Web page. Navigate to your folder where you are storing your documents for this course. **Save** the Web page as **2H_Security_Firstname_Lastname**

3. Near the top of the page, point to the **Topics** link and then click the **Overview** link. Read the practices for safer computing. On the toolbar, click the **Print** button to print the entire Web page. The Web page is sent directly to the printer without any additional options for setting the footer.

(Project 2H–Guarding Against Security Risks continues on the next page)

Assessments

Mastering the Internet

(Project 2H–Guarding Against Security Risks continued)

4. Click the **Topics** link again, and then click the **Phishing** link. Read the article on phishing. Then continue to click the **Topics** link, selecting two more articles about topics that interest you.

5. **Start** Notepad and if necessary, **Maximize** the **Notepad** window. Type a title and a brief paragraph summarizing what you learned about each of the three topics. In your paragraph, create a brief list of recommendations for online safety.

6. At the top of the **Notepad** window, on the menu bar, click **File**, and then from the displayed **File** menu, click **Page Setup**. In the displayed **Page Setup** dialog box, click the **Header** box, and then delete any existing text. Click in the **Footer** box, delete any existing text, and then using the underscore character as indicated, and your own first and last names, type **2H_Security_Recommendations_Firstname_Lastname** Click **OK** to close the dialog box.

7. At the top of the **Notepad** window, on the menu bar, click **File**, and then from the displayed **File** menu, click **Save As**. In the displayed **Save As** dialog box, click the **Save in arrow**, and then navigate to the folder where you are storing your documents for this course. In the **File name** box, type **2H_Security_Recommendations_Firstname_Lastname** For any additional Web pages you want to use to support your findings, print them using the **Print** button on the toolbar.

8. On the toolbar, click the **Tools** button, then **Delete Browsing History**. In the **History** section, click the **Delete history** button. In the **Delete History** box that displays, click **Yes**.

9. Check your *Chapter Assignment Sheet* or *Course Syllabus* or consult your instructor to determine whether you are to submit your assignments by printing on paper, or electronically by using your college's course information management system. Electronically, you can submit the *.txt* file created in Notepad. To print on paper from Notepad, under the **File** menu, click **Print**, and then print accordingly. To submit the document electronically, follow the instructions provided by your instructor.

10. **Close** the **Notepad** window. **Close** the **Internet Explorer** window.

End **You have completed Project 2H**

Assessments

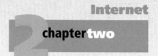

Project 2I — Protecting Your Computer from Viruses

Objectives: 1. *Perform Commands with Internet Explorer;* **2.** *Perform Commands with the Toolbar;* **4.** *Browse the World Wide Web Using Links, the Address Bar, History, and Favorites;* **5.** *Print, Save, and E-mail a Web Page;* **11.** *Identify Safe Browsing Strategies.*

Shane Washington's training initiative for office staff of the City of Desert Park, Arizona includes a unit on computer virus protection. In this Assessment, you will use the Address bar to locate information on recent virus threats at the Web site for McAfee anti-virus software. The Web site provides a virus page that contains an extensive collection of information including:

- Recent virus threats
- Search tool to locate information on a specific virus
- Virus removal tools
- Virus hoaxes
- Virus glossary
- Virus calendar
- Worldwide virus map

You will visit the Web site to identify the most recent virus threat and explore some of the Web site's features. Then you will locate and save a world map of recent virus outbreaks.

For Project 2I, you will need the following files:

New blank Notepad document

You will save your files as
2I_Map_Firstname_Lastname
2I_Virus_Firstname_Lastname

1. On the left side of the Windows taskbar, point to, and then click the **Start** button. On the **Start** menu that displays, click **Internet** to start the Internet Explorer program. Then in the upper right corner of the **Internet Explorer** window, click the **Maximize** button to enlarge the window to fill the computer screen completely.

2. In the **Address bar**, click one time to select the existing text, type **http://us.mcafee.com/virusInfo/default.asp** and then press [Enter] to display the **McAfee Virus Information** Web page. Take a moment to read the Web page, and then locate the **Recent Threats** area. Locate the name, threat level, and date of the most recent virus threat area. Click the name of the most recent virus to display more information

(Project 2I–Protecting Your Computer from Viruses continues on the next page)

Assessments

(Project 2I–Protecting Your Computer from Viruses continued)

about the virus. Note the risk to home users and corporate users and the date the virus was discovered.

3. Click **Back**. Under **Recent Threats**, click **Virus Hoaxes**. Read about virus hoaxes, and then click **Back**. Click **Virus Removal Tools**. Locate and read about the list of recent virus threats in the table and the links that lead tools to get rid of the virus threat.

4. In the upper left corner of your screen, click the **Back** button to return to the **McAfee Virus Information** Web page. Scroll down the page until you locate an area labeled **Virus Map**. Click the **Virus Map** to open it in a new window.

5. Locate and click the **United States** to show a closer view of the country. In the lower left corner of the United Stages, locate and click **Arizona** to show an enlarged view of the state.

6. Right click the map, and then click **Save Picture As** to display the **Save Picture** dialog box. Click the small **down arrow** on the right side of the **Save In** box to display locations for saving the graphic. **Save** the map to your storage area as **2I_Map_Firstname_Lastname**

7. **Start** Notepad and if necessary, **Maximize** the **Notepad** window. Type a title and a brief paragraph summarizing what you learned about the most recent virus threats, virus hoaxes, and removal tools.

8. At the top of the **Notepad** window, on the menu bar, click **File**, and then from the displayed **File** menu, click **Page Setup**. In the displayed **Page Setup** dialog box, click the **Header** box, and then delete any existing text. Click in the **Footer** box, delete any existing text, and then using the underscore character as indicated, and your own first and last names, type **2I_Virus_Firstname_Lastname** Click **OK** to close the dialog box.

9. At the top of the **Notepad** window, on the menu bar, click **File**, and then from the displayed **File** menu, click **Save As**. In the displayed **Save As** dialog box, click the **Save in arrow**, and then navigate to the folder where you are storing your documents for this course. In the **File name** box, type **2I_Virus_Firstname_Lastname**

10. Check your *Chapter Assignment Sheet* or *Course Syllabus* or consult your instructor to determine whether you are to submit your assignments by printing on paper, or electronically by using your college's course information management system. Electronically, you can submit the *.txt* file created in Notepad. To print on paper from Notepad, under the **File** menu, click **Print**, and then print accordingly. To submit the document electronically, follow the instructions provided by your instructor.

11. **Close** the **Notepad** window. **Close** the **Internet Explorer** window.

End **You have completed Project 2I**

Assessments

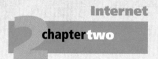
Project 2J—Comparing Browser Plug-ins

Objective: 4. *Browse the World Wide Web Using Links, the Address Bar, History, and Favorites;* **8.** *Describe How Plug-ins Work.*

Courtney Shrever, Executive Assistant for Mayor David Parker, has asked you to help her update all of the computers in the office with plug-ins. Using the concepts presented in this chapter, research where you can download the most recent versions of the four most commonly used plug-ins. Include one plug-in for each: text, audio, video, and animation. Create a summary document listing each plug-in by name, the URL where you can download it, what kind of files are handled by the plug-in, and any costs or licensing associated with the plug-in. Save your document as **2J_Plug_Ins_Firstname_Lastname** and submit to your instructor as directed.

For Project 2J, you will need the following file:

New blank Notepad document

You will save your file as
2J_Plug_Ins_Firstname_Lastname

End **You have completed Project 2J** ————————————

3 chapterthree

Searching the World Wide Web

OBJECTIVES

At the end of this chapter, you will be able to:

1. Formulate a Keyword Query to Implement a Search
2. Search with the Address Bar
3. Search with the Instant Search Feature
4. Locate Expert Resources
5. Find Online Library Catalogs and Scholarly Resources

6. Search with Boolean Operators
7. Locate News and Opinion Resources
8. Find Invisible Web Resources and Specialized Databases

9. Implement a Search Using a Directory Search Site
10. Implement a Search Using a Meta-Search Engine

11. Explore How a Search Engine Works
12. Evaluate Search Results

OUTCOMES

Mastering these objectives will enable you to:

Project 3A
Implement Basic Search Techniques

Project 3B
Perform Advanced Searches

Project 3C
Explore Search Tools

Project 3D
Develop Search Strategy Guidelines

Greater Atlanta Job Fair

The Greater Atlanta Job Fair is a nonprofit organization supported by the Greater Atlanta Chamber of Commerce and the Atlanta City Colleges. The organization holds targeted job fairs in and around the greater Atlanta area several times each year. Candidate registration is free and open to area residents and students enrolled in certificate or degree programs at any of the City Colleges. Employers pay a nominal fee to display and present at the fairs.

The fairs are widely marketed to companies nationwide and locally to prospective candidates to provide a wide and varied pool of employers and candidates. When candidates register for a fair, their resumes are scanned into an interactive, searchable database that is provided to the employers. A few of the industries targeted by fairs this year will be: aerospace, temporary office personnel, government, K-12 education, information technology, and financial planning/brokerage.

In addition to the targeted fairs throughout the year, the organization also presents an annual Atlanta Job Fair that draws over 2,000 employers in more than 70 industries and generally registers more than 5,000 candidates.

Searching the World Wide Web

The World Wide Web supplies you with information ranging from artifacts to information on the nearest zoological garden. Because the Web has experienced a tremendous burst of development and growth since its introduction, the organization of information is not always obvious and straightforward. A search engine or a directory will help you locate information on the Web. Search techniques help you efficiently target the right materials as you search for results. Evaluation strategies help you identify valid resources within the search results.

Project 3A Implementing Basic Search Techniques

The staff of the Greater Atlanta Job Fair is preparing for the next job fair. In Activities 3.1 through 3.9, the Greater Atlanta Job Fair staff and you will explore several specialized search tools to help find information that will be helpful in the planning phase of the staff's preparations. You will formulate and perform a keyword query to identify several search engines and their characteristics. After categorizing these search engines, you will develop a set of guidelines to help the staff determine when to use a specific search engine.

You will use the browser's Address bar to perform a keyword search and the Instant Search feature for Internet searches. You will also locate expert resources, online library catalogs, and other scholarly resources to locate information. Finally, you will create documents to summarize your findings.

For Project 3A, you will need the following files:

New blank Notepad documents
Web page printouts

You will save your files as
3A_Guidelines_Firstname_Lastname
3A_Address_Bar_Firstname_Lastname
3A_Instant_Search_Firstname_Lastname
3A_Expert_Tools_Firstname_Lastname
3A_Library_Firstname_Lastname

Figure 3.1

Objective 1
Formulate a Keyword Query to Implement a Search

Finding good information on the Web quickly and efficiently depends on several factors. Knowing the right keywords to use or how to structure your **keyword query** or **natural language query** takes practice to generate the most appropriate search results list for your needs. A keyword query is a word or phrase that represents the subject you want to find out about and is used to begin a search. A natural language query is a query that uses a complete sentence or question to begin a search.

Alert!

Assessing Project 3A and Project 3B

For Projects 3A and 3B of this chapter, you and your instructor can evaluate your approach to the problem and your result by consulting the scoring rubric located in the end-of-chapter material. For these hands-on projects, there is no online quiz.

Activity 3.1 Developing Queries for a Search

In this activity, you will formulate a search query by developing a topic statement, identifying keywords, and creating a natural language query.

1 Review the following guidelines for conducting an effective search, and then develop a topic statement that summarizes the type of information you want to find.

To develop a topic sentence, you identify several search engines and explore their characteristics. First, you find search engines and URLs. For example, you might use the topic statement, *What are some commonly used search engines?*

- Identify the type of information you want to find. It is helpful to develop a topic statement that you can refer back to as you evaluate your search results. For example, a topic statement to help you find an information technology job in Atlanta, Georgia is *What kinds of information technology jobs are available in Atlanta Georgia?*

- Think about words you might use as keywords. Do a quick directory search to see what words are used as subject categories and subcategories and use those words as your keywords. Then think of several **synonyms**—words that mean almost the same thing— for your keywords. For example, for *information technology jobs*, you might use *Atlanta Georgia jobs*, or *Atlanta technology jobs*. Synonyms, such as the words *employment*, *careers*, or *work*, can be used instead of the word *jobs*.

- Formulate questions or sentences to use as natural language queries. Use the fewest number of words to capture what you want to know. Compare results that come from your natural language queries with results that come from your keyword queries. An example is, *What information technology jobs are available in Atlanta Georgia?* Other examples include *What Atlanta Georgia employers have information technology jobs available?* or *Is there an IT employment service in Atlanta Georgia?*

After you understand the information you are looking for and how to ask for that information, you need to select a **search engine**. A search engine is a computer program used to locate files, documents, and Web pages containing specific keyword queries or natural language queries. Search engines have three main components:

- **Spider**—The spider, also called the **crawler**, or **bot** (short for robot), is a program that searches the Internet for new documents and Web files, and then catalogs the words found within the documents and files for use in a search engine.

- **Index**—The index is a large database used in a search engine that stores references to words found in documents and Web files located by the spider. The index also stores the frequency of appearance and the location of the words within each file and the URL.

- **Search engine software**—The search engine software is a program that compares the keyword or natural language query to the words and references stored in the index. When you make a query, the search engine software generates the search results list that displays in the browser window.

Because each search engine works in a slightly different way and provides different results, do not limit yourself to just one search engine. Try the same keywords and natural language queries at a couple of search engines to determine which one gives you the type of information you need. Competition among search engines is intense, so try search engines that you may not have tried before.

2 From your topic statement, identify keywords to summarize the statement. You should also think of any synonyms for the keywords and other forms of the words to use as alternatives.

These keywords and synonyms will be used as your keyword query. In this example, you will use the keyword *search engine.* Some synonyms include *search site, directory search site,* or *Web search site.* Other forms of the word include *searching* or *searches.*

3 From your topic statement, develop a natural language query.

In this example, you might try your topic statement *What are some commonly used search engines?* or *Where can I find a directory search site?*

You will use your keyword query and natural language query in the next activity.

Activity 3.2 Identifying Search Engines and Their Characteristics

In this activity, you will use the topic statement, keywords, and a natural language query to identify four search engines. You will analyze the main characteristics of each search engine.

1 **Start** Internet Explorer and if necessary, **Maximize** the window to fill the screen. In the **Address bar**, click one time to select the existing text, and then type **http://www.yahoo.com** Press ⏎.

The Yahoo! home page displays. Yahoo! is one of the most popular search engines. It started in 1994 as a directory search site that people maintained. Although it still has a directory component, the prominent feature is its search engine.

2 On the toolbar, click the **Add to Favorites** button ⌖. From the menu that displays, click **Add to Favorites**. In the **Add a Favorite** dialog box, click the **New Folder** button, and then in the **Favorites** list, create a folder. Name it **Chapter_3_Searching** and then click the **Create** button. Then click the **Add** button to add the Yahoo! Web page to the folder.

The Yahoo! Web site is added to your Favorites folder for this chapter and the Add a Favorites dialog box closes. Adding the Yahoo! home page to your Favorites folder for this chapter enables you to refer back to the Web site at any time.

3 At the top of the **Yahoo!** Web page, locate the **Search** text box, and then type your keyword query developed in the previous activity or use the keyword query **search engine** Then click the **Web Search** button.

Several search results display. The results are shown in a *search results list*. A search results list is a list of Web pages containing the query and displayed as links that are located by any given search engine. Each individual link in the search results list is called a *hit*.

The results of a search are organized into categories that require further investigation. *Sponsored sites* are included as part of the search results list. Sponsored sites, also called *sponsored results* or *sponsored links*, are Web sites that try to market themselves by paying search engine owners to be shown as a listing in search result lists. Typically, sponsored sites are commercially oriented. The information found at a sponsored site may or may not be appropriate for the purposes of your search.

4 Evaluate the search results list by identifying those results that most closely match your query. Look carefully to determine if any are sponsored sites. Compare your screen with Figure 3.2. Your search results list may look different.

Yahoo! Search
URL in Address bar

Query in
Search text box

Sponsor results

Figure 3.2

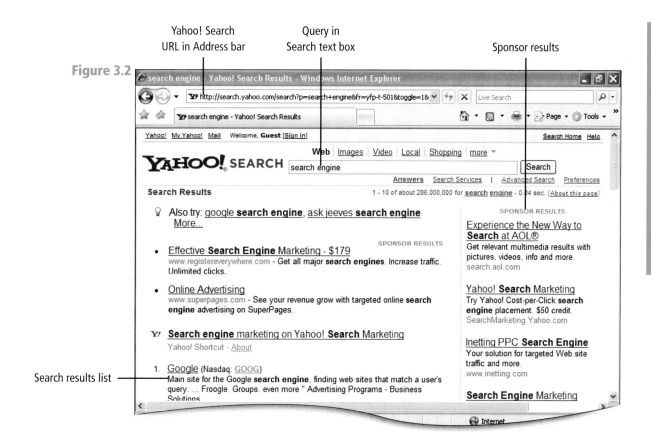

Search results list

5 In the search results list, in the results that are not sponsored, right-click the first search engine link. From the context-sensitive menu that displays, click the **Open in New Tab** option. After the search engine Web page opens in a new tab, take a moment to review the Web site.

Determine the type of search engine you have found by noting if it is a **directory**, a search engine that uses keyword queries, a search engine that uses natural language queries, or a combination of the three types. Recall that a directory is an alphabetical list of subject categories arranged in a hierarchy starting from a set of broad subject areas to more detailed subcategories for individual Web sites or Web resources.

If the search engine is a **meta-search engine**, identify the search engines that are available for use. A meta-search engine is a search tool that uses several search engines to locate results for a single query and returns the results as a single list. Meta-search engines do not use their own index or database; instead, they use other search engines, directories, and multimedia resources to compile search results at the meta-search engine Web site.

6 Using the skills you have practiced, add this search engine or meta-search engine Web site to your **Favorites** folder for this chapter, so that you can refer back to the Web site at any time.

7 On the home page of the search engine, identify the types of file formats that can be located using the search engine. Review the table in Figure 3.3, which shows some of the search categories and the file types that are located by search engines.

A series of links or tabs located near the search text box indicates the categories or file types you will find.

Search Categories and File Types that May Be Located	
Category	**File Type**
Web	HTML files
Images	GIF, JPG, Flash, or Shockwave files
Audio	MP3, RA, WAV, or WMA files
Video	ASX, AVI, MPG, MOV, or WMV files

Figure 3.3

8 On the home page of the search engine, click the **Advanced** or **Advanced Search** link. Scroll down the new page to identify and review how you can refine your search at that search engine.

Boolean operators can be used at most search engines. Boolean operators are mathematical or logic terms used to make a query more specific by showing the relationship of the words used in the query. Each search engine has its own preferred syntax for formulating a query with Boolean operators. Remembering how each Boolean operator works for each search engine is a cumbersome task. You can use the *advanced search* feature found at most search engines. The advanced search feature is a search engine feature that provides options for refining a keyword query by specifying additional criteria for returned search results.

Advanced search features work by enabling you to put in keywords and then selecting options from a menu or series of check boxes instead of typing the Boolean operators.

You can further refine search results by using *search filters* found under the advanced search feature. The search result list that is returned contains not only the keywords but also meets the additional filtering criteria. Search filters limit the search results to specific criteria, such as the format of the results. For example using search filters, a search can be limited to finding audio, video, graphics, HTML, PowerPoint, or Excel files. Filters limit the results to a certain file size. They also limit search results by the language used on the Web pages, or you can set the filters for a range of dates.

You may be able to filter the top-level domain name or the URL. Spiders notate where they find words within the document as well as the URL where they are found. Because of this, you can limit the results to finding the keywords in certain parts of the documents, such as the title or URL. A search filter can limit the results to specific top-level domains, such as educational institutions (*.edu*) or government sites (*.gov*). In addition, some search filters are used to locate documents created in a certain language or country. Other filters limit the results to documents created or updated on certain dates. Some search engines provide filters that enable you to filter out adult content.

9 Locate the **Help** section, and then review the content for tips on maximizing searches. Then click the **Back** button ⬅️. Locate the **Frequently Asked Questions (FAQ)** section, if available, and review the content.

Most search engines provide a Help section or FAQ section; however, they may be labeled something other than *Help* or *FAQ*. Both of these sections are excellent resources for discovering the best techniques to use with the search engine. Over time, you will develop a repertoire of search engines and understand the circumstances for when to use each.

10 After you have created notes about the characteristics of the search engine, click **Close** ❌ to close the second tab and return to the Yahoo! Search the search results list. Select a new search engine to explore. Using the techniques you have practiced, open the link in a new tab, and then add it to your **Favorites** folder for this chapter. Review and make notes about the type of search engine, the type of files that can be located with the search engine, and how to refine a search with advanced options. Research a total of three search engines.

Activity 3.3 Creating a Document to Compare Search Engines

In this activity, you will create a summary document that compares three search engines that can be used the Greater Atlanta Job Fair staff.

1 Decide on a location where you will store your document—either in a folder on your computer's hard drive or a folder on a removable storage device such as a USB flash drive. Click the **Start** button 🏁 *start* , and then click **My Computer**. Navigate to the desired location, and if necessary, create a folder for this course into which you can store documents. Name the folder **Chapter_3_Searching** and then press Enter. Close **My Computer** when you are finished.

2 From the Windows taskbar, click the **Start** button 🏁 *start* . Point to **All Programs**, point to **Accessories**, and then click **Notepad** to open a blank Notepad document. If necessary, **Maximize** the **Notepad** window.

3 In the **Notepad** window, at the insertion point, type **3A_Guidelines_ Firstname_Lastname** Press Enter two times. Type the name of the first search engine you identified, and then type the URL of that search engine. Press Enter two times.

4 Type **Types of Files:** and then type the types of files that can be located at that search engine. Press Enter two times, and then type

Advanced Search Options: Type one or two sentences that describe the way searches can be refined using this search engine. Press Enter two times.

5 Repeat the previous steps for each of the two remaining search engines you identified.

6 At the top of the **Notepad** window, on the menu bar, click **File**, and then from the displayed menu, click **Page Setup**. In the displayed **Page Setup** dialog box, click in the **Header** box, and then delete any existing text. Click in the **Footer** box, and then delete any existing text. In the **Footer** box, using the underscore character as indicated and your own first and last names, type 3A_Guidelines_Firstname_ Lastname Click **OK** to close the dialog box.

7 At the top of the **Notepad** window, on the menu bar, click **File**, and then from the displayed **File** menu, click **Save As**. In the displayed **Save As** dialog box, click the **Save in arrow**, navigate to the **Chapter_3_Searching** folder, and then in the **File name** box, type 3A_Guidelines_Firstname_Lastname Click **OK** to close the dialog box.

Your document is saved to your course work folder as 3A_Guidelines_ Firstname_Lastname.

8 Check your *Chapter Assignment Sheet* or *Course Syllabus* or consult your instructor to determine if you are to submit your assignments by printing on paper, or electronically by using your college's course information management system. Electronically, you can submit the *.txt* file that you created in Notepad. To print on paper from Notepad, from the **File** menu, click **Print**, and then print accordingly. To submit electronically, follow instructions provided by your instructor.

9 **Close** ⊠ the **Notepad** window.

Objective 2
Search with the Address Bar

One of the easiest ways to begin a search is to use the Address bar in the browser window. Using the Address bar to search is most appropriate when you want to find out about organizations or when you are looking for names of associations, specific products, or services. You simply type a keyword query into the Address bar text box—instead of a URL—and press Enter.

Activity 3.4 Searching with the Address Bar

The Greater Atlanta Job Fair staff wants to find out if there are any organizations, associations, products, or services that should be included in the upcoming Job Fair. In this activity, you will conduct a search using the Address bar of the browser window.

1 In the **Address bar**, click one time to select the existing text, and then type **information technology jobs in Atlanta Georgia** Figure 3.4 shows a keyword query using the Address bar with Internet Explorer as the browser.

Whatever you use as the keyword query displays as part of the search result. For example, if you wanted to search for information technology jobs in Atlanta Georgia, you could try a single keyword such as *jobs*. You may get more specific results if you use a query such as *information technology jobs in Atlanta Georgia*.

Each browser uses a search engine to locate Web pages relating to the keyword query. But not all browsers use the same search engine. Recall that a search engine is a computer program used to locate files, documents, and Web pages containing specific keywords. Microsoft Internet Explorer uses Live Search as its default search engine. Netscape Browser and Firefox use Google as the default search engine.

More Knowledge

Changing the Default Search Engine in Internet Explorer

You change the default search engine used by Internet Explorer by clicking the down arrow to the immediate right of the Search button on the toolbar. When the submenu displays, click the Find More Providers command. In the Web page that displays, click the name of the search engine in the list of providers. Then in the Add Search Provider dialog box, click the Make this my default search provider check box and finally, click the Replace Provider button.

Address bar   Keyword query

Figure 3.4

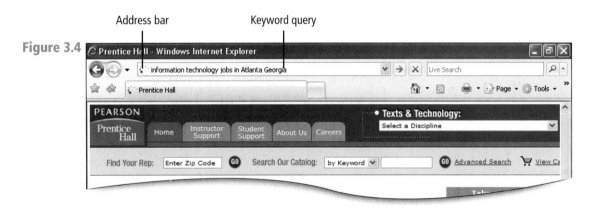

2 Press Enter. Compare your screen with Figure 3.5.

A search using the Address bar will produce many results— numbering into the thousands or even millions—in a matter of a fraction of a second as a search results list. Typically a search results list will contain the total number of results, the length of time it takes to find the hits, the search engine's logo, and several sponsored sites.

Alert!

Does your search results list differ?

Your search results lists may differ from the one shown. The World Wide Web adds new pages every day. Search engines differ in how often they are updated and how they display the results. The number of results in the list and the location of sponsored results within the search results, the placement within the browser window, and other features may vary on your screen for any search you perform in this chapter.

Search engine   Hit   Sponsored sites

Figure 3.5

Total number of results

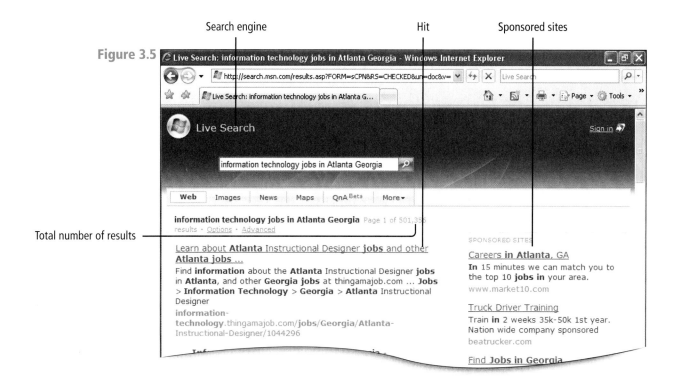

3 From the search results list displayed in the browser, on the toolbar, click the **Page button down arrow** [⌄], and then click **Save As** to open the **Save Webpage** dialog box. In the top part of the **Save Webpage** dialog box, on the right side of the **Save in** text box, click the **down arrow** [⌄] to display the locations for saving the Web page.

A hierarchy of folders and drives displays. You can choose where to save your Web page. If you click *Desktop*, the Web page will save on the desktop of the computer you are currently using. If you choose a storage disk or drive such as your *USB Flash drive, 3 1/2 Floppy*, or *CD-RW*, the Web page will be saved to that device and you will be able to open it at different computer.

4 Click your preferred storage disk or device and navigate to the **Chapter_3_Searching** folder. In the lower part of the **Save Webpage** dialog box, on the right side of the **Save as type** text box, click the **down arrow** [⌄] to display the options for saving the Web page. Click the **Webpage, complete** option to save the entire Web page as an HTML file.

The File name text box will already contain the search query by default.

5 In the **File name** text box, click one time to select the existing text, and then type **3A_Address_Bar_Firstname_Lastname** Click the **Save** button.

The Save Webpage dialog box closes and the Web page is saved onto your storage device or desktop.

6 On the toolbar, click the **Print button down arrow** [·] , and then click **Page Setup** to open the **Page Setup** dialog box.

The Page Setup dialog box is divided into four sections: Paper, Headers and Footers, Orientation, and Margins. Under Headers and Footers, you can type information into the text boxes to annotate the printout.

7 In the **Page Setup** dialog box, click in the **Header** box, and then delete any existing text. Click in the **Footer** box, and then delete any existing text. Then, using the underscore character as indicated and your own first and last names, in the **Footer** box, type **3A_Address_Bar_Firstname_Lastname** Click **OK** to add this information as the footer to the Web page and to close the **Page Setup** dialog

box. On the toolbar, click the **Page button down arrow** [·] , and then click **Print Preview** to display the **Print Preview** dialog box.

The Print Preview dialog box shows what the Web page will look like when it prints. You can print directly from this dialog box.

Alert!

Check Your Settings

Some security software and pop-up blockers may prevent you from modifying your system's settings. In addition, some schools prevent computer lab or classroom computers from being modified from their default settings or may prevent certain activities from being performed. You may need to change the system's settings back to the default settings for your school or business after completing this chapter's activities. Check with your instructor for additional instructions before completing this chapter.

8 In the **Print Preview** toolbar, click the **Print Document** button to open the **Print** dialog box. In the **Print** dialog box, click **Print**.

9 In the **Print Preview** dialog box, click the **Close** button ⊠ .

Objective 3
Search with the Instant Search Feature

Instant Search is located on the toolbar. It is a search tool that enables you to locate Web sites, images, and maps on the Internet.

Activity 3.5 Searching with the Instant Search Feature

In this activity, you and the staff of the Greater Atlanta Job Fair use the Instant Search feature to find information about technology jobs in Atlanta, Georgia.

1 On the toolbar, locate the **Instant Search** text box. In the **Instant Search** text box, click one time to select the existing text, and then type **What is the availability of information technology jobs in Atlanta?** Click the **Search** button.

Although you can type just a keyword query into the text box, you may also type in a complete sentence or question—a natural language query.

After the search is complete, a new page displays in a tab with several links to Web sites about your topic. The search results list generated by the default search engine displays in the browser window. Information such as the number of total search results and a list of sponsored sites is included with the search results list. In addition, at the top of the search result list, your natural language query displays.

2 Scroll down the page and notice each hit displays only the most important words of your natural language query in bold text. The **stop words** have been removed. Stop words are short words that connect the more important words of a natural language query. Stop words have little impact on the meaning. Figure 3.6 shows typical Instant Search results.

Figure 3.6

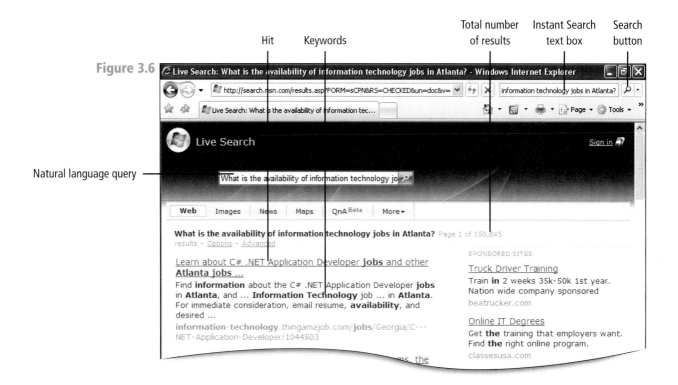

3 Save the **Search Results** Web page to the **Chapter_3_Searching** folder as **3A_Instant_Search_Firstname_Lastname**

4 Add the **footer 3A_Instant_Search_Firstname_Lastname** to the document.

5 On the toolbar, click the **Print button down arrow** [˙], and then click **Print Preview** to display the **Print Preview** dialog box.

6 In the **Print Preview** toolbar, click the **Print Document** button to display the **Print** dialog box. In the **Print** dialog box, click **Print**.

7 In the **Print Preview** dialog box, click the **Close** [X] button.

Objective 4
Locate Expert Resources

When you are looking for factual and accurate information, you need to use Web sites that provide information authored by subject matter experts. The author's name, area of expertise, and reputation are important facts to note as you gather information from credible sources. You need to verify the author's affiliation to make sure the credentials are appropriate for your topic area.

Knowing who sponsors a Web site also helps determine the relevance of the information on a Web site. For example, if you need employment statistics, you can use a government Web site to gather the statistics.

You might also use a directory search site to locate expert resources. Recall that a directory is an alphabetical list of subject categories arranged in a hierarchy leading from a set of broad subject areas to more detailed subcategories to individual Web sites or Web resources. Directories are sometimes referred to as *subject catalogs*. You locate information with a directory search by *drilling down*—clicking into more specific areas—into the subject categories, or, until you locate the information you want. A *breadcrumb trail* forms as you click the subject categories to keep track of each successive level of category. A breadcrumb trail is a navigation tool that lists each category and subcategory in the order in which they are clicked. Typically, the breadcrumb trail displays in a horizontal row at the top of the Web page.

Activity 3.6 Exploring Expert Resources

The Greater Atlanta Job Fair staff wants to find a listing of credible experts on a variety of employment-oriented areas. In this activity, you will explore two expert resource sites and evaluate them for credibility.

1 In the **Address bar**, click one time to select the existing text, type **http://www.refdesk.com/expert.html** and then press Enter.

The home page of the refdesk.com Ask The Experts Web site displays. Started in 1995, the refdesk.com Web site provides several types of reference materials and access to facts of all kinds. The Ask The Experts page of the refdesk.com Web site is a directory that links to several expert resources. A brief description of each expert resource is provided.

The refdesk.com Ask The Experts Web page enables you to search with two different methods: the directory search and the search engine method. Remember, for searches where you do not know which keywords to use, it is a good idea to use the directory search method.

The search engine, labeled Search the Web, is powered by Google. Results from the search engine are found anywhere on the Web and not necessarily on the Ask The Experts Web site.

2 Using the techniques you practiced, add the refdesk.com **Ask The Experts** Web page to the **Favorites** folder, so that you can refer back to the Web site at any time.

3 In the upper left corner of the refdesk.com **Ask the Experts** Web page, locate the **Search the Web** text box. Further down on the left side of the screen, locate the heading *Services*, under which there are numerous links to expert resources. Scroll down the page and locate the *Subjects* heading, which contains links for very specific subject categories of expert resources. On the right side of the screen, notice the advertisements for sponsored sites. Compare your screen with Figure 3.7. Both headings—*Services* and *Subjects*— provide links leading to expert sources. You can read the descriptions to help you determine which experts you want to use.

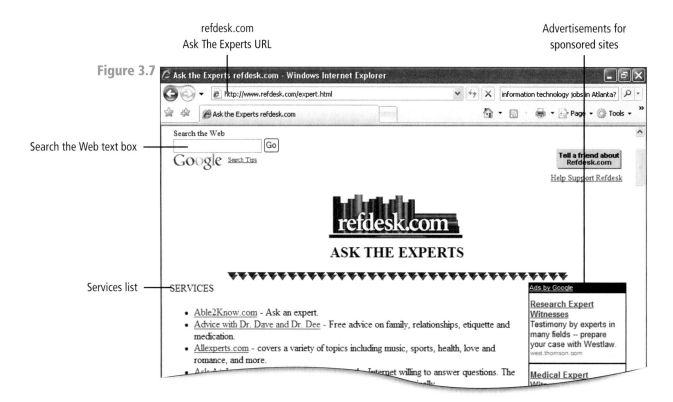

Figure 3.7

refdesk.com
Ask The Experts URL

Advertisements for
sponsored sites

Search the Web text box

Services list

4 Scroll down the page and review the **Services** and **Subjects** sections to see what expert resources are offered. Click any links that have descriptions relating to employment such as census or salary. After you have finished viewing the census or salary expert Web site, click **Close** [X] to close the new browser window and return to the refdesk.com **Ask The Experts** Web page.

Another Way ┌─ **To Open Links in a New Browser Window**

You can also open a link to a new Web page in a new browser window, so that you can easily return to the original Web page. Open a link in a new browser window by right-clicking the link. Then from the context-sensitive menu that displays, click the Open in New Window command. When you are done viewing the new Web page, click the Close button to return to the original Web page.

5 Using the following criteria, evaluate the refdesk.com **Ask The Experts** Web site. Specifically, make notes so you will remember the following items. You will use these notes in the next activity.

- The name of this Web site
- Its URL
- The type of information you find here
- The site's sponsor
- The author of the site if the author is listed

Note any outstanding characteristics and how the information is organized at this site. Typically, the name of the Web site is found at the top of the browser window and in the title bar. The sponsor's name may be at the top of the Web site and displayed as a brand or logo. Knowing who sponsors a site helps you determine the objectives of the Web site. The author's name is found either at the top or the bottom of the Web page. The author's name helps to determine his credentials and affiliation.

6 On a **New Tab**, click one time to open a new tab. In the **Address bar** of the new tab, click one time to select the existing text, type **http://www.allexperts.com** and then press Enter.

The AllExperts home page displays in a new tab. Opening a Web site in a new tab enables you to easily navigate between two or more sites by clicking each tab.

The AllExperts Web site offers a question-and-answer service manned by experts who volunteer their responses. It is organized into several subject categories and associated keywords.

7 Add the **AllExperts** home page to the **Favorites** folder for this chapter, so that you can refer back to the Web site at any time.

8 Scroll to review the Web site. Then, at the top of the **AllExperts** home page, locate the **Search for** text box that can be used with a keyword query. At the top and bottom of the Web page, locate the sponsored links.

9 In the middle of the page, locate the subject categories. Click the **Jobs/Careers** link. On the **Jobs/Career** page that displays, scroll to find the *Career Planning/Job Searching* heading, and then click the **Job Searching** link. On the **Jobs Searching** page that displays, click the **Headhunters & Employment Agencies** link. As an alternative, you can right-click any of these links to open them in a new browser window.

A list of experts on headhunting and employment agencies displays. The name, area of expertise, and the expert's status is listed.

10 Click the first **View Profile** link.

The expert profile provides a description of the expert's area of expertise, and ratings on the knowledge, and reviews from recent users. Consumer feedback such as the reviews from users can help you judge the credibility of the Web site.

11 Click the **Back** button to return to the list of experts. Then click the next profile. Notice this expert's area of expertise, and ratings on his knowledge, and his reviews.

12 Click the **Back** button as necessary to return to the **AllExperts** home page. As an alternative, if you right-clicked the link, so that it

displayed in a new browser window, click **Close** to close the new browser window and return to the **AllExperts** home page.

13 Using the same criteria as before, evaluate the **AllExperts** Web site. Make notes so that you will remember the name of this Web site, its URL, and the type of information you find on the site. Identify the site's sponsor and the author if the author is listed. Make note of any outstanding characteristics and how the information is organized at this site. You will use your notes in the next activity.

Activity 3.7 Creating a Document to Compare Expert Resources

In this activity, you will create a summary document that evaluates two expert resources that can be used whenever a list of experts on employment-oriented information is needed by the Greater Atlanta Job Fair.

1 **Start** Notepad, and in the **Notepad** window, at the insertion point, type **3A_Expert_Tools_Firstname_Lastname** Press [Enter] two times to create a blank line. Type **Ask The Experts:** and then type the URL of the refdesk.com **Ask The Experts** Web site. Press [Enter] two times.

2 Type the Web site's sponsor and the author—if the author is listed at the Web site. Next, type one or two sentences that summarize the characteristics and how the information is organized at this site. Press [Enter] two times to create a blank line.

3 Type **AllExperts:** and then type the URL of the **AllExperts** Web site. Press [Enter] two times.

4 Type the site's sponsor and the author—if the author is listed at the Web site. Next, type one or two sentences that summarize the characteristics and how the information is organized at this site.

5 Using the techniques you have practiced, add the **footer 3A_Expert_ Tools_Firstname_Lastname** to the document.

6 Using the techniques you have practiced, navigate to the **Chapter_3_ Searching** folder and then save the document as **3A_Expert_ Tools_Firstname_Lastname** Click **OK** to close the dialog box.

7 Check your *Chapter Assignment Sheet* or *Course Syllabus* or consult your instructor to determine if you are to submit your assignments by printing on paper, or electronically by using your college's course information management system. Electronically, you can submit the *.txt* file created in Notepad. To print on paper from Notepad, from the **File** menu, click **Print**, and then print accordingly. To submit electronically, follow instructions provided by your instructor.

8 **Close** ⊠ the **Notepad** window.

Objective 5
Find Online Library Catalogs and Scholarly Resources

Searching for research and reference materials often starts at the local library. The research materials you find at the library are often supported by electronic resources. Many public and academic libraries now offer their catalogs online, so that you can search for books, electronic journals, powerful subscription-based databases, and full-text articles from any Internet-connected computer. This gives you access to larger libraries with specialized collections and materials for your research needs.

Most libraries offer an easy-to-use interface for accessing their catalogs and collections online. Some library sites may be set up for directory searches. At other library sites you start your search with a keyword query and a search engine. Then typically, you can refine the search by selecting specific types of resources.

Activity 3.8 Finding Online Library Catalogs and Other Scholarly Resources

In Activity 3.8, you will explore several types of online library catalogs and other scholarly resources for the Greater Atlanta Job Fair staff. Because so much research must be performed prior to each job fair, the staff needs a better understanding of what types of library resources are available online. You will locate several online resources including a local library and a national library.

1 In the **Address bar**, click one time to select the existing text, type **http://lists.webjunction.org/libweb** and then press ⏎. Compare your screen with Figure 3.8.

The Libweb home page displays. Using directory searches, Libweb connects you to libraries all over the world including academic, public, national, state, and regional libraries. The libraries are organized by location. Notice there is also a search text box to use if you already know the location, the library type, the name, or other information about a particular library.

Figure 3.8

Libweb URL   Directory search by location

Keyword Search text box

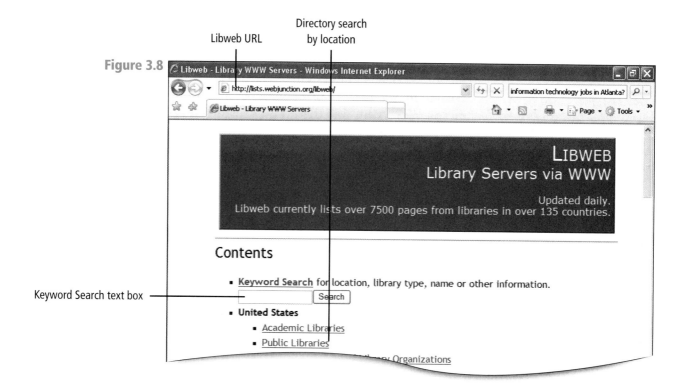

2. Add the **Libweb** home page to your **Favorites** folder for this chapter, so that you can refer back to the Web site at any time.

3. Under the heading for the *United States*, locate the types of library links offered. Click the **Public Libraries** link to view the locations of public library Web sites in United States. Scroll down the page to locate the heading for *Southeast* and the link for **Georgia**. On the page that displays next, click the **Atlanta-Fulton Public Library** link.

The Atlanta-Fulton Public Library System home page displays.

4. Add the **Atlanta-Fulton Public Library** home page to your **Favorites** folder for this chapter, so that you can refer back to the Web site at any time.

5. At the top of the **Atlanta-Fulton Public Library** home page, locate the links labeled **Home**, **Library Locations**, **Events & Classes**, **Books & Materials**, **Services**, **Support AFPLS**, and **About AFPLS**. Point to **Books & Materials**, and then in the submenu that displays, click **Catalog Search**.

The Atlanta-Fulton Public Library Quick Search page displays. The Web page provides links for directory searches and search engine capabilities to help you locate books and materials at the library.

6. In the **Quick Search** section, click the round button on the left of the **Catalog** choice. Then in the **Search for** text box, type **jobs report** Click the **words or phrase** button to begin the search.

The search is conducted using only items found in the Atlanta-Fulton Public Library System catalog. The search result list contains several titles of books and materials that contain the keyword query. Across the top of the page, you can find options to limit the search, begin a new search, or keep the search. You may also begin another search by scrolling down the page to the search text box located under the search results list.

7 Evaluate the **Atlanta-Fulton Public Library** Web site. Make notes so you will remember the name of this Web site, its URL, and the type of information you find here. Identify the site's sponsor and the author if the author is listed. Make note of any outstanding characteristics and how the information is organized at this site. You will use your notes in the next activity.

8 Click the **Back** button as needed to return to the **Atlanta-Fulton Public Library** home page.

9 On a **New Tab**, click one time to open a new tab. Then in the **Address bar** of the new tab, click one time to select the existing text, type **http://www.loc.gov** and then press Enter.

The Library of Congress home page displays in a new tab. The Library of Congress is the largest library in the world. It serves as the research resource for Congress and it also serves the American people. The ability to access the library online has enabled more people to view the library's historic collections than would ever have the opportunity to visit the library in person.

10 Add the **Library of Congress** Web site to your **Favorites** folder for this chapter, so that you can refer back to the Web site at any time.

11 Notice how the Web site is organized. On the left are resources of various interest groups. At the top of the Web page are broad categories that show types of collections from multimedia to maps to multilingual resources. At the top of the page is also the **Search** text box used for keyword searching. In the center of the Web page are links to highlighted collections or special events at the Library. Compare your screen with Figure 3.9, and then in the **Search** text box, type the keyword query **jobs report** Click the **Search** button.

After several seconds, a search results list displays. Results are found at several different URLs and may be in several formats, such as HTML files, *PHP files*, and *PDF files*. Recall that HTML files are simply Web pages. Files with the extension. *php* are HTML files with scripting embedded within the HTML coding so that *dynamically generated* results from databases are displayed onscreen. Dynamically generated is a term representing a method of instantly creating Web pages in response to specified criteria.

Files with the extension *.pdf* are in *portable document format*, a special file format created in Adobe Acrobat—a program that translates output from other programs into the portable document format. PDF files can be opened and viewed with a free software program called Adobe Reader. There is a version of Adobe Reader for many different versions of operating systems. Typically, you can read a *.pdf* file but you cannot modify it unless you have been given rights to do so by the document's creator.

Figure 3.9

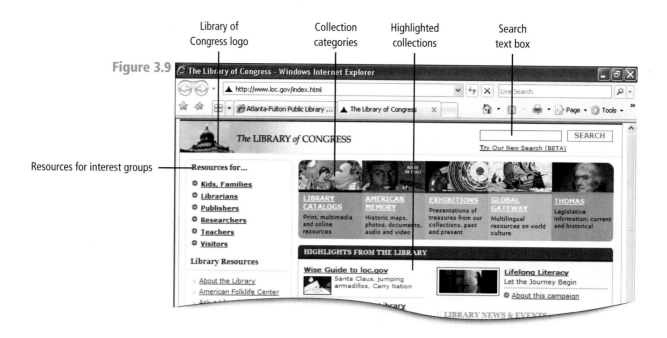

Library of Congress logo   Collection categories   Highlighted collections   Search text box

Resources for interest groups

12 On the left side of the search results list, click the **More Search Options** link. Compare your screen with Figure 3.10.

The Library of Congress provides options for searching Library Web Pages or for searching several Online Catalogs. There are options for searching Other Library Resources such as access to copyright records, historical archives, and legislative records.

A breadcrumb trail forms at the top of the page. Recall that a breadcrumb trail is a navigation tool that lists each category and subcategory in the order in which it has been clicked. You can click any part of the breadcrumb trail to return to that part.

Breadcrumb trail

Figure 3.10

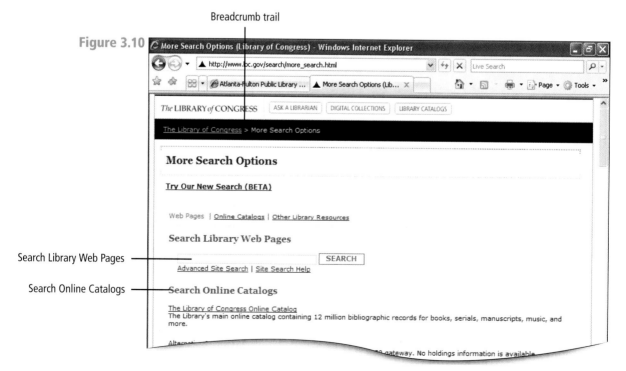

Search Library Web Pages

Search Online Catalogs

13 In the upper left corner of the Web site, click the **Library of Congress** link in the breadcrumb trail. As an alternative, click the **Library of Congress** logo to return to the **Library of Congress** home page.

14 Evaluate the **Library of Congress** home page. Make notes so you will remember the name of this Web site, its URL, and the type of information you find here. Identify the site's sponsor and the author if the author is listed. Make note of any outstanding characteristics and how the information is organized at this site. You will use these notes in the next activity.

Activity 3.9 Creating a Document to Compare Library Resources

In this activity, you will create a summary document that provides a listing of library resources including a local library and a national library with an extensive collection of historical and government resources.

1 **Start** Notepad, and in the **Notepad** window, at the insertion point and using your own name, type **3A_Library_Firstname_Lastname** Press Enter two times to create a blank line. Type **Atlanta-Fulton Public Library:** and then type the URL of the **Atlanta-Fulton Public Library** Web site. Press Enter two times to create a blank line.

2 Type the site's sponsor and the author—if the author is listed at the Web site. Next, summarize in one or two sentences any outstanding characteristics and how the information is organized at this site. Press Enter two times.

3 Type **Library of Congress:** and then type the URL of the **Library of Congress** Web site. Press Enter two times.

4 Type the site's sponsor and the author—if the author is listed at the Web site. Next, summarize in one or two sentences any outstanding characteristics and how the information is organized at this site.

5 Add the **footer 3A_Library_Firstname_Lastname** to the document.

6 Navigate to the **Chapter_3_Searching** folder and then save the document as **3A_Library_Firstname_Lastname** Click **OK** to close the dialog box.

7 Check your *Chapter Assignment Sheet* or *Course Syllabus* or consult your instructor to determine if you are to submit your assignments by printing on paper, or electronically by using your college's course information management system. Electronically, you can submit the *.txt* file created in Notepad. To print on paper in Notepad, from the **File** menu, click **Print**, and print accordingly. To submit electronically, follow instructions provided by your instructor.

8 **Close** ☒ the **Notepad** window. **Close** ☒ the **Internet Explorer** window. If prompted to close all tabs, click **Close Tabs**.

End **You have completed Project 3A**—————————

Project 3B Performing Advanced Searches

The Greater Atlanta Job Fair holds several job fairs each year. The organization is staffed by volunteers so it is hard to maintain a consistent group of workers. Research is an important part of the staff's duties. With so many options for searching available, making sure that all of the volunteers know when to use the right search tool is important. In Activities 3.10 through 3.16, you will identify several Boolean operators and advanced search features. After performing an advanced search you will save the search results Web page. You will search for news at several news and opinion Web sites. You will create a document to compare the news sources. Then you will help the staff explore the Invisible Web, also called the Deep Web, and specialized databases. Finally, you will create a document to compare the Invisible Web resources.

For Project 3B, you will need the following files:

New blank Notepad documents
Web page printout

You will save your files as
3B_Boolean_Firstname_Lastname
3B_News_Firstname_Lastname
3B_Invisible_Firstname_Lastname

Objective 6
Search with Boolean Operators

When a search engine responds to a query with more than one word in it, the search engine gives each word roughly equal weight for retrieval. The words may or may not be found next to each other in the resulting documents or files. The term *proximity* describes how each word in the query displays on the Web page in relation to the other words of the query. You may find extra words that go with the query but have no added value for your search. For example if you use the query *Atlanta information technology jobs*, you may get results for anything having to do with Atlanta, results for Atlanta information, Atlanta technology, or Atlanta jobs. You may get results for information technology jobs in other cities or any type of job offered in any city.

Recall that Boolean operators are mathematical or logic terms used to make a query more specific by showing the relationship of the words used in the query. Showing the relationship of the words to each other makes the search results list align more closely to the kind of information you want to find.

Activity 3.10 Searching with Boolean Operators and Advanced Search Features

In this activity, you and the Greater Atlanta Job Fair staff practice searching using Boolean operators and other advanced search features to try to find information on Atlanta jobs.

1 **Start** Internet Explorer, and then **Maximize** the window.

2 In the **Address bar**, click one time to select the existing text, and then type **http://vlib.org** Press Enter.

The WWW Virtual Library home page displays. Recall that a ***virtual library*** is a specialized type of directory that has resources organized by information professionals such as librarians. Typically virtual libraries contain excellent, reliable resources that have been analyzed and rated in the same way that public libraries do. The WWW Virtual Library is considered a virtual library.

The WWW Virtual Library is the oldest catalog for scholarly resources. It was started by Tim Berners-Lee in the 1990s. The WWW Virtual Library is an online collection of high–quality resources gathered and evaluated by experts in the different categories who volunteer their time. The home page provides a listing of several subject categories and a brief list of associated keywords that can be searched as a directory. The WWW Virtual Library home page also contains a search engine text box called *Quick search.*

3 Add the **WWW Virtual Library** Web site to your **Favorites** folder for this chapter, so that you can refer back to the Web site at any time.

4 At the top of the **WWW Virtual Library** Web page, locate the **Quick search** text box. Locate the pair of open book logos. Compare your screen with Figure 3.11.

The WWW Virtual Library uses the open book logos as a navigation tool to return you to the home page from any Web page in the site. The logos are found on both the upper left and upper right corners of the Web page.

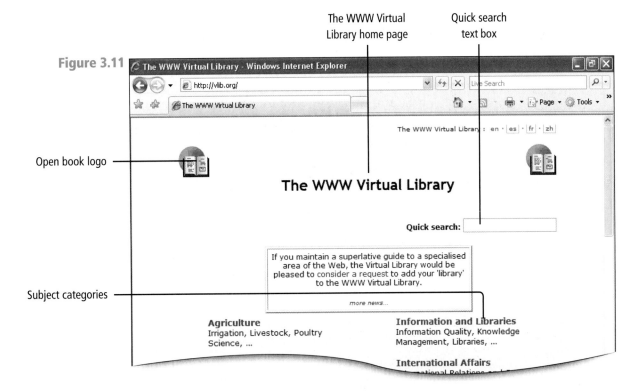

Figure 3.11

5 In the **Quick search** text box, type the keyword query **Atlanta jobs** and then press Enter.

After several seconds, a search results list displays. Because you did not include any Boolean operators such as quotation marks around the keywords, each word was given equal weight and numerous results were returned for each word in the query.

When you put quotation marks around the words in the keyword query, the search results list contains Web pages with that exact phrase—keywords in the same order and proximity.

6 On the search results page, on the right side of **Search!** button, click the **Advanced** link.

Options are displayed to refine the search in several ways including the use of Boolean operators. Most search engines enable you to search using Boolean operators as an advanced search option. However, each search engine interprets the Boolean operators in a slightly different way. You should check each search engine's Help section, so that you use the proper syntax when formulating your query using Boolean operators.

The most commonly used Boolean operators include AND, OR, and NOT. They are always capitalized, so that the search engine does not get them confused with keywords being searched. Some search engines use symbols instead of words such as + (plus sign) in place of the Boolean operator AND. The − (minus sign) may stand for NOT at some search engines.

The Boolean operator NEAR will return Web pages that have all of the keywords in the query, but the words may display no more than 10 to 20 words apart on the Web page. The asterisk (*) is called a *wildcard character* because it takes the place of any number of missing letters in a keyword. Figure 3.12 summarizes several Boolean operators, other characters used in queries, and the results they produce.

7 Be sure the query *Atlanta jobs* still displays in the **Search for** text box, and then add quotation marks around the query. Click the **down arrow** in the match box, and then click **Boolean**. Click the **Search** button.

After a few seconds, the search results list displays. This time no results were found that contain the phrase *Atlanta jobs*—both words next to each other on the Web page.

8 Add the **footer 3B_Boolean_Firstname_Lastname** to the document.

9 Navigate to the **Chapter_3_Searching** folder and then save the document as **3B_Boolean_Firstname_Lastname**

Boolean Operator	Search Query	Results
AND	Atlanta AND Jobs	Returns results for pages that contain both words.
OR	Atlanta OR Jobs	Returns results for pages that contain either word.
NOT	Atlanta NOT Jobs	Returns results for pages that contain the word *Atlanta* but not the word *Jobs*.
NEAR	Atlanta NEAR Jobs	Returns results for pages that contain both words and the words are placed within 10–20 words apart.
" "	"Atlanta Jobs"	Returns results for pages that contain the exact phrase.
*	Technology* Atlanta	Returns results for pages that contain words beginning with *Technology something* before the word *Atlanta*. For example, *Technology employment Atlanta* or *Technology jobs Atlanta*.
+	Atlanta+Jobs	Returns results for pages that contain both words.
−	Atlanta−Jobs	Returns results for pages that contains *Atlanta* but not the word *Jobs*.

Figure 3.12

Objective 7
Locate News and Opinion Resources

The World Wide Web has made it easy to stay connected to the news wherever you are. Several different types of news such as archived news, breaking news, local and regional news, business news, world news, or editorial pieces are available. News is provided by several online sources such as newspapers, magazines, wire services, radio station, or television station Web sites. You can get the news in several different formats including searchable Web sites, e-mail alerts, live **RSS** feeds, or **podcasts**. Recall that **Really Simple Syndication** (RSS) is a system developed to automatically alert subscribers of updates made to sites such as blogs, news, weather, or sports sites. Podcasts are the download of MP3 audio files from the World Wide Web to MP3-compatible computers or portable audio players using RSS technology. Typically, you subscribe to a specific podcast and RSS alerts you when there have been updates. With so many places to get the news, it is helpful to be familiar with several news-related search tools.

Activity 3.11 Finding News at Google

The Greater Atlanta Job Fair staff members are putting together a report that requires several types of information including recent news stories about unemployment. In this activity, you and the Greater Atlanta Job Fair staff will explore a resource for reading about current news and searching for other news stories.

1 In the **Address bar**, click one time to select the existing text, type **http://www.google.com** and then press [Enter]. In the displayed **Google** home page, click the **News** link.

The Google News home page displays. Google is a search engine that also provides news on its Web site. Besides current world, U.S., and business news, you can find sciences, sports, entertainment, and health news.

2 Add the **Google News** Web site to your **Favorites** folder for this chapter, so that you can refer back to the Web site at any time.

3 At the top of the **Google News** Web page, locate the **Search News** text box, and then type the keyword query **unemployment**. Click the **Search News** button.

A search results list displays with links to stories about unemployment that come from several sources. By default the list is sorted by *relevance* to the keyword. Relevance is how closely the search results relate to your keyword query. If you want to find the most recent news, you sort the search results list by date by clicking the Sort by date link located in the upper right corner of the screen.

4 In the search results list, review the story listed first. Notice the keyword is in bold text. Notice the source, date of publication, and the brief summary that is provided. Click the **link** to go directly to the full story, and then read it. Click the **Back** button 🔙 to return to Google News search results list.

As an alternative, you may want to right-click the link to open it in a new browser window. After you have finished reading the news story, click **Close** ❎ to close the new browser window and return to the Google News search results list.

5 At the top of the page, click the **Google News** logo.

The Google News home page displays.

6 Evaluate the **Google News** home page. Make notes so you will remember the name of this Web site, its URL, and the type of information you find here. Identify the site's sponsor and the author if the author is listed. Make note of any outstanding characteristics and how the information is organized at this site. You will use these notes in an upcoming activity.

Activity 3.12 Searching for News Using Advanced Search Features

In this activity, you will use the advanced search options to locate news stories at another news search engine.

1 In the **Address bar**, click one time to select the existing text, and then type **http://www.altavista.com** Press [Enter]. When the **AltaVista News** home page displays, click the **News** tab. Compare your screen with Figure 3.13.

The AltaVista News home page displays.

AltaVista is a search engine that enables searches for many types of Web files such as Web pages, MP3 files, and video files. They have an added feature that enables you to locate news using advanced search features. Recall that an advanced search feature is a search engine feature that provides options for refining a keyword or specifying criteria for returned search results. A search begins at AltaVista by putting a keyword query into the text box. Then you can refine the search by specifying a topic category, or a geographic region where the news event occurred using the menus provided at the top of the Web page. You can also specify a date or range of dates.

AltaVista News
Web site

News tab

Figure 3.13

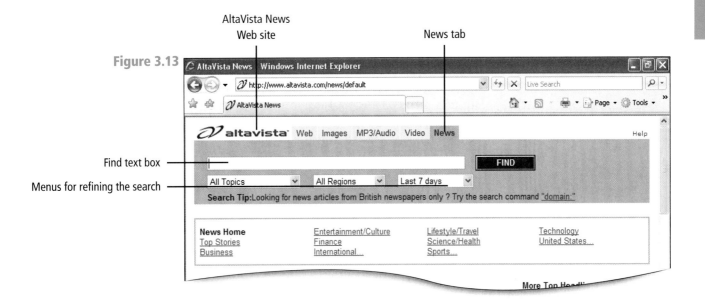

Find text box

Menus for refining the search

2 Add the **AltaVista News** Web site to your **Favorites** folder for this chapter, so that you can refer back to the Web site at any time.

3 In the **Find** text box, type the keyword query **unemployment** From the **All Topics** menu, click **Business.** From the **All Regions** menu, click **United States**. Do not make a choice in the **Last 7 days** menu. Click the **Find** button.

The search result list displays. By default it sorts the returns by relevance but you can choose to sort them by date by clicking the sorted by date link located at the top of the search results list. All of the results are recent and from United States news sources.

4 Scroll down the search results list and notice the results provide a brief summary of the article, the news source, and the time of publication. At the bottom of the page, click the **Next** link to review one more page of search results.

5 On the breadcrumb trail in the upper left corner, click the **News Home** link to return to the **AltaVista News** home page.

6 Evaluate the **AltaVista News** home page. Make notes so you will remember the name of this Web site, its URL, and the type of information you find here. Identify the site's sponsor and the author if the author is listed. Make note of any outstanding characteristics and how the information is organized at this site. You will use these notes in an upcoming activity.

7 Keep your browser open for the next activity.

Activity 3.13 Searching for Business News Resources

In this activity, you will locate audio-enhanced business news resources on the Web.

1 In the **Address bar**, click one time to select the existing text, and then type **http://www.npr.org** Press Enter.

The National Public Radio home page displays. NPR is a non-profit organization that provides non-commercial news and entertainment on the radio and on the Web. NPR offers a full range of categories including current national news stories, business news, politics, and opinion pieces. NPR enables you to search archives of old programs by date, by program name, or by topic. Transcripts of old programs are available for purchase at the Web site.

Many of the stories have audio enhancements including podcasting. You can search the podcasts by topic, title, or provider. To use the podcasting feature you need software to manage the podcast subscription. NPR provides links to several podcasting software programs.

2 Add the **NPR** Web site to your **Favorites** folder for this chapter, so that you can refer back to the Web site at any time.

3 On the left side of the home page, click the **Business** link.

The NPR Business Web page displays. The categories for the Business stories include *Economy, Your Money, Technology,* and *Media.*

4 Scroll down the Web page and on the right side of the **NPR Business** Web page, click the **Podcast Directory** link. Review the list of available business podcasts.

The NPR Podcast Directory Web page displays with several of the business podcasts visible. Other podcast categories include Arts & Culture, Books, Classical Music, and Commentary. Several other categories are available. NPR partners with public radio stations to develop and offer the podcasts.

5 In the upper left corner, click the **NPR** logo to return to the **NPR** home page. Evaluate the **NPR** home page. Take notes so you will remember the name of this Web site, its URL, and the type of information you find here. Identify the site's sponsor name and the author's name if the author is listed. Note any outstanding characteristics and how the information is organized at this site. You will use these notes in the next activity.

Activity 3.14 Creating a Document to Compare News and Opinion Resources

In this activity, you will create a summary document that provides a listing of news and opinion resources including a search engine, news located using an advanced search features, and business news resources.

1 If necessary, **Start** Notepad, and then **Maximize** the **Notepad** window.

2 In the **Notepad** window, type **3B_News_Firstname_Lastname**—use your own first and last names—and then press Enter two times. Type **Google News:** and then type the URL of the **Google News** Web site. Press Enter two times.

3 Type the name of Google's sponsor and the author—if the author is listed at the Web site. Next, summarize in one or two sentences any outstanding characteristics and how the information is organized at this site. Press Enter two times.

4 Type **AltaVista:** and then type the URL of the **AltaVista News** Web site. Press Enter two times.

5 Type the **AltaVista News** Web site's sponsor name and the author's name—if the author is identified on the Web site. Next, summarize in one or two sentences any outstanding characteristics and how the information is organized at this site. Press Enter two times.

6 Type **NPR:** and then type the URL of the **NPR** Web site. Press Enter two times.

7 Type NPR's sponsor name and the author's name—if the author is listed at the Web site. Next, summarize in one or two sentences any outstanding characteristics and how the information is organized at this site.

8 Add the **file name** to the document.

9 Navigate to the **Chapter_3_Searching** folder and then save the document as **3B_News_Firstname_Lastname**

10 Check your *Chapter Assignment Sheet* or *Course Syllabus* or consult your instructor to determine if you are to submit your assignments by printing on paper, or electronically by using your college's course information management system. Electronically, you can submit the *.txt* file created in Notepad. To print on paper from Notepad, from the **File** menu, click **Print**, and print accordingly. To submit electronically, follow instructions provided by your instructor.

11 **Close** ☒ the **Notepad** window. **Close** ☒ the **Internet Explorer** window.

Objective 8
Find Invisible Web Resources and Specialized Databases

The *Invisible Web*, or *Deep Web*, is much larger than the World Wide Web. The Invisible Web represents documents and files stored on Web servers or in electronic databases that are not accessible using directories and search engines typically used when searching the World Wide Web.

Directories and search engines enable you to retrieve large amounts of valuable information. However, there is more information that is never included in search result lists. There are several reasons why these resources are difficult to find.

Originally, the World Wide Web was composed of HTML documents. Search engines were developed to index the HTML content. As the WWW developed, different file formats became part of Web sites. Search engine development lagged behind by not being able to locate the newer file formats such as multimedia files, Word, PowerPoint, or Adobe Acrobat files. This started the development of the Invisible Web.

Other files are invisible because the files are stored in **specialized databases**. A specialized database is an electronic database that contains information and materials on a specific topic. Specialized databases require registration before access to the files in the database is enabled. A user ID and password is created during the registration process and must be used to access the files. Search engine spiders do not know the passwords so those types of files cannot be added to the search engine index and cannot be retrieved during a search engine or directory search.

Specialized databases pose additional barriers for directories and search engines. Many Web pages are dynamically generated—instantly created in response to specified criteria. Parts of the Web page are stored in the database and put together at the last moment to display as an entire Web page when the criteria are specified. Spiders are unable to categorize and store these dynamically generated Web pages.

Some specialized databases such as research journals or government databases will return abstracts or partial documents during a search but will not show the full text or entire documents without a payment. Libraries often subscribe to these journals and databases. Then members of the library can access the journals free of charge if they know how to locate them through the library system.

Activity 3.15 Locating the Invisible Web and Specialized Databases

In this activity, you will help the Greater Atlanta Job Fair staff use Invisible Web resources. Many types of information are stored in databases that are not searchable using a typical search engine. Some of the information is free, but other kinds of the information are located in subscription-based databases.

1 In the **Address bar**, click one time to select the existing text, and then type **http://completeplanet.com** Press Enter. Compare your screen with Figure 3.14.

The CompletePlanet home page displays. CompletePlanet is a directory that leads to thousands of Invisible Web resources. All of the resources are located in publicly available databases. You can locate resources by either selecting a topic in the directory listing or by typing in a keyword query into the *Find databases relevant to* text box. Links in the upper part of the Web page lead to a Help/FAQ page, a

Contact Us page, and an About CompletePlanet page. The Help/FAQ page provides many useful tips for conducting successful searches at CompletePlanet and links to other Invisible Web resources.

Figure 3.14

Help/FAQ link   Contact Us link   About CompletePlanet link

Find databases relevant to text box

Directory listing of topics

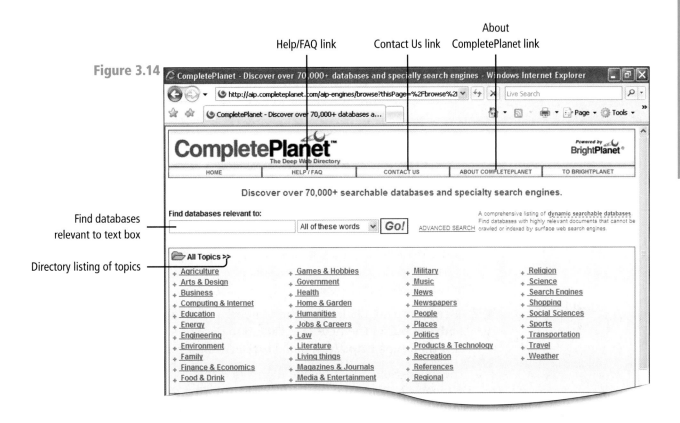

2. Add the **CompletePlanet** Web site to your **Favorites** folder so that you can refer back to the Web site at any time.

3. In the middle of the Web page, click the **Government** link. In the middle of the search results page that displays, click the **Statistics** link.

Several government sponsored databases are displayed in the search result list. You may want to right-click any of these links to open them in a new browser window.

4. After you have finished viewing the new Web site, click **Close** ⊠ to close the new browser window and return to the **CompletePlanet** Web page. At the top of the **CompletePlanet** Web page, click one time into the **Find databases relevant to** text box, type the keyword query **jobs report** and then click the **Go** button.

A new search result list displays with several databases that contain the keywords but not necessarily that phrase.

You may want to right-click any of these links to open them in a new browser window.

5 After you have finished viewing the Web site in a new browser window, click **Close** ☒ to close the new browser window and return to the **CompletePlanet** Web page. At the top of the **CompletePlanet** Web page, click the **Help/FAQ** link.

The Help/FAQ Web page displays. It is organized into broad categories to help you learn more about how and where to search for Invisible Web resources.

6 Right-click the **Deep Web FAQs** link to open the link in a new browser window. Review the FAQs that you find interesting.

After you have finished viewing the Deep Web FAQ, click **Close** ☒ to close the new browser window and return to the **CompletePlanet Help/FAQ** Web page.

7 In the upper left corner of the window, click the **Back** button ◀ as necessary to return to the **CompletePlanet** home page. Evaluate the **CompletePlanet** Web site. Take notes so you will remember the name of this Web site, its URL, and the type of information you find here. Identify the site's sponsor and the author's name if the author is listed. Make note of any outstanding characteristics and how the information is organized at this site.

8 On a **New Tab**, click one time to open a new tab. Then in the **Address bar** of the new tab, click one time to select the existing text, and then type **http://www.dialogselect.com** Press ⏎.

The DialogSelect home page displays. DialogSelect provides an extensive collection of abstracts and full-text articles from well-respected databases, newswires, journals, business publications, and business releases. DialogSelect is a *subscription-based* search engine. You can access information found at DialogSelect by subscribing for a flat fee or by using a per use plan. Research areas include business, chemistry, energy, food, government, patents, medicine, news, pharmacy, reference, and technology.

9 Add the **DialogSelect** Web site to your **Favorites** folder for this chapter, so that you can refer back to the Web site at any time.

10 On the left side of the screen, click the **DialogGov** link.

The DialogGov page displays. This page provides access to a list of original patent filings, explains how to use Automatic Alerts, enables you to sign up for a newsletter on a topic of interest, and search their newsroom for information you are interested in finding.

11 Scroll to locate and then click the **Search NewsRoom Now** link.

The Dialog NewsRoom Web page displays. You begin your search here by supplying a title, company name, publication name, publication type, and other criteria to help locate resources for your search.

12 In the **Words in Title** text box, type **jobs report** and then click the **Search** button.

You will be prompted for your user ID and password to conduct the actual search. Because you are not registered on this site, you will not be able to complete your search. DialogSelect is a subscription-based search engine.

13 In the upper left corner of the window, click the **Back** button 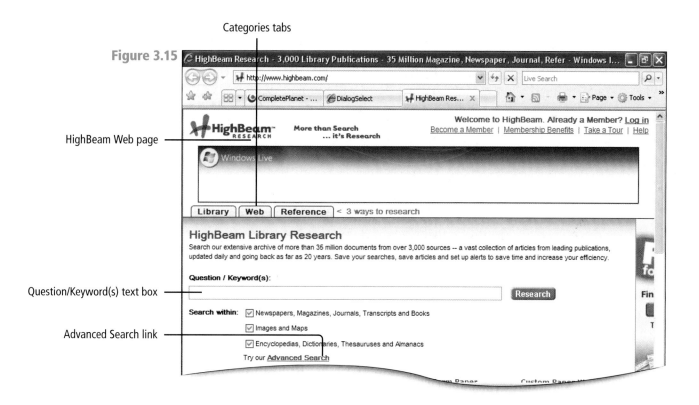 as necessary to return to the **DialogSelect** home page. Evaluate the **DialogSelect** Web site. Take notes so you will remember the name of this Web site, its URL, and the type of information you find here. Identify the site's sponsor and the author's name if the author is listed. Make note of any outstanding characteristics and how the information is organized at this site. You will use these notes in the next activity.

14 On a **New Tab**, click one time to open a new tab. In the **Address bar** of the new tab, click one time to select the existing text, type **http://www.highbeam.com** and then press Enter. Compare your screen with Figure 3.15.

The HighBeam Research home page displays. HighBeam Research is a meta-search engine that provides access to both free Web resources and paid resources. You can search under Library, Web, or Reference categories. You search by using a keyword query or natural language query. HighBeam provides for advanced searches using Boolean operators. You can also refine searches by publication type, date, author, article title, or type of publication that you are interested in.

Categories tabs

Figure 3.15

HighBeam Web page

Question/Keyword(s) text box

Advanced Search link

15 Add the **HighBeam** Web site to your **Favorites** folder for this chapter, so that you can refer back to the Web site at any time.

16 At the top of the Web page, locate three research tabs labeled *Library*, *Web*, and *Reference*. In the default **Library** tab, locate the **Question/Keyword(s)** text box, and then type **What information technology jobs are available in Atlanta Georgia?** as a natural language query. Leave the check boxes for various documents, images, and reference resources checked so that they will be included. Click the **Research** button, and then evaluate the types of search results that are returned.

Notice that links are sorted by relevance and include both Free and Premium articles. Articles marked *Premium* require a fee to view the full-text article.

You can modify the results by showing only Premium articles or only Free articles. You may further refine the search by sorting the results by date, or relevance, or both. You may specify where the results are gathered.

17 In the **search results** list, scroll down the page, and then review the description of the articles.

As an alternative, you may want to right-click the link to open the article in a new browser window. Once you have finished viewing article, click **Close** ⊠ to close the new browser window and return to the search results list.

18 In the upper left corner, click the **HighBeam Research** logo to return to the **HighBeam** home page. Evaluate the **HighBeam** Web site. Make notes so you will remember the name of this Web site, its URL, and the type of information you find here. Identify the site's sponsor and the author if the author is listed. Make note of any outstanding characteristics and how the information is organized at this site. You will use these notes in the next activity.

Activity 3.16 Creating a Document to Compare Invisible Web Resources

In this activity, you will create a summary document that provides a listing of Invisible Web resources including a directory search site, a specialized database resource that is available on a subscription basis, and a metasearch engine providing links to both free and subscription resources.

1 If necessary, **Start** Notepad, and then **Maximize** the **Notepad** window.

2 In the **Notepad** window, at the insertion point, type **3B_Invisible_Firstname_Lastname** Press `Enter` two times. Type **CompletePlanet:** and then type the URL of the **CompletePlanet** Web site. Press `Enter` two times.

3 Type the site's sponsor name and the author's name—if the author was listed at the Web site. Next, type one or two sentences that summarize outstanding characteristics and how the information is organized at this site. Press `Enter` two times.

4 Type **DialogSelect:** and then type the URL of the **DialogSelect** Web site. Press [Enter] key two times.

5 Type the site's sponsor name and the author's name—if the author was listed at the Web site. Next, type one or two sentences that summarize outstanding characteristics and how the information is organized at this site. Press [Enter] two times.

6 Type **HighBeam:** and then type the URL of the **HighBeam** Web site. Press the [Enter] key two times to create a new line.

7 Type the site's sponsor name and the author's name—if the author was listed at the Web site. Next, type one or two sentences that summarize outstanding characteristics and how the information is organized at this site. Press [Enter] two times.

8 Add the **footer 3B_Invisible_Firstname_Lastname** to the document. Then save the document as **3B_Invisible_Firstname_Lastname**

9 Check your *Chapter Assignment Sheet* or *Course Syllabus* or consult your instructor to determine if you are to submit your assignments by printing on paper, or electronically by using your college's course information management system. Electronically, you can submit the *.txt* file created in Notepad. To print on paper from Notepad, from the **File** menu, click **Print**, and then print accordingly. To submit electronically, follow instructions provided by your instructor.

10 **Close** ☒ the **Notepad** window. **Close** ☒ the **Internet Explorer** window. If prompted to close all tabs, click **Close Tabs**.

End **You have completed Project 3B** ――――――――――

Project 3C Exploring Search Tools

In Objectives 9 and 10, you will see how a directory search site can be helpful in locating information. You will identify how to use a meta-search site to broaden your search results.

Objective 9
Implement a Search Using a Directory Search Site

How do I use a directory to search the Web? You can locate information on the Web using a directory search site. Directories generally cover a smaller amount of Web sites than search engines because directories are compiled and updated by humans. Some directories are organized and evaluated by professional editors, whereas other directories are managed by volunteers. Some directory search sites partner with search engines to provide more usability at the search site. An example of this is Yahoo! The table in Figure 3.16 shows popular directory search sites and their URLs.

Popular Directory Search Sites	
Directory	**URL**
About.com	http://about.com
Galaxy	http://www.galaxy.com
Librarians' Internet Index	http://lii.org
LookSmart	http://looksmart.com
Open Directory Project	http://dmoz.org
Yahoo!	http://www.yahoo.com

Figure 3.16

What kind of search results will I get with directories? You locate information with a directory search by drilling down into the categories, or clicking into more specific areas, until you locate the information you want. Many directory search sites provide abstracts or descriptive summaries for each category and subcategory. This is a helpful feature because you find out more about the category before you decide to click it as you drill down. A breadcrumb trail typically displays at the top of the directory Web page.

When should I use a directory? Directory search sites are helpful as a starting point for any type of Web research because they are so easy to use. You do not need to think of keywords for the search. In fact, the subject categories can be used as keywords for other types of searches. Directories are a great choice when you are searching for a general overview of a topic or when you want information about a popular or commonly researched topic. However, the information found through a directory search may not be the most current because people update directories.

Objective 10
Implement a Search Using a Meta-Search Engine

What is a meta-search engine?   Recall that a meta-search engine is a search tool that uses several search engines to locate results for a single query and returns the results as a single list. Meta-search engines do not use their own index or database; instead they use other search engines, directories, and multimedia resources to compile search results at the meta-search engine Web site. Figure 3.17 lists some popular meta-search engines and their URLs.

Popular Meta-Search Engines	
Meta-Search Engine	**URL**
Clusty	*http://clusty.com*
Dogpile	*http://dogpile.com*
Ixquick	*http://ixquick.com*
Mamma	*http://mamma.com*
MetaCrawler	*http://www.metacrawler.com*
Proteus Internet Search	*http://www.thrall.org/proteus.html*
Search.com	*http://www.search.com*
SurfWax, Inc.	*http://surfwax.com*

Figure 3.17

When should I use a meta-search engine?   Meta-search engines are good for basic searches. You use a meta-search engine when you need a lot of information on a topic that comes from different perspectives. Meta-search engines save a lot of time because they access several search engines at once. Most meta-search engines enable you to select from a list that the search engines to use for the query.

What are the disadvantages of using a meta-search engine?   Because each search engine works with advanced search options in a different way, meta-search engines are limited to working within a common set of advanced search options. The number of results returned in the search results list is also limited at a meta-search engine. In addition, sponsored links can be included as part of the search result list.

What is clustering?   Even when you use filters and other advanced search features, the search results lists may contain several thousand or more hits. *Clustering* is used at certain search engines to help organize search results lists. Clustering is a technology that groups the top-ranked search results from multiple sources into a hierarchy of folders representing the main ideas of the keyword query. Hits are placed into the folders based on relationships among the results. The task of evaluating the search result is much easier because you can browse through the folders and focus on the relationships. Figure 3.18 shows a clustered search result list.

Figure 3.18

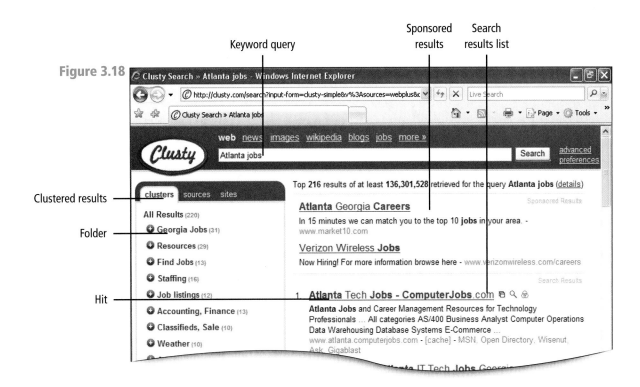

Keyword query · Sponsored results · Search results list

Clustered results
Folder
Hit

End You have completed Project 3C ——————————

Online Quiz

Project 3C

Take the online self-study quiz for this chapter:

1. Go to **www.prenhall.com/go** and select the textbook *GO!* **with the Internet**.

2. Select **chapter 3**.

3. Select Self-Study Quiz Project 3C.

Project 3D **Developing Search Strategy Guidelines**

In Objectives 11 and 12, you discover how search engines work. You will examine and evaluate search results.

Objective 11
Explore How a Search Engine Works

What are some popular search engines? Search engines help us get the most out of the Web; understanding how search engines work will help you get the most out of using a search engine. Recall that search engines work using three main components—the spider, the index, and the search engine software. Figure 3.19 lists some popular search engines and their URLs.

Popular Search Engines	
Search Engine	**URL**
Alltheweb	*http://alltheweb.com*
AltaVista	*http://www.altavista.com*
Ask.com	*http://www.ask.com*
Gigablast	*http://www.gigablast.com*
Google	*http://www.google.com*
Lycos	*http://www.lycos.com*
MSN	*http://www.msn.com*
Wisenut	*http://wisenut.com*
Yahoo!	*http://www.yahoo.com*

Figure 3.19

Do all search engines work the same way? The same keyword query used at different search engines will turn up search results that, for the most part, are quite different. However, there may be some *overlap* between the search result lists. Overlap is the number of times different search engines turn up the same Web site on a search results list in response to the same queries.

Search engines return different results because the spiders collecting words and references do so in different ways. Some spiders search the entire file or document noting where the words are located within the file or document and how often they display within the content of the Web page. This is called ***full-text indexing***. Special attention is paid to the titles of the Web pages and to words at the beginning of lengthy documents. Stop words are ignored in full-text indexing.

Although all spiders take note of the URL where the files and documents are located, some spiders search the **metatags** of each file. Metatags are tags found in HTML coding that provide information such as the author, a listing of keywords, and a description of the content of the Web page.

It is not possible for each spider to search the entire collection of Web files and documents every day. Spiders look for new Web files at regularly scheduled intervals but not every spider uses the same schedule. Because of this, it is possible that new Web pages are available but are not yet showing up in search result lists.

The results returned by search engines are ranked in order of relevance of the keywords to the Web pages containing them. **Rankings** provide a reason why search result lists vary. When you create a query, the results are listed in order of relevance according to their rankings. Rankings are the algorithms used to retrieve and list words from the search engine's index. Typically, a Web page that has a term in the title will rank higher than a page where the same term is found well down in the content of the Web page. Pages that are linked to numerous, high-quality pages will rank higher than those that receive fewer authoritative links.

Some search engines are commercially motivated or make extensive use of sponsored sites. Sponsored sites are marked, although not always clearly. Figure 3.20 shows how ranked search results and sponsored sites may display in a search result list.

Figure 3.20

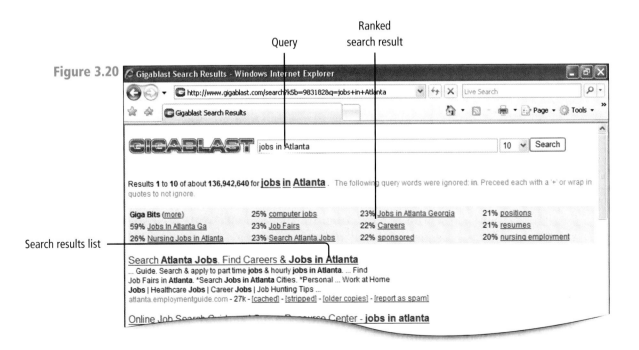

How do I begin my search? There are several types of search engines to use when looking for information. Whether you are doing research for a school project or trying to find out information on your favorite hobby, the right search tool helps you search efficiently. Figure 3.21 provides some guidelines for helping you decide on the right search tool to use.

Search Guidelines to Help You Get Started

Search in the Right Place	Search using the tools that you expect will have your information including dictionaries, reference books, encyclopedias, and the Internet.
	Use directory search sites to find a general overview of a topic or when you are just starting with a search.
	Use a search engine when you have specific terms that you need to find.
	Use a meta-search engine when you need varied results returned quickly.
	Use a specific source affiliated with your topic when you need expert information.
	Use your local or school library to access their subscription-based databases and electronic journals.
	Don't be afraid to try new search engines.
Search with the Right Words	Use specific keywords to limit the results to those that will be most helpful to you.
	Spell the keywords correctly.
	Check the Help page or FAQ page to see how a particular search engine uses Boolean operators.
	Use the advanced features or filters to narrowly define your keywords and refine your results.
	Enrich common terms to clarify the context before the search begins.

Figure 3.21

Objective 12
Evaluate Search Results

How do I evaluate the search results list? Search results lists return a large number and variety of results and categories, some of which may be for sponsored sites. The best results from the search results list will be those hits that mostly closely align with the topic statement.

How do I evaluate the hits? As you visit the hits that seem to be aligned with your topic, you can quickly identify the location of specific keywords within the hit by using the browser's Find command located on the Edit menu. This will help you screen the results and eliminate those hits that do not contain enough relevance to your topic.

After you identify those hits from the search results list that may be useful, you need to determine the validity of those hits. Some of the Web sites in the search results list may provide legitimate and factual information. Other sites seem to be ***primary sources*** but are actually commercial Web sites or editorial sites. Primary sources are those sources that provide direct evidence, testimony, or facts related to the research subject. Careful evaluation is necessary to determine which sites are credible and provide the kind of the kind of information you need.

Who sponsors the Web site?   The first step in determining the purpose of a Web resource is to look for the name of the organization sponsoring the site. Recall that knowing who sponsors a site helps you determine the objective of the Web site. Often this information is clearly indicated as a prominent logo, brand name, or parent company in the upper portion of the Web page. Similar information is sometimes located at the bottom of the Web page or on an *About Us* Web page within the Web site. You should be able to locate contact information at the bottom of the Web page such as an e-mail address, a street address, or a phone number.

Look at the URL and notice the domain name for the site. Make sure the domain name coincides with the type of information you seek. Domain names are issued to certain groups and organizations. For example, *.gov* indicates a government Web site while *.edu* is used for an educational institution. Non-profit organizations are likely to have *.org* as the domain name while *.com* indicates a commercial or personal site. For example, when looking for specific employment statistics, you may want to use a government Web site.

Who is the author of the Web site?   When determining if a Web site is a credible source, try to identify who wrote the material found at the Web site. Although not all Web sites list an author for the content of the site, you may locate the author's name by looking at the top of the Web page or by scrolling down to view the bottom of the Web page. If an author's name is found, try to verify that the author is an authority on the topic by performing a search on the author's name to determine his or her credentials and affiliation. Make sure the author's credentials are appropriate for the topic area.

What is the quality of the content?   Review the content of the Web site with a critical eye. Can the date be verified or cross-checked? Are the facts similar to those found in other reliable sources? Data that can be verified from more than one authoritative source can normally be considered accurate.

You should check for design considerations, language usage, and depth of coverage. Design considerations include the overall style of the site and the use of pleasing color combinations. The graphics should be focused and proportionate to the Web page. There should not be any missing images on the Web page. All links should work as expected and not produce any errors.

Look for an indication of when the page was last updated or some type of ***date stamp***. A date stamp is a statement of year or a range of years to indicate how long the Web site has existed or the most recent update for the Web site. A date stamp is typically found at the bottom of a Web site. You may also want to check for a ***copyright*** notice. Copyright is the legal protection given to the authors of intellectual works including but not limited to art, music, or writings. Both of these elements—date stamp and copyright notice—are important in assessing the quality of a Web site. A date stamp helps you determine if you are getting the most recent information. A copyright notice indicates that the work is original and more likely to be a primary source. Copyright notices are typically found at the bottom of the Web page. Figure 3.22 shows where you can look for criteria to evaluate the quality of a Web page.

Domain name

Figure 3.22

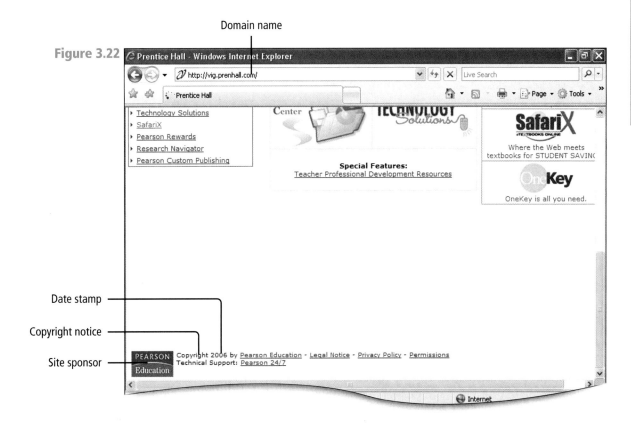

Date stamp

Copyright notice

Site sponsor

As another step, you will want to scan the Web page for grammatical errors and misspelled words. Read the content and look for obvious misinformation or biased statements. Look for indications that it might be a cleverly disguised advertisement or sales pitch for a product. Finally, check the amount of detail and the depth of coverage for the topic to ensure that it adequately meets your needs. Figure 3.23 provides a quick checklist to help you evaluate your search results.

Search Results Checklist

To Evaluate the . . .	Ask These Questions . . .
Search results list	• Which hits align most closely with my topic statement?
	• Can I find my keywords in any of the results?
Sponsor of the Web site	• Do you see a logo or brand name on the Web site?
	• Do you see contact information for the sponsor?
	• What is the domain name for the Web site?

(Continued)

(Continued)

Search Results Checklist

To Evaluate the . . .	Ask These Questions . . .
Author of the Web site	• Do you recognize the author's name as an authority?
	• Can you determine the affiliation of the author?
	• Are the credentials appropriate for the topic area?
Site design considerations	• Can the data be verified or located in other authoritative sources?
	• Has the site won any awards?
	• What is the overall style of the site?
	• Is a pleasing color scheme used?
	• Are the graphics clear and proportionate?
	• Is the site accessibility-compliant?
	• Are there any missing images?
	• Do all the links work correctly?
	• Is there a date stamp or date for the last update?
	• Is there a copyright notice?
Language usage	• Are there any grammatical errors?
	• Are there any misspellings?
Depth of coverage	• Is there any obvious misinformation?
	• Are there any biased statements?
	• Does it link to a variety of authoritative sites?
	• Is there enough detail and depth of coverage?
	• Does it seem like an advertisement or sales pitch?

Figure 3.23

End You have completed Project 3D —————————

Online Quiz

Project 3D

Take the online self-study quiz for this chapter:

1. Go to **www.prenhall.com/go** and select the textbook *GO!* **with the Internet**.

2. Select **chapter 3**.

3. Select Self-Study Quiz Project 3D.

Assessments

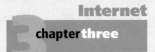

Summary

In this chapter, you tried several techniques for searching. You formulated a keyword query to identify search engines and their characteristics. You used the Address bar and the Instant Search feature to search for Web pages on the World Wide Web. You located specialized search tools such as expert resources, online library catalogs, and scholarly databases. You performed searches using Boolean operators and other advanced search features. You located news and opinion resources. You found Invisible Web resources and specialized databases. You discovered when to use a directory search site. You explored the use of a meta-search engine to conduct a search. You examined how a search engine works. You developed search strategy guidelines including how to evaluate the search results.

Key Terms

Advanced search 150

Boolean operators 150

Bot 147

Breadcrumb trail 157

Clustering 181

Copyright..................186

Crawler 147

Date stamp 186

Deep Web 173

Directory 149

Drilling down 157

Dynamically
    generated 163

Full-text indexing 184

Hit 148

Index 147

Instant Search..........155

Invisible Web 173

Keyword query 146

Metatags 184

Meta-search
    engine.....................149

Natural language
    query 146

Overlap 183

PDF or .*pdf* file 163

PHP file 163

Podcast 169

Primary sources 185

Proximity..................166

Rankings 184

Really Simple
    Syndication
    (RSS).....................169

Relevance 170

Search engine 147

Search engine
    software 147

Search filter..............150

Search results
    list 148

Specialized
    database 174

Spider 147

Sponsored links........148

Sponsored results 148

Sponsored sites 148

Stop words................156

Subject catalog 157

Synonyms 146

Virtual library 167

Wildcard character ..168

Assessments

Rubric

Projects 3A and 3B in the front portion of this chapter, and Projects 3E through 3K that follow have no specific correct result; your result will depend on your approach to the information provided. Make Professional Quality your goal. Use the following scoring rubric to guide you in how to approach the search problem, and then to evaluate how well your approach solves the search problem.

The *criteria*—Internet Mastery, Content, Format and Layout of Search Results, and Process—represent the knowledge and skills you have gained that you can apply to solving the search problem. The *levels of performance*—Professional Quality, Approaching Professional Quality, or Needs Quality Improvements—help you and your instructor evaluate your result.

	Your completed project is of Professional Quality if you:	Your completed project is Approaching Professional Quality if you:	Your completed project needs Quality Improvements if you:
1–Internet Mastery	Choose and apply the most appropriate search skills, tools, and features and identify efficient methods to conduct the search and locate valid results.	Choose and apply some appropriate search skills, tools, and features, but not in the most efficient manner.	Choose inappropriate search skills, tools, or features, or are inefficient in locating valid results.
2–Content	Conduct a search that is clear and well organized, contains results that are accurate, appropriate to the audience and purpose, and are complete.	Conduct a search in which some results are unclear, poorly organized, inconsistent, or incomplete. Misjudge the needs of the audience.	Conduct a search that is unclear, incomplete, or poorly organized, containing some inaccurate or inappropriate content.
3–Format and Layout of Search Results	Format and arrange all search results to communicate information and ideas, clarify function, illustrate relationships, and indicate relative importance.	Apply appropriate format and layout features to some search results, but not others. Overuse search techniques, causing minor distraction.	Apply format and layout that does not communicate the search results clearly. Do not use format and layout features to clarify function, illustrate relationships, or indicate relative importance. Use available search techniques excessively, causing distraction.
4–Process	Use an organized approach that integrates planning, development, self-assessment, revision, and reflection.	Demonstrate an organized approach in some areas, but not others; or, use an insufficient process of organization throughout.	Do not use an organized approach to solve the problem.

Assessments

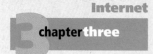

Rubric

Projects 3A and 3B in the front portion of this chapter, and Projects 3E through 3K that follow have no specific correct result; your result will depend on your approach to the information provided. Make Professional Quality your goal. Use the following scoring rubric to guide you in how to approach the search problem, and then to evaluate how well your approach solves the search problem.

The *criteria*—Internet Mastery, Content, Format and Layout of Search Results, and Process—represent the knowledge and skills you have gained that you can apply to solving the search problem. The *levels of performance*—Professional Quality, Approaching Professional Quality, or Needs Quality Improvements—help you and your instructor evaluate your result.

	Your completed project is of Professional Quality if you:	Your completed project is Approaching Professional Quality if you:	Your completed project needs Quality Improvements if you:
1–Internet Mastery	Choose and apply the most appropriate search skills, tools, and features and identify efficient methods to conduct the search and locate valid results.	Choose and apply some appropriate search skills, tools, and features, but not in the most efficient manner.	Choose inappropriate search skills, tools, or features, or are inefficient in locating valid results.
2–Content	Conduct a search that is clear and well organized, contains results that are accurate, appropriate to the audience and purpose, and are complete.	Conduct a search in which some results are unclear, poorly organized, inconsistent, or incomplete. Misjudge the needs of the audience.	Conduct a search that is unclear, incomplete, or poorly organized, containing some inaccurate or inappropriate content.
3–Format and Layout of Search Results	Format and arrange all search results to communicate information and ideas, clarify function, illustrate relationships, and indicate relative importance.	Apply appropriate format and layout features to some search results, but not others. Overuse search techniques, causing minor distraction.	Apply format and layout that does not communicate the search results clearly. Do not use format and layout features to clarify function, illustrate relationships, or indicate relative importance. Use available search techniques excessively, causing distraction.
4–Process	Use an organized approach that integrates planning, development, self-assessment, revision, and reflection.	Demonstrate an organized approach in some areas, but not others; or, use an insufficient process of organization throughout.	Do not use an organized approach to solve the problem.

Assessments

Fill in the Blank

Write the correct answer in the space provided for each statement.

1. You search for HTML files at a search engine Web site under the category named _____.

2. You search for GIF or JPG files at a search engine Web site under the category named _____.

3. A query that uses a complete sentence or question to begin a search is called a(n) _____.

4. A term referring to how closely the search results relate to your keyword query is called _____.

5. Documents and files stored on Web servers or in electronic databases that are not accessible using directories and search engines typically used when searching the World Wide Web are found on the _____.

6. An electronic database that contains information and materials on a very specific topic is called a(n) _____.

7. The most commonly used Boolean operators include OR, NOT and _____.

8. In the query *Atlanta* _____ *Jobs*, the Boolean operator that returns results for pages that contain either word in a query is _____.

9. In the query *Atlanta* _____ *Jobs*, the Boolean operator that returns results for pages that contain only the first word instead of both words is _____.

10. The Boolean operator that returns results that have all of the keywords in the query but the words may display no more than 10–20 words apart on the Web page is _____.

11. To return results that contain the exact phrase, use the symbol _____.

12. A symbol that can be used as a wildcard character is the _____.

13. To return results for pages that contain both words of a query use the Boolean Operator AND or the symbol _____.

14. You can use the Boolean operator NOT or the _____ symbol to return the same kind of results.

15. The download of MP3 audio files from the World Wide Web to MP3-compatible computers or portable audio players using RSS technology is called a(n) _____.

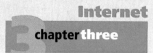

Matching

Match each term in the second column with its correct definition in the first column by writing the letter of the term on the blank line in front of the correct definition.

_____ **1.** A search tool that enables you to locate Web sites, images, and maps on the Internet from the toolbar of the Internet Explorer window.

_____ **2.** A system developed to automatically alert subscribers of updates made to sites such as blogs, news, weather, or sports sites.

_____ **3.** An alphabetical list of subject categories arranged in a hierarchy leading from a set of broad subject areas to more detailed sub-categories for individual Web sites or Web resources.

_____ **4.** A specialized type of directory that has resources organized by information professionals such as librarians.

_____ **5.** Short words connecting the more important words of a natural language query.

_____ **6.** HTML files with scripting embedded within the HTML coding so that dynamically generated results from databases are displayed onscreen.

_____ **7.** Files translated as output from other programs using the Adobe Acrobat program.

_____ **8.** A method of instantly creating Web pages in response to specified criteria.

_____ **9.** The download of MP3 audio files from the World Wide Web to MP3-compatible computers or portable audio players using RSS technology.

_____ **10.** An electronic database that contains information and materials on a very specific topic.

_____ **11.** Mathematical or logic terms used to make a query more specific by showing the relationship of the words used in the query.

_____ **12.** How near each word in the query displays to each other on the Web page of a hit.

_____ **13.** An asterisk that is used to take the place of any number of missing letters in a keyword.

_____ **14.** Words that mean almost the same thing.

_____ **15.** A search engine feature used to limit the search results to specific criteria.

A Boolean operators

B Dynamically generated

C Instant Search

D PDF files

E PHP files

F Podcast

G Proximity

H Really Simple Syndication (RSS)

I Search filter

J Specialized database

K Stop word

L Subject catalog

M Synonyms

N Virtual library

O Wildcard character

(P

El Cuero Specialty Wares

El Cuero de Mexico is a Mexico City-based manufacturer of high-quality, small leather goods for men and women. Its products include wallets, belts, handbags, key chains, and travel bags. The company distributes its products to department and specialty stores in the United States and Canada through its San Diego-based subsidiary, El Cuero Specialty Wares.

The CEO of El Cuero de Mexico, Miguel Hernandez, will be visiting the offices of El Cuero Specialty Wares next month. He will attend marketing presentations, review advertising plans, meet with several large customers, present company budget figures, and attend a dinner party for the San Diego employees. El Cuero Specialty Wares President, Alejandra Domene, will work with the Vice President of Marketing, Richard Kelly, and the Chief Financial Officer, Adriana Ramos, to prepare for the meetings and events.

Communication Using E-mail

E-mail use has grown to become the most popular Internet tool used today. E-mail is used for both professional, work-related interactions and personal communications. Communications take place at a much faster rate because of e-mail. E-mail attachments move documents and files across countries, saving time and money. Ideas can be shared nearly instantaneously instead of waiting several days for traditional mail to arrive. Access to Web-based e-mail is available at any Internet-connected computer at any time.

Project 4A Signing Up for a Web-Based E-mail Account

The CEO of El Cuero de Mexico, Miguel Hernandez, is coming to the San Diego subsidiary, El Cuero Specialty Wares for meetings and presentations. His Executive Administrative Assistant, Cristina Mandala, needs to finalize the details of his trip. Having a Web-based e-mail account will help facilitate the planning that must take place. In Activities 4.1 through 4.3, you will set up a free Web-based e-mail account. You will help Cristina compose an e-mail message and attach the itinerary for Miguel's trip to the e-mail message. You will send a carbon copy of the e-mail message and add an e-mail address to the address book. You will create a signature file and send an e-mail message. Then you will sign out of the e-mail account.

For Project 4A, you will need the following files:

i04A_Itinerary
Web page printout

You will save your file as
4A_Registration_Confirmed_Firstname_Lastname

Figure 4.1

Objective 1
Locate and Set Up a Web-Based E-mail Account

Electronic mail, or *e-mail*, is a service that provides for the exchange of messages and documents over the Internet or over an organization's network. E-mail is the most frequently used Internet service.

E-mail's popularity is due to the way in which e-mail speeds up the communication process. E-mail messages can be composed and sent to a recipient in a matter of seconds and the recipient—if online and logged into their e-mail account—can quickly compose a reply to send back. Because e-mail is a form of **asynchronous communication**, all participants do not need to be online at the same time. Recall that asynchronous communication is an electronic communication in which the participants do not need to be online at the same time, and all participants can view the communication when they want to do so. This provides a great convenience, enabling communications to take place around the clock.

E-mail is also cost-effective. Stationary and postage is not necessary for sending simple messages. Multiple page documents can be sent as attachments saving courier costs and delivery time. E-mail messages are easy to save, organize into *folders*, and store for future reference. A folder is an e-mail feature used to collect, organize, and store your e-mail.

Alert!

Assessing Project 4A and Project 4B

For Projects 4A and 4B of this chapter, you and your instructor can evaluate your approach to the problem and your result by consulting the scoring rubric located in the end-of-chapter material. For these hands-on projects, there is no online quiz.

Activity 4.1 Setting Up a Web-Based E-mail Account

Cristina Mandala, the Executive Administrative Assistant for Miguel Hernandez is in the midst of making arrangements for his upcoming trip to the United States. Cristina works from several locations and needs flexible access to her e-mail account. In Activity 4.1, you will locate a Web-based e-mail account for Cristina to use and help her register for the account.

1 **Start** Internet Explorer and if necessary, click the **Maximize** button to enlarge the window to fill the computer screen completely. In the **Address bar**, click once to select the existing text, type **http://mail.yahoo.com** and then press Enter. If a Security Alert dialog box displays, click OK.

The home page for Yahoo! Mail displays. Yahoo! Mail is an easy-to-use, Web-based e-mail system that offers many features, such as an address book and the ability to block addresses from your **Inbox**. The Inbox is the default folder in an e-mail system where incoming messages are placed.

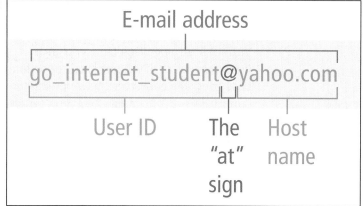

Yahoo! Mail also offers other features such as a spam blocker and antivirus protection. It enables you to share photos and attachments, and it has a mobile feature that enables users to access a Yahoo! Mail account by using an Internet-enabled cell phone.

Yahoo! Mail can offer a free e-mail account because it sells space to advertisers. The ads display within your e-mail account Web page when you are logged in.

2 Locate the **Don't have a Yahoo! ID?** section, and then click the **Sign Up** link. If a Security Alert dialog box displays, click **OK** to continue to the next Web page.

The Yahoo! Registration Web page displays. It contains a form to gather the information needed to set up your account and create your e-mail address. An ***e-mail address*** is a code used to specify *where* and to whom to send and receive e-mail. An e-mail address is composed of three main parts: the user ID, the "at" sign or @, and the host name:

- The ***user ID*** is a unique name that identifies who uses the e-mail account. Schools and businesses typically issue a user ID that is based on a combination of your first and last name. At other times, you may be able to select your own preferred user ID—as long as it is not being used by anyone else—that follows a predetermined syntax, such as a certain number of characters or pattern of letters.

- The next part of the e-mail address is the ***"at" sign*** or @. This character is always part of an e-mail address and separates the user ID from the host name. Originally, the "at" sign was used to indicate that user's account was set up *at* a specific server.

- The ***host name*** is the name of the server where e-mail is received and stored within the organization. It includes the domain name of the organization. For example in the e-mail address, go_internet_student@yahoo.com, the .com is the domain name for the Yahoo! organization. Figure 4.2 identifies each of the three main parts of an e-mail address.

Figure 4.2

3 On the **Yahoo! Registration** Web page, in the section labeled **Create Your Yahoo! ID**, locate the text boxes where you should type your first and last name, and then type the correct responses. Then from the **Preferred content** menu, click **Yahoo! U.S.** or the country where you reside. Click the **down arrow** and select your gender. Next, type your preferred Yahoo! ID.

Your Yahoo! ID is the user ID that will enable you to sign into your e-mail account. It also becomes part of your e-mail address that others will use when they want to send e-mail to you. Your e-mail address will follow the syntax—*Yahoo! ID*@yahoo.com.

Yahoo! IDs may include any letter, the numbers 0 through 9, the underscore character, and a single period. You should not use spaces or characters other than what is mentioned on the Web page.

You may need to try a couple of different Yahoo! IDs. Some Yahoo! IDs may already be in use. Yahoo! Mail provides a link where you may check the availability of a user ID that you are considering before you complete the registration process.

Other points to keep in mind when choosing your Yahoo! ID:

- Do not use your real name as your Yahoo! ID so your identity is protected online.

- Try to choose something that is short—five to eight characters work well—so it easy to type and easy to remember.

- Keep your Yahoo! ID politically neutral and socially correct.

4 In the **Password** text box, type a password that will be used to access your e-mail account. Notice the password characters display as dots to preserve security. Then in the next text box, carefully retype the password to confirm that is the one you want to use.

A **password** is a string of characters—letters, numbers, and often other punctuation marks—that is used in combination with a user ID to verify authorization to use a network, server, or computer. Because passwords help to protect unauthorized access to your account, choose your password carefully. After the password is chosen, do not reveal it to others to help guard against unauthorized use of your password.

Yahoo! Mail specifies that you must use at least six characters in your password. Typically, passwords are six to nine characters so that they are easy to remember. Make the password a character combination that is easy to type quickly so that you do not need to look down at the keyboard. This helps to prevent anyone looking over your shoulder from seeing the characters you type. Use a combination of uppercase and lowercase letters. It is also a good idea to include both letters and numbers in the password.

When creating a password, avoid the following:

- Do not use your first or last name, your spouse's or child's name, or your pet's name in any form—reversed, capitalized, or doubled.

- Do not use the months of the year, your birthday, or the birthday of anyone you know.

- Do not use your telephone number, house number, driver's license number, car license plate number, or Social Security number.

- Avoid any other information such as street name or city name that can be associated with you.

- Do not use all numbers, all letters, or a password composed entirely of the same letter.

- Do not use a word found in the dictionary because it is too easy to guess.

5 In the **If You Forget Your Password** section, locate the **Security question** menu, and then click the **down arrow**. Click one of the questions listed. Then type the answer to the security question in the **Your answer** text box. Next, using the **Birthday** menu, click the **down arrow** to choose the month, and then type in your birthday and year. Type your Zip/Postal code into the next text box. If you have an alternate e-mail address, type that address into the last text box. Compare your screen with Figure 4.3.

All of the information entered in this section of the form helps to confirm your identity if you ever forget your password. The alternate e-mail address is where Yahoo! Mail sends a new password.

Figure 4.3

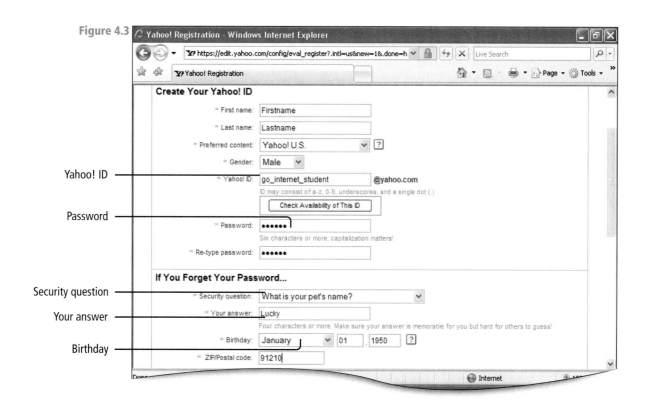

Yahoo! ID

Password

Security question

Your answer

Birthday

6 In the **Verify Your Registration** section, notice the scrambled code displayed beneath the text box. In the **Enter the Code Shown** text box, type the code displayed on your screen.

The code displays as wavy letters and numbers that have been distorted or rotated to a small degree. This type of text is referred to as *CAPTCHA*. CAPTCHA stands for *Completely Automated Public Turing test to tell Computers and Humans Apart*. CAPTCHA was developed and trademarked by Carnegie Mellon University and helps prevent computer programs from performing events online instead of humans performing events online. This code is used by Yahoo! Mail as a security measure to prevent mass automatic registrations generated by computers.

7 In the **Terms of Service** section, use the scroll bars to read through the Terms of Service statement. Alternatively, click the Printable Version link to print out the Terms of Agreement or click the link labeled Terms of Service to view the terms in a separate window.

The Terms of Service provides important legal information about Yahoo!, your responsibilities in using the Yahoo! services, general information, a description of Yahoo! services, disclaimers of warranty, limitations of liability, and violation information.

8 In the **Terms of Service** section, locate and click the **Privacy Policy** link. In the **Security Alert** dialog box, click **Yes**.

The Yahoo! Privacy Policy displays. The Yahoo! Privacy Policy states how Yahoo! collects and uses your information, the Yahoo! policy for children under the age of 13, how Yahoo! uses cookies, and how you can edit your personal information and preferences. You will need to review both the Terms of Service and the Privacy Policy before you proceed with your registration.

9 At the bottom of the screen, click the **I agree** button to agree with the Terms of Service and Privacy Policy if you agree with the stated legal requirements.

A Web page confirming the completion of your registration displays.

10 Using the techniques you have practiced, add the **footer 4A_Registration_Confirmed_Firstname_Lastname** and then print the Web page.

You should print this page and keep it for future reference. The page lists your Yahoo! ID, your alternate e-mail address, your security question, and the answer you selected.

11 Decide on a location where you can store a document—either in a folder on your computer's hard drive or a folder on a removable storage device such as a USB flash drive. Click the **Start** button ![start] and then click **My Computer**. Navigate to the desired location, and if necessary, create a folder for this course into which you can store documents. Name the folder **Chapter_4_E-mail**. Close **My Computer** when you are finished.

12 Save the confirmation Web page to the **Chapter_4_E-mail** folder as **4A_Registration_Confirmation_Firstname_Lastname**

Note — Using Your Alternate E-mail Address

The Web page confirming the completion of your registration states that a confirmation message has been sent to an alternate e-mail address that you provided during the registration process. The alternate e-mail address is used for problem resolution such as when you forget your password and cannot log into your Yahoo! Mail e-mail account. A temporary password is sent to the alternate address.

13 At the bottom of the **Registration Completed** Web page, click the **Continue to Yahoo! Mail** button. In the **Security Alert** box, click **Yes**.

The Yahoo! Mail home page displays. Take a moment to review the screen and locate the features shown in Figure 4.4.

Another Way ── To Verify Your Yahoo! Password

At times, Yahoo! randomly prompts you to verify your password. If this happens, simply type your user ID and password in the correct text boxes and click the Sign In button. You may also be prompted with a screen displaying the Already Have A Yahoo! ID? section. If this occurs, type your Yahoo! ID and password that you just established, and then click the Sign In button. If a Security Alert box displays, click OK to continue to your Yahoo! Mail account. If a second Security Alert Box displays, click Yes to continue.

Figure 4.4

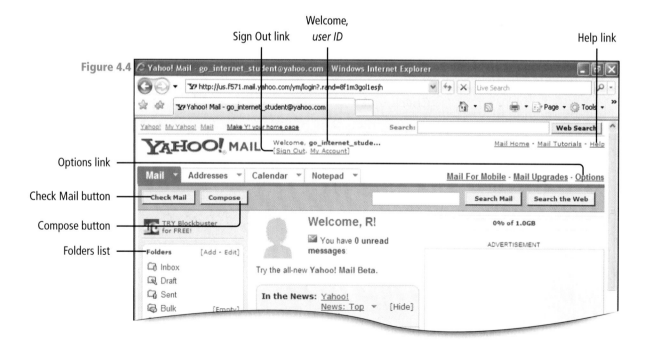

14 Keep your browser window open for the next activity.

Objective 2
Compose and Send a Basic E-mail Message

Recall that there are two major e-mail systems: Web-based and client-based. Regardless of the type of e-mail system you use, all e-mail messages contain similar features. The parts of an e-mail message can be grouped into two main components: the ***mail header*** and the ***message body***. The mail header is located at the top of the e-mail message and contains information about the message, such as the sender's e-mail address, the recipient's e-mail address, and the subject. Some e-mail programs include the date and time the message was sent as part of the header.

The message body contains the content of the e-mail message. It is important to treat e-mail with some formality by including a greeting and by signing your name at the closing of the e-mail message body. Some messages are short and quick; others are lengthy. The content can be text or hyperlinks you want to share with the recipient. Some e-mail programs enable you to include a background or other graphics as part of the message body. The message body may also include a link to an ***attachment***. E-mail attachments are additional files sent along with the e-mail message to support the meaning or subject matter of the e-mail.

Activity 4.2 Creating a Basic E-mail Message

Plans for Miguel Hernandez's trip to the United States to visit Alejandra Domene, President of El Cuero Specialty Wares, continue to develop. In Activity 4.2, you will help Cristina Mandala, the Executive Administrative Assistant for Miguel Hernandez, compose a basic message notifying Miguel and Alejandra of the itinerary for the trip.

1 In the upper left corner of your **Yahoo! Mail Inbox**, click the **Compose** button. Compare your screen with Figure 4.5.

A form displays where you can address your e-mail, compose your e-mail message, format the message, attach a file, use the Spell Check tool, use a signature file, and send the e-mail.

Figure 4.5

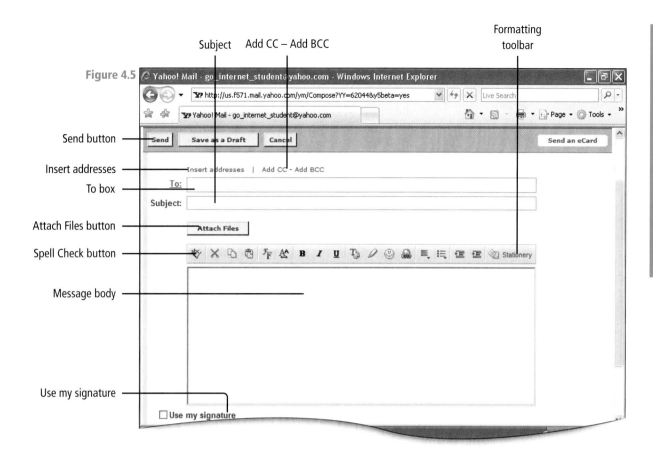

- Subject
- Add CC – Add BCC
- Formatting toolbar
- Send button
- Insert addresses
- To box
- Attach Files button
- Spell Check button
- Message body
- Use my signature

2 At the top of the form, click the **Add CC** link to add an additional line. In the **To** text box, type your own e-mail address—your new Yahoo! Mail e-mail address. In the **Cc** line, type a classmate's Yahoo! Mail e-mail address. Alternatively, you may want to type your instructor's e-mail in the Cc line.

The *To line* provides the name and e-mail address of the recipient or recipients of the e-mail message. The *carbon copy* line, or *Cc*, lists people who will receive a copy of the e-mail message for informational purposes.

The names specified in the *blind carbon copy* line, or *Bcc*, also receive the message, but their names will not display when the recipients mentioned in the To or Cc lines open the e-mail message. Names listed in the Bcc line display only to the sender and the Bcc recipient. This feature can be helpful when you need to shield the privacy of certain e-mail recipients but still share the information contained in the message.

More Knowledge

Carbon Copies

The first "C" in Cc or Bcc can refer to either *carbon* copy or *courtesy copy* (*blind courtesy copy*). Both are considered correct. However, certain organizations prefer one translation over another. Check with your instructor for your school's preference.

3 In the **Subject** line, type **Chapter_4_Itinerary**

The ***Subject line*** is created by the sender and should summarize in a couple of words the main idea of the e-mail message. Subject lines need to be specific because the recipient often uses the subject line to determine the importance or urgency of the e-mail message. You should not leave the Subject line blank.

4 In the largest text box—the message body—type the following message, pressing ⟨Enter⟩ at the end of each line.

Dear Senor Hernandez and Senora Domene,

Please open the file attached to this e-mail, i04A_Itinerary. It contains your itinerary for your upcoming trip. Feel free to contact me if you have any questions about your travel arrangements.

Sincerely,

Cristina Mandala

Executive Administrative Assistant

El Cuero de Mexico

011-525-555-5555

5 Between the **Subject** line and the message body, locate and click the **Attach Files** button.

A form displays where you can browse for up to five files to attach to the e-mail message. The Attach Files button enables you to add an attachment to the message. When the message arrives in the recipient's Inbox, e-mail attachments are noted with the file name, the file format, and size of the file.

Attachments can be almost any type of file format such as a word-processed document, a presentation, an audio file, or a video file. The e-mail recipient must have the appropriate plug-in installed on his computer in order to open and display the attachment's content.

Some organizations do not enable all file types to be sent as attachments to help prevent the spread of viruses. In those cases, attachments may be automatically deleted before arriving in the recipient's Inbox. In addition, file size for attachments may also be limited. It is helpful to check with the recipient to see if there any restrictions on attachment file size at their organization before sending e-mail attachments to them.

6 On the **Attach Files** Web page, click the first **Browse** button, and then navigate to where you are storing the files for this chapter and locate the **i04A_Itinerary** file. Click that file to select it, and then click **Open** to add it to the **Attach Files** page. Then at the bottom of the **Attach Files** page, click the **Attach Files** button. Compare your screen with Figure 4.6.

A message displays that the file is being attached. The i04A_Itinerary file is added to your e-mail message and then the Attachments confirmation Web page is displayed. You can return to the message when you click the Continue to Message button.

Attached file name

Figure 4.6

Continue to Message button

Attachments confirmation Web page

7 Click the **Continue to Message** button, and then click the **Spell Check** button. Compare your screen with Figure 4.7.

The Spell Check tool displays at the top of the message body. Any word that may be misspelled displays in red text. A list of suggestions displays or you may type in your own version. For any of the suggestions, you may click **Change** to change that instance of the word. The down arrow next to Change provides the option to *Change this word* or *Change all occurrences*. Or you may click **Ignore down arrow** to *Ignore this word* or *Ignore all occurrences* of the word. When you have worked through all of the suggestions, click **Close** to close the Spell Check tool.

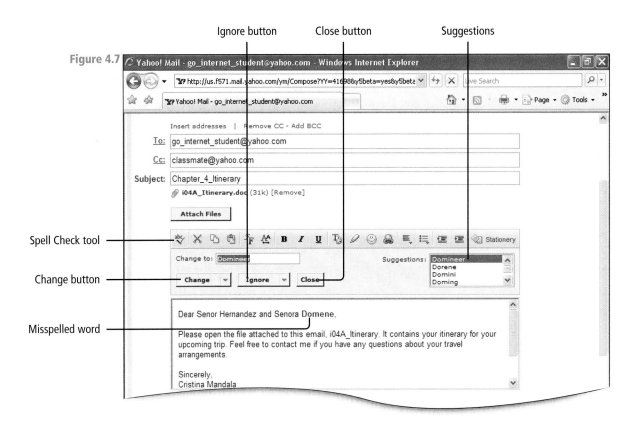

Figure 4.7

Ignore button   Close button   Suggestions

Spell Check tool

Change button

Misspelled word

8 Click the **Send** button to send your e-mail message to the e-mail addresses you typed in the **To** and **Cc** lines.

A Message Sent confirmation page displays on your screen. You have the option to add the address where you sent the message to your address book or return to the Inbox without adding it. Recall that an address book is a feature that stores the names and e-mail addresses of your friends, colleagues, or other contacts that you would like to communicate with using e-mail.

9 Click the **Add to Address Book** button. On the **Add Recipients to Address Book** Web page that displays, notice the e-mail addresses of the recipients are listed. For each recipient, fill in the first name, last name, and any nickname for that recipient. Then click the **Add to Address Book** button.

You will see a confirmation statement that a contact has been added to the Address Box. Then you are returned to the Inbox and any new e-mail messages will display in your Inbox. Because you used your own address in the To line, you should have a copy of the message you just sent in your Inbox.

10 Keep your browser open for the next activity.

Activity 4.3 Creating a Signature File and Signing Out of Your Account

Cristina Mandala, the Executive Administrative Assistant for Miguel Hernandez, has discovered she will need to add her name and contact information to all of the e-mail she sends. She would like to have this information automatically added to all outgoing e-mails. In Activity 4.3, you will create a signature file to make adding contact information to e-mails easier. You will also sign out of a Web-based e-mail account.

1 In the top right side of the **Yahoo! Mail Inbox**, locate and click the **Options** link to display the **Mail Options** Web page.

The Mail Options feature provides several ways to customize your Web-based e-mail account including spam protection, blocking addresses, and managing features of your e-mail account. Some of the options are considered *Premium Services* that require a monthly fee.

2 Scroll down the **Mail Options** Web page, and then locate the **Signature** link. Compare your screen with Figure 4.8.

The Signature option lets you create and add a signature file to any e-mail message. A **signature file** is often included at the end of an e-mail. A signature file is a file that you create that contains your name and other information that can be automatically added to every e-mail you send. Typically, professional signature files include a name, title, and contact information. Personal signature files may include a favorite quotation or your nickname.

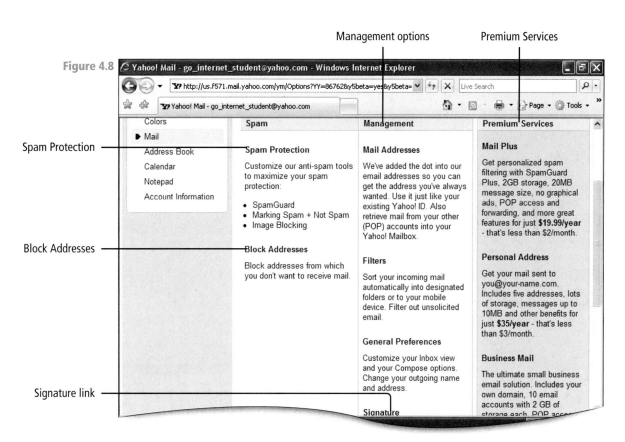

Figure 4.8

Management options

Premium Services

Spam Protection

Block Addresses

Signature link

3 Click the **Signature** link.

The form to create a signature displays.

4 At the top of the form, locate and if necessary click Plain, so the message is created as plain text. In the large text box, type your first name and last name, your school's name, and your Yahoo! Mail e-mail address. Click the **Add signature to all outgoing messages** check box. Compare your screen with Figure 4.9.

The *Plain* option creates the signature in plain text. It can be read by all e-mail programs that receive your e-mail message. If you choose *Color and Graphics* option, the e-mail program receiving your message may not be able to interpret the color or graphics as you designed them to look.

Signature files can be added to every message that you send by choosing the *Add signature to all outgoing messages* option. If you do not choose that option now, you have the choice to add your signature file to each individual e-mail message that you compose.

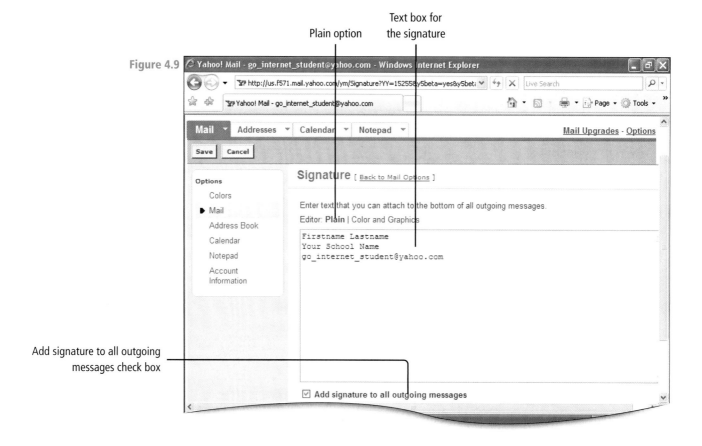

Figure 4.9

5 At the bottom left of the **Signature** Web page, click the **Save** button to save your signature file.

The Mail Options Web page displays.

6 At the top left corner of the **Mail Options** Web page, click the **Check Mail** button to return to the **Inbox**. In the upper left corner of your **Yahoo! Mail Inbox**, click **Compose**. In the **To** line, type your Yahoo! Mail address, and then in the **Subject** line, type **Testing My Signature File**. In the message body, type **Testing my signature file** and then click the **Send** button.

The Message Sent confirmation page displays. Because you have already added your address to the address book, you are not prompted to add this address again.

7 Near the top left of the **Yahoo! Mail Inbox**, click **Check Mail**.

The message displays in your Yahoo! Mail Inbox.

8 At the top of the **Inbox** screen, click the **Sign Out** link.

You will be signed out of your Yahoo! Mail account and the Yahoo! Mail home page displays.

It is important to remember to sign out your Yahoo! Mail account so that anyone else using the same computer after you is not able to access your account. The next time you want to sign back into your e-mail account, go to *http://mail.yahoo.com* and sign in using your Yahoo! ID and password.

9 **Close** Internet Explorer.

End **You have completed Project 4A** ————————————

Project 4B Managing Web-Based E-mail Programs

Cristina Mandala is pleased with her new Web-based e-mail account. She uses it frequently to plan for her boss's upcoming trips. Now she needs to practice using several important features to manage the e-mail account. In Activities 4.4 through 4.9, you will receive and open an e-mail message, open an e-mail attachment, reply to an e-mail message, and forward an e-mail message. You will print an e-mail message. You will create a folder to help organize e-mail messages and then manually move a message into the folder. You will set up a filter to automatically send certain incoming messages to a folder other than the Inbox. You will look for messages in the Bulk folder. You will delete e-mail messages from the Trash folder and sign out of your account.

For Project 4B, you will need the following files:

E-mail message printout

You will print the message
Re: Chapter_4_Itinerary

Objective 3
Receive and Reply to an E-mail Message with an Attachment

E-mail moves along the Internet by using the client-server computing architecture just as the viewing of a Web page uses the client-server architecture. In a client-based e-mail system, the **e-mail client** resides on your computer—the client. An e-mail client is a software program that is used to compose, send, and receive e-mail messages. Common client-side programs include Outlook Express, Mozilla Thunderbird, Netscape Mail, and Eudora.

With a Web-based e-mail system, you can access and use the features of your e-mail system from any computer that is connected to the Internet. Examples of Web-based e-mail systems include Yahoo! Mail, Gmail, and MSN Hotmail.

For any e-mail system, you must use a password to log into the e-mail account and access your e-mail messages. After you compose and send an e-mail message, it is broken down into data packets by using packet switching, and the packets are passed between **mail servers**. A mail server is a large computer that receives, stores, and sends e-mail messages. When the data packets reach the correct destination, they are reassembled back into an e-mail message and stored on a mail server until you log into your e-mail account and request the e-mail messages. The e-mail message is then sent to your e-mail client's Inbox and displayed onscreen. E-mail is not completely secure and may be intercepted at any point as it is sent between the client and server.

Activity 4.4 Checking for E-mail and Opening E-mail with an Attachment

As part of the preparation for the upcoming trip, many files need to be passed between the staff of El Cuero de Mexico and the staff at El Cuero Specialty Wares by using e-mail. In this activity, you and Cristina Mandala will check for new e-mail, open an e-mail message, and open an attachment.

1 **Start** Internet Explorer and if necessary, click the **Maximize** button 🔲 to enlarge the window to fill the computer screen completely. In the **Address bar**, click one time to select the existing text, type **http://mail.yahoo.com** and then press ⏎.

2 In the **Sign in to Yahoo!** section, type your Yahoo! ID and password. Click the **Sign In** button. In the **Security Alert** dialog box that displays, click **Yes**.

Your Yahoo! Mail Inbox displays.

3 In the upper left corner of the **Inbox**, locate and click the **Check Mail** button.

The Check Mail button checks for new e-mail messages on the mail server and then opens your Inbox and displays all messages in a list. The new messages display in the center of the screen in bold text to indicate that they are unread messages. You can see the Sender, the Subject, the Date, and the Size. The Sender is the same as a *From line* and indicates the name or user ID of the person who sent the e-mail. The Subject line is determined by the sender when the e-mail message is composed. The Date indicates when the message was sent. Size refers to the size of the e-mail and is measured in kilobytes (K). A paper clip button is displayed to the immediate left of the Subject line and indicates a message that has an attachment.

You should receive two messages. One message has the Subject line *Chapter_4_Itinerary* and the other message has the Subject line *Testing My Signature File*. You may also see one or more messages from your classmates as a result of the previous activity.

4 In the list of unread messages, under the **Subject** heading, click **Testing My Signature File**.

The message displays in the center of your screen. Recall that you sent this message to yourself. The message contains your signature file.

5 Click the **Back to Messages** link to return to the **Inbox**. Then in the list of unread messages under the **Subject** heading, click the **Chapter_4_Itinerary** message. Compare your screen with Figure 4.10.

The message displays in the center of the screen. The date and time that the e-mail was sent, the From line, the Subject line, the To line, the CC line, and a link to the attachment are displayed.

Date and time   CC line   Message body

Figure 4.10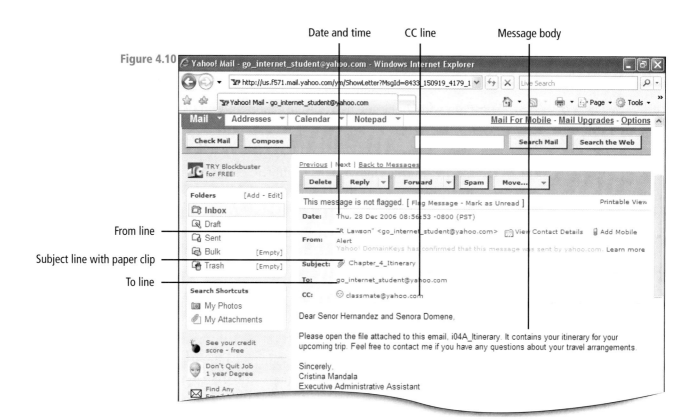
From line
Subject line with paper clip
To line

6 Near the bottom of the message, in the section labeled **Attachments**, locate the **Scan and Save to Computer** link. Compare your screen with Figure 4.11.

All attachments for the e-mail are listed under *Files*. The paper clip button is visible. The size of the list is also listed. A link labeled Preview enables you to view the attachment within the browser window. The link labeled Scan and Save to Computer checks the attachment for virus and then prompts you to open the attachment if no virus is found.

File name and size   Scan and Save to Computer

Figure 4.11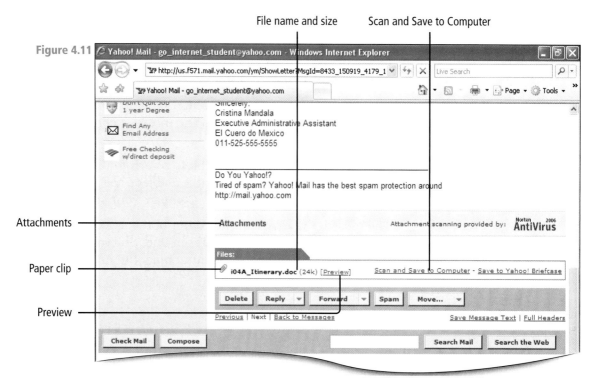
Attachments
Paper clip
Preview

7 Click the **Scan and Save to Computer** link.

Yahoo! Mail automatically scans the attached file for viruses and displays a Virus Scan Results Web page. E-mail attachments can be used to start a *virus* or a malicious *executable file*. Recall that a virus is an unwanted piece of code or a program sent to you that runs on your system and causes unexpected or damaging effects. An executable file is a program that the computer runs directly from the file. Like a virus, a malicious executable file may cause unexpected or damaging effects.

Even if the e-mail appears to come from someone you know, do not open an e-mail attachment until you have scanned it with an antivirus software program. The sender may not be aware that a virus is being sent from his computer.

8 On the **Virus Scan Results** Web page, read the **Scan Results**. If the results state *No virus threat detected*, click the **Download Attachment** button. Then in the **File Download** dialog box, click the **Open** button.

The appropriate plug-in for the attachment automatically opens and the attached itinerary displays in a new window. For this file, Microsoft Word is used to open the attachment because it has *.doc* as the file extension. The *.doc* file extension is the extension added at the end of files created in the Microsoft Word program.

9 Read the itinerary, and then in the upper right corner of the Microsoft Word window, click **Close** ☒ to return to the e-mail message. Click the **Back to Message** button to return to the message. Keep the message on your screen for the next activity.

Activity 4.5 Using the Reply and Forward Features

Miguel Hernandez and Alejandra Domene have approved the itinerary. In Activity 4.5, you will use the Reply feature and the Forward feature to help Cristina Mandala send the itinerary to other staff members that are helping to plan the trip.

1 Near the top of the e-mail message, notice the **Delete**, **Reply**, and **Forward** buttons. Click the **Reply down arrow**. Compare your screen with Figure 4.12.

The Delete button enables you to remove e-mail messages from your Inbox. The Forward button enables you to send the message to someone other than the sender of the original message.

Many e-mail messages require you to provide a response. A *Reply* is your electronic response to an e-mail message. It enables you to send the original e-mail and additional information or comments back to the sender. There are two options to use. *Reply To Sender* sends your reply only to the sender of the original message and the *Reply To Everyone* option enables you to send the original e-mail and additional information or comments back to the original sender and all recipients of an e-mail message.

Typically, when you reply to a message, the original message is included as part of the reply message. However, some organizations prefer that you do not include the original message with your reply message to help keep account sizes within the quotas established by the organization.

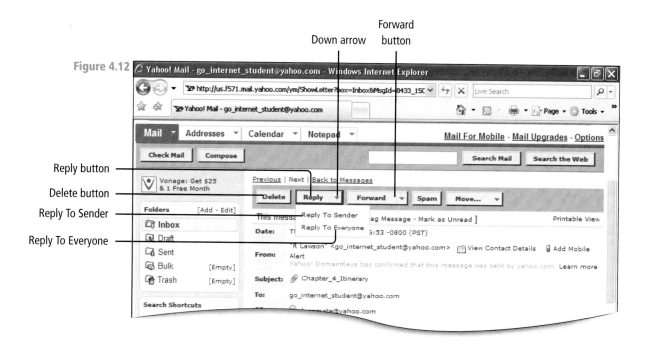

Figure 4.12

Down arrow

Forward button

Reply button

Delete button

Reply To Sender

Reply To Everyone

2 Click the **Reply To Everyone** option.

The e-mail message displays in a new window similar to the form used when you compose a message. The To and the Cc lines are already filled with the names of the sender and the other recipients. The Subject line contains the phrase *Re:* and then the same Subject line as the original message. In the message body, the original message is visible.

Re: stands for *regarding* and is automatically added to the beginning to the Subject line of all Reply messages. Each time the message is replied to, another *Re:* is added. If a message has been passed back and forth several times, the subject line may contain a lengthy string of *Re:* before the original subject line.

3 In the message body, if necessary, position the insertion point at the upper left corner of the message area, and then type the following reply message:

Dear Cristina,

Thank you for all of your hard work to organize our trip. I would like you to now schedule the caterer for the dinner on the last night of the trip.

Please make sure that the food for the party is authentic Mexican cuisine. The caterer should be made aware that Senora Alejandra Domene is allergic to seafood. My wife is allergic to peanuts.

Sincerely,

Miguel Hernandez, CEO
El Cuero de Mexico
011-525-555-5599

4 When you have finished typing your message, make sure the **Use my signature** check box is selected, and then click the **Send** button.

The Reply Sent Web page displays to confirm where the message was sent. Your Reply message will arrive in the Inbox of the sender and the Inbox of each of the recipients of the original message.

5 In the upper left corner, click the **Check Mail** button to return to the **Inbox**. In the **Inbox**, click the **Subject** line of the original message **Chapter_4_Itinerary**. When the message displays in the center of the screen, click the **Forward down arrow**. Figure 4.13 shows the two Forward options, *As Inline Text* and *As Attachment*.

Forward means to send a message you have received, modified, or left in its original entirety, to another recipient who is not the original sender. Two options for forwarding display. ***As Inline Text*** forwards the message embedded into the message body. ***As Attachment*** forwards the message as a separate file that must be viewed as an attachment by the recipient.

Forward Down
button arrow

Figure 4.13

As Inline Text

As Attachment

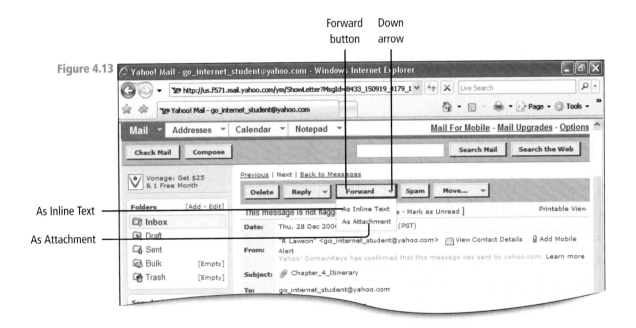

6 Click **As Inline Text**.

The new window displays similar to the form used whenever you compose a message. The To line is blank so that you can type in an e-mail address. Alternatively, you may select a name from your address book by clicking Insert addresses and then the name.

The Subject line is filled in with the same Subject line as the original message with the phrase *Fwd:* in front of it. *Fwd:* indicates the message is being forwarded to someone who was not on the original list of recipients.

The message body contains the original message. The attachment is visible and will be forwarded along with the e-mail message unless you choose to remove it. By default, the Use my signature check box is selected.

7 In the **To** line, type your own e-mail address, and then click the **Send** button.

The Message Forwarded Web page displays indicating where the forwarded message was sent. The forwarded message will arrive in your Inbox.

8 In the upper left corner, click the **Check Mail** button to display your **Inbox**. Compare your screen with Figure 4.14. Keep the **Inbox** on your screen for the next activity.

Figure 4.14

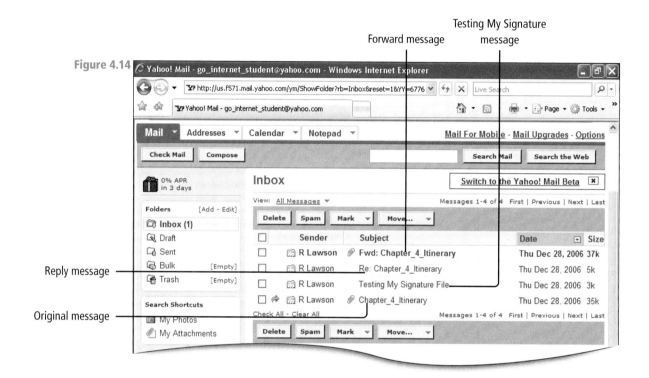

Objective 4
Print an E-mail Message

Although e-mail is a convenient form of communication with several benefits, it does require that you are at a computer or using a handheld computing device when you read your messages. At times, you may want a printed version of an e-mail message to read or to keep on file as a matter of record.

Activity 4.6 Printing an E-mail Message

Cristina Mandala must meet with the caterer to plan the menu for the dinner party at the close of the business trip. Miguel Hernandez has approved the itinerary and has e-mailed her important dietary requirements that Cristina must share with the caterer. It is easier to show the caterer a copy of the e-mail because she will not have access to a computer during the meeting. In Activity 4.6, you will print an e-mail message.

1 In the upper left corner of the **Inbox**, locate and click the **Check Mail** button.

The new messages display in the center of the screen as unread messages and are indicated by bold text. The default sort order is chronological so the newest messages display at the top of the list. You may have received one or more messages from your classmates as a result of the previous activity.

2 In the list of unread messages, click the **Subject** line of the **Re: Chapter_4_Itinerary** message that you sent to yourself or that was sent by a classmate.

3 When the e-mail opens, on the far right of screen, locate and click the **Printable View** link.

The e-mail message displays in a pop-up box containing a *printer-friendly version*. A printer-friendly version is a version of the message that has no ads and has been formatted and centered to fit correctly on a standard 8 ½-by-11 sheet of paper. It can be printed by using the Print button of the browser or the Print link provided as part of the printer-friendly version.

4 Compare your screen with Figure 4.15 where two windows are displayed onscreen—the original message window and the printer-friendly version window. Then in the printer-friendly version, click the **Print** link to display the **Print** dialog box.

Figure 4.15

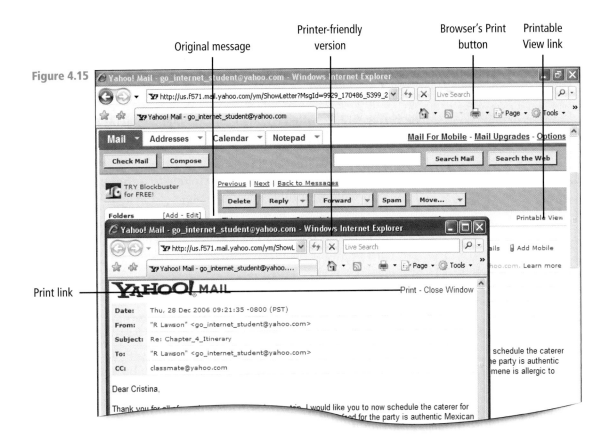

Original message
Printer-friendly version
Browser's Print button
Printable View link
Print link

5 In the **Print** dialog box, click the **Print** button.

The dialog box closes, the message prints, and you return to the printer-friendly version.

6 In the upper right corner of the printer-friendly version, click the **Close** button ☒ to close the window and return to the original message window.

7 On the left side of the screen, click the **Check Mail** button. Keep the **Inbox** on your screen for the next activity.

Objective 5
Create Folders and Filters

E-mail arrives in your Inbox in chronological order. However, you may want to read and store your e-mail according to the content or subject of the e-mail by using a series of folders. Recall that folders are used to collect, organize, and store your e-mail. *Filters* are a feature used to automatically sort your e-mail messages into folders as the messages arrive instead of placing them directly into in the Inbox by default. Filters are created based on specified rules for keywords contained in the From, To or Cc lines, the Subject line, or the body of the message. Filters can be very helpful to organize incoming messages. Filters enable you to determine the organization of the e-mail not necessarily by when the e-mail arrives in your Inbox but by criteria that you establish. Because filters perform based on predetermined rules, a poorly structured Subject line or From line can fool a filter into sorting an e-mail message into a folder where it does not actually belong.

Activity 4.7 Creating a Folder and Moving E-mail into It

Cristina Mandala finds it difficult to locate certain e-mails that she must refer back to because there are so many regarding the upcoming trip. In this activity, you will create a new folder to organize e-mail messages. Then you will manually move messages into the folder.

1 On the left side of the **Inbox**, in the section labeled **Folders**, notice that several folders have already been created. Compare your screen with Figure 4.16.

Several default folders come with your Yahoo! Mail account. Recall that the Inbox folder is the default folder in an e-mail system where incoming messages are placed. The *Draft folder* stores e-mail messages that you have composed but not yet sent. The *Sent folder* stores a copy of all of the e-mail messages that you send out. The *Bulk folder* is used to collect incoming e-mail that appears to be spam. You may periodically empty this folder by using the Empty link. The *Trash folder* stores e-mail that you have deleted until you empty this folder.

The Add link enables you to create a new folder. The Edit link enables you to set options, empty folders, rename folders, or delete folders.

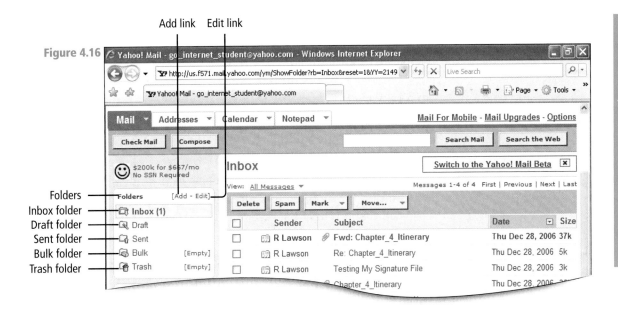

Figure 4.16

Add link Edit link

Folders
Inbox folder
Draft folder
Sent folder
Bulk folder
Trash folder

▓2▓ In the upper right corner of the **Folders** section, locate and click the **Add** link.

A pop-up box labeled Explorer User Prompt displays. It contains a text box where you can enter a name for a new folder.

▓3▓ In the **Explorer User Prompt** text box, type **Chapter_4** and then click **OK**.

The pop-up box closes and a new section labeled My Folders displays. Your new folder displays in the My Folders section. You can store messages from your work with Chapter 4 in this new folder. If you add more new folders, they will display alphabetically in the My Folders section.

▓4▓ On the left side of the **Inbox**, click the **Inbox** folder to display a list of read and unread messages. Click the **check box** next to the message that was forwarded in the previous activity—**Fwd: Chapter_4_ Itinerary**. Directly above the list of e-mail messages, locate and click the **Move down arrow**.

A list of folders displays. The down arrow on the Move button enables you to select a folder where you can move the e-mail message.

▓5▓ In the list of folders, click the **Chapter_4** folder.

The Fwd: Chapter_4_Itinerary message is no longer visible in the Inbox because it has been moved into the Chapter_4 folder.

▓6▓ Under **My Folders**, click the **Chapter_4** folder and notice the **Subject** line of the forwarded message is displayed—**Fwd: Chapter_4_ Itinerary**.

▓7▓ Click the **Inbox** folder one more time, and then keep the **Inbox** open for the next activity.

Activity 4.8 Creating a Filter

You can also organize your e-mails to be automatically placed into the folders so that you can read them at a more convenient time. In Activity 4.8, you will create and use a filter that sends incoming e-mails directly to a folder other than the Inbox.

1 In the upper right corner of the **Inbox**, locate and click the **Options** link. Near the middle of the **Mail Options** Web page that displays, click the **Filters** link.

The Filters Web page displays. The left and right panels should be empty. If any filter has already been created, the name of the filter will display in the left panel. The rules of the filter will display in the right panel.

2 Just above the left panel, click the **Add** button. Compare your screen with Figure 4.17.

The Add Message Filter Web page displays. You can enter a filter name, set the rules for the filter to follow, determine where to move e-mail that meets the criteria of the filter, and add the filter to your e-mail account.

The rules for the filter can be set to identify words in four e-mail components. If an e-mail meets any of the rules, it is automatically moved to a folder instead of remaining in the Inbox. The e-mail components include:

- From line or header—The user ID, host name, e-mail address, or the name of the sender originating the e-mail

- To/Cc line or header—The user ID or the name of the person receiving the mail or anyone who is being copied on the e-mail

- Subject—Any word or all words in the subject line

- Body—Any word or phrase contained in the message body

Figure 4.17

Choose Folder

Add Filter button

Filter Name

If all of the following rules are true

Then

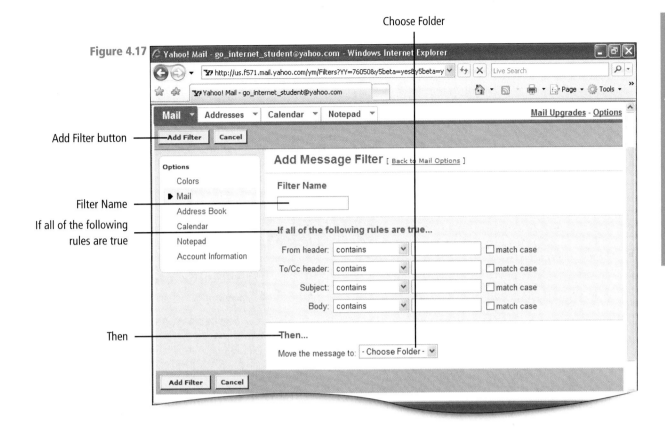

3 In the **Filter Name** text box, type **Chapter_4** In the **If all of the following rules are true** section, click the **Subject down arrow**, and then click **contains**. In the next text box, immediately to the right of **Subject contains**, type **Chapter_4** Leave the match case check box unchecked. In the **Then** section, click the **Choose Folder down arrow**, and then click the **Chapter_4** folder that you created in the previous activity. Click the **Add Filter** button to finish creating the filter. Compare your screen with Figure 4.18.

The Filters Web page displays. The Chapter_4 filter displays on the left and the rules of the filter display on the right.

Chapter_4 filter rules

Figure 4.18

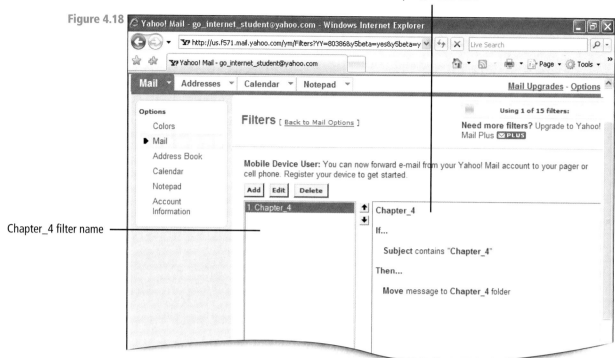

Chapter_4 filter name

4️⃣ At the upper left of the screen, click the **Mail tab**, and then click the **Check Mail** link to return to the **Inbox**.

5️⃣ At the upper left of the screen, click the **Compose** button, and then type your own e-mail address in the **To** line to test the filter. In the **Subject** line, type **Chapter_4 filter** In the message body, type your name and the phrase **Testing the filter** Click **Send** to send the message.

The Message Sent Web page displays to confirm where the e-mail was sent. By sending the message with Chapter_4 in the Subject line to your own e-mail address, you can test the filter to see how well it works.

6️⃣ On the **Message Sent** Web page, click **Check Mail** to refresh your **Inbox**.

You should not see any new e-mail in your Inbox. However, you should notice a number next to the Chapter_4 folder. The number indicates how many new messages have been routed to the folder by the filter.

7️⃣ Under **My Folders**, click the **Chapter_4** folder.

The forwarded message that you moved to the Chapter_4 folder in the previous activity is displayed in this folder. You should also see the new unread message that the filter automatically placed in the Chapter_4 folder.

8️⃣ Click the **Subject** line of the **Chapter_4 filter** e-mail, read it, and then click the **Inbox** folder to return to your **Inbox**. Keep the **Inbox** displayed on your screen for the next activity.

Objective 6
Delete E-mail from Your Account

Most e-mail accounts have generous storage limits, but eventually you will need to delete e-mail messages to make room in your account. You may want to delete spam or messages that are no longer important to you on a regularly scheduled basis.

Activity 4.9 Deleting E-mail and Signing Out

Miguel Hernandez, CEO of El Cuero de Mexico, had a successful trip to San Diego to meet with Alejandra Domene of El Cuero Specialty Wares. Cristina Mandala, his Executive Administrative Assistant, wants to clean out her Web-based e-mail account so it will be ready for the next trip that she must plan for Senor Hernandez. In this activity, you will delete e-mail and then sign out of the Web-based e-mail account.

1 In the upper left corner of the **Inbox**, click the **Check Mail** button to refresh your **Inbox**.

2 On the left side of the screen, click the **Bulk** folder.

If you have received any spam messages, they automatically are listed in the Bulk folder instead of your Inbox folder. These messages are listed in the right side of the screen.

3 For any messages stored in the **Bulk** folder, scroll to the bottom of the message list, and then click the **Check All** link. Click the **Delete** button. If you are prompted by a pop-up box to confirm the deletion, click the **OK** button.

It is possible that you do not have any messages in your Bulk folder. But for any messages that were in the Bulk folder have now been deleted from the Bulk folder and stored temporarily in the Trash folder.

4 On the left side of the screen, click the **Chapter_4** folder. When the folder displays, click the check box next to the message you sent in the previous activity—**Chapter_4 filter**—and then click the **Delete** button.

The message will be deleted from the Chapter_4 folder and stored temporarily in the Trash folder.

5 On the left side of the screen, click the **Trash** folder to open it and view the list of any e-mail messages that have been deleted. Near the top of the screen, notice that the **Messages in Trash** do not count toward your mailbox quota.

Web-based e-mail systems impose storage limits on the accounts. These storage limits vary in size with each provider. It is not uncommon to find storage limits in the 1 and 2 gigabyte (GB) range. Most e-mail messages are small so these limits are generous.

Yahoo! Mail provides 1.0 GB for each free account. E-mail messages in your Trash folder and your Bulk folder do not count toward your storage quota. However, other Web-based e-mail providers may count the Trash or Bulk folder toward your quota.

6 Next to the **Trash** folder, locate and click the **Empty** link. In the **Yahoo! Mail Confirm** dialog box that displays, click **Empty**.

Your Trash folder is emptied and a Web page displays with a message to confirm there are no messages in your Trash folder.

7 Near the top of the screen, click the **Sign Out** link.

The Yahoo! Mail home page displays and you are signed out of your Yahoo! Mail account.

8 **Close** ☒ Internet Explorer.

End You have completed Project 4B ─────────────

Project 4C Exploring E-mail Systems, Protocols, Netiquette, and Nuisances

In Objectives 7 through 9, you will compare e-mail systems and explore the protocols needed to use each system. You will identify appropriate e-mail netiquette. You will minimize nuisances associated with sending and receiving e-mail.

Objective 7
Compare E-mail Systems

How does an e-mail system work? E-mail messages can be sent over many types of networks, using two major systems: client-based e-mail systems and Web-based e-mail systems.

- *Client-based e-mail systems* are accessed by using a software program installed on your computer—the client. Your ISP provides an e-mail account that works with the ISP's mail servers to send and store your e-mail messages.

- *Web-based e-mail systems* are e-mail systems that use the World Wide Web in a similar way as the client. Web-based e-mail accounts are accessible from any computer that has an Internet connection and a Web browser installed. This enables you to conveniently read and send e-mail from almost anywhere. Most Web-based e-mail accounts are provided free of charge as part of a larger Web site.

  There are several providers for Web-based e-mail accounts. When choosing a provider, you will likely consider recommendations from your friends or family.

Client-Based E-mail Systems

What is Outlook Express? *Outlook Express* is one of the most commonly used client-based e-mail systems because it is the default e-mail client that comes with the Windows operating system. The Outlook Express program works with your ISP to send and receive e-mail messages. Do not confuse Outlook Express with *Microsoft Outlook*, which is part of the Microsoft Office Suite. Microsoft Outlook provides features in addition to e-mail such as calendaring and other collaboration tools. Outlook Express does not have these features.

You start Outlook Express just as you start other software programs. Figure 4.19 shows where Outlook Express is located on the Start menu.

Figure 4.19

Outlook Express

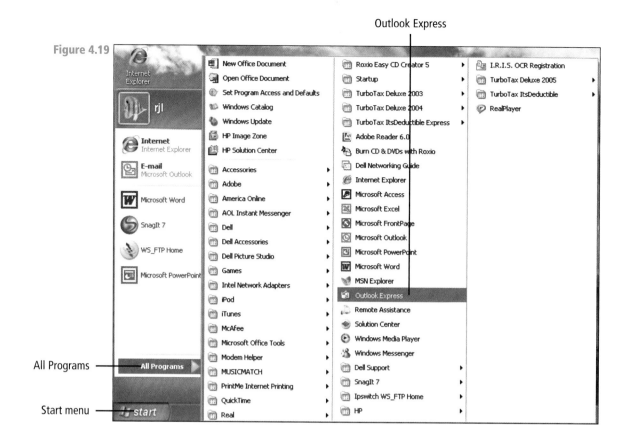

All Programs

Start menu

How do I configure Outlook Express? After Outlook Express is started, it must be configured—or set up—before you can begin to send and receive e-mail. The first time you start the program, a wizard displays to help you configure it. After configuring the program, you need to supply your user ID and password each time you start up the program to access your e-mail with Outlook Express.

You need to know several pieces of information to complete the wizard. If you do not already know some of the information, such as the mail server name and the protocols used, you should contact your ISP to find the information. The information you will need to know to complete the wizard is:

• Your e-mail address

• Your user ID and password

• The names of both the incoming and outgoing mail servers

• The protocols used on the mail servers (SMTP, POP3, IMAP, or HTTP)

After completing the wizard, you can add additional accounts or modify existing accounts in Outlook Express. There are several options available to customize the Outlook Express layout so that you can manage your e-mail efficiently.

Web-Based E-mail Systems

What are the features of Web-based e-mail systems? Web-based e-mail systems provide most of the basic features you find in client-based e-mail systems. Typically, you can send and receive e-mail, use spell check, create folders, maintain an address book, and include attachments with e-mail messages. Many providers offer message filtering, spam blocking, and virus protection. Some also provide advanced features such as voice mail or the ability to send e-mail messages to a mobile device.

What are advantages of Web-based e-mail systems? Web-based e-mail systems enable you to send and receive e-mail from any computer that has an Internet connection. This is an important advantage for people who travel frequently or who use multiple computers. Your e-mail messages are not downloaded and stored on the computer you use to access your Web-based e-mail account so the messages can be accessed wherever you go or from whatever computer you choose. You do not have to own a computer to use Web-based e-mail because you can access it at any Internet-connected computer such as computers found at the library, school computer lab, or wherever you can access public computers.

Many people use Web-based e-mail accounts as their primary e-mail accounts. Others use Web-based e-mail accounts to communicate with friends and family instead of using a work-related account. Still other people open Web-based e-mail accounts to help shield their identity when they visit online auction sites, buy products, or participate in online discussion groups. Having a separate Web-based e-mail account for these purposes prevents spam from being sent to your work-related e-mail account.

How do I get a Web-based e-mail account? Most Web-based e-mail systems provide free service. The service can be provided free of charge to the user because the Web-based e-mail provider sells advertising. Advertisers purchase ads that display in the interface of e-mail users' accounts as pop-ups and banner ads. You can usually upgrade to a fee-based account that will eliminate the ads if you find them annoying.

There are several providers for Web-based e-mail systems. Among the most popular are Yahoo! Mail, Gmail, and MSN Hotmail. The table in Figure 4.20 shows several providers and their Web site addresses.

Web-Based E-mail Providers and Their Web Site Addresses

Web-Based E-mail Provider	URL
AOL Mail	http://webmail.aol.com
Fastmail	http://www.fastmail.fm
Gmail	http://gmail.google.com
Lycos Mail	http://mail.lycos.com
Mail.com	http://www.mail.com
MSN Hotmail	http://www.hotmail.com
Yahoo! Mail	http://mail.yahoo.com

Figure 4.20

You start a Web-based e-mail account by visiting the Web site of the provider to request an account. You do not have to configure your computer to use a Web-based e-mail system as you do with a client-based e-mail system. After the account is established, you can access your e-mail by connecting to the Internet and then going to the provider's Web site. You must type in your user ID and password before you can send and receive your e-mail.

Features of E-mail Systems

What features do e-mail systems offer?   At a minimum, these features should include plenty of storage space—many providers offer at least 1 gigabyte (GB) of storage. Other desirable features include a well-designed and easy-to-use interface, antivirus protection, and *spam* filtering. Spam is unsolicited and unwanted e-mail sent to several recipients at once generally for the purpose of advertising.

What is an address book?   Most providers enable you to create an *address book*. To send an e-mail message, you must address the e-mail message. Recall that an address book is a feature that stores the names and e-mail addresses of your friends, colleagues, or other contacts that you would like to communicate with using e-mail. Most providers enable you to create folders to organize your mail; some also provide a search function for locating e-mails based on the date or by keywords in the message. Other providers enable you to manage multiple accounts or forward your Web-based e-mail to another e-mail client or a mobile device. Many providers now integrate other forms of online communication into the e-mail client such as:

- Calendaring—*Calendaring* is a feature that tracks events and alerts you when an event's time and date has arrived. Often calendaring features enable you to create a group calendar that all group members can access.

- Chat—Recall that chat is an interactive, text-based synchronous discussion among two or more participants performed using an Internet-connected computer and specialized software.

- Instant messaging—Recall that IM is also an interactive, text-based synchronous discussion similar to chat, however usually only two people are participating within one window.

- Photo sharing—*Photo sharing* is a feature that enables you to upload digital photos so that the photos can be viewed by others as part of a Web page.

- Voice messaging—*Voice messaging* is a feature that enables you to record and send a digital voice message in place of an e-mail message.

E-mail Protocols

What protocols are necessary for e-mail systems to work correctly?
The two types of e-mail systems perform similar functions—communicating electronically—but do so in very different ways. Both systems use

protocols to exchange information, but each system uses a different protocol. Recall that a protocol is a common set of rules for how computers communicate and exchange information. Several protocols help e-mail systems work correctly. **Simple Mail Transfer Protocol**, or **SMTP**, is the protocol that handles outgoing messages and routes them to their destination. SMTP looks carefully at the e-mail address for the domain name. SMTP then uses **name resolution** to determine the IP address where the e-mail message should be sent. Recall that name resolution is the translation performed by the Domain Name System (DNS) that translates a text-based URL into a numeric IP address for the purpose of locating the computer being requested. In this case, the e-mail address is used in place of a text-based URL.

The e-mail message is broken down into data packets and sent along the Internet to the destination. After the data packets of the e-mail message arrive at the correct IP address, they are reassembled into an e-mail message on a mail server. The incoming message can be handled by three other protocols depending on the type of e-mail system that is used. Two of the protocols, POP3 and IMAP, work with client-based e-mail systems.

• **Post Office Protocol 3**, or **POP3**, is a protocol that enables the e-mail client to connect to the mail server and download all of the messages being stored for that e-mail address to the user's computer. Typically, after the messages are downloaded, they are removed from the POP3 server and can be read only from that user's computer.

• **Internet Message Access Protocol**, or **IMAP**, handles incoming a bit differently. IMAP is the protocol that enables the e-mail client to read and manage e-mail messages using the user's computer but the messages remain stored on the server. Because the messages remain stored on the server, the user can read their e-mail messages from several different computers without losing any messages.

Incoming Web-based e-mail systems work with the third protocol, **Hypertext Transfer Protocol**, or **HTTP**. Recall that HTTP is the protocol used to carry the request from the Web browser on the client computer to the server computer, and then to transport pages from the server computer back to the client computer. With Web-based e-mail systems, the request is for e-mail messages.

When using a Web-based e-mail system, your e-mail is sent as hypertext markup language (HTML), using an HTTP server so you do not need a POP3 or IMAP server. A Web site provides the access to the e-mail messages so that e-mail can be read at any computer that has Internet access and has a Web browser installed.

What protocol handles attachments? E-mail attachments are handled by **Multipurpose Internet Mail Extensions**, or **MIME**. MIME is a protocol that takes care of decoding non-text documents such as images, audio, and video files that may be attached to e-mail messages. When the attachments are opened, MIME makes sure the attachments open and display using the correct software program for that file type.

Objective 8
Identify Appropriate E-mail Netiquette

What is netiquette? *Network etiquette*, or *netiquette*, is a set of principles developed to express courtesy and to help people act appropriately while sending e-mail and using the Internet. E-mail is a written form of communication with its meaning coming from the interpretation of the recipient. Misunderstanding an e-mail message is easy to do and can cause problems in work environments, among family members, and numerous other circumstances. Netiquette helps to prevent those types of misunderstandings.

Netiquette Guidelines

What are some netiquette guidelines? Several netiquette guidelines exist. These guidelines include:

- Use a descriptive subject line and signature to help the recipient know who is sending the message and why he is sending it. Never leave the subject line blank as it is considered rude to do so.

- Keep the message body short and focused on the main topic.

- Use the spell check feature of your e-mail client so the recipient will understand what you are trying to say.

- DO NOT TYPE with all capital letters. It is the online equivalent of **shouting** or raising your voice. You can add emphasis to certain words in your e-mails by surrounding them with a pair of *asterisks* or _underscores_.

- Do not forward chain letters, executable files, or unsolicited messages for entertainment value. Because these types of messages may carry viruses, it is recommended to enable your antivirus software to scan all incoming and outgoing e-mail messages.

- Always remember there is a person on the other end of the message. Choose your words carefully so that your e-mail message is respectful and carries the message that you intend to send.

- Be aware of all recipients' perspectives when sending an e-mail to a group. Phrase your ideas appropriately for the entire group and do not spread gossip.

Expressing Emotion in E-mail

What are emoticons? An *emoticon* is a series of keyboard characters, text, or inline images that create a face to represent an emotion. Emoticons are used in e-mail messages, instant messaging, or chat because they express the emotions of the sender. Emoticons should only be used in informal communications. Most emoticons must be viewed by tilting your head to the left to visualize a face showing the emotion. More recent versions of e-mail clients automatically convert the series of keyboard characters into a small graphic showing the emotion. Some common emoticons and their meanings are shown in Figure 4.21.

Common Emoticons and Their Meanings

Emoticon	Meaning
:-{	I'm angry.
:-!	I'm bored.
:-S	I'm confused.
:")	I'm embarrassed.
:-/	I'm frustrated.
:-D	I'm laughing.
:-(	I'm sad.
:-)	I'm smiling or happy.
:-O	I'm surprised.
;-)	I'm winking.

Figure 4.21

Acronyms and Text Shortcuts

What are acronyms? An *acronym* is a series of letters that stand for the first letter of words in a phrase. It takes much longer to type a message than it does to speak the message. An acronym is a way to make communication easier. Like emoticons, acronyms should be used only in informal communications. The main disadvantage with using an acronym is that the recipient may not know what the letters stand for and so the meaning becomes obscured. Figure 4.22 shows some common acronyms and their meanings.

Common Acronyms and Their Meanings

Acronym	Meaning
AAF	As a friend.
AFC	Away from computer.
BAC	Back at computer.
BTW	By the way.
ETA	Estimated time of arrival.
FYI	For your information.
HAND	Have a nice day.
IBRB	I will be right back.
IMHO	In my humble opinion.
LOL	Laughing out loud.

Figure 4.22

How are text shortcuts different from acronyms? *Text shortcuts* are a way to shorten communication using a series of letters that sound like the word they stand for. Both acronyms and text shortcuts may be used in informal e-mails to friends and family, but they are not recommended for use in business e-mails. Figure 4.23 shows some text shortcuts and their meanings.

Common Text Shortcuts and Their Meaning

Text Shortcut	Meaning
AAR8	At any rate.
B4	Before.
CU	See you.
GR8	Great.
Kewl	Cool.
L8R	Later.
NRG	Energy.
OIC	Oh, I see.
PLS	Please.
TNX	Thanks.

Figure 4.23

Objective 9
Minimize Nuisances Associated with E-mail

What kind of nuisances are associated with e-mail? It is important to be aware of nuisances that are associated with e-mail. Several types of e-mail messages can be considered nuisances and can pose risks. These nuisances include spam, the transmission of hoax e-mail messages, phishing schemes, and virus attacks.

All of these types of e-mail are costly for the general public and for businesses in terms of lost time and productivity. Identifying and deleting these types of e-mail takes a lot of time and takes a lot of storage space on the mail servers.

What is spam? Unsolicited e-mail marketing, or spam, is a major problem on the Web. Recall that spam is unsolicited and unwanted e-mail sent to many recipients at once generally for the purpose of advertising and is the electronic equivalent of junk or bulk mail. Individuals, organizations, and companies purchase marketing lists that contain thousands of e-mail addresses and then send spam to everyone on the list.

Typically, spam is sent by automatic programs that make it difficult to track the exact location of origination. Spam can originate from any country but research shows spam most often comes from the United States, China, Russia, Japan, Canada, and South Korea.

How can I protect myself from spam? You need to be cautious when giving out your e-mail address online. Filling out an online form or joining an online discussion group can put you on one or more marketing lists that are used for spam. Always check the privacy policy of any Web site requesting your e-mail address to see how your address will used and with whom it will be shared.

You can set filters for your e-mail account to filter out e-mails containing keywords that are commonly used in spam messages. The most commonly advertised products in spam messages include prescription drugs, mortgage offers, stock market tips, and pornography sites.

You can install spam-blocking software on your computers to help minimize the onslaught of spam. However, even with these programs some spam messages may still be delivered.

What else is being done about spam? Spam has become such a major issue that legislation has been introduced to try to resolve the problem. Legislation, such as the CAN-SPAM Act, has been introduced to deal with firms sending spam by establishing rules about the types of e-mail that can be sent. Consumers can file a complaint with the Federal Trade Commission Bureau of Consumer Protection regarding any spam they receive. Other countries have established similar legislation.

What is a hoax? A *hoax* is an e-mail making false statements or outrageous offers. Like spam, this type of e-mail is costly and causes lost time and productivity. Typically, a hoax will offer something too good to be true such as a free trip to Europe if you send a small amount of money to cover administrative expenses. Other hoaxes play on your sympathies by asking you to donate to fraudulent charities. Some hoaxes are sent so many times that they become *urban legends*. An urban legend is a story or hoax that has been circulated for extended time periods and may actually have been acted on by recipients of the e-mail. There are several Web sites where you can check about the authenticity of any e-mail if you have doubts about any e-mail you receive. Figure 4.24 give the names of some helpful Web sites and their URLs where you can check for hoaxes or urban legends.

Checking for Hoaxes and Urban Legends

Web Site	URL
About.com The Urban Legends and Folklore	*http://urbanlegends.about.com*
dmoz Open Directory Project	*http://dmoz.org/Society/Folklore/Literature/Urban_Legends*
HOAXBUSTERS	*http://hoaxbusters.ciac.org*
McAfee Virus Hoax	*http://vil.mcafee.com/hoax.asp*
ScamBusters.org	*http://www.scambusters.org*
Snopes.com	*http://www.snopes.com*
Sophos Hoaxes	*http://www.sophos.com/security/hoaxes*
Symantec Hoaxes	*http://www.symantec.com/avcenter/hoax.html*

Figure 4.24

What is the problem with phishing? *Phishing* is the practice of sending an e-mail that attempts to illegally solicit personal information by requesting information for account verification, passwords, account numbers, or other personal data. The e-mail may appear to come from an official entity such as a bank or credit card company because it may contain the logo of the business or refer you to a Web site that appears legitimately associated with that business or organization. If you receive a suspicious e-mail, you can call the organization to make sure the e-mail is legitimate. However, most organizations—banks, credit card companies, or a company who would have reason to ask about your credit card account number—do not use e-mail to communicate with you about your account or your password, or to verify other personal information.

How can I prevent virus attacks? Although viruses can get into your computer from downloading infected program files, they also come through e-mail messages and attachments. A virus can be transmitted to your computer when you click a link sent to you in an e-mail message. The link may appear to go to a Web site that you are interested in but may actually lead to an executable file that starts a viral infection. Viruses are also spread by attachments carrying executable files.

Use caution when clicking links within e-mail messages or opening attachments sent to you. Make sure they are from a reputable, credible, and trustworthy source and that they are sent to you with your permission. To prevent viruses from causing damage, keep your antivirus software up-to-date. Set your antivirus program to scan all e-mail and attachments for viruses. Delete any e-mail without opening it from any sender you do not recognize.

End You have completed Project 4C ————————————————

Project 4C

Take the online self-study quiz for this chapter:

1. Go to **www.prenhall.com/go** and select the textbook *GO!* **with the Internet**.

2. Select **chapter 4**.

3. Select **Self-Study Quiz Project 4C**.

Project 4D **Exploring Mailing Lists and Newsletters**

Not only is e-mail used for personal and business communications, but it is also used for community interest, education, and public service. Mailing lists, listservs, and newsletters are efficient means of communicating because several people—from two to two thousand or more—receive the same information from a single e-mail. Mailing lists, listservs, and newsletters are different from spam because the recipients have requested to receive the e-mail messages. In Objectives 10 and 11, you will explore mailings lists, listservs, and newsletters.

Objective 10
Explore Mailing Lists

What is a mailing list?   A *mailing list*, or *listserv*, is a subscription-based list of several names and e-mail addresses combined under one e-mail address generally managed by software and used for the discussion of specific topic areas. Many schools use listservs to keep in contact with their alumni. Clubs and other organizations also use mailing lists. Listservs may be used to conduct research by searching the archives of a mailing list for information on any specialized topic you are interested in. For example, to learn more about marketing imports, it may be useful to be part of a listserv focused on marketing, particular countries, or specific product types.

The use of mailing lists is an efficient method for sharing information. When an e-mail is sent to the mailing list address, everyone who is part of that mailing list receives the same message at nearly the same time. In addition, any reply made to that original e-mail is received by everyone on the mailing list. In other words, every message and every reply is made available to everyone on the list.

Many mailing lists archive all messages sent on the mailing list so that they can be referred to again. The archives are stored by the mailing list on servers and can be accessed at Web sites that provide an **internal search engine**. An internal search engine is a search engine that indexes only a particular Web site in order to create a search results list that contains only results from that Web site. For example, Tile.Net's search engine enables you to narrow your search to just Tile.Net. Some mailing lists permit their archives to be visible to any search engines. For that type of mailing list, messages may turn up in a search result list from a search conducted at Google, Yahoo!, or any other search engine.

What does a mailing list manager do?   A *mailing list manager* is a software program installed on a server that handles accepting messages and *posting* them on the list. Posting is the act of sending an e-mail messages to a mailing list or listserv. An individual message is called a *post*. The mailing list manager sends these messages to everyone who is part of the list and processes requests from the list members to subscribe or unsubscribe from the list. *Majordomo* and *LISTSERV* are two

Project 4D: Exploring Mailing Lists and Newsletters | **Internet**   247 programs that are commonly used to manage mailing lists. The server where the mailing list manager software is installed is called the **list server**. For this reason mailing lists are also referred to as *listservs*.

What is a moderated list?   Some mailing lists are moderated; others are unmoderated lists. A **moderated list** is a mailing list where all messages are screened by a human—the **moderator**—before being enabled to be sent to a mailing list. The moderator may determine some posts need editing before being enabled to be sent to the list. Other postings may be deleted and not enabled on to the rest of the mailing list members.

In an **unmoderated list**, messages are not screened before they are posted—sent out—to all members of the mailing list. Any message or reply sent on an unmoderated list will automatically be sent to all of the members of the list.

What is a closed list?   For some lists, a moderator reviews all requests to join the mailing list and approves or denies list membership requests. This is known as a **closed list**. In an **open list**, requests to join a mailing list are not screened by a moderator. An open list accepts everyone who tries to join the list by using the correct commands.

Finding Mailing Lists

Where can I find a mailing list?   Mailing lists support specific discussion topics that range from professional interests such as business and finance discussions to hobby-oriented interests such as crafting leather goods. There are several ways to find a mailing list. You can find a mailing list to join by searching through Web sites such as Tile.Net or CataList that are set up specifically to house large collections of mailing lists.

You can also use a search engine to help you locate a mailing list. You can type the topic and the words mailing list at a search engine Web site. You can further refine your search results by using the advanced search feature of the search engine.

After you have located and joined a mailing list, use your e-mail account to send and receive messages on the mailing list.

Are there any Web-based mailing lists?   Some lists enable you to subscribe by using either your e-mail address or by using the Web site as the mailing list interface. Web-based mailing lists are easy to use and provide additional features such as photo sharing and polling features. You can start your own mailing list at these Web sites as well.

Typically, Web-based mailing lists are open and unmoderated. Anyone can join the mailing list and any post is accepted. Because of this, you may discover messages that are unrelated to the topic of the mailing list.

With Web-based mailing lists, it is a good idea to join them using an alternate e-mail address protect your primary e-mail account. The table in Figure 4.25 shows the names and addresses for Web sites where you can find information on searching for, joining, or creating your own mailing lists.

Mailing List Providers

Where To Find Mailing Lists	URL
Bravenet Mailing Lists	*http://www.bravenet.com/webtools*
CataList	*http://www.lsoft.com/lists/listref.html*
Google Groups	*http://groups.google.com*
Tile.Net	*http://tile.net/lists*
Topica	*http://lists.topica.com*
Yahoo! Groups	*http://groups.yahoo.com*

Figure 4.25

Subscribing and Unsubscribing to Mailing Lists

Why are there two e-mail addresses associated with a mailing list?
Mailing lists have two e-mail addresses that are used. Before you can participate in a mailing list, you must subscribe to the list. To subscribe to a mailing list, you send an e-mail message to the ***administrative address***. The administrative address is reserved for sending commands such as *Subscribe* and *Unsubscribe* to the mailing list. E-mail sent to the administrative address is only received by the mailing list manager or the moderator if it is a moderated list. In the case of unmoderated lists, no one reviews the request; the mailing list manager automatically takes care of the request.

The other address used in a mailing list is the ***list address***, which is the e-mail address used for posting messages and replying to messages. Everyone who is on the mailing list will see the messages sent to the list address. If you happen to use the wrong e-mail address for the wrong task, you may get flamed. A ***flame*** is an abusive or insulting e-mail sent to someone on the list. For example, if you use the list address to ask to unsubscribe from the mailing list instead of using the administrative address, everyone subscribed to the list will see your post. You may get flamed by another mailing list member because you should have used the administrative address for that type of request.

After you have subscribed to a mailing list, it is a good idea to ***lurk*** for a while to get a feel for the type of messages that are being sent. When you lurk, you receive and read the posts, but you do not reply to any of them. On many lists, it is possible to lurk and read posts without being a member of the mailing list. However, if you want to create your own post, you must subscribe to the list. Lurking helps you get oriented to the culture of the list by enabling you to observe the type of discussion that is taking place. If you feel comfortable with the mailing list discussion, you can reply and contribute to the discussion by adding posts. If you do not feel comfortable, you can unsubscribe from the mailing list and try another one. There are literally thousands of lists created for any given topic so there is no reason to remain subscribed to a list that you do not consider useful or interesting.

How do I subscribe and unsubscribe from a mailing list? The e-mail messages sent for subscribing and unsubscribing have very little content but are structured in a very specific way. Lists may have different rules for subscribing and unsubscribing. Typically unless you are joining a Web-based mailing list, the To line should be addressed to the administrative address for the mailing list.

For many lists, the list rules dictate that the Subject line should be left intentionally blank. In the message body, you type the word *Subscribe* and the *name of the list*. For other lists, these rules vary and you put the word *Subscribe* in the Subject line and leave the message body blank. Figure 4.26 shows an example of how you might address an e-mail asking to subscribe to a mailing list.

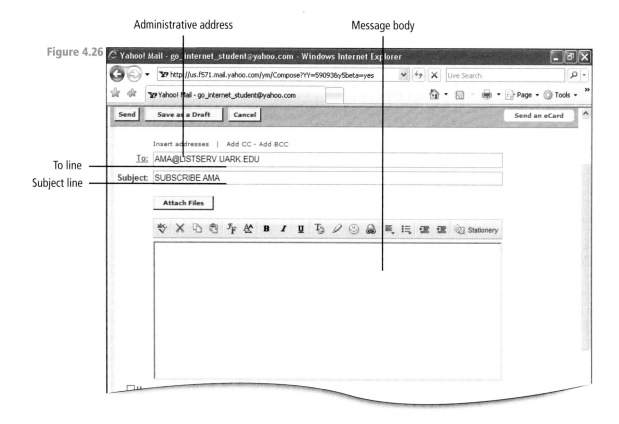

Figure 4.26

Whatever the rules are for a particular list, if you compose and send the Subscribe e-mail correctly, the mailing list manager or moderator sends a confirmation e-mail. You must confirm that you do want to join the list by replying to it within a set period of time—usually 24 hours. After confirming you want to join the mailing list, you will receive an e-mail from the mailing list manager or moderator welcoming you to the mailing list. The welcome e-mail provides instructions for using the list such as the list rules. It also provides the correct syntax for commands that can be used at the list.

To unsubscribe from the mailing list, you must follow the same rules for composing the e-mail as you did when you subscribed. You send an e-mail message with the administrative address in the To line and then put the word *Unsubscribe* in either the Subject line or message body of the e-mail. If you compose and send this e-mail correctly you will receive a confirmation e-mail message that you have been removed from the mailing list.

Mailing List Commands

What are mailing list commands? Both *Subscribe* and *Unsubscribe* are examples of commands. Mailing list commands help you manage the volume of e-mail messages generated by a mailing list. Other commands can be used to let you know who is on the mailing list and their e-mail addresses. However, you can hide your name and address on a mailing list to protect your privacy using another command.

Most mailing lists generate a lot of e-mail. You may find it helpful to use the *Digest* command to request that all of the messages generated by the mailing list each day be sent to you once as a single message instead of being sent one at a time.

Not all mailing lists enable the use of all commands. When you join a mailing list, the welcome e-mail will provide a list of commands accepted by that mailing list. Figure 4.27 summarizes several commonly used commands in a generic format. Recall that each mailing has its own syntax preferences for writing commands. In addition, when using each command, you must replace *listname* with the correct name of the list.

A Summary of Mailing List Commands

Commands	Task Performed by the Command
REVIEW listname	Enables you to see the names and addresses of mailing list members.
SET listname conceal	Hides your name and address from members using the Review command.
SET listname digest	Enables you to receive a single message that contains all of the posts for a day instead of getting each post separately.
SET listname noconceal	Un-hides your name and address from members using the Review command.
SUBSCRIBE listname	Enables you to subscribe to a mailing list.
UNSUBSCRIBE listname or SIGNOFF listname	Enables you to unsubscribe from a mailing list.

Figure 4.27

Objective 11
Find Special Interest Newsletters

What is a newsletter?   A *newsletter* is an electronic publication regularly sent out to subscribers to provide information on a specific topic. Some newsletters are free of charge, others are paid subscriptions. Newsletters can be oriented toward marketing, news, partisan politics, hobbies, or any other specialized areas of interest. A newsletter is similar to a mailing list because it arrives by e-mail and is sent to many subscribers at once. However, newsletters are different from spam because the recipients have requested to *opt-in* or receive these types of e-mails.

How can I find a newsletter?   Often newsletters are offered at Web sites as a special service. For example, many online news sites will offer newsletters notifying you of breaking news or other news articles on a specific topic sent directly to your e-mail address.

You find newsletters by using methods similar to those used to finding mailing lists. Just as with a mailing list, you can locate newsletters by using a search engine. You type the topic and the word *newsletter* at the search engine. You can further refine your search results by using the advance search feature of the search engine. In addition, there are several Web sites providing large listings or a searchable database of available newsletters. Figure 4.28 gives the URLs for several newsletters and listing sites.

A Summary of Newsletter Listings

Newsletter Resources	URL
CNET	*http://nl.com.com/gen_login.jsp?brand=cnet*
InfoWorld	*http://subscribe.infoworld.com*
JupiterMedia Newsletters	*http://e-newsletters.internet.com*
MarketResearch Newsletter	*http://www.marketresearch.com*
MediaFinder	*http://www.mediafinder.com*
MSNBC Newsletters	*http://www.msnbc.msn.com/id/7422001*
Newsletter Access Directory	*http://www.newsletteraccess.com*

Figure 4.28

How can I receive a newsletter?   After you find a newsletter that sounds interesting, you must subscribe to the newsletter before you can receive it. Subscriptions are handled in a couple of ways. Typically, for newsletters offered as a special service at a Web site, you simply will need to fill out a short form and submit it online at that Web site. If you find out about the newsletter at one of the large listing sites, you may also be able to subscribe by simply filling out a form at that Web site.

Other newsletters can be accessed from listing sites that provide the name of the newsletter, the frequency of publication, and an e-mail address where you write and ask to subscribe to the newsletter.

Information on how to unsubscribe from a newsletter is often provided near the bottom of each newsletter message. If you subscribed to the newsletter by clicking a link at a Web site, you may be able to unsubscribe by clicking a link at the same Web site you used to subscribe. For other newsletters, you must send an e-mail asking to be taken off the newsletter subscription list.

End **You have completed Project 4D** ———————————

Online Quiz

Project 4D

Take the online self-study quiz for this chapter:

1. Go to **www.prenhall.com/go** and select the textbook *GO!* **with the Internet.**

2. Select **chapter 4.**

3. Select **Self-Study Quiz Project 4D**.

Assessments

Summary

In this chapter, you set up and used a Web-based e-mail account. You composed a basic e-mail message and added an attachment before sending the message. You sent a carbon copy of the e-mail message. You created a signature file. You added a name to the address book. You signed out of your Web-based e-mail account and signed back into your account. You received an e-mail and opened its attachment. You replied, and forwarded the e-mail message. You printed the e-mail message. You managed your e-mail account by creating folders and filters. Then you used a filter to put e-mail into a folder. You deleted e-mail from your account and signed out of it. You compared e-mail systems and the protocols needed to run them. You identified appropriate netiquette and nuisances associated with e-mail. You found out where to locate and use mailing lists, listservs, and special interest newsletters.

Key Terms

Acronym 243

Address Book 240

Administrative address 249

As Attachment 227

As Inline Text 227

Asynchronous communication 208

"At" sign (@) 209

Attachment 214

Blind carbon copy (Bcc) 215

Blind courtesy copy (Bcc) 215

Bulk folder 230

Calendaring 240

Carbon copy (Cc) 215

Client-based e-mail system 237

Closed list 248

Completely Automated Public Turing test to tell Computers and Humans Apart (CAPTCHA) 212

Courtesy copy (Cc) ..215

Draft folder 230

Electronic mail (or e-mail) 208

E-mail address 209

E-mail client 222

Emoticon 242

Executable file 225

Filters 230

Flame 249

Folder 208

Forward 227

From line 223

Hoax 245

Host name 209

Hypertext Transfer Protocol (HTTP) 241

Inbox 208

Internal search engine 247

Internet Message Access Protocol (IMAP) 241

List address 249

LISTSERV 247

Listserv 247

List server 248

Lurk 249

Mail header 214

Mail server 222

Mailing list 247

Mailing list manager 247

Majordomo 247

Message body 214

Microsoft Outlook ..237

Moderated list 248

Moderator 248

Multipurpose Internet Mail Extension (MIME) 241

Name resolution 241

Network etiquette (or Netiquette) 242

Newsletter 252

Open list 248

Opt-in 252

Outlook Express 237

Password 210

Phishing 246

Photo sharing 240

Post 247

(Continued)

Assessments

Internet
chapter four

Key Terms

Posting 247

Post Office Protocol 3
(POP3) 241

Printer-friendly
version 229

Protocol 241

Reply 225

Reply To Everyone 225

Reply To Sender 225

Sent folder 230

Shouting 242

Signature file 219

Simple Mail
Transfer Protocol
(SMTP) 241

Spam 240

Subject line 216

Text shortcut 244

To line 215

Trash folder 230

Unmoderated list 248

Urban legend 245

User ID 209

Virus 225

Voice messaging 240

Web-based
e-mail system 237

Assessments

Matching

Match each term in the second column with its correct definition in the first column by writing the letter of the term on the blank line in front of the correct definition.

_____ **1.** A service that provides for the exchange of messages and documents over the Internet or over an organization's network.

_____ **2.** An e-mail folder that stores e-mail that you have deleted until you empty this folder.

_____ **3.** The default folder in an e-mail system where incoming messages are placed.

_____ **4.** A unique name that identifies who uses the e-mail account.

_____ **5.** The name of the server where e-mail is received and stored within the organization and the domain name of the organization.

_____ **6.** An e-mail component, located at the top of the e-mail message, that contains information about the e-mail message such the sender's e-mail address, the recipient's e-mail address, and the subject.

_____ **7.** An e-mail component that provides the name and e-mail address of the recipient or recipients of the e-mail message.

_____ **8.** An e-mail component listing a person who will receive an e-mail message but whose name is only visible to the sender and that person.

_____ **9.** Additional files sent along with the e-mail message to support the meaning or subject matter of the e-mail.

_____ **10.** A software program that is used to compose, send, and receive e-mail messages.

_____ **11.** An e-mail component that indicates the name or user ID of the sender of the e-mail.

_____ **12.** A file that you create and is automatically added to every e-mail you send.

_____ **13.** Large computers that receive, store, and send e-mail messages.

_____ **14.** An e-mail feature that sends a message you have received and modified, or in its original entirety, to another recipient.

_____ **15.** An e-mail feature that is used to automatically sort your e-mail messages into folders as the messages arrive in the Inbox.

A Attachment

B Blind carbon copy or Bcc

C Electronic mail or e-mail

D E-mail client

E Filters

F Forward

G From line

H Host name

I Inbox

J Mail header

K Mail server

L Signature file

M To line

N Trash folder

O User ID

Assessments

Fill in the Blank

Write the correct answer in the space provided.

1. An e-mail feature used to collect, organize, and store your e-mail is called a(n) _____.

2. A feature that stores the names and e-mail addresses of your friends, colleagues, or other contacts that you would like to communicate with using e-mail is called a(n) _____.

3. A code used to specify where and to whom to send and receive e-mail is called a(n) _____.

4. A character that is always part of an e-mail address and separates the user ID from the host name is called the _____.

5. A string of characters—letters, numbers and punctuation—that is used in combination with a user ID to verify authorization to use a network, server or computer is called a(n) _____.

6. An e-mail component containing the content of the e-mail message is called a(n) _____.

7. An e-mail component that lists people who will receive a copy of the e-mail message for informational purposes is called a(n) _____.

8. An e-mail component created by the sender that summarizes in a couple of words the main idea of the e-mail message is called a(n) _____.

9. An e-mail client's feature that tracks events and alerts you when an event's time and date has arrived is called a(n) _____.

10. An e-mail folder that stores e-mail messages that you have composed but not yet sent is called a(n) _____.

11. An e-mail client's feature that enables you to record a digital voice message in place of an e-mail message is called _____.

12. Your electronic response to an e-mail message that enables you to send the original e-mail and additional information or comments back to the sender is called a(n) _____.

13. An e-mail folder that stores a copy of all of the e-mail messages that you send out is called a(n) _____.

14. A program that the computer runs directly from the file is called a(n) _____.

15. An e-mail message formatted without ads or other Inbox features showing so that the message will fit well on standard printer paper is called a(n) _____.

Assessments

Internet
chapter four

Rubric

Projects 4A and 4B in the front portion of this chapter, and Projects 4E through 4J that follow, have no specific correct result; your result will depend on your approach to the information provided. Make Professional Quality your goal. Use the following scoring rubric to guide you in how to approach the search problem and then to evaluate how well your approach solves the search problem.

The criteria—Internet Mastery, Content, Format and Layout of Search Results, and Process—represent the knowledge and skills you have gained that you can apply to solving the search problem. The levels of performance—Professional Quality, Approaching Professional Quality, or Needs Quality Improvements—help you and your instructor evaluate your result.

	Your completed project is of Professional Quality if you:	Your completed project is Approaching Professional Quality if you:	Your completed project Needs Quality Improvements if you:
1–Internet Mastery	Choose and apply the most appropriate search skills, tools, and features and identify efficient methods to conduct the search and locate valid results.	Choose and apply some appropriate search skills, tools, and features, but not in the most efficient manner.	Choose inappropriate search skills, tools, or features, or are inefficient in locating valid results.
2–Content	Conduct a search that is clear and well organized, contains results that are accurate, appropriate to the audience and purpose, and are complete.	Conduct a search in which some results are unclear, poorly organized, inconsistent, or incomplete. Misjudge the needs of the audience.	Conduct a search that is unclear, incomplete, or poorly organized, containing some inaccurate or inappropriate content.
3–Format and Layout of Search Results	Format and arrange all search results to communicate information and ideas, clarify function, illustrate relationships, and indicate relative importance.	Apply appropriate format and layout features to some search results, but not others. Overuse search techniques, causing minor distraction.	Apply format and layout that does not communicate the search results clearly. Do not use format and layout features to clarify function, illustrate relationships, or indicate relative importance. Use available search techniques excessively, causing distraction.
4–Process	Use an organized approach that integrates planning, development, self-assessment, revision, and reflection.	Demonstrate an organized approach in some areas, but not others; or, use an insufficient process of organization throughout.	Do not use an organized approach to solve the problem.

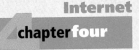

Project 4E — Searching for Web-Based E-mail Providers

Objectives: 1. *Locate and Set Up a Web-Based E-mail Account;* **7.** *Compare E-mail Systems.*

You and Cristina Mandala, Executive Administrative Assistant for the CEO of El Curero de Mexico, meet to discuss options for free Web-based e-mail accounts. Cristina sometimes accompanies her boss, Miguel Hernandez, who travels frequently for business-related matters. Cristina needs an e-mail account that can be accessed from anywhere in the world. In this Assessment, you will locate and compare the features of Web-based e-mail providers. Then you will make a recommendation for a provider for Cristina to use as she travels.

For Project 4E, you will need the following file:

New blank Notepad document

You will save your file as
4E_Providers_Firstname_Lastname

1. **Start** Internet Explorer and if necessary, click the **Maximize** button to enlarge the window to fill the computer screen completely. In the **Address bar**, click one time to select the existing text, type **http://www.e-mailaddresses.com** and then press [Enter] The **E-mailAddresses.com** home page displays. E-mailAddresses.com provides a directory of e-mail services providers, information on how to find e-mail addresses of friends and family and tips on using e-mail.

2. On the right side of the window, locate and click the **Free web mail** link. Scroll down the **Web-based E-mail Providers A-D** Web page to view the providers listed. At the bottom of the Web page, notice the section labeled **More Reviews**, and then click each of the links to continue your review until you have seen all of the providers. Among the providers, choose two providers that you are familiar with or that you are interested in finding out more about and make note of the cost, storage quotas, spam protection, and any other features for each provider.

3. **Start** Notepad and if necessary, click the **Maximize** button to enlarge the window to fill the computer screen completely. At the blinking insertion point in the **Notepad** window, type **4E_Providers_Firstname_Lastname** Press [Enter] two times to create a new line. Type the name of the first e-mail provider, and then type the URL of the e-mail provider's Web site. Press [Enter] two times to create a blank line. Write a brief paragraph summarizing the costs, storage

(Project 4E–Searching for Web-Based E-mail Providers continues on the next page)

Assessments

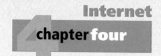

Mastering the Internet

(Project 4E–Searching for Web-Based E-mail Providers continued)

quotas, spam protection, and any unique features. Press Enter two times to create a blank line. Type the name of the second e-mail provider, and then type the URL of the e-mail provider's Web site. Press the Enter key two times to create a blank line. Summarize the costs, storage quotas, spam protection, and any unique features for the second provider.

4. Add the **footer 4E_Providers_Firstname_ Lastname** to the document. Then **save** your document as **4E_Providers_Firstname_ Lastname** in the storage location you set up for this chapter's work.

5. Check your *Chapter Assignment Sheet* or *Course Syllabus* or consult your instructor to determine if you are to submit your assignments by printing on paper, or electronically by using your college's course information management system—for example, Blackboard or WebCT. To print on paper from Notepad, under the **File** menu item, click **Print**. To submit electronically, follow the instructions provided by your instructor.

6. **Close** the **Notepad** window. **Close** the **Internet Explorer** window.

End **You have completed Project 4E**

Assessments

Mastering the Internet

Project 4F — Searching for a Mailing List by Using CataList

Objectives: 2. *Compose and Send a Basic E-mail Message;* **3.** *Receive and Reply to an E-mail Message with an Attachment;* **4.** *Print an E-mail Message;* **10.** *Explore Mailing Lists.*

Richard Kelly, Vice President for Marketing at El Cuero Specialty Wares, wants to join a mailing list focused on marketing products in the United States. You have been asked to help him find a mailing list that will provide this type of information. In this Assessment, you will use CataList to locate the American Marketing Association's mailing list.

For Project 4F, you will need the following file:

E-mail message printout

**You will print the message as
4F_CataList_Firstname_Lastname**

1. **Start** Internet Explorer and if necessary, click the **Maximize** button to enlarge the window to fill the computer screen completely. In the **Address bar**, click one time to select the existing text, and then type **http://www.lsoft.com/lists/listref.html** Press Enter. The **CataList** home page displays. CataList has a searchable database listing over 55,000 public mailing lists.

2. Scroll down the page slightly until you locate the section labeled **List information**. Click the **Search for a mailing list of interest** link to display the **List Search** Web page. In the **Look for** box, type **marketing** and then select the **List Name** and **List Title** check boxes. Then click the **Start the Search!** button. A search result list displays containing several names and list addresses for mailings lists with the word *marketing* in either the list name or list title.

3. Near the top of the Web page, scroll down as necessary and review the **Search Results** page until you locate the mailing list for the **American Marketing Association**. Click its link and review specific information about this list. Make note of the list name, the host name, the number of subscribers, and features of the mailing list. Note the address and command syntax to subscribe to the list. Note the administrative address.

4. Near the middle of the Web page, locate and click the **Web archive interface** link to view the archives. Click the date of the most recent archive. You will not be able to log in to view the archives unless you

(Project 4F–Searching for a Mailing List by Using CataList continues on the next page)

Assessments

Mastering the Internet

(Project 4F—Searching for a Mailing List by Using CataList continued)

are a member of the list. Click the **Back** button as needed to return to the **American Marketing Association** Web page.

5. Near the bottom of the **American Marketing Association** Web page, locate and click the **Take a look at the list's configuration** link. Note the owner of the list.

6. Using the techniques you have practiced, log into your **Yahoo! Mail** e-mail account, and compose an e-mail addressed to your e-mail address and your professor's e-mail address. Type the Subject line **4F_CataList_ Firstname_Lastname** In the message body, write a summary of the features of the American Marketing Association mailing list. Specify the list name, the host name, the number of subscribers, and features of the mailing list. Also include the address and command syntax to subscribe to the

list, the administrative address, and the list owner.

7. Using the techniques you have practiced, when it arrives in your **Inbox**, print the **4F_CataList_Firstname_Lastname** e-mail.

8. Check your *Chapter Assignment Sheet* or *Course Syllabus* or consult your instructor to determine if you are to submit your assignments by printing on paper, or electronically by using your college's course information management system—for example Blackboard or WebCT. To print on paper from Notepad, from the **File** menu, click **Print**. To submit electronically, follow the instructions provided by your instructor.

9. Log out of your **Yahoo! Mail** e-mail account and **Close** the **Internet Explorer** window.

End **You have completed Project 4F**

Assessments

Mastering the Internet

Project 4G — Signing Up for a Newsletter

Objectives: 5. *Create Folders and Filters;* **11.** *Find Special Interest Newsletters.*

Miguel Hernandez, President of El Cuero de Mexico, is preparing for his upcoming business trip to San Diego. He would like to learn more about issues associated with start-up companies in the United States. You offer to subscribe to a newsletter to learn more and then update him weekly on your findings. You explain to Miguel that the *Wall Street Journal* is a well-respected news organization for both print and online journalism. In this Assessment, you will subscribe to the Startup Journal newsletter offered through the *Wall Street Journal* Web site. Then you will create a filter and a folder in your Yahoo! Mail accounts to receive the newsletter in a folder that will let you to keep them organized as you receive them.

For Project 4G, you will need the following file:

Web page saved as a file

You will save your file as
4G_Newsletter_Firstname_Lastname

1. **Start** Internet Explorer and if necessary, click the **Maximize** button to enlarge the window to fill the computer screen completely. In the **Address bar**, click one time to select the existing text, and then type **http://www.startupjournal.com** Press Enter. The **Startup Journal The Wall Street Journal Center for Entrepreneurs** home page displays.

2. Near the bottom of the Web page, scroll to locate the section labeled **E-mail Alerts**. Click the **e-mail newsletters** link to begin the subscription process.

3. On the **E-mail Center** Web page that displays, scroll down slightly and locate the text boxes labeled **Your Name** and **Your E-mail Address**. Use your own name and e-mail address to fill in the text boxes. Scroll down and click the **On StartupJournal Today** newsletter check box. Then click the **Submit** button. A confirmation page displays.

4. Using the techniques you have practiced, **Save** the confirmation Web page as **4G_Newsletter_Firstname_Lastname** in the **Chapter_4_E-mail** folder.

5. Using the techniques you have practiced, log into your **Yahoo! Mail** account and create a folder named **Newsletters** Then create a filter

(Project 4G–Signing Up for a Newsletter continues on the next page)

Assessments

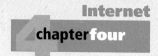

Mastering the Internet

(Project 4G–Signing Up for a Newsletter continued)

with **On StartupJournal Today** as the rule for both the **From** header and the **Subject** header. Although it may take a few days before you begin receiving your newsletters, this filter should make the newsletter arrive in the Newsletter folder instead of arriving in your Inbox.

6. After you receive a few newsletters, compose an e-mail addressed to your e-mail address and your professor's e-mail address. Type the **Subject** line **4G_Newsletter_Firstname_Lastname** In the message body, specify how long it took to begin receiving the newsletters, and whether the filter worked. Before sending the e-mail, attach the **confirmation Web page** that

you saved as **4G_Newsletter_ Firstname_Lastname**.

7. Check your *Chapter Assignment Sheet* or *Course Syllabus* or consult your instructor to determine if you are to submit your assignments by printing on paper, or electronically by using your college's course information management system—for example Blackboard or WebCT. To print on paper from Notepad, under the **File** menu item, click **Print**. To submit electronically, follow the instructions provided by your instructor.

8. Log out of your **Yahoo! Mail** e-mail account and **Close** the **Internet Explorer** window.

End **You have completed Project 4G**

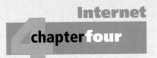
Project 4H—Searching for an Online Netiquette Quiz

Objectives: 2. *Compose and Send a Basic E-mail Message;* **8.** *Identify Appropriate E-mail Netiquette.*

The President of El Cuero Specialty Wares, Alejandra Domene, wants everyone in the San Diego office to take a quiz on netiquette. Because the parent company is located in Mexico, she knows a lot of e-mail will be exchanged and she wants to prevent the possibility of misunderstandings due to poor online manners and poor communication. You and Hector Guzman from the El Cuero Specialty Wares IT Department must search for an online quiz over netiquette rules. In this Assessment, you will search for and take an online netiquette quiz.

For Project 4H, you will need the following file:

Web page saved as a file

You will save your file as
4H_Netiquette_Firstname_Lastname

1. **Start** Internet Explorer and if necessary, click the **Maximize** button to enlarge the window to fill the computer screen completely. In the **Address bar**, click one time to select the existing text, and then type **http://www.ask.com** Press Enter. The **Ask.com** home page displays. Ask.com is a search engine.

2. In the **Search** text box, type **netiquette quiz** and then click the **Search** button. A Web page displays with several search results listed. Notice along the right side of the screen that there are suggestions to narrow your search. Using either of the search results list or the suggestions, locate three online netiquette quizzes.

3. Click the link to the first online netiquette quiz and evaluate the Web site. Note the author or sponsor of the site and the date of the last update for the site. Click the **Back** button to return to the search results list and then visit the other two online netiquette quizzes. Note the author or sponsor of each site and the date of the last update for each site. Of the three sites, determine which site has been most recently updated or which site has the most well-known author or sponsor, and then take the quiz at that Web site.

4. When you have filled in all of your quiz answers, and before submitting the quiz, save the completed quiz Web page as **4H_Netiquette_Firstname_Lastname** in the storage location you set up for this chapter's work.

(Project 4H–Searching for an Online Netiquette Quiz continues on the next page)

Assessments

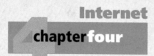

(Project 4H–Searching for an Online Netiquette Quiz continued)

5. Using the techniques you have practiced, compose an e-mail addressed to your e-mail address and your professor's e-mail address. Type the **Subject** line **4H_Netiquette_Firstname_Lastname** In the message body, explain why you chose the netiquette quiz that you did and if you were surprised by any of the questions. Before sending the e-mail, attach the **completed quiz Web page** that you saved as **4H_Netiquette_Firstname_Lastname**.

6. Check your *Chapter Assignment Sheet* or *Course Syllabus* or consult your instructor to determine if you are to submit your assignments by printing on paper, or electronically by using your college's course information management system—for example Blackboard or WebCT. To print on paper from Notepad, under the **File** menu item, click **Print**. To submit electronically, follow the instructions provided by your instructor.

7. Log out of your **Yahoo! Mail** e-mail account and **Close** the **Internet Explorer** window.

End   You have completed Project 4H _____

Assessments

Mastering the Internet

Project 4I — Sending a Free E-Card, Using Your Web-Based E-mail Account

Objectives: 2. *Compose and Send a Basic E-mail Message;* **6.** *Delete E-mail from Your Account;* **9.** *Minimize Nuisances Associated with E-mail.*

The Office Manager for San Diego-based El Cuero Specialty Wares, Michelle Carlton, wants you to find a clever way to remind everyone of the dangers of phishing. You have found an e-card at the Federal Trade Commission Web site that can be sent from Web-based e-mail accounts, is available as a printed version, or can be viewed in Spanish. In this Assessment, you will sign into your Web-based e-mail account and send the e-card to your e-mail account and your professor's e-mail account.

For Project 4I, you will need the following file:

Web page saved as a file
E-mail message printout

You will save your file as
4I_Phishing_Firstname_Lastname

---

1. **Start** Internet Explorer and if necessary, click the **Maximize** button to enlarge the window to fill the computer screen completely. In the **Address bar**, click one time to select the existing text, and then type **http://www.ftc.gov/bcp/conline/ecards/phishing/index.html** Press Enter. The **Federal Trade Commission's e-card** home page displays. Click the **click to play** button to view the e-card's tips on phishing. If you have a sound card and speakers on your computer, you will hear background music as you view the tips.

2. In the tabbed area of your screen, click **New Tab** to open a second tab in the browser. In the **Address bar** of the second tab, click one time to select the existing text, and then type **http://mail.yahoo.com** Press Enter. Then log into your **Yahoo! Mail** e-mail account and compose an e-mail addressed to your e-mail address and your professor's e-mail address. Type the **Subject** line **4I_Phishing_Firstname_Lastname** In the message body, type **http://www.ftc.gov/bcp/conline/ecards/phishing/index.html** and then send the e-mail message.

3. Near the top of the **Inbox**, click the **Sign Out** link to sign out of your **Yahoo! Mail** account. Click the **Close** button to close this second tab of the browser. The e-card should still display in the original browser window.

(Project 4I—Sending a Free E-Card, Using Your Web-Based E-mail Account continues on the next page)

Assessments

(Project 4I–Sending a Free E-Card, Using Your Web-Based E-mail Account continued)

4. Along the left side of the e-card tab, click **Printable Tips** to display a FTC Consumer Alert *How Not to Get Hooked by a 'Phishing' Scam*. In the browser window, click the **Page down arrow**, and then **Save** the **FTC Consumer Alert** Web page as **4I_Phishing_Firstname_Lastname** in the **Chapter_4_E-mail** folder.

5. Check your *Chapter Assignment Sheet* or *Course Syllabus* or consult your instructor to determine if you are to submit your assignments by printing on paper, or electronically by using your college's course information management system—for example Blackboard or WebCT. To print on paper from Notepad, under the **File** menu item, click **Print**. To submit electronically, follow the instructions provided by your instructor.

6. **Close** the **Internet Explorer** window.

End **You have completed Project 4I**

GO! Search

Project 4J — Comparing E-mail Protocols

Objectives: 2. *Compose and Send a Basic E-mail Message;* **7.** *Compare E-mail Systems.*

For Project 4J, you will need the following file:

New blank Notepad document

You will save your file as
4J_Protocols_Firstname_Lastname

Cristina Mandala, the Executive Administrative Assistant for Miguel Hernandez, CEO of El Cuero de Mexico, is interested in protocols that e-mail systems use. Specifically, she would like to know more about SMTP, POP3, IMAP, and MIME. Using the techniques you have practiced, form one or more keyword queries to perform an advanced search at your preferred search engine. Locate information about each of these protocols and how they affect e-mail storage. Create a comparison document listing the search engine that you used to locate the information, the keyword query or queries used, the advanced search strategies or Boolean operators used, and the results of your search. Provide a brief statement about each of the protocols and how they affect e-mail storage as well as the URL where you located this information. Save your document with the footer **4J_Protocols_Firstname_Lastname** and with the same file name. Then submit it to your instructor as directed.

End **You have completed Project 4J**

chapterfive

Collaborating on the World Wide Web

OBJECTIVES

At the end of this chapter, you will be able to:

OUTCOMES

Mastering these objectives will enable you to:

1. Locate Existing Blogs
2. Set Up an Account at a Blogging Web Site
3. Publish Posts to Your Blog

Project 5A
Create Your Own Blog

4. Search for USENET Newsgroups
5. Locate a Web-Based Newsgroup
6. Read and Reply to Threads at a Web-Based Newsgroup

Project 5B
Locate Newsgroups

7. Discover Wikis and Vlogs
8. Identify Message Boards, Web-Based Forums, and Bulletin Boards
9. Explore Instant Messaging and Compare Instant Messengers

Project 5C
Explore Other Web-Based Communication Tools

10. Identify Types of IRC and Chat
11. Define Internet Telephony and VoIP
12. Describe Video Conferencing

Project 5D
Compare Synchronous Communication Tools

Southland Gardens

Gardening is booming! Retail sales of lawn and garden equipment and supplies total over $30 billion a year, and over 65 percent of households engage in some type of lawn care or gardening activity (according to the U.S. Census Bureau). Southland Media, a television production company headquartered in Irvine, California, saw a need for practical, useful, and entertaining information on the subject and developed the show *Southland Gardens*.

In sunny southern California, lawn care and gardening are year-round activities, so *Southland Gardens* covers all aspects of the subjects in 30 half-hour episodes per year. Show topics include challenges unique to urban gardening, vegetable gardens, landscape design, and flower gardens. Shows also include expert tips and inspiration from other gardeners, gardening basics, and timesaving tips. This year the producers plan to expand the show's format to one hour and include tours of historical and notable public and private gardens, yard and garden "makeovers," garden projects for kids, and indoor and container gardening. Additionally, a companion Web site has been established, where viewers can get more information about show segments, purchase supplies, and e-mail guests of the show.

Collaborating on the World Wide Web

The world has grown smaller because of the capability to collaborate using many World Wide Web tools. Blogs help people share thoughts and ideas with each other. Newsgroups provide a way to find out what others think about specific topics. Communication takes place at a much faster pace using chat and instant messaging. In this chapter, you will explore several ways to communicate and collaborate using Web-based tools.

Project 5A Creating Your Own Blog

The president of Southland Media, Danny Golden, wants to find out more about blogs and how they can be used to enhance the company's companion Web site for the Southland Gardens television show. He wants the blog to take the form of a gardening journal with entries on a variety of topics including garden design plans, tips for combating insects without using pesticides, and methods for growing organic foods. Mr. Golden also wants to provide how-to videos on gardening tasks, such as pruning rose bushes and planting bulbs.

In Activities 5.1 through 5.4, you will show Mr. Golden and the Southland Media staff how to locate existing blogs, find a free blogging site, and set up an account with a hosting provider. You also will show them how to publish entries for the blog.

For Project 5A, you will need the following files:

New blank Notepad document
Web page printout

You will save your files as
5A_Blog_Search_Firstname_Lastname
5A_Blog_Post_Firstname_Lastname

Figure 5.1

Objective 1
Locate Existing Blogs

A **blog** is becoming a commonly used communication tool on the World Wide Web. A **Web log**, or blog, is a Web site that takes the form of a journal or news site, is updated frequently, and represents the personality of the author of the Web site. Blogs are used for many purposes, including news, political and financial opinion, marketing, and personal journaling.

You can locate a blog on the World Wide Web by searching with a search engine such as Google. For example, to locate a blog about gardening, you could use a keyword query such as *gardening blog*. Some general search engines, such as Ask.com, provide search tools that are dedicated to finding search results only from blog content on the Web.

Alert!

Assessing Project 5A and Project 5B

For Projects 5A and 5B of this chapter, you and your instructor can evaluate your approach to the problem and your result by consulting the scoring rubric located in the end-of-chapter material. For these hands-on projects, there is no online quiz.

Activity 5.1 Locating Blogs with a Search Engine

Danny Golden, the president of Southland Media, wants to know about various gardening blogs currently on the Web. In this activity, you will formulate a keyword query to locate existing gardening blogs by using both a general search engine and a specialized blog search engine.

1 **Start** Internet Explorer and if necessary, click the **Maximize** button. In the **Address bar**, click to select the existing text, type **http://www.google.com** Press Enter to display the **Google** home page.

Alert!

Does your screen display vary?

Web sites, including blogs, change their layout or content frequently. Your screen may vary from several of the screen shots used in this book. However, you should still be able to identify the key points being illustrated.

2 Using the techniques you have practiced, in the **Google Search** text box, type **gardening blog** as your keyword query, and then click the **Google Search** button.

The search results list displays on the left. Sponsored Web sites may be displayed on the right side of the screen. Recall that sponsored Web sites pay to be listed as search results. In addition to gardening blogs, you may notice sites that provide blogging space or sites that sell gardening supplies.

The Google search engine searches for individual entries, or **posts**, made to blogs. Posts are **timestamped** and listed in reverse chronological order so that the newest post displays first. A timestamp is an expression of time—hour or day—that indicates the most recent update for a blog or a Web site.

More Knowledge

Using Google Blog Search

Google offers a search tool dedicated to searching only for content found in blogs. The tool can be found when you click the more link on the Google home page. You use Google Blog Search the same way you use Google—by typing in a keyword and clicking the Search Blogs button. The search results list is sorted by relevance to the keyword or by date. Typically, you will not see any sponsored sites listed on the right side of the screen when using the Google Blog Search tool. However, some of the search results may be blog postings for commercial products or advertisements.

3 Scroll down the search results list, and then evaluate the hits as you previously practiced. Read the description for each hit and look for your keyword. Be sure to notice both the URL and the top-level domain of the hit to help you determine the sponsor of the blog. Then from the search results list, identify a blog that you will evaluate.

Recall that a **top-level domain** is the highest level in the Domain Name System expressed as the last part of the domain name and represented by a period followed by three letters.

Some of the hits may be from magazines or gardening organizations. Others may be columns from well-known gardeners or hobbyists who enjoy communicating about their gardens.

4 In the search results list, click the link to the blog that you identified. Take a moment to review the posts of the blog you chose. The post may be similar to the one shown in Figure 5.2.

Several characteristics are common among blogs. Blogs are generally organized into a series of tables containing the content of the blog. Most blogs contain a title, the author's name, the date of the post, and a **permalink**. A permalink is the unique URL for a blog post that users can use to locate the post by typing the permalink—URL of the blog post—into the Address bar of the browser.

The content found at a blog may include text, images, audio, video, **blogrolls**, and links to Web pages. A blogroll is a series of links found in a blog that connects to other blogs that are related in some way to the original blog. A **blogger**—the author of a blog Web site—builds site traffic by linking to other blogs through the use of reciprocal blogrolls.

The posts are listed with the most recent entry first. Comments can be made to the posts, and may display underneath the post. At some blog sites, comments display on a separate page that opens after you click the comment link. The **trackback** feature notifies a blogger when comments are made to one of the posts. The ability to generate a trackback is programmed into the blog software to automate the notification process.

Permalink

Figure 5.2

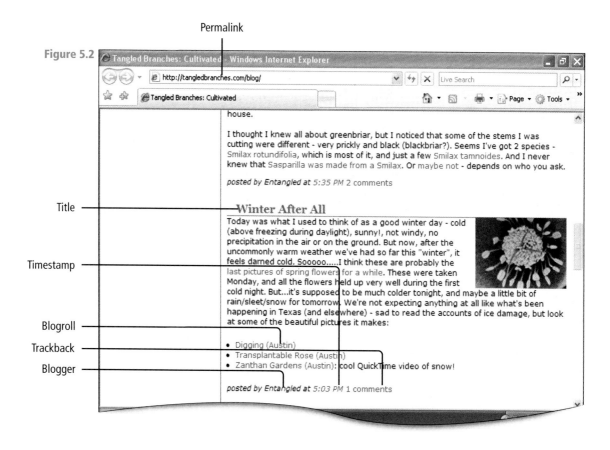

5 Using the following criteria, evaluate the blog that you identified in the previous step. Specifically, make notes so you will remember the following items. You will use these notes in the next activity.

- The name of the blog, the title of the post, and its author

- The current date and the date the blog was last updated

- The blog's permalink—URL

- Any blogrolls and comments that are displayed

This information can be found at any blog post and helps you to determine the relevance of the blog post in terms of your objective for searching for it. Recall that blogs are commonly written as opinion pieces or journal entries so you may not want to rely on blog posts as primary sources when creating research reports for your school work.

6 Click the **Back** button 🔙 to return to the search results list. Click the link of a second blog. Review the posted comments and evaluate it using the same criteria as in the previous step.

7 In the **Address bar**, click to select the existing text, type **http://www.technorati.com** and then press ⏎.

The Technorati home page displays. Technorati enables you to search the *blogosphere*. The blogosphere encompasses the collection of blogs found on the World Wide Web and includes the entire blogging community of authors and readers.

Specialized blog search engines, such as Technorati, locate blogs by using a keyword query. Typically, blog search engines allow you to use Boolean operators and other advanced search features to increase the relevance of the search results list. Some blog search engines provide both keyword searches and directory searches organized by subject to help you locate blogs on your favorite topics. Figure 5.3 lists the URLs for some search engines that locate blog content.

Specialized Blog Search Engines

Blog Search Engine	URL
Ask.com	*http://www.ask.com*
Bloglines	*http://www.bloglines.com*
Daypop	*http://www.daypop.com*
Digg	*http://digg.com*
Feedster	*http://feedster.com*
Google Blog Search	*http://blogsearch.google.com*
Technorati	*http://technorati.com*

Figure 5.3

Each type of blog search engine monitors blogs and keeps track of the frequent updates made to blogs. You can subscribe to receive notification of the updates to the blogs that you choose by using *Really Simple Syndication*, or **RSS**. Recall that RSS is a system developed to automatically alert subscribers of updates made to sites such as blogs, news, weather, or sports sites. As new content is posted to a blog, you receive notification of the update with an RSS feed called a **blog feed**. A blog feed is also called an **aggregator**.

8 Near the top of the **Technorati** home page, locate the **Search for** text box. Then scroll down and across the Web page and take a moment to review the various components that make up the Technorati home page, as shown in Figure 5.4.

The *Search for* text box enables you to search by keywords found in blog posts, tags, or blog directories. **Tags** are categories for the organization of blog topics that are added to the blog when the blog is written. When you search for a blog using a keyword query, the search engine matches the keyword with the tags established for any given blog post.

On the left side of the page, you can review Top Searches by clicking them in the directory. On the right side of the home page, the **Advanced search** link allows you to search by keyword modified by Boolean operators, URLs linked to a blog, tags, or blog directories.

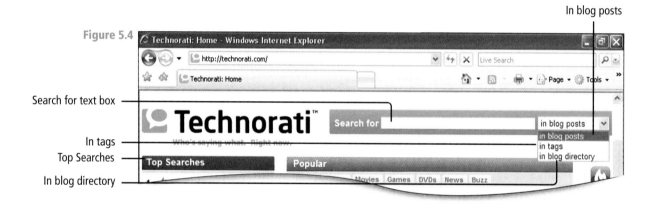

Figure 5.4

Search for text box
In tags
Top Searches
In blog directory
In blog posts

9 On the **Technorati** home page, click the **Advanced search** link. On the **Technorati Search** Web page that displays, review the features of the Web page. Scroll down the page, to the section labeled **Keyword Search**. In the box below **Show posts that contain**, type **gardening blogs**. Notice that you can use Boolean operators by typing into specific text boxes within this section.

10 In the **Search in** section, click to select the **Blogs about** button to locate only blogs matching the keyword query. In the text box that displays to the right of the **Blogs about** button, type **gardening** Click the **Search** button.

The search results list displays. Just like a general search engine, sponsored sites and links to actual blogs may display together as part of the search results list.

11 Compare your screen with Figure 5.5. Then scroll down the search results list, and evaluate the hits using the same criteria that you used with the Google search results list. Read the description for each hit and look for your keyword. Try to determine the sponsor of the blog by using the URL and top-level domain if it's given as part of the hit. Then from the search results list, identify a blog that you would like to evaluate.

Figure 5.5

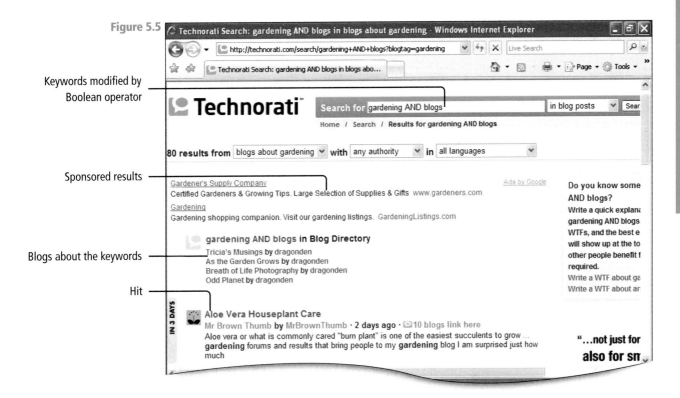

Keywords modified by Boolean operator

Sponsored results

Blogs about the keywords

Hit

12 In the search results list, click the link to the blog that you identified. Review the post, evaluate it using the same criteria as in Step 5, and take notes.

13 On the toolbar, click the **Back** button 🔙 to return to the search results list. Click the link of a second blog. Review the post, evaluate it using the same criteria as in Step 5, and take notes.

14 Take a moment to review your notes for the four blog posts and determine which search engine provided the most relevant blogs. Identify the search engine—either Google or Technorati—that you would recommend for locating blogs. You will use your notes in the next activity.

Activity 5.2 Comparing Blog Search Tools

Now that you have located blogs using two different types of blog search tools, Danny Golden and the staff of Southland Media would like to know if one blog search tool is preferred over another. In this activity, you will create a summary document that evaluates the quality of four blog posts. Then you will make a recommendation for the blog search engine that you feel is most useful.

1 **Start** Notepad and if necessary, **Maximize** the Notepad window. In the **Notepad** window, at the insertion point, type **5A_Blog_Search_ Firstname_Lastname** and then press Enter two times.

2 Type the name of the search tool used, the name of the blog, the title of the post, and the author. Press Enter two times, and then type the date the blog was last updated and its permalink. Press Enter two

times, and then type the names of any blogrolls or any comments. Press (Enter) two times.

3 Type the name of the second blog, the title of the post, and the author. Press (Enter) two times, and then type the date the blog was last updated and its permalink. Press (Enter) two times, and then type the names of any blogrolls or any comments. Press (Enter) two times.

4 Type the name of the second search tool used, the name of the third blog, the title of the post, and the author. Press (Enter) two times, and then type the date the blog was last updated and its permalink. Press (Enter) two times, and then type the names of any blogrolls or any comments. Press (Enter) two times.

5 Type the name of the fourth blog, the title of the post, and the author. Press (Enter) two times, and then type the date the blog was last updated and its permalink. Press (Enter) two times, and then type the names of any blogrolls or any comments. Press (Enter) two times.

6 Type the name of the search engine you recommend for locating blogs, and then press (Enter) two times. Type a single paragraph that describes why you chose the search engine that you recommend. In making your recommendations, consider the evidence gathered from your evaluation of blogs returned on each of the search results lists. Also consider the difficulty level for using each search tool.

7 Decide on the location where you will store your document—either in a folder on your computer's hard drive or a folder on a removable storage device such as a USB flash drive. Check with your instructor if necessary. Click the **Start** button ![start], and then click **My Computer**. Navigate to the location where you have decided to store your document. On the left side of your screen, under **File and Folder Tasks**, click **Make a new folder**. In the text box labeled **New Folder** that displays, using your own first and last names, type **Chapter_5_Collaborating** Then press (Enter). **Close** ![X] the **My Computer** window when you are finished.

8 Using the techniques you have practiced, add the **footer 5A_Blog_ Search_Firstname_Lastname** to the document.

9 Using the techniques you have practiced, navigate to the folder created in Step 7 and save the document as **5A_Blog_Search_ Firstname_Lastname**

10 Check your Chapter Assignment Sheet or Course Syllabus or consult your instructor to determine whether you are to submit your assignments by printing on paper or electronically, using your college's course information management system. Electronically, you can submit the *.txt* file created in Notepad. To print on paper from Notepad, under the **File** menu, click **Print**, and print accordingly. To submit the document electronically, follow the instructions provided by your instructor.

11 **Close** ![X] the **Notepad** window. Keep your browser open for the next activity.

Objective 2
Set Up an Account at a Blogging Web Site

Before you can begin creating posts, you must create an account with the **hosting provider**. A hosting provider is an organization that provides server space for Web sites or blogs either free of charge or for a monthly fee. The table in Figure 5.6 lists several popular providers and their URLs.

Blog Providers

Blog Provider	URL
21Publish	*http://www.21publish.com*
Blog-City	*http://www.blog-city.com/bc*
Blogger	*http://www.blogger.com*
LiveJournal	*http://www.livejournal.com*
Typepad	*http://www.typepad.com*
WordPress	*http://wordpress.com*

Figure 5.6

Another Way

To Use a Blog Software Program

You also can create blogs using a blog software program installed on your computer. In addition to the software, you will need a host server to upload the blog content so that your blog posts will be visible on the World Wide Web. Although using blog software requires more technical knowledge, software, and hardware, it offers more control of the layout and available features of the blog.

Activity 5.3 Signing Up for a Blogging Account

The staff at Southland Media has enjoyed reading several gardening blogs. The staff members are anxious to get started creating their own blogs. In this activity, you will set up an account with a hosting provider.

1 **Start** Internet Explorer and **Maximize** 🔲 the window. In the **Address bar**, click one time to select the existing text, type **http://www.blogger.com** and then press [Enter] to display the **Blogger** home page.

Blogger is a hosting provider where you can search for blogs from all across the Web or click recommended links to view recently updated blogs. Blogger is now part of Google and has been merged with other Google services.

Blogger has a profile system that enables you to choose to hide or reveal your blog to the general public. If you do allow the general public to read your blog, you may choose to hide or reveal your name and identity. You can also choose to accept or delete any comments made to your blog.

Blogger provides services such as photo sharing, as well as group blogs for families, small groups, or teams. In addition to more traditional methods for posting materials to your blog, you can post text and photos using your cell phone or through e-mail. You can also send MP3 files using any telephone.

Alert!

Does your version of Blogger differ?

Your version of the Blogger Web site may differ as Blogger merges with Google. If this occurs, work through the steps according to the instructions provided at the Web site.

2 Scroll down the **Blogger** home page, and then click the **Create Your Blog Now** link. In the **Security Alert** dialog box that displays, click **OK**.

The Blogger: Create Blogger Account Web page displays. This form allows you to first create a Google account by providing your e-mail address. You will use this e-mail address as your user ID each time you want to log into your Blogger account. This also becomes your user ID for all Google services.

3 Fill in the **Create Blogger account form**. At the top of the form, type in the e-mail address that you want to use when you access this account. Next, type a password that is at least six characters long, and in the next text box, retype the same password to confirm it. The Password strength is indicated below the **Retype password** text box. Type a display name that will be used to sign all of your blog posts. Next, type a word verification code. Compare your screen with Figure 5.7.

Alert!

Did you use your real name?

Do not use your real name as your display name so that you can shield your identity while online. You may not want to use your primary e-mail address for the same reason, especially if your name is part of your e-mail address.

When choosing a password, be sure to include punctuation marks and mix upper- and lowercase letters with numbers. Do not use passwords that contain personal information, words that can be found in a dictionary, or repeating or sequential numbers or letters.

Most sites offering free services such as e-mail or blogging space use some type of verification as a security measure to prevent automatic registrations. Typically, this verification is a code that displays as letters and numbers that have been distorted or rotated—**CAPTCHA**.

Recall that CAPTCHA stands for Completely Automated Public Turing test to tell Computers and Humans Apart. CAPTCHA is a program that makes certain text visible onscreen appear to be composed of wavy and distorted letters in order to prevent computer programs from performing events online instead of humans performing events online. The program was developed and is trademarked by Carnegie Mellon University.

Figure 5.7

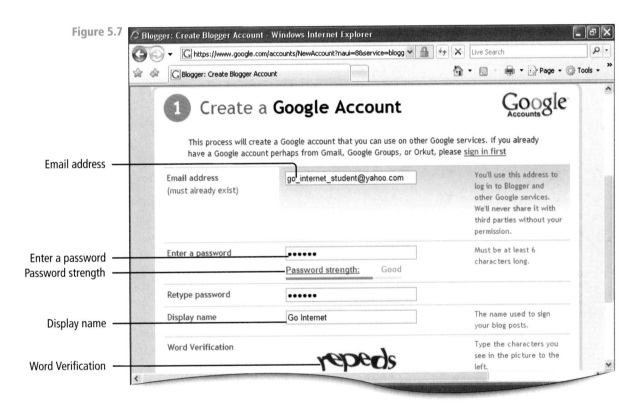

Near the bottom of the form, click the **Terms of Service** link, and then take a moment to review the Terms of Service in the pop-up window that displays. After reading the terms of service, **Close** ☒ the pop-up window. If you agree with the terms of service, click the **I accept the Terms of Service** check box. Review what you have typed into the entire form, and then click the **Continue** button.

After a few moments, a confirmation page displays where you type in your e-mail address and newly created password to sign into Blogger, using your Google account information. If the **AutoComplete Passwords** dialog box displays, click **No.** Then, if a **Security Alert** dialog box displays, click **Yes**. If a second **Security Alert** dialog box displays, click **OK.** Compare your screen with Figure 5.8.

The *dashboard* displays. A dashboard is a user interface, or a Web page, that provides one location to perform several tasks such as viewing or editing your profile. You also can access your account to change your password or edit your personal information. You create and manage your blog here as well.

Figure 5.8

6 Keep your browser open for the next activity.

Objective 3
Publish Posts to Your Blog

After an account is created, you must create the blog before you can add content or blog posts. You use forms to create the blog and add the blog content. The hosting provider takes the content from the form and places it into a *template*. A template is a predesigned document that can be added to or modified for use in a blog, Web page, or word-processed document. Then the hosting provider uploads the template to a host server, which *publishes* the post to the blog. The term, publish, means to make available after writing. After the content is published, the blog can be located by a search engine and can be viewed by anyone.

Activity 5.4 Posting to a Blog

The staff members at Southland Media are excited to begin posting to their new blog accounts. In this activity, you will show the staff how to create a blog and make a post a blog.

1 Near the top of the dashboard, click the **Create a Blog** link to display the **Name your blog** Web page. The page contains a form you can use to name your blog and establish the blog address, or permalink.

The blog address can be used by anyone who wants to view your blog. All Blogger Web addresses begin with *http://*. You may want to use the blog's title to make up the next part of the Web address or other descriptive name. The word *blogspot* makes up the next part of the domain name, and *.com* is the top-level domain.

2 On the **Name your blog** Web page, in the **Blog title** box, type a title for your blog. If you need help, click the question mark button next to the text box. In the **Blog address (URL)** box, type your blog's title, your display name, or other descriptive words in the text box. Click the **Check Availability** link to determine if your blog address is available. Compare your screen with Figure 5.9.

The title of your blog should represent the main focus of your blog. For example, if your blog will be about growing herbs, the title could be *The Herb Gardener* or *Flavorful Garden.*

If the blog address you have chosen has already been taken, you will be prompted to choose a different blog address. If your blog address is available, you will see the confirmation text *This blog address is available.*

If you already have a domain name that you would like to use instead of the Blogger's blog address, you may do so by clicking the Advanced Setup link. Use Advanced Setup also if you have your own server to host the blog.

Figure 5.9

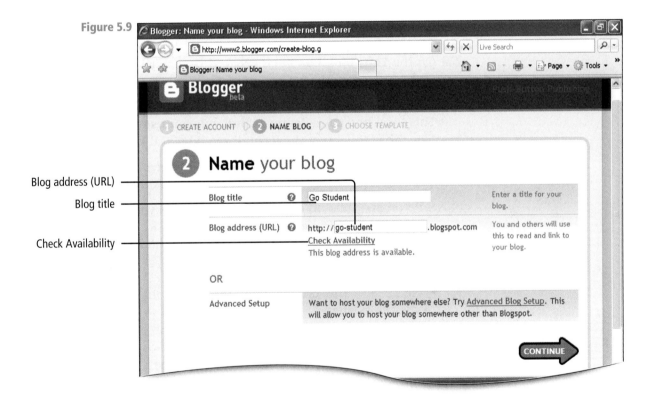

3 Click the **Continue** button to display the **Choose a template** Web page. On the **Choose a template** Web page, scroll down and review the templates. Compare your screen with Figure 5.10. Click any of the **Preview template** links to view the individual templates that interest you. Decide which template you want to use for your blog, and then click the template name to select the template. Click **Continue**.

The **Your Blog has been created confirmation** Web page displays. You may now begin to makes posts to your blog.

Figure 5.10

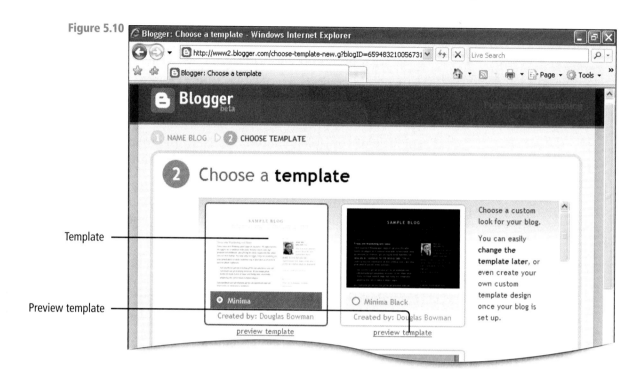

Template

Preview template

On the **Your blog has been created** page, click **Start Posting** to display a form you may use to compose your blog content. Compare your screen with Figure 5.11.

This form has many features that you can use to customize your blog. Near the top of the form, three tabs and a link display:

- Posting—This is the default tab that enables you to create posts, edit posts, moderate comments, and check the status of your blog.

- Settings—This tab enables you to manage your blog by making choices about Basic account information, Publishing, Formatting, Comments, Archiving, Site Feed, E-mail, and Members.

- Template—This tab enables you to modify the current template.

- View Blog—This link enables you to see your blog as it will display when published.

Figure 5.11

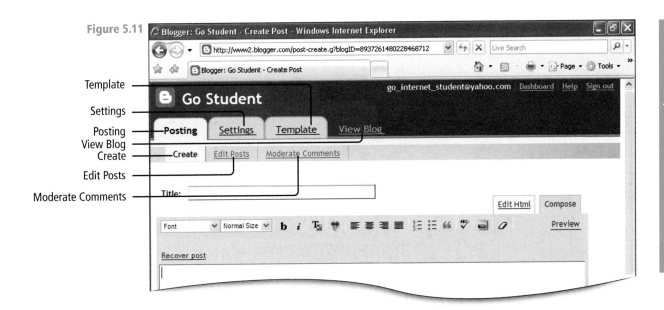

Template

Settings

Posting
View Blog
Create

Edit Posts

Moderate Comments

5 In the **Title** box, click to select the existing text, and then type **My Favorite Plant**

Not all templates allow you to choose a title. Some templates automatically fill in the title for you. If the Title text box is already filled in with the blog title you chose when you created your blog, you can make a new title for this post. To do so, click to select the existing text, and then type your preferred title.

6 In the large text area located under the Formatting toolbar, click to position the insertion point, and then type **Welcome to my gardening blog!** Select the text you just typed, and on the Formatting toolbar, click the **Font down arrow**, and then click **Arial**.

The *Formatting toolbar* contains a set of onscreen tools that enables you to customize the appearance of text. Here, you choose the *font* style, size, and emphasis, and you also add color, create hyperlinks, and align the text. You also can add lists, quotes, and images. A font is a certain named style of text that represents qualities of size, spacing, and shape of letters.

Hold the mouse over each button to display a *ScreenTip*, which describes what each button can do. Recall that a ScreenTip is a Windows feature that temporarily displays a small box providing information about, or the name of, a screen element as you hold the mouse pointer over buttons or images in Internet Explorer or other Web browsers.

7 With the text still selected, on the Formatting toolbar, click the **Normal Size down arrow**, and then click **Large**. If necessary, click the **Align Left** button to align the message to the left. Position the insertion point after the word *blog!*, and then press Enter two times.

8 Type a short paragraph about your favorite flower or tree. Include the name of the plant, how large it grows or its shape, the color of its flowers, and any other information you feel is important in describing your favorite plant.

⬚9 In the paragraph that you wrote, click and drag to select the name of your favorite plant. On the Formatting toolbar, click the **Bold** button, and next click the **Italic** button. Then click anywhere in the text area. Compare your screen with Figure 5.12.

Figure 5.12

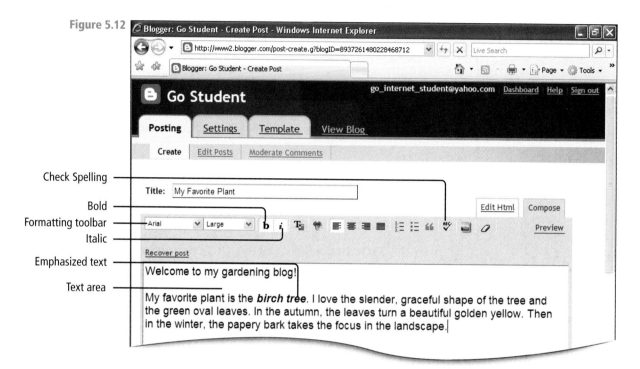

Check Spelling
Bold
Formatting toolbar
Italic
Emphasized text
Text area

Avoid Invisible Text

The background color and the text color must contrast each other so that your audience can read the text of your blog. Typically, the default text color is black. If you chose a template with a black background, the text will not be visible unless you change the color of the text to something other than black. To change the text color, first select the text. Then, on the Formatting toolbar, click the Text Color button, and then click to select the desired color.

⬚10 On the Formatting toolbar, click the **Check Spelling** button. In the displayed **Spell Checker** dialog box, work through the suggested changes by clicking the **Replace** or **Ignore** buttons as appropriate.

Because your blog will be visible to others, you must take the time to spell check your posts. When all corrections have been made, the Spell Checker dialog box closes.

More Knowledge
Working with Pop-Ups

The Spell Checker dialog box is a pop-up. You will not be able to spell check your document using this feature if you have configured your browser to block pop-ups.

11 Near the bottom of the form, locate the **Labels for this post** text box, and then type **gardens** and **gardening** Then click the **Publish** button.

The Labels for this post will be used as tags for the blog. Recall that tags are matched with keyword queries when people search for blogs at search engines.

The Publishing is in progress Web page displays while the Blogger server publish your post. The percentage of files published is updated as the process progresses. When your post has been published, the *Your blog published successfully* confirmation displays.

12 On the **Your blog published successfully** page, click the **View Blog (in a new window)** link.

The first post for your blog displays in a new window separate from the original blog window.

13 Take a moment to review the post. Notice several features along the top, left, and center of the Web page. Compare your screen with Figure 5.13. Your screen may differ if you chose a different template, but all of the features should be located somewhere on your post.

Figure 5.13

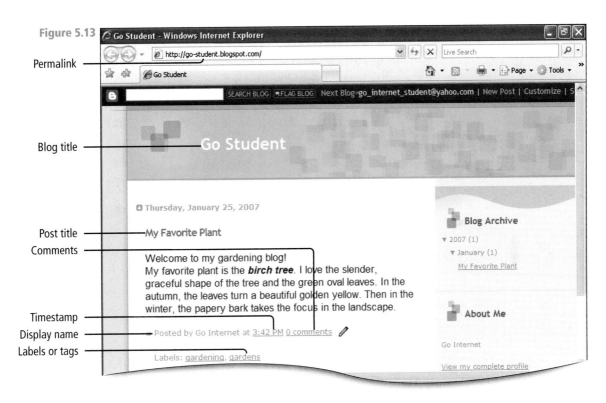

- Permalink
- Blog title
- Post title
- Comments
- Timestamp
- Display name
- Labels or tags

14 On your post, locate and click the **comments** link. In the **Security Alert** dialog box, click **OK**.

The Post a Comment On page displays.

15 On the right side of the screen, in the **Leave your comment** text box, type **Congratulations on your first post** Then click the **Publish Your Comment** button.

A confirmation page indicates your comment has been saved.

16 On the **confirmation** page, locate and click the **Show Original Post** link. In the **Security Alert** dialog box, click **Yes**. Notice that your comment displays under the original post.

17 Using the techniques you have practiced, add the **footer 5A_Blog_ Post_Firstname_Lastname** Then using the techniques you have practiced, navigate to the **Chapter_5_Collaborating** folder created for this chapter and save the Web page as **5A_Blog_Post_Firstname_Lastname**

18 Check your Chapter Assignment Sheet or Course Syllabus or consult your instructor to determine whether you are to submit your assignments by printing on paper or electronically, using your college's course information management system. Electronically, you can submit the *.txt* file that you created in Notepad. To print on paper from Notepad, under the **File** menu, click **Print** and print accordingly. To submit the document electronically, follow the instructions provided by your instructor.

19 In the upper right hand corner of the **Blogger** window, click the **Sign Out** link. In the **Security Alert** dialog box, click **OK.** In the **Security Alert** dialog box that displays, click **Yes**. Then **Close** ☒ all **Internet Explorer** windows.

You are logged out of Blogger. When you are ready to create a new blog post, go to the Blogger home page and use your e-mail address and password to log in.

End **You have completed Project 5A**————————————

Project 5B Locating Newsgroups

Elizabeth Robinson and Victor Ortiz are the cohosts for the new gardening television show *Southland Gardens*. Both Elizabeth and Victor would like to have a resource that is easy to access because they must know about a wide range of gardening topics in order to converse with their weekly guests on the show. They want to join a gardening-related newsgroup. In Activities 5.5 through 5.8, you will demonstrate techniques for locating a newsgroup, reading a newsgroup thread, and performing other common tasks such as sorting articles by date. You will also explore how to join a newsgroup and post a reply to an article.

For Project 5B, you will need the following files:

Web page printouts

You will save your files as
5B_USENET_Firstname_Lastname
5B_Newsgroup_Firstname_Lastname
5B_Newsgroup_Post_Firstname_Lastname

Objective 4
Search for USENET Newsgroups

Recall that **asynchronous communication** is electronic communication in which the participants do not need to be online at the same time, and all participants can view the communication when they want to do so. A **newsgroup** is an example of asynchronous communication.

A newsgroup is an Internet forum that provides a threaded discussion on specific topics such as financial aid or gaming. A newsgroup is composed of a series of articles and posts. An **article** is the original message, and recall that a post is any of the subsequent replies to an article. Together, an article and all of the posts create the **thread** that follows a specific topic.

The original newsgroups were sponsored by **USENET**. Recall that USENET is an electronic bulletin board for research discussion among researchers and scientists where individuals could read, post, or reply on a specific topic of interest by using a system of threaded discussion boards. It was first used early in the development of the Internet.

Activity 5.5 Locating a USENET Newsgroup

In this activity, you will locate a newsgroup about gardening.

1 **Start** Internet Explorer and if necessary, click the **Maximize** button to enlarge the window to fill the computer screen completely. In the **Address bar**, click one time to select the existing text, type **http://www.tile.net** and then press Enter.

The TILE.NET Web page displays. **_TILE.NET_** is a well-respected search tool used for locating Internet resources. TILE.NET provides references for newsletters and discussion lists, USENET newsgroups, vendors for computer products, Internet Service Providers, and Web design companies. The TILE.NET URL has *.net*—instead of *.com*—as its top-level domain. Recall that top-level domains are used to identify Web sites belonging to certain types of organizations. In this case, TILE.NET is a Web site that provides information on topics related to the structure of the Internet.

2 On the **TILE.NET** home page, click the **Usenet Newsgroups** link. Compare your screen with Figure 5.14.

The TILE.NET/NEWSGROUP Web page displays. Sponsored sites display on the left and bottom of the Web page. You can search for newsgroups using keyword queries or by using a directory search. When using the directory search, you locate newsgroups by index, description, or newsgroup hierarchy.

Figure 5.14

Search text box

Sponsored sites

Directory searches

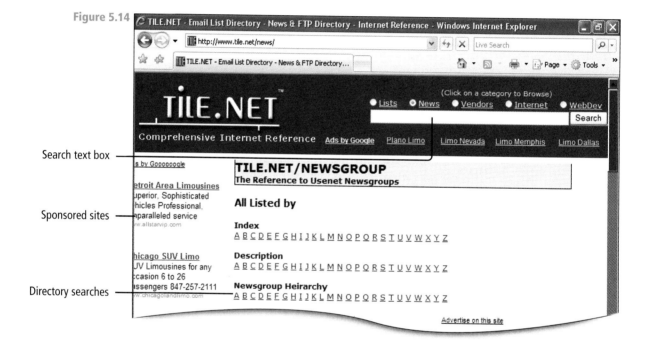

3 In the **Search** text box, type the keyword query **gardening** and then press [Enter]. Compare your screen with Figure 5.15.

On the displayed TILE.NET Search Results page, several USENET newsgroups are listed. The name of a newsgroup is structured into a topic category called a **_hierarchy_**.

Figure 5.15

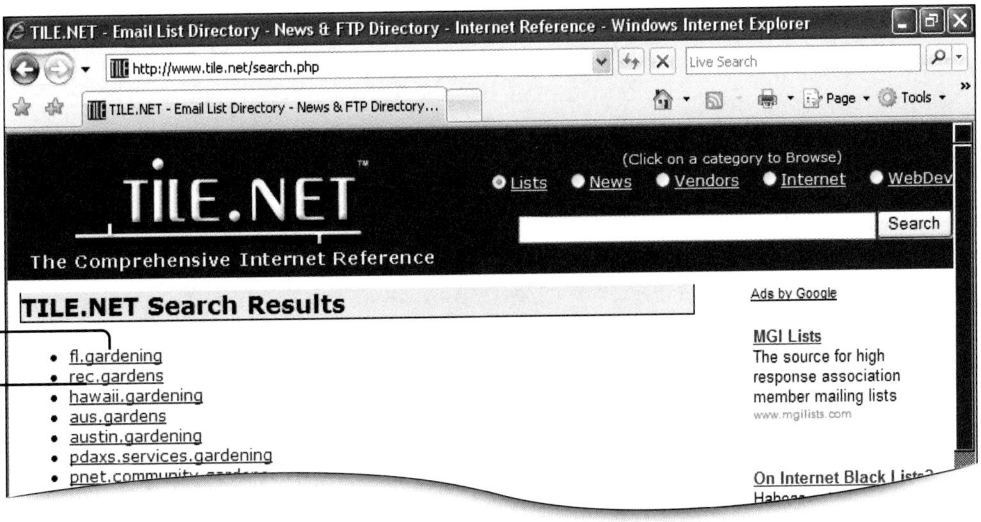

Search results list

Hierarchy

More Knowledge
The Big Seven

When USENET was developed, seven top-level hierarchies grouped all discussion threads into general categories. These categories were comp.*, misc.*, news.*, rec.*, sci.*, soc.*, and talk.*. Permission was needed to create a new newsgroup within these seven categories. Another category was created, alt.*, for discussions that did not fit into the seven top-level hierarchies. Permission was not needed to create a new newsgroup in the alt.* category. As a result, in the alt.* category you will find a variety of topics, including some unusual or obscure topics.

The seven original top-level USENET hierarchies were called the *Big Seven*. In 1995, another group, humanities.*, was formed, and the Big Seven became the *Big Eight*. In 2000, biz.* was created for the discussion of business issues. The biz.* newsgroup is the only newsgroup that permits the posting of advertisements.

4 Take a moment to review the table shown in Figure 5.16, which describes the ten hierarchies and the types of discussions included within each hierarchy. The asterisk (*) is a wildcard that stands in place of the rest of the newsgroup name.

Each part of a newsgroup name gets more specific as you read from left to right. Each newsgroup name begins with the general top-level hierarchy followed by more specific levels within the hierarchy. Dots, or periods, separate each level of the hierarchy. For example, for the newsgroup *rec.gardens.orchids*, the discussion is focused on growing orchids for recreation.

Newsgroup Hierarchies

Top-Level Hierarchy	Discussion Topic
alt.*	Alternative discussions outside of the Big Seven categories. Permission is not needed to create a newsgroup in this hierarchy.
biz.*	Business-oriented discussions. This is the newest hierarchy.
comp.*	Computer hardware, software, and other computer-related discussions.
humanities.*	Humanities, art, and literature discussions.
misc.*	Discussions that don't fit into the other Big Seven categories. Permission is needed to create a newsgroup in this hierarchy.
news.*	Discussions that deal with newsgroup policy and issues.
rec.*	Recreation-related discussions.
sci.*	Scientific research and application discussions.
soc.*	Current events and social issues discussions.
talk.*	Debate and controversial discussions.

Figure 5.16

5 In the **Search Results** list, look closely at the names of several newsgroups and determine how many are in the rec.* hierarchy. Right-click the first link for the rec.* hierarchy and open it in a new window. Review the newsgroup threads and then **Close** ☒ the window to return to the search results list. Right-click another link for the rec.* hierarchy, open it in a new window, and review the threads. When you are finished, **Close** ☒ the window to return to the search results list.

6 Add the **footer 5B_USENET_Firstname_Lastname** to the Web page.

7 Navigate to the **Chapter_5_Collaborating** folder and save the Web page as **5B_USENET_Firstname_Lastname**

Objective 5
Locate a Web-Based Newsgroup

In addition to USENET, another newsgroup system developed was called **Deja News**. Deja News provided access to several thousand newsgroups until the late 1990s. Google Groups now manages and hosts the Deja News newsgroups, and Google has created searchable **archives** of the threads. An archive is an electronic copy of a file that can be stored in a separate location and retrieved at a future date. Google Groups makes it easy to join a newsgroup or even start your own newsgroup. You can access Web-based newsgroups and read the threads by using any computer that has a browser installed and that is connected to the Internet.

Activity 5.6 Locating a Web-Based Newsgroup

In this activity, you will locate a newsgroup using Google Groups.

1 In the **Address bar**, click one time to select the existing text, type **http://www.google.com** and then press ⏎. Alternatively, you can reach Google Groups at http://groups.google.com.

The Google home page displays. Recall that Google is a search engine that enables searches among several categories. One of the categories is Groups, which is used to search for newsgroups. You can also start your own group using Google Groups.

2 In the middle of the **Google** Web page, click the **more** link, and then click the **Groups** link. Compare your screen with Figure 5.17.

From the displayed Google Groups home page, you can search for groups by using a keyword query in the Search Groups text box. In the Explore Groups section, you can perform a directory search to locate a group by category. This directory search is loosely organized according to the USENET hierarchy although some categories have been combined with others. In addition, you can use the Popular Groups area to perform a directory search to read threads at the most popular newsgroups.

Figure 5.17

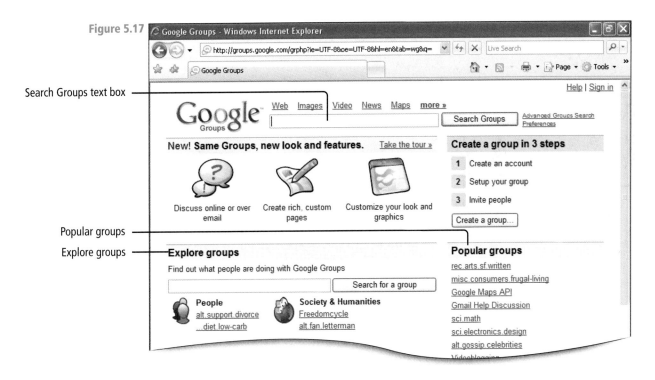

Search Groups text box

Popular groups

Explore groups

3 At the top of the page, in the **Search Groups** text box, type **gardening** and then click the **Search Groups** button. Take a moment to review the search results list and notice that there are hundreds of results.

You can sort the results by relevance or by date. Sponsored links may be mixed in with other search results or display on the right of the search results list.

4 Click the **Sort by date** link. Compare your screen with Figure 5.18.

The most recent articles display at the top of the Web page. You can determine when they were posted by their timestamp. You can also see which newsgroup they were posted under.

Figure 5.18

Sorted by date ——

Sort by relevance ——
Newsgroup ——
Sponsored links ——
Timestamp ——

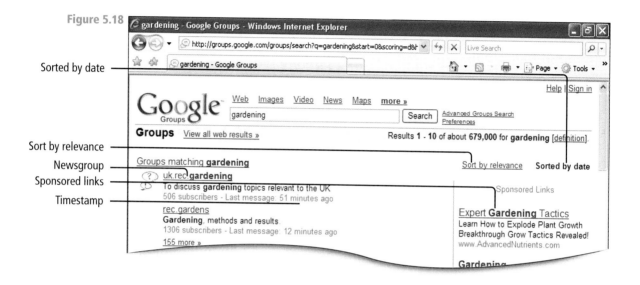

5 Keep your browser open for the next activity.

Objective 6
Read and Reply to Threads at a Web-Based Newsgroup

Newsgroups use several *news servers* to store and manage the articles, posts, and threads. A news server is a server that hosts several newsgroups. News servers exchange articles, posts, and threads from their hosted newsgroups with other news servers and their hosted newsgroups. By using this distribution process, all threads from all news servers can be viewed by anyone participating in the newsgroup—even if the individual's computer is not directly connected to the news server hosting the newsgroup. A *newsfeed* is the exchange of articles and posts between news servers. The *Network News Transfer Protocol*, or *NNTP*, is the protocol used to distribute the articles, posts, and threads within newsgroups.

Activity 5.7 Reading Threads at a Web-Based Newsgroup

In this activity, you will read newsgroup threads. Google Groups enables you to locate existing newsgroups using keyword queries, just as you do for typical Web searches.

1 In the **Google Groups** search results list, click the first newsgroup listed. Compare your screen with Figure 5.19.

Some ISPs have a news server and offer access to a select number of newsgroups. Many people find that it is convenient to access newsgroups using either an e-mail client or a newsreader. E-mail clients, such as Microsoft Outlook or Outlook Express, can be set up to access newsgroups.

In addition, some browsers provide a built-in ***newsreader***. A newsreader is a program that supports NNTP and is used to read newsgroup threads. With either method you need to specify the name of the news server you would like to access and subscribe to the newsgroup on that news server.

If your ISP doesn't support newsgroups or you do not know the name of any news servers, you can still access a newsgroup by using a newsgroup search engine found on the World Wide Web. Web sites, such as Google Groups, enable you to search for newsgroups and read the threads using your browser to access the Web-based interface instead of NNTP and a newsreader.

Because people frequently create newsgroups or make new threads and posts, it is likely that your newsgroup will be different from the one in the figure. However, you should be able to locate the same features.

The most recent articles for that newsgroup display. The name of the newsgroup displays near the top of the Web page. The default view is Topic summary where you see the title and some of the message text. You may also use the Topic list view for the messages. Active older topics are also available.

Figure 5.19

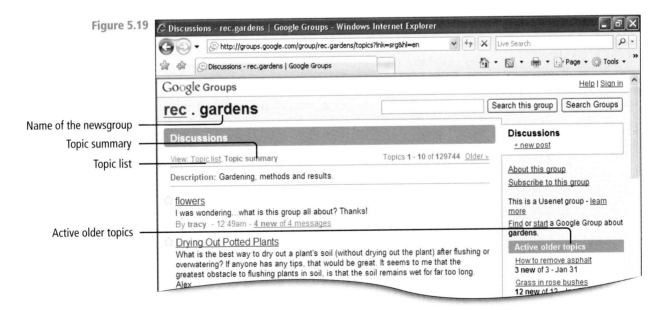

Name of the newsgroup
Topic summary
Topic list
Active older topics

2 In the list of articles, click the link to the most recent article. Read the article and any posts to the article. Compare your screen with Figure 5.20.

The article and all replies to it display. You can see the newsgroup name, the title of the article, the author of the article, and the time-stamp. You can reply or forward the article by clicking the More options link.

Figure 5.20

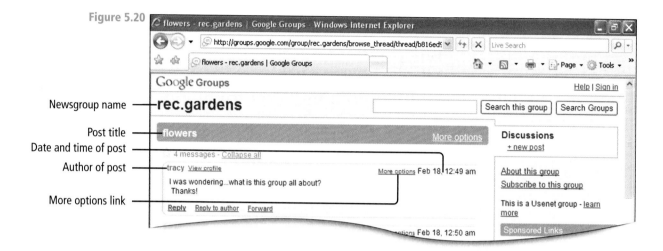

3 Click the **More options** link. Compare your screen with Figure 5.21.

The More options link provides several useful options. You can reply to the article so that everyone will see the reply or you can reply to the author so that only the author sees the reply. You can print the thread, show the individual message, just show the original message, or find other messages by the same author. In addition, you can report the message if you find an article that appears to be spam or contains illegal content. You can return to the default view by clicking Hide options.

You do not need to be a Google Groups member to complete any of these tasks. However, you must be a member of the newsgroup in order to reply or forward the message.

Figure 5.21

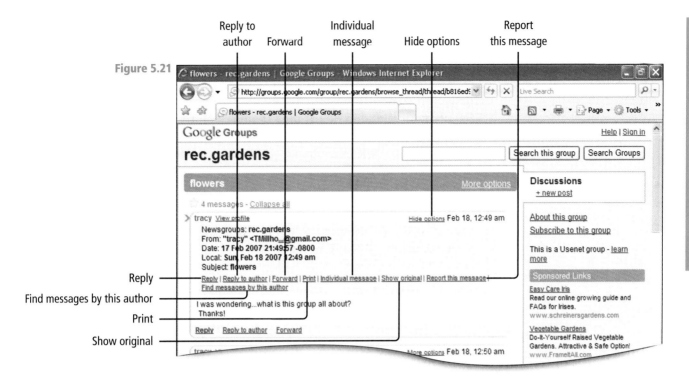

Reply to author · Forward · Individual message · Hide options · Report this message

Reply

Find messages by this author

Print

Show original

More Knowledge
Moderated Newsgroups

In *moderated newsgroups,* your post will be reviewed or filtered for content and relevance, prior to being sent to the news server. If the content of the post meets the criteria set for the newsgroup, the *moderator* will forward the message for posting. A moderator is the human who screens newsgroup posts to determine if the posts should be allowed to be sent to the news server. Your post becomes visible to everyone who has subscribed to that newsgroup if it is approved by the moderator.

Just as you find in unmoderated listservs, there is no review process in place for *unmoderated newsgroups*. An unmoderated newsgroup is a newsgroup where articles and posts are not screened before being sent to the news server. All posts are accepted.

4 In the **More options** view, click the **Individual Message** link to display just the article. Using the techniques you have practiced, add the **footer 5B_Newsgroup_Firstname_Lastname** to the Web page, and then save the Web page as **5B_Newsgroup_Firstname_Lastname** in the **Chapter_5_Collaborating** folder.

Activity 5.8 Joining a Newsgroup and Posting a Reply

In this activity, you will join a newsgroup at Google Groups using your the Google account information you created previously. Then you will reply to an article.

1 Click the **Reply** link.

You must be a member of Google Groups and signed into your account to reply to any newsgroup article. If you are already signed into your Google account, you will not need to sign in again.

As an alternative, you may be prompted to sign in by a link displayed at the bottom of the message. When you click the link, two Security Alert dialog boxes may display before allowing you to view the Google Groups Sign-in Web page. If the first Security Alert dialog box displays, click OK. If a second Security Information dialog box displays, click Yes.

2 On the right side of the **Google Groups Sign-in** Web page, in the area labeled **Google Account**, click the **E-mail** text box, and then type your e-mail address. Click in the **Password** text box and type your password. If there is a check mark in the **Remember me on this computer** check box, click one time to remove the check mark.

You can use the same e-mail address and password that you used to create your Google account in earlier in the chapter. Blogger and Google Groups, as well as other Google services, use this same account information.

If you are using a publicly available computer in your classroom or a lab, it is not a good idea to have the computer remember your account information. Leaving the default check mark in the *Remember me on this computer* check box could allow someone other than you to access your Google account.

3 Click the **Sign in** button. In the **AutoComplete Passwords** dialog box, click **No**.

The Welcome to Google Groups Web page displays.

Alert!

Did Internet Explorer save your password?

Internet Explorer offers to remember your password for you. If you are using a publicly available computer in your classroom or a lab, it is not a good idea to have the browser remember your account information.

4 In the **Getting Started with Google Groups** section, locate the **Nick name** text box and type the same display name that you use to access your blog at Blogger. Then click the **Continue** button.

The Reply to topic Web page displays.

More Knowledge

Verifying Your Google Account

You may be prompted to verify your Google account by accessing your e-mail account. If this occurs, follow the instructions provided by Google.

5 On the **Reply** Web page, in the large text box, position your insertion point in the upper left corner at the beginning of any article text and type a brief reply to the article. Compare your screen with Figure 5.22. Scroll down the page and click the **Send** button.

A confirmation page displays with a note that your message will display in the newsgroup momentarily. It may take a few seconds for the servers to update.

Figure 5.22

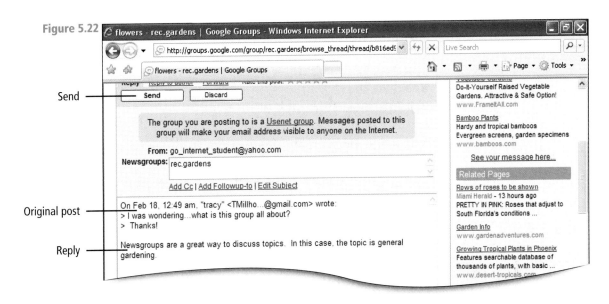

Send
Original post
Reply

6 On the **confirmation page**, click the **Click here to continue** link to display the original article. Scroll down the page as necessary to locate your post.

7 Add the **footer 5B_Newsgroup__Post_Firstname_Lastname** to the Web page. Navigate to the **Chapter_5_Collaborating** folder, and then save the Web page as **5B_Newsgroup_Post_Firstname_Lastname**

8 Check your Chapter Assignment Sheet or Course Syllabus or consult your instructor to determine whether you are to submit your assignments by printing on paper or electronically, using your college's course information management system. Electronically, you can submit the *.txt* file that you created in Notepad. To print on paper from Notepad, under the **File** menu, click **Print** and print accordingly. To submit the document electronically, follow the instructions provided by your instructor.

9 In the upper left corner of the **Google Group** page, click the name of the newsgroup to return to the group. Then, in the upper right corner of the Web page, click the **Sign Out** link to sign out of Groups.

Close ☒ the **Internet Explorer** window.

End **You have completed Project 5B**

Project 5C Exploring Other Web-Based Communication Tools

In Objectives 7 through 9, you will compare several Web-based communication tools. You will discover that wikis provide a text-based communication outlet and that wikis support collaboration among participants of the wiki. Then, you will explore vlogs, which combine text and multimedia for communication. You will identify message boards and Web-based forums. Finally, you will explore instant messaging and compare instant messaging clients.

Objective 7
Discover Wikis and Vlogs

Wikis and vlogs create unique opportunities for interactivity on the World Wide Web. Both of these Web-based communication tools enable many types of information to be shared among large audiences. Not only can wikis and vlogs be used for entertainment, but many schools, businesses, and organizations also use them as part of their Web sites to state policies and procedures or to show how to perform tasks. For example, a college may offer a wiki as an explanative Web site created by peer advisors and counselors that shows the steps to enroll in the school and how to register for classes.

Vlogs are helpful in online courses where students must observe or perform activities as part of their homework. For example, a science instructor may develop a series of vlogs demonstrating specific topics of the course. The instructor could show the correct technique for taking a cutting from a plant so that the student could do the same procedure at their home. Another vlog might show the root development on the cutting over a series of days so that the student could compare and check the progress of his cutting against what is shown in the vlog.

Wikis

What is a wiki? Wikis provide a collaborative digital writing environment similar to blogs. A *wiki* is a Web site that enables anyone to add, edit, or delete content after registering with the Web site. A wiki is different from a blog because a blog permits visitors to respond with comments and to create blogrolls. A wiki permits people to change the actual content of the wiki page. Figure 5.23 shows a wiki on gardening.

Figure 5.23

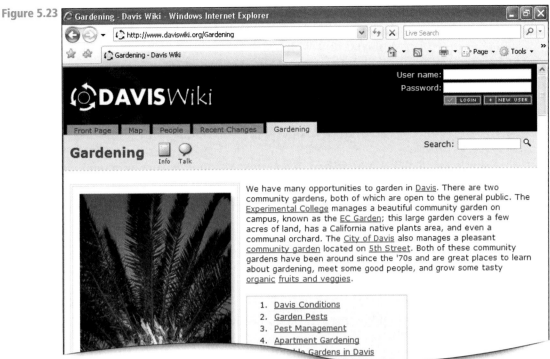

Where can I find a wiki? *Wikipedia* is the largest, most well-known wiki. Wikipedia is an online encyclopedia created by contributing editors. Anyone can edit Wikipedia without logging in, but all changes are tracked. Governance has been established to resolve editing disputes. In case of disputes, inappropriate edits are removed and the previous content is restored.

Wikis are also used at some schools for group-developed presentations or other types of team projects. Students work together by researching a topic and then creating a wiki to present their findings. The table shown in Figure 5.24 lists some popular resources for locating wikis and creating wikis.

Popular Wikis Resources

Wiki Resource	URL
Twiki	*http://twiki.org*
WikiFarms	*http://c2.com/cgi/wiki?WikiFarms*
WikiIndex	*http://www.wikiindex.com/Wiki_Index*
Wikipedia	*http://en.wikipedia.org/wiki/Main_Page*
Wiktionary	*http://www.wiktionary.org*
Xwiki.com	*http://www.xwiki.com*

Figure 5.24

How does a wiki work?   A *wikiengine* is the software that runs the wiki on a Web server. Wiki visitors edit the content by using a form displayed in a Web browser, and the wikiengine converts the edits into a revised version of the Web page. Many wikiengines are **open source** software programs. Recall that an open source software program consists of software program instructions that are available for free distribution; users provide feedback and debug the software in cooperation with the original developers, or even modify and redistribute the programs.

A *WikiWord* is the navigational feature of a wiki that functions as a hyperlink. It is easy to create new hyperlinks in a wiki by taking two or more capitalized words and then running them together, such as NewLink or NextPage. The wikiengine recognizes this pattern, which is known as *CamelCase*. Then the wikiengine creates a link that you click to create a new page. CamelCase is a pattern used in many programming languages where words are written as compound words and each word is capitalized. The capital letters resemble a camel's back.

What do I need to edit a wiki?   Although little technical knowledge is required to edit a wiki, the wiki pages use HTML tags to mark up the content of the wiki. This can make it difficult for some wiki contributors to locate the content among the tags. Therefore, most wikis have a *sandbox*. A sandbox is a practice area where individuals new to wikis can practice making edits without damaging the real content of the wiki.

Vlogs

What is a vlog?   A *video log*, or *vlog*, is a blog that uses video as its primary content. Just as with blogs, there is a growing community, called the *vlogosphere*. The vlogosphere is the collection of vlogs found on the World Wide Web including the entire vlogging community of vloggers and readers. A *vlogger* is the author of a vlog.

Several hosting providers are available where you can create a free account. Then, after making a video and compressing it, you upload the video to the hosting providers. Popular vlogs include vacation videos or videos created for artistic expression such as up-and-coming independent bands or singers trying to break into show business. Increasingly, vlogs are used for *citizen journalism*. Citizen journalism can be defined as citizens reporting breaking news events as they occur at their location in the form of a blog or vlog.

How do I find vlogs?   If you have a computer with a browser, Internet access, and a plug-in that supports video, you can search for and view vlogs using a keyword query at a general search engine. Several search engines have also been created that specialize in locating video content on the Web. The table shown in Figure 5.25 lists several resources for locating vlogs.

Vlog Resources and Directories

Vlog Resource	URL
01vlog.com	*http://www.01vlog.com*
Blip.tv	*http://blip.tv*
Lulu.tv	*http://www.lulu.tv*
Mefeedia	*http://mefeedia.com*
YouTube	*http://www.youtube.com*

Figure 5.25

What problems will I encounter with vlogs?   Although the majority of vlogs are created for entertainment value—representing educational, environmental, personal, or political content—you will find vlogs with copyrighted or offensive content. Anyone who has video-recording equipment and an Internet connection can create and upload vlogs. Because of the ease with which people can create and post vlogs, vlogging can create privacy concerns for those posting vlogs. Most vlog hosting providers have strong statements and guidelines that help you protect your identity and location if you appear in a video. However, these guidelines are sometimes ignored by vloggers.

Vlog hosting providers have privacy policies and Terms of Service agreements in place for everyone who uses the hosting provider. In addition, most hosting providers include guidelines on keeping vloggers safe. In accordance with the Children's Online Privacy Protection Act (COPPA), children under 13 are not allowed to post vlogs. Because of the volume of vlog posts, it is almost impossible for vlog-hosting providers to screen vlogs before they are made accessible to the public. You can report objectionable vlogs at the Web site. Most vlog providers have easy-to-locate links labeled as abuse reporting mechanisms. The vlog providers appreciate receiving this type of feedback.

Objective 8
Identify Message Boards, Web-Based Forums, and Bulletin Boards

What is a message board?   A *message board* is a Web-based discussion area similar to a newsgroup where topics are discussed in threads. A message board is different from a newsgroup because it is entirely Web-based and uses HTTP as the protocol. Recall that even though you can use a Web site to read posts at a newsgroup, the protocol that makes a newsgroup function is NNTP.

Message boards are also called ***Web-based forums***, or simply ***forums***, or ***bulletin boards***. Message board discussions are laid out in tables. The discussion threads are organized chronologically in the order the posts are made. Figure 5.26 shows an example of a message board.

Figure 5.26

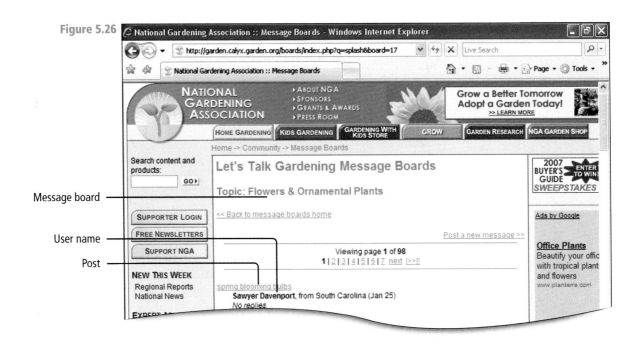

Message board

User name

Post

How does a message board work? You do not need special software or a newsreader to read or post messages to a message board. Message boards are publicly accessible so anyone can create a new thread. However, many messages boards require you to create an account before posting to it.

Message board software sets up accounts with user IDs and passwords. Typically, posts display the user ID as part of the post. When using message boards, it is a good idea to use an alternative name for your user ID, instead of your given name, to help protect your personal identity. You do not know who will read the threads because they are easily accessed. Some message boards enable you to set preferences to hide your identity so that any posts that you make are anonymous.

What is an avatar? Some message boards enable you to create an *avatar*. An avatar is a graphic used to represent a message board—instant message or chat—participant. For example, if you are interested in growing roses, you may choose to be represented by an avatar depicting a rose or someone holding a rose.

What are message board communities? Often, virtual communities develop among message board participants. Rules of netiquette develop within the message board community. Moderators are able to edit, delete, or move postings according to established rules for the message board.

Message boards are commonly used to provide support and customer service at many commercial Web sites. You find these message boards linked to the home page of a Web site. These moderated message boards are used to provide FAQs, or frequently asked questions, to customers. Problems are posted, and answers are offered by other message board participants. For example, you might use a message board to find out why your printer has suddenly stopped working. You would locate the answer in a message board FAQ offered by the printer's manufacturer before using e-mail, chat, or a telephone to contact a live service representative.

Other messages boards are focused on one topic, such as gardening, sports, popular music, or current movies. Sometimes rivalries develop in the message board, and public conflict and flaming erupts. The moderator must then remind the participants of the message board rules. Participants who break the rules risk having the moderator delete their threads.

Where can I locate a message board?   You can locate existing message boards by using either a keyword query at a search engine or a directory search. For example, to locate a gardening message board, type the query *gardening message board* into the search text box. The search results list will provide links to several gardening-oriented forums and message boards.

Some Web sites combine message board search capabilities with message board creation tools. There are several opportunities to create your own message board free of charge or for a modest fee. Figure 5.27 lists some providers.

Message Board Providers	
Message Board Provider	**URL**
123Forum.com	*http://www.123forum.com*
Big-Board	*http://www.big-boards.com*
iVillage Message Boards	*http://www.ivillage.com/messageboards*
Yahoo! Message Boards	*http://messages.yahoo.com*

Figure 5.27

Objective 9
Explore Instant Messaging and Compare Instant Messengers

Instant messaging, or IM, is quickly becoming the second most commonly used World Wide Web service behind e-mail. Because of its popularity, several IM clients exist. IM is an easy and convenient communication tool. Each IM client offers nearly the same features. However, many clients are proprietary so that messages are sent only between others using that same IM client.

Instant Messaging

What is instant messaging?   *Instant messaging*, or *IM*, is an interactive, text-based synchronous discussion where, typically, only two people participate within one window. Many IM programs, or *IM clients*, allow multiple windows to be open at once. An IM client is an instant messaging program installed on your computer that enables you to send and receive messages instantly. IM clients provide a service that alerts you when your friends or colleagues are online and enables you to communicate with them in real time.

How does IM work?   After you have an IM client installed on your computer, the IM client can be configured to start automatically when you start your computer. You may set other preferences to permit the IM client to contact the server with notification that you are online or to forward your ***contact list*** to the server. A contact list is a list of people you know and their user IDs.

You control the ability to communicate with others through the contact list. The IM client runs in the background until someone from your contact list sends a message to you or you send a message. If someone from your contact list is online, that user ID is marked as active, or online, in your contact list. The contact list is updated as more contacts come online. In the same way, your contacts display in your contact list, your user ID displays to your contacts so that they are able to see when you are online.

You can mark yourself as being away from the computer, or mark that you are busy when you want to be left alone but still want to know if any of your contacts are online. You can also block or ignore individuals you want to avoid. As contacts go offline, the contact list is updated again.

How do I send an instant message?   To send an instant message to a contact who is online, click or double-click the name of the contact. In the displayed window, type your message, and then click the Send button. Any responses are displayed in the same window. When you have finished the conversation, you can close the window and choose either to save or delete the conversation. Figure 5.28 shows an IM conversation.

Figure 5.28
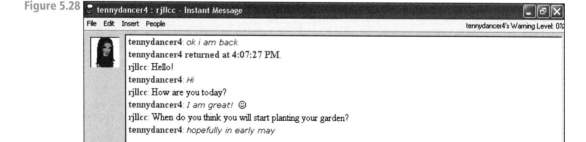

What are the features of an IM client?   Because instant messages are text-based, most people add ***emoticons*** to express feelings, or use ***acronyms*** to reduce the amount of typing. Recall that emoticons are a series of keyboard characters, text, or inline images that create a face displaying an emotion and are commonly used in chat or instant messaging. For example, when you type :-), you are saying *I'm smiling* or *I'm happy.* When you type :-D, you are saying *I'm laughing.* Acronyms are a series of letters that stand for the first letter of words in a phrase commonly used in chat or instant messaging. For example, AFC stands for "away from the computer" and BAC stands for "back at the computer."

Instant messaging was an entirely text-based service when it was first introduced. Now many IM clients allow you to insert graphics to replace typed emoticons. Avatars can be used with some IM clients to represent individuals. Additional features have been integrated into most IM clients, including chat, voice, and video capabilities. IM clients support file sharing, e-mail, and streaming information such as news, sports, and weather updates. You can include hyperlinks as part of your messages. All of these updates make IM an easy and convenient way to communicate.

In addition, you can display your photos along with your message or use a **Web cam** for sending live video content. A Web cam is a small camera that connects to your computer and transmits your image or whatever is immediately in front of the camera lens across the Internet to a receiving computer for display on that computer's monitor. Audio messages are now available with several IM clients, and instant messages can be routed to mobile phones.

Many IM clients include chat and **whiteboard** features so that more than two people can participate in the same conversation. A whiteboard is a feature that allows each participant to view and interact with a screen, Web page, document, or drawing. Most IM clients allow you to attach and share files during the conversation. You can initiate an e-mail and send a file as an attachment using your IM client. Streaming content, such as news, headlines, weather, and stock market quotes, is available with some instant messaging programs, with RSS feeds that alert you to updated content.

What precautions should be taken with instant messaging?   Instant messages are susceptible to viruses. Most antivirus software programs do not automatically scan all instant messages unless you set them to do so. To help guard against virus infection, avoid clicking on any unknown or unexpected links or attachments that may be sent to you.

Follow safe computing practices by talking only to those people you know and trust. It is not a good idea to share passwords, account information, or personal information in instant messages because third parties can intercept the messages. In addition, because instant messages can be saved, avoid typing or saying anything that you would not want shared with others in the future.

Comparing Instant Messengers

What are the most popular IM clients?   Popular instant messaging programs are available as free downloads on the World Wide Web. After the client is downloaded and installed on your computer, you are able to connect to the IM provider's server to communicate with anyone who has the same IM client. The table shown in Figure 5.29 lists the names of several IM clients, and the URLs where you can find out more about and download each program.

Instant Messaging Clients

IM Client	URL
AIM	*http://www.aim.com*
ICQ	*http://www.icq.com*
Jabber	*http://www.jabber.org*
meebo	*http://www.meebo.com*
Miranda	*http://www.miranda-im.org*
Trillian	*http://www.ceruleanstudios.com*
Windows Live Messenger	*http://get.live.com/messenger*
Yahoo! Messenger	*http://messenger.yahoo.com*

Figure 5.29

Can I use one IM client to communicate with all the other IM clients?   Typically, IM clients are proprietary and work only with others using that same client. For example, if you use AIM, then you will be able to communicate only with your friends who also have AIM. You may need several IM clients installed on your computer to communicate with everyone you know.

Because there are so many IM clients that are available, it may be helpful to have a unifying utility program that can communicate with all IM clients. The Miranda and Trillian clients support most of the major IM clients and are available free of charge. By installing either one of these two programs, you can communicate with nearly anyone else regardless of the IM client they use.

Miranda is an open source program, so you can participate in its development. At their Web sites, both Trillian and Miranda offer forums where you can find support or provide answers to others. Both Web sites also feature a blog for the discussion on development issues.

 You have completed Project 5C

Project 5C

Take the online self-study quiz for this chapter:

1. Go to **www.prenhall.com/go** and select the textbook *GO!* **with the Internet.**

2. Select **chapter 5.**

3. Select **Self-Study Quiz Project 5C.**

Project 5D **Comparing Synchronous Communication Tools**

In Objectives 10 through 12, you compare **synchronous communication** tools. Recall that synchronous communication is electronic communication in which two or more participants are online at the same time and communicating with each other. To begin, you will identify types of IRC and chat. Then, you will define Internet telephony and VoIP. Finally, you will explore video conferencing options.

Objective 10
Identify Types of IRC and Chat

IRC and chat enable individuals to participate in real-time conversations over the Internet. Chat is popular and is often used for entertainment and conversation among friends. Many organizations host live events using chat. For example, a symposium held as a chat may be used to introduce a new product to customers living across many states. In addition, chat may be used to provide customer support at some business Web sites. Some online classes use chat to communicate with the teacher during online office hours or to talk to a classmate.

IRC

What is an IRC and how is it used? *Internet Relay Chat*, or **IRC**, is the first system developed to enable multiple individuals to participate in text-based, real-time conversations over the Internet. Although it takes more skill to use than typical Web-based chat, IRC is still a popular option for chat today.

To use IRC, you must download an IRC client so that you can connect to an IRC server. Unlike self-installing IM clients that are downloaded from a Web site, you typically download an IRC client from an **anonymous FTP** site. An anonymous FTP site permits you to log in and access files on a server without identifying yourself to the server with a user ID and password. An anonymous FTP site accepts the word *guest* or *anonymous* as the user ID and supplying a password is unnecessary.

After you have downloaded and installed the IRC client, you must configure it, or set it up, to connect to an IRC server. Several IRC servers join together, forming a network. There are several separate networks, with several thousand individuals on each network. Individuals using IRC are known by nicknames. You will be unable to talk with individuals who are on a different network but you will be able to talk with individuals who are on different servers.

What is a channel? IRC conversations are held in **channels**. Channels are chat rooms that focus on a specific topic. Some channels are public, indicated by the abbreviation *pub*; other channels are private, indicated by the abbreviation *prv*. You will see private channels listed only if you are member of that private channel.

All channel names begin with the pound sign (#), such as *#zengarden*. A **channel operator** is the first person to join a channel who therefore, gets to control the channel. A channel operator can choose whether to share the operator status. A channel operator's nickname is preceded by the "at" sign (@). The channel operator determines who joins a channel and who speaks in the channel.

How are IRCs used?   Most IRC clients use text-based commands to perform common tasks. IRC clients for computers running the Windows operating system, such as mIRC, use buttons and icons to perform common tasks. However, even if you are using mIRC, it is a good idea to become familiar with the text-based commands because the commands work in all IRC clients. IRC commands begin with a forward slash (/) followed by a single word. For example, the command */help* will provide help information. You must type all commands carefully, paying close attention to spacing and capitalization. The table shown in Figure 5.30 lists some of the common IRC commands.

IRC Commands

Typed Command	Result
/join#zengarden	Enables you to join the channel named zengarden.
/me is a redrose	Tells everyone in #zengarden that your nickname is redrose. The result displays as * *yournick is a redrose.*
/who#zengarden	Provides a list of user nicknames for the channel. The result displays as *Pub: #zengarden @greenleaf froggey redrose toadster.*
hello everyone	Tells everyone in #zengarden that you say hello. Your nickname is automatically shown in brackets. The result displays as *<redrose> hello everyone.*
/leave#zengarden	Enables you to leave #zengarden.
/quit good night!	Enables you to quit IRC and gives a final message to everyone in #zengarden. The result displays as *** *Signoff: redrose (good night!).*

Figure 5.30

Chat

What is chat?   Recall that **chat** is interactive, text-based synchronous discussion among two or more participants, performed using an Internet-connected computer and specialized software. Some clients require software that is downloaded to your computer as freeware before you can send or receive chat messages.

Other clients are Web-based and require no software other than a browser and may require a subscription to the Web-based service. Web-based chat allows individuals to access some IRC networks and channels using a Web browser. Web-based chat also allows individuals to access other chat rooms set up at the Web site of provider.

Web-based chat is easy to use. Unlike IRC, individuals who want to chat do not need to know any special commands. Each participant types text into a text box and then clicks the Send button to post the message. The text then displays on the screens of all active participants. The table shown in Figure 5.31 lists the names of some popular chat clients and the URLs where you can find out more about each program.

Popular Chat Clients

Chat Client	URL
Gmail Chat	*http://mail.google.com/mail/help/intl/en/chat.html*
mIRC	*http://www.mirc.com*
MSN Chat	*http://chat.msn.com*
Yahoo! Chat	*http://chat.yahoo.com*

Figure 5.31

What are the features of chat? There are several providers of Web-based chat. Each provider may have a slightly different interface, but some features are common to all clients. Typically, a series of menus is located on the top edge of the chat window. These menus allow individuals to perform commands such as starting a private chat, recording the chat session, asking a question of a participant, or exiting the program.

Chat participants are displayed in a list, usually found along one side of the window. A text box for entering messages is generally located at the bottom of the window.

To participate, users type a message into the text box and then click a Send button onscreen or press the Enter key on the keyboard. The message displays in the main window next to the participant's name. Typically, each participant's messages are written in a different color to help distinguish the messages. Emoticons and acronyms are used to help speed up the typing of the messages. Figure 5.32 shows a typical chat room.

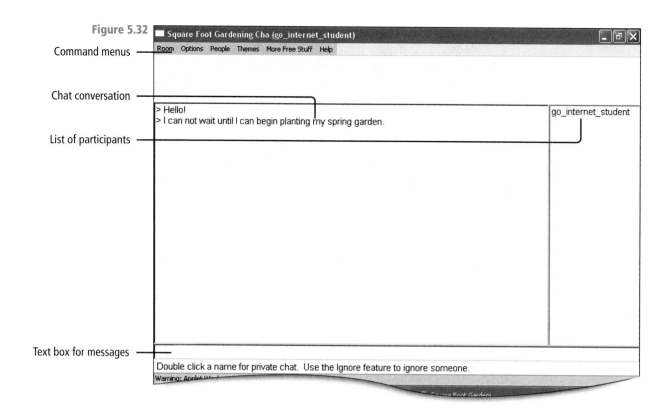

Figure 5.32

Command menus

Chat conversation

List of participants

Text box for messages

Is chat always text-based? Although chat began as a text-based service, most chat providers now provide additional enhancements. You can display multimedia and hyperlinks along with the text. You can send files to other participants as attachments. Most Web-based chats include whiteboards and allow you to share files onscreen.

What precautions should be used in chat rooms? Web-based chat rooms provide both public and private conversations. Public chat rooms allow anyone to use the service. If you are new to chat and do not know how it works, you are called a *newbie*. It is a good idea for a newbie to *lurk* in a chat room to get a feel for the flow of conversation before joining in. When you lurk, you receive and are able to read the messages, but you do not reply to any of the messages. Sometimes, flaming occurs in public chat rooms. Recall that the term *flame* refers to sending an abusive or insulting message to someone on a mailing list, listserv, or in a chat room.

Keep in mind that because many chat rooms are public. You can never be certain that participants are who they say they are. Be careful abut what you say in the chat room. Never reveal your name or location, and always protect your personal information.

Objective 11
Define Internet Telephony and VoIP

What is Internet telephony? *Internet telephony* is the transmission of voice communication over the Internet by using packet switching and TCP/IP. Internet telephony is also called *Voice over Internet Protocol*, or **VoIP**. Calls can be made between two computers or between a computer and a telephone or cellular phone.

VoIP takes analog voice data and converts it to digital form. When it is in digital form, the data is broken into packets and sent over IP networks. When the packets arrive at their destination, they are reassembled and converted back into analog form.

What are the benefits of VoIP?   VoIP providers are found world-wide—a great advantage in today's global economy. Some businesses have switched to VoIP as a cost savings measure. Calls made using VoIP are cheaper than traditional telephone calls because VoIP calls are not taxed and long distance charges are not incurred. Calls made between computers are free. VoIP providers charge a flat rate for calls within the United States and Canada. Calls made to other countries are generally cheaper than traditional overseas telephone rates.

What do I need to make a VoIP call using my computer?   Several providers are available that allow you to make VoIP calls from your computer. The table in Figure 5.33 includes the names and URLs for several popular providers.

VoIP Providers	
VoIP Provider	**URL**
Net2Phone	*http://web.net2phone.com*
NetZeroVoice	*http://www.netzero.net/voip*
Skype	*http://www.skype.com*
Vonage	*http://www.vonage.com*
Windows Live Messenger	*http://get.live.com/messenger/overview*
Yahoo! Messenger	*http://messenger.yahoo.com*

Figure 5.33

You need Internet access before you can make a call using VoIP. Your computer needs speakers and either a microphone or a headset. Calls can be made from computer to computer or computer to phone. A software program provides a contact list, which you use to enter names and phone numbers.

Most software for VoIP also has an interface resembling a phone pad so that you can click the numbers to dial the call. Sound effects may be built into the program to simulate dialing and ringing sounds. Features such as call waiting, conference calling, and voice-mail are available with most programs. It is a good idea to research providers for benefits and disadvantages before switching to VoIP.

Objective 12
Describe Video Conferencing

What is video conferencing? *Video conferencing* is the transmission of video and audio data for the purpose of synchronous communication between two or more geographically separated participants. Although video conferencing originally took place over telephone or network lines, it now takes place using a high-bandwidth connection and Internet Protocol.

Video conferencing may be used to support collaboration and team project development. Video conferencing saves money for businesses by reducing travel time and ticketing costs associated with out-of-town meetings. Many families enjoy using video conferencing to stay in touch with relatives who may live far away.

What equipment is needed for video conferencing? Video conferencing takes place on a computer with Internet access. The computer must have speakers, a headset or microphone, a Web cam, sound and video cards, and video conferencing software.

Several video conferencing software packages are available, as shown in the table in Figure 5.34. Most of these packages integrate several services, such as a text-based chat, a whiteboard, and document sharing. Video conferencing can be recorded and archived for viewing at a later time.

Video Conferencing Programs	
Video Conferencing Software	**URL**
Acrobat Connect Professional	*http://www.adobe.com/products/breeze/index.html*
GoToMeeting	*https://www.gotomeeting.com*
MS Office Live Meeting	*http://www.microsoft.com/uc/livemeeting/default.mspx*
WebEx	*http://www.webex.com*

Figure 5.34

Several video conferencing options are available on the Web free of charge. Most of the major instant messaging clients, such as Windows Live Messenger and Yahoo! Messenger, also offer video conferencing. However, these options are not for large groups of participants but rather one-on-one conversations. As long as both participants have the same equipment, high bandwidth connections, and are using the same IM client, it is easy to set up and use the video conferencing feature.

When should you use each of the collaboration tools? Knowing when to use each one of the collaboration tools discussed in this chapter can be confusing. Each has its own best use. The table in Figure 5.35 lists each tool, gives other names for the tools, and describes when you might want to use each.

Collaborative Tools

Commonly Called	Also Called	When To Use
Blog	Web log	Sharing thoughts and ideas with others with frequent updates.
Chat		Brief, quick, synchronous communication among two or more participants.
Instant message	IM	Brief, quick, synchronous communication between two participants.
IRC	Internet Relay Chat	Brief, quick, synchronous communication typically using special commands.
Message board	Web-based forum, forum, or bulletin board	Publicly accessible, threaded, Web-based discussion board typically used for FAQs, customer support, and troubleshooting.
Newsgroup	USENET	Networked, threaded discussion boards set up for seven or eight hierarchies of topics.
Video conferencing		Communication made between two or more computers with voice and video data to support collaboration and team project development.
Vlog	Video log	Similar to blogs but including video content typically used for citizen journalism or entertainment
VoIP	Internet telephony	Voice communication made between computers and telephones.
Wiki		Digital writing environment used for collaborative projects.

Figure 5.35

 End You have completed Project 5D ————————

Online Quiz

Project 5D

Take the online self-study quiz for this chapter:

1. Go to **www.prenhall.com/go** and select the textbook *GO!* **with the Internet.**

2. Select **chapter 5.**

3. Select **Self-Study Quiz Project 5D**.

Assessments

Summary

In this chapter, you located blogs using a general search engine and a specialized search engine. You read blogs and compared blog search tools. You set up an account at a blogging Web site and published a post to your blog. Next, you searched for USENET newsgroups. You searched for Web-based newsgroups and read threads. Then you joined a Web-based newsgroup and posted a reply. You explored other Web-based communication tools, such as wikis and vlogs. You identified message boards, Web-based forums, and bulletin boards. You explored instant messaging and compared types of IM clients. You identified types of IRC and chat. You looked at Internet telephony and VoIP, which enables you to use your computer for making phone calls. Finally, you described video conferencing.

Key Terms

Acronym 308

Aggregator 278

Anonymous FTP 311

Archive 294

Article 291

Asynchronous
  communication 291

Avatar 306

Big Eight 293

Big Seven 293

Blog 274

Blog feed 278

Blogger 276

Blogosphere 277

Blogroll 276

Bulletin Board 305

CamelCase 304

CAPTCHA 283

Channel 311

Channel operator 312

Chat 312

Citizen
  journalism 304

Contact list 308

Dashboard 284

Deja News 294

Emoticon 308

Font 287

Formatting
  toolbar 287

Forum 305

Flame 314

Hierarchy 292

Hosting provider ...281

IM client 307

Instant
  messaging (IM) 307

Internet Relay
  Chat (IRC) 311

Internet telephony ..314

Lurk 314

Message board 305

Moderated
  newsgroup 299

Moderator 299

Newbie 314

Newsfeed 296

Newsgroup 291

Newsreader 297

News server 296

Network News
  Transfer Protocol
  (NNTP) 296

Open source 304

Permalink 276

Post 275

Publish 284

Really Simple
  Syndication (RSS) ..277

Sandbox 304

ScreenTip 287

Synchronous
  communication 311

Tags 278

Template 284

Thread 291

TILE.NET 292

Timestamp 275

(Continued)

Assessments

Key Terms

Top-level domain 275

Trackback 276

Unmoderated
    newsgroup 299

USENET 291

Video
    conferencing 316

Video log 304

Vlog 304

Vlogger 304

Vlogosphere 304

Voice over Internet
    Protocol (VoIP) 314

Web-based forum 305

Web cam 309

Web log 274

Whiteboard 309

Wiki 302

Wikiengine 304

Wikipedia 303

WikiWord 304

Assessments

Matching

Match each term in the second column with its correct definition in the first column by writing the letter of the term on the blank line in front of the correct definition.

_____ **1.** A Web site that takes the form of a journal or news site, is updated frequently, and represents the personality of the author of the Web site.

_____ **2.** Electronic communication in which the participants do not need to be online at the same time, and all participants can view the communication when they want to do so.

_____ **3.** An RSS feed that notifies you of an update to a blog.

_____ **4.** The original message of a thread found in a newsgroup.

_____ **5.** The author of a blog.

_____ **6.** An article and all of the posts that follow along a specific topic in a newsgroup.

_____ **7.** A series of links found within a blog that connects to other blogs.

_____ **8.** A well-respected resource used for locating Internet references for newsletters, discussion lists, USENET newsgroups, vendors for computer products, Internet Service Providers, and Web design companies.

_____ **9.** The collection of blogs found on the World Wide Web including the entire blogging community of authors and readers.

_____ **10.** The seven original top-level hierarchies: comp.*, misc.*, news.*, rec.*, sci.*, soc.*, and talk.*.

_____ **11.** A user interface, or a Web page, that provides one location to perform several tasks such as viewing or editing your profile, changing your password, editing your personal information, and creating or managing your blog.

_____ **12.** An early newsgroup system that provided access to several thousand newsgroups until the late 1990s, when it was taken over by Google Groups.

_____ **13.** The protocol used to distribute the articles, posts, and threads among newsgroups.

_____ **14.** The exchange of articles and posts between news servers.

_____ **15.** The software program that supports NNTP and is used to read newsgroup threads.

A Aggregator

B Article

C Asynchronous communication

D Big Seven

E Blog

F Blogger

G Blogosphere

H Blogroll

I Dashboard

J Deja News

K Newsfeed

L Newsreader

M NNTP

N Thread

O TILE.NET

Assessments

Fill in the Blank

Write the correct answer in the space provided.

1. A system developed to automatically alert subscribers of updates made to sites such as blogs, news, weather, or sports site is called _____.

2. An Internet forum that provides a threaded discussion on specific topics is called a(n) _____.

3. An individual entry in a blog or any of the subsequent replies to an article found in a newsgroup is called a(n) _____.

4. The unique URL for a blog post so that users can locate the post by typing the URL into the Address bar of the browser is called a(n) _____.

5. A networked discussion board for discussion among researchers and scientists in the early development of the Internet is known as _____.

6. A blog feature that notifies a blogger when comments are made to one of the posts is called the _____.

7. A topic category that provides the structure of a newsgroup name is called a(n) _____.

8. Categories for the organization of blog topics that are added to the blog when the blog is written are called _____.

9. An expression of time—hour or day—to indicate the most recent update for a blog or a Web site is called a(n) _____.

10. A server that hosts several newsgroups to exchange articles, posts, and threads from their hosted newsgroups with other news servers and their hosted newsgroups is called a(n) _____.

11. An RSS feed that notifies you of an update to a blog is called a(n) _____.

12. A program that makes certain text visible onscreen appear to be composed of wavy and distorted letters in order to prevent computer programs from performing events online instead of humans performing events online is known as _____.

(Continued)

Assessments

Fill in the Blank

13. A predesigned document that can be added to or modified for use in a blog, Web page, or word-processed document is called a(n) _____.

14. An electronic copy of a file that can be stored in a separate location and retrieved at a future date is called a(n) _____.

15. The human who screens newsgroup posts to determine whether the posts should be allowed to be sent to the news server is called the _____.

Assessments

Rubric

Projects 5A and 5B in the front portion of this chapter, and Projects 5E through 5K that follow have no specific correct result; your result will depend on your approach to the information provided. Make Professional Quality your goal. Use the following scoring rubric to guide you in how to approach the search problem and then to evaluate how well your approach solves the search problem.

The *criteria*—Internet Mastery, Content, Format and Layout of Search Results, and Process—represent the knowledge and skills you have gained that you can apply to solving the search problem. The *levels of performance*—Professional Quality, Approaching Professional Quality, or Needs Quality Improvement—help you and your instructor evaluate your result.

	Your completed project is of Professional Quality if you:	Your completed project is Approaching Professional Quality if you:	Your completed project Needs Quality Improvement if you:
1–Internet Mastery	Choose and apply the most appropriate search skills, tools, and features and identify efficient methods to conduct the search and locate valid results.	Choose and apply some appropriate search skills, tools, and features, but not in the most efficient manner.	Choose inappropriate search skills, tools, or features, or are inefficient in locating valid results.
2–Content	Conduct a search that is clear and well organized, contains results that are accurate, appropriate to the audience and purpose, and are complete.	Conduct a search in which some results are unclear, poorly organized, inconsistent, or incomplete. Misjudge the needs of the audience.	Conduct a search that is unclear, incomplete, or poorly organized, containing some inaccurate or inappropriate content.
3–Format and Layout of Search Results	Format and arrange all search results to communicate information and ideas, clarify function, illustrate relationships, and indicate relative importance.	Apply appropriate format and layout features to some search results, but not others. Overuse search techniques, causing minor distraction.	Apply format and layout that does not communicate the search results clearly. Do not use format and layout features to clarify function, illustrate relationships, or indicate relative importance. Use available search techniques excessively, causing distraction.
4–Process	Use an organized approach that integrates planning, development, self-assessment, revision, and reflection.	Demonstrate an organized approach in some areas, but not others; or, use an insufficient process of organization throughout.	Do not use an organized approach to solve the problem.

Project 5E—Finding Garden Design Blogs

Objective: 1. *Locate Existing Blogs.*

Yumiko Sato, garden design consultant for Southland Media, is looking for blogs on garden design for an upcoming show. Previous searches have not brought the kind of information Yumiko wants. In this Assessment, you will find blogs related to garden design using a search engine. After gathering the information, you will use Notepad to summarize your findings.

For Project 5E, you will need the following file:

New blank Notepad document

You will save your file as
5E_Garden_Design_Firstname_Lastname

1. **Start** Internet Explorer and if necessary, click the **Maximize** button to enlarge the window to fill the computer screen completely. In the **Address bar**, click one time to select the existing text, type **http://www.feedster.com** and then press Enter. The **Feedster** home page displays. Feedster is a search engine for newsfeeds. You can locate blogs, news, and podcasts at this search engine.

2. At the top of the **Feedster** home page, click the **Search Help** link. Take a moment to review how Feedster uses Boolean operators and read any other suggestions about searches. When you are finished, return to the **Feedster** home page.

3. In the **Search** text box, type the keyword query **garden design** Above the **Search** text box, locate and click **Blogs**, and then click the **Search** button.

4. Scroll down the search results list and evaluate the hits by reading the description and noting the location of the blog posting. Determine how recently the post was made and decide if the post is relevant to garden design. If necessary, click the **Next** button as needed to locate a blog on garden design.

5. Evaluate the blogs for the following:

   - The name of the blog
   - The permalink of the post
   - The timestamp for the post

(Project 5E–Finding Garden Design Blogs continues on the next page)

Assessments

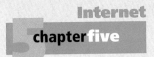

(Project 5E–Finding Garden Design Blogs continued)

Then repeat the evaluation process for two more blogs.

6. Start Notepad, and then save a document in Notepad as **5E_Garden_Design_ Firstname_Lastname** Use the file name as the title of the document. After the title, press Enter two times.

7. Type the name of the first blog post you evaluated, the permalink of the post, and the timestamp. Repeat this for two other posts. Create a paragraph after the list of posts and type a summary that explains how you located and evaluated the blog posts.

8. Add the **footer 5E_Garden_Design_ Firstname_Lastname** to the document. **Save** the document as **5E_Garden_Design_**

Firstname_Lastname in the **Chapter_5_ Collaborating** folder.

9. Check your Chapter Assignment Sheet or Course Syllabus or consult your instructor to determine whether you are to submit your assignments by printing on paper or electronically, using your college's course information management system. Electronically, you can submit the *.txt* file created in Notepad. To print on paper from Notepad, under the **File** menu, click **Print** and print accordingly. To submit the document electronically, follow the instructions provided by your instructor.

10. Close the **Notepad** window. **Close** the **Internet Explorer** window.

End **You have completed Project 5E**

Assessments

Project 5F—Locating Active Message Boards

Objective: 8. *Identify Message Boards, Web-Based Forums, and Bulletin Boards.*

Miguel Harris, a technology assistant for Southland Media, needs to determine if a message board is a good idea for the *Southland Gardens* companion Web site. Before he puts a message board into place, he wants to see other garden message boards. In this Assessment, you will locate a message board and then read and evaluate the posts.

For Project 5F, you will need the following file:

Web page printout

**You will save your file as
5F_Message_Board_Firstname_Lastname**

1. **Start** Internet Explorer. In the **Address bar**, click one time to select the existing text, and then type **http://peopleconnection. aol.com/messageboards** Press ⏎. The **AOL People Connection** home page displays. This is a service of AOL where you can find discussion on a variety of topics. You can use the home page as a directory search engine or you can perform a keyword query.

2. On the left side of the screen, locate and click the **Home, Hobbies & Family** link. In the middle of the Web page that displays, locate and click the **Home & Garden** link. Several broad topics display. Locate and click the **Gardens & Yard Discussions** link. At the top of the Web page, notice the breadcrumb trail for navigating through the message boards. Click the **Community Standards** link. Some message boards are managed by AOL; others are managed by members. You can report off-topic posts, and you can also control settings to filter unwanted content. Close the **Community Standards** pop-up window to return to the list of messages.

3. In the main content area of the table, notice the **Title**, **Latest Message**, and **Items** columns. Click the **Title** link of a message board that has more than zero posts. For the message board that displays, in the main content area, notice the **Title** of the posts, the **Latest Message**, and the **Messages (Unread)** columns. Click one of the messages—threads—and then review all posts looking for relevance to the message topic and the timestamp.

(Project 5F–Locating Active Message Boards continues on the next page)

Assessments

(Project 5F–Locating Active Message Boards continued)

4. Add the **footer 5F_Message_Board_ Firstname_Lastname** to the Web page **Save** the Web page to the **Chapter_5_ Collaborating** folder as **5F_Message_ Board_Firstname_Lastname**

Check your Chapter Assignment Sheet or Course Syllabus or consult your instructor to determine whether you are to submit your assignments by printing on paper or electronically using your college's course information management system.

5. Close the **Internet Explorer** window.

End You have completed Project 5F

Assessments

Mastering the Internet

Project 5G—Evaluating IM Clients

Objectives: 3. *Publish Posts to Your Blog;* **9.** *Explore Instant Messaging and Compare Instant Messengers;* **12.** *Describe Video Conferencing.*

In this Assessment, you will help Miguel Harris, a technology assistant for Southland Media, develop a recommendation for an IM client that can be used by the Southland Media staff. Because there are so many additional features available with IM clients, he wants to compare two different IM clients.

For Project 5G, you will need the following file:

Web page printout

You will save your file as
5G_IM_Clients_Firstname_Lastname

1. **Start** Internet Explorer. In the **Address bar**, click one time to select the existing text, and then type **http://www.aim.com** Press Enter. The **AIM** home page displays. Review the home page and evaluate the site for the following features:

   - Use of emoticons or avatars
   - Ability to include hyperlinks with your messages
   - Photo sharing
   - Audio messages or video conferencing
   - Route instant messages to mobile phones

2. Make notes about these features. You will transfer these notes to a post at your blogging site created for an activity earlier in this chapter.

3. In the **Address bar**, click one time to select the existing text, type **http://messenger.yahoo.com** and then press Enter. The **Yahoo! Messenger** home page displays. Review the home page and evaluate the site for the same features used in Step 1. Then make notes about these features for your blog post.

4. In the **Address bar**, click to select the existing text, type **http://www.blogger.com/start** and then press Enter. The **Blogger** home page displays. Using your user ID and password that you established earlier, log into your Blogger account.

(Project 5G–Evaluating IM Clients continues on the next page)

Assessments

(Project 5G–Evaluating IM Clients continued)

5. Using the dashboard, make a new post titled **5G_IM_Clients_Firstname_Lastname** Create a paragraph for each IM client that lists the name of the IM client and the results of the evaluation that you completed in the previous steps.

6. Type a final paragraph that provides your recommendation on the IM client for Southland Media to use. Format the blog post and check the spelling. Then publish your post. After the post is confirmed and published, view the blog post.

7. Add the **footer 5G_IM_Clients_Firstname_ Lastname** to the Web page and **Save** the

Web page to the **Chapter_5_Collaborating** folder as **5G_IM_Clients_Firstname_ Lastname**

Check your Chapter Assignment Sheet or Course Syllabus or consult your instructor to determine whether you are to submit your assignments by printing on paper or electronically using your college's course information management system.

8. Sign out of Blogger and **Close** the **Internet Explorer** window.

End **You have completed Project 5G** ———————————————

chaptersix

Locating Resources on the World Wide Web

OBJECTIVES

At the end of this chapter, you will be able to:

1. Perform a Directory Search and Evaluate a Special-Interest Web Site
2. Perform a Search for Special-Interest Web Sites Using a Search Engine and an Advanced Search
3. Compare Types of Special-Interest Web Sites

4. Access Weather Information Online
5. Install a Feed on Your Computer
6. Manage Travel Arrangements Online

7. Find People Using Online Resources
8. Locate Legal Information and Educational Opportunities

9. Identify Award-Winning Web Sites and Portals
10. Compare Gaming Sites
11. Explore Multimedia Resources

OUTCOMES

Mastering these objectives will enable you to:

Project 6A
Access a Special-Interest Web Site for Health Information

Project 6B
Compare Push and Pull Content on the Web

Project 6C
Find Informational Resources on the Web

Project 6D
Locate Entertainment Sites

University Medical Center

The University Medical Center is a premier patient-care and research institution serving the metropolitan area of Orange Beach, Florida. Because of its outstanding reputation in the medical community and around the world, the Medical Center is able to attract top physicians and researchers in all fields of medicine and achieve a level of funding that enables it to build and operate state-of-the-art

facilities. Preserving and developing that sterling reputation is the responsibility of the Medical Center Office of Public Affairs. The Office of Public Affairs conducts community and national promotion of the services, achievements, and professionals of the Medical Center. The staff interacts with the media, writes and distributes press releases and announcements, prepares marketing materials, develops public awareness campaigns, maintains a speaker's bureau of experts on a number of medical and research topics, and conducts media training for physicians and researchers. The Office of Public Affairs has recently been informed that the Medical Center will be announcing successful results of a clinical trial of a new surgical technique, so preparations for the announcement will be a high priority for the staff for the next several weeks.

Locating Resources on the World Wide Web

The World Wide Web has become an integral component of our culture. It is now common practice to consult the Web for information and advice on how to care for our health, our homes, and many other aspects of our lives. Using the Web, you can find the latest weather report, sports scores, or information about favorite hobbies. The Web helps us locate people and businesses, make travel arrangements, and find maps. It is easy to access legal resources, training, and educational opportunities. The Web is also used for entertainment, such as playing online games or enjoying multimedia content. In this chapter, you will explore many ways to locate special-interest Web sites and other helpful resources.

Project 6A Accessing a Special-Interest Web Site for Health Information

The University Medical Center is developing a Web site as part of its marketing strategy. Because the University Medical Center has a reputation as a premier patient care and research institution, people from across the country need to know more about it. The Center would like people to be able to access the Web site to learn more about the services offered at the Center. In Activities 6.1 through 6.4, you will help Rachel Foster, Web Content Manager, explore existing health-related Web sites. You will search for and evaluate special-interest Web sites in the health field using two different search techniques: a directory search and a search engine. Then you will compare your findings.

For Project 6A, you will need the following files:

New blank Notepad document
Web page printouts

You will save your files as
6A_Directory_Firstname_Lastname
6A_Medical_Center_Firstname_Lastname
6A_Government_Firstname_Lastname
6A_Health_Info_Firstname_Lastname

Figure 6.1

Objective 1
Perform a Directory Search and
Evaluate a Special-Interest Web Site

Several types of Web sites are devoted to the discussion of health-related issues ranging from prevention to treatment of disease. The federal and state governments provide recommended guidelines for health and nutrition. Many university medical centers now have Web sites where you can locate information on symptoms, disease treatments, and research. Pharmaceutical companies provide information about their products. While visiting any of these Web sites is not a substitute for obtaining information from your health care provider, many people find a visit to these types of Web sites helpful as a first step in understanding and caring for their health. Performing a search and evaluating the results are good ways to begin looking for information about special-interest topics such as health.

Alert!

Assessing Project 6A and Project 6B

For Projects 6A and 6B of this chapter, you and your instructor can evaluate your approach to the problem and your result by consulting the scoring rubric located in the end-of-chapter material. For these hands-on projects, there is no online quiz.

Activity 6.1 Locating Health Information Using a Directory

In this activity, you will help Rachel Foster, Web Content Manager for University Medical Center, begin a search for existing Web sites in the health field. You will look for information from frequently visited and well-respected hospitals.

1 **Start** `start` Internet Explorer and if necessary, **Maximize** the Internet Explorer window. In the **Address bar**, click one time to select the existing text, and then type **http://dir.yahoo.com/Health** Press `Enter`.

The Yahoo! Health Directory home page displays. This Web site provides several categories for health-related topics, which are reviewed and organized by a staff of professional editors. Sponsored sites are clearly marked and displayed under *Sponsor Results* on the right side of the Web page.

2 Scroll down the page, locate and click the **Hospitals and Medical Centers** link. Compare your screen with Figure 6.2.

The Hospital and Medical Centers Web page is organized into several sections including Inside Yahoo!, Categories, Sponsor Results, and Site Listings. The Site Listings are ranked by popularity, but you can also sort them alphabetically by clicking the Alphabetical link.

Figure 6.2

Sponsor Results

Inside Yahoo!

Categories

By Popularity link

Site Listings

Alphabetical link

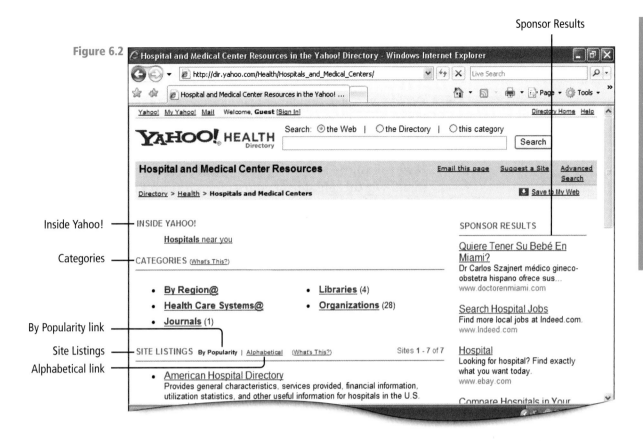

3 Under **Site Listings**, click the **American Hospital Directory** link to display the **American Hospital Directory** home page. Using the techniques you have practiced, create a **Favorites** folder with the name **Chapter_6_Firstname_Lastname** Then, add this Web site to the folder as one of your **Favorites** for this chapter.

4 Using the following criteria, evaluate the **American Hospital Directory** Web site. Write notes so that you remember the following items. You will use these notes in an activity later in the project.

- Sponsorship of the Web site—Do you see a logo or brand name on the Web site? Do you see contact information for the sponsor? What is the domain name for the Web site?

- Author of the Web site—Do you recognize the author's name as an authority? Can you determine the affiliation of the author? Are the credentials appropriate for the topic area?

- Site design considerations—Can the data be verified or located in other authoritative sources? Has the site won any awards? What is the overall style of the site? Is the color scheme pleasing? Are the graphics clear and proportionate? Is the site accessibility compliant? Are there any missing images? Do all the links work correctly? Is there a date stamp or date for the last update? Is there a copyright notice?

- Language use—Are there any grammatical errors? Are there any misspellings?

- Depth of coverage—Is there any obvious misinformation? Are there any biased statements? Does the Web site link to a variety of authoritative sites? Is there enough detail and depth of coverage? Does the information read like an advertisement or sales pitch?

5 Decide on a location where you can store a document—either in a folder on your computer's hard drive or a folder on a removable storage device such as a USB flash drive. Check with your instructor if necessary. Click the **Start** button, and then click **My Computer**. Navigate to the location where you have decided to store your document. On the left side of your screen, under **File and Folder Tasks**, click **Make a new folder**. In the text box labeled *New Folder* that displays, type **Chapter_6_Resources** Then press Enter. **Close** the **My Computer** window when you are finished.

6 Add the footer **6A_Directory_Firstname_Lastname** to the Web page.

7 Navigate to the **Chapter_6_Resources** folder that you just created for this chapter and save the Web page as **6A_Directory_Firstname_Lastname**

8 Check your *Chapter Assignment Sheet* or *Course Syllabus* or consult your instructor to determine if you are to submit your assignments by printing on paper or electronically by using your college's course information management system. Print the Web page and submit it as instructed.

9 Keep your browser open for the next activity.

Objective 2
Perform a Search for Special-Interest Web Sites Using a Search Engine and an Advanced Search

When you need specific information, you should search for specific sources affiliated with your topic of interest. Special-interest Web sites can be located easily by performing a basic search with a search engine. All searches begin by formulating a keyword query. Try to use keywords that are specific to your topic of interest so that the search results returned to you are limited to those results that will be the most helpful.

Recall that advanced search features or filters may be used to help define keywords and refine search results. For example, if you are interested in finding only government Web sites, you can request that only Web sites with that top-level domain—*.gov*—be returned. Most advanced search features also enable you to use Boolean operators, and they enable you to specify a language, file format, or a date range for updates made to the Web page. This saves time because only Web sites meeting the criteria specified in the advanced search or filter will display in your search result list.

Activity 6.2 Locating Health Information Online Using a Search Engine

University medical centers are well respected in the health industry. Because universities receive a lot of research funding, university medical centers typically perform advanced or cutting-edge medical procedures. In this activity, you will use a search engine to locate and compare several university medical center Web sites.

1 If necessary, **Start** ![start] Internet Explorer and **Maximize** ![maximize] the window. In the **Address bar**, click one time to select the existing text, and then type **http://www.google.com** Press Enter.

The Google home page displays.

2 In the **Google Search** text box, type **University Medical Centers** as the keyword query and press Enter. Compare your screen with Figure 6.3.

The search results list displays with links to several medical centers. Some sponsored links may be included on the right side of the screen.

Alert!

Does your search results list differ?

Your search results lists may differ from the one shown. The World Wide Web adds new pages every day. Search engines differ in how often they are updated and how they display the results. The number of results in the list and the location of sponsored results within the search results, the placement within the browser window, and other features may vary on your screen for any search you perform in this chapter.

Sponsored Links

Figure 6.3

Keyword query

Search results list

3 In the search results list, locate and right-click the link to the first university medical center so that it will open in a new window or new tab. When the university medical center Web site displays, add it to your **Favorites** folder created for this chapter.

4 With the same criteria you used in Activity 6.1, evaluate the Web site. Write notes so that you remember what you discovered. You will use these notes in an activity later in the project.

5 In the upper right corner of the university medical center Web page, click the **Close** ☒ button or close the tab to return to the Google search results list. Right-click the link to the second university medical center in the search results list so that it will open in a new window or a new tab. When this university medical center Web site displays, add it to your **Favorites** folder created for this chapter.

6 Using the same criteria used for the first Web site, evaluate this second university medical center Web site. Take notes to use later in this project.

7 In the upper right corner of the second university medical center Web page, click the **Close** ☒ button or close the tab to return to the Google search results list. Add the footer **6A_Medical_Center_Firstname_Lastname** to the Google search results list Web page.

8 Navigate to the folder you created for this chapter and save the Web page as **6A_Medical_Center_Firstname_Lastname**

9 Check your *Chapter Assignment Sheet* or *Course Syllabus* or consult your instructor to determine if you are to submit your assignments by printing on paper or electronically by using your college's course information management system. Print the Web page and submit it as instructed.

10 Keep your browser open for the next activity.

Activity 6.3 Locating Health Information Online Using an Advanced Search

The federal government provides current research findings and general information at several health-related Web sites. In this activity, you will search for health information using the advanced search feature at a search engine to locate only health-related Web sites created by the government.

1 In the **Address bar**, click one time to select the existing text, and then type **http://www.google.com** Press Enter.

The Google home page displays.

2 On the right side of the **Google Search** text box, click the **Advanced Search** link to display the **Advanced Search** Web page. In the section labeled **Find Results**, click in the **with all of the words** text box, and type **health** Scroll to locate the section labeled **Domain**. Make sure the word *Only* displays in the menu, and then type **.gov** in the text box. Press Enter. Compare your screen with Figure 6.4.

A search results list displays with all of the hits from federal and state government Web sites. You can verify the Web sites are government Web sites because the top-level domain is *.gov* for each of the Web sites. The exception is the list of sponsored links located on the right side of the screen.

Recall that each search engine may use Boolean operators or filters in a slightly different way. For example, as an alternative, when using Google, you can type a keyword followed by a colon, and then the top-level domain—*health:.gov.* This query should give you the same set of search results. Consult each search engine's Help or FAQ area to learn exactly how to write your query. Not all search engines respond to the query if it is typed as *health:.gov.*

Figure 6.4

Keyword query

Government Web site

Top-level domain

3 In the search results list, locate and right-click the link to the first government Web site in the search results list so that it will open in a new window or tab. When this Web site displays, add it to your **Favorites** folder created for this chapter.

4 With the same criteria you used in Activity 6.1, evaluate the Web site. Write notes so that you remember all the information. You will use these notes in an activity later in the project.

5 In the upper right corner of the Web page, click the **Close** ⊠ button to return to the Google search results list. Right-click the link to the second government Web site in the search results list so that it will open in a new window. When this Web site displays, add it to your **Favorites** folder created for this chapter. Then, using the same criteria used for the first Web site, evaluate this second government Web site. Take notes to use later in this project.

6 In the upper right corner of the government Web site, click the **Close** ⊠ button to return to the Google search results list. Add the footer **6A_Government_Firstname_Lastname** to the Google search results list Web page.

7 Navigate to the folder created for this chapter, and then save the Web page as **6A_Government_Firstname_Lastname**

8 Check your *Chapter Assignment Sheet* or *Course Syllabus* or consult your instructor to determine if you are to submit your assignments by printing on paper or electronically by using your college's course information management system. Print the Web page and submit it as instructed.

9 Keep your browser open for the next activity.

Objective 3
Compare Types of Special-Interest Web Sites

The World Wide Web provides access to many different types of Web sites providing information on special interests. In addition, these special-interest Web sites can be located using different search techniques. Developing a method to evaluate and compare search techniques, the types of Web sites available, and the information found at each type of Web site helps you determine the credibility and usefulness of the Web sites.

Activity 6.4 Comparing Health Information Web Sites

In this activity, you will create a summary document for Rachel Foster, Web Content Manager at the University Medical Center. She will use your summary document as a research aid to guide her as she develops a Web site for the University Medical Center.

1 If necessary, **Start** [*start*] Notepad and **Maximize** [ ] the window.

2 At the blinking insertion point in the **Notepad** window, type **6A_Health_Info_Firstname_Lastname** Press [Enter] two times. Type **Yahoo! Health Directory:** and press [Enter] two times to create a new line. Type **American Hospital Directory:** and then type the URL of the **American Hospital Directory** Web site. Press [Enter] two times to create a new line. Write a brief paragraph summarizing the information you found for the sponsor and the author of the Web site. Then type the information you found for the site design considerations, language use, and the depth of coverage.

3 Press [Enter] two times to create a new line. Type **Google Search Engine:** and then press [Enter] two times to create a new line. Type **University Medical Centers:** and the name and URL of the first university medical center that you visited. Write a brief paragraph summarizing the information you found for the sponsor of the Web site. Then provide information about the site design considerations and the depth of coverage. Press the [Enter] key two times, and then type the name and URL of the second university medical center that you visited. Write a brief paragraph summarizing the information you found for the sponsor and author of the Web site. Then provide information about the site design considerations, language use, and the depth of coverage.

4 Press the [Enter] key two times to create a new line. Type **Google Search Engine Advanced Search:** and press the [Enter] key two times to create another new line. Type **Government Health Sites:** and the name and URL of the first government Web site that you visited. Write a brief paragraph summarizing the information you found for the sponsor and author of the Web site. Then provide information about the site design considerations, language use, and the depth of coverage. Press the [Enter] key two times, and then type the name and URL of the second government Web site that you visited. Write a brief paragraph summarizing the information you found for the sponsor and author of the Web site. Then provide information about the site design considerations, language use, and the depth of coverage.

5 Add the footer **6A_Health_Info_Firstname_Lastname** to your document.

6 Navigate to the folder created for this chapter and save the document as **6A_Health_Info_Firstname_Lastname**

7 Check your *Chapter Assignment Sheet* or *Course Syllabus* or consult your instructor to determine if you are to submit your assignments by printing on paper or electronically by using your college's course information management system. Electronically, you can submit the *.txt* file created in Notepad. To print on paper from Notepad, from the **File** menu, click **Print**, and then print accordingly. To submit electronically, follow instructions provided by your instructor.

8 **Close** ☒ the **Notepad** window. **Close** ☒ the **Internet Explorer** window.

End **You have completed Project 6A** ————————————————

Project 6B Comparing Push and Pull Content on the Web

The University Medical Center is ready to develop a new public awareness campaign about the relationship between weather and health. They hope to raise awareness with regard to the risks of sun exposure, air quality, and common allergens. These issues are of major concern to several patients in the "special risk" category—for patients with long-term and acute illnesses such as asthma or cancer. In Activities 6.5 through 6.8, you show Gerard Kim, Media Specialist for the University Medical Center, where to locate weather information and how to add a Really Simple Syndication (RSS), feed to keep him alerted to weather changes. Gerard will share this information with "special risk" category patients so that they can add an RSS feed to their computers. You will also show Gerard how to access maps or travel directions and manage travel arrangements online.

For Project 6B, you will need the following files:

Web page printouts

You will save your files as
6B_Feed_Firstname_Lastname
6B_Map_Firstname_Lastname
6B_Travel_Firstname_Lastname

Objective 4
Access Weather Information Online

Access to current weather conditions is valuable to many people such as construction workers, farmers, or air traffic controllers. These jobs are weather-dependent. Families often check the weather before starting their day or when planning for vacations. People with health issues may also need to carefully track changing weather conditions.

The World Wide Web provides easy access to current weather conditions and extended weather forecasts. **RSS feeds** are becoming a common way to keep up with the constant change of weather-related content on the Web. Recall that Really Simple Syndication, or RSS, is a system developed to automatically alert subscribers of updates made to sites such as blogs, news sites, weather, or sports sites. An RSS feed is an individual Web document in XML format that contains content such as news, weather, or blog posts. **Extensible Markup Language**, or **XML**, is a markup language developed to allow the description of data for the purpose of sharing the data over many devices.

Activity 6.5 Locating Weather Information Online

Most of the patients at University Medical Center have access to both a television and a computer. After conducting a survey, Gerard Kim has concluded many patients would like to use the computer for weather updates. In this activity, you help Gerard Kim, Media Specialist for the University Medical Center, locate weather information online.

1 If necessary, **Start** 🎯 start Internet Explorer and **Maximize** 🔲 the window. In the **Address bar**, click one time to select the existing text, type **http://www.nws.noaa.gov** and then press [Enter].

The **National Oceanic and Atmospheric Administration's National Weather Service (NOAA NWS)**, home page displays. The NWS provides the information that television and private meteorological companies use to prepare the forecasts. It is considered the primary source for weather information in the United States. NOAA is a government organization that is part of the U.S. Department of Commerce. It conducts research and provides recommendations on climates, oceans, fisheries, air quality, and weather. Each organization—NOAA and NWS—has its own logo.

2 On the left side of the screen, locate the **Local forecast by "City, St"** text box. Type the name of your city, followed by a comma, and the two-letter abbreviation for your state. Then click the **Go** button. Compare your screen with Figure 6.5.

The most recently updated Forecast at a Glance displays on a Web page dynamically generated for the city and state you typed. You can get a Detailed 7-day Forecast and the Current Conditions. Recent radar and satellite images are available further down the page. Additional types of forecasts are also available on the Web page.

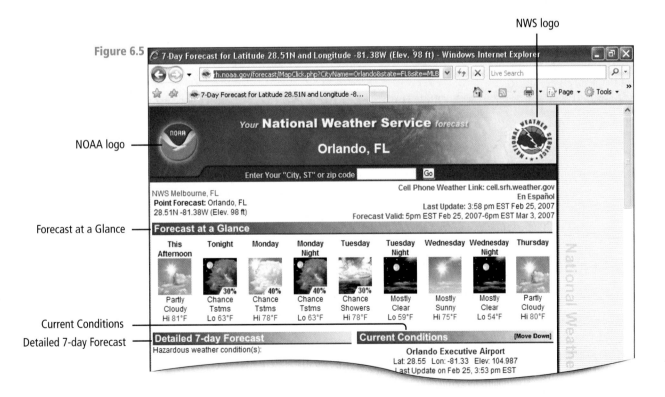

Figure 6.5

NWS logo

NOAA logo

Forecast at a Glance

Current Conditions

Detailed 7-day Forecast

3 Click the **Back** button 🔙 to return to the **NOAA NWS** Web page. Under the **Local forecast by "City, St"** text box, locate and click the **RSS Feeds** link.

The NOAA NWS RSS Library Web page displays. The NWS Web site provides RSS feeds, *podcasts*, and *vodcasts*. Vodcasts are the download of video files from the World Wide Web to compatible computers or portable video players using RSS technology. Recall that a podcast is the download of MP3 audio files from the World Wide Web to MP3-compatible computers or portable audio players using RSS technology.

RSS feeds are considered one form of *push technology*. Push technology is a technology that works on the World Wide Web where users are provided with new and updated information either automatically or at specified intervals. With push technology, you do not have to visit each Web site to find the most recent updates. Instead you receive a notification on your computer whenever updates are made to the Web sites.

4 Scroll down the page and review the list of available RSS feeds. Notice that the list includes information about severe weather and local storm reports. Scroll up the page and click the **Download an RSS Reader** link.

NOAA NWS provides a link to a Web page within the dmoz Open Directory Project Web site where you can download an RSS reader. The dmoz Open Directory Project is a popular directory search site. NOAA NWS links you directly to the part of the dmoz Open Directory Project Web site that provides links to several RSS readers. To use an RSS feed, you need an *RSS reader*. An RSS reader is a software program or Web-based service that provides access to RSS feeds. Typically these readers are free of charge.

5 Click the **Back** button 🔙 two times to return to the **NOAA NWS RSS Library** Web page. Scroll down until you are near the bottom of the page, and then locate the section labeled **Podcasts**. Under the heading *NOAA Weather Radio*, click the first link.

The NOAA NEWS Experimental MP3 Podcast Forecasts Web page displays. This is a new service offered by the NOAA NWS. Currently just a few regions are available for subscription using RSS or for the download of MP3 audio files.

6 In the upper right corner of the screen, click the **NWS** logo to return to the **NWS** Web page.

7 Keep your browser open for the next activity.

Objective 5
Install a Feed on Your Computer

Although many people visit weather-related Web sites to check on conditions and forecasts, improvements to technology such as RSS feeds provide easier ways to access this information. With an RSS reader, feeds automatically notify you when an update is posted at a site. You do not need to visit the Web site; the information comes to your computer and you simply click a link to view the information.

Activity 6.6 Installing and Using an RSS Feed

Gerard Kim knows that several patients at University Medical Center use computers and would appreciate being automatically alerted to changing weather conditions. In this activity, you help Gerard Kim install an RSS reader on his computer so he can begin using RSS feeds.

1 If necessary, **Start** 🔲 *start* Internet Explorer and **Maximize** 🔲 the window. In the **Address bar**, click one time to select the existing text, type **http://www.weather.com** and then press Enter.

The *Weather.com* home page displays. Weather.com is a well-known television resource, providing weather forecasts and information 24 hours a day, seven days a week. It has a Web site that provides resources aimed at specific markets, such as people interested in local weather, international weather, special forecasts for travelers, recreational reports, and school day forecasts.

In addition, the Web site provides several interactive tools such as photo sharing, videos, and weather maps customized for any zip code. Programs are available so you can download weather information to your Web site, and get reports on your mobile phone or on your computer with RSS feeds. Feeds are also used to access other types of content at the Web site such as podcasts.

2 At the bottom right corner of the Web page, locate and click the **RSS feeds** link. You can also find an RSS link under the Downloads category. Compare your screen with Figure 6.6.

The RSS Feeds From The Weather Channel Web page displays. The Weather Channel offers RSS feeds for national weather, local weather, or the Weather Channel blog. When you subscribe to a feed, it is added to a list stored on your computer.

Internet Explorer detects when there is a feed offered at a Web site. The Feeds button activates and displays as an orange square on the toolbar at the top of the browser window. If you click the Feeds down arrow, you can see the list of available feeds. If you subscribe to any of the available feeds, you can simply click it to access the content with an RSS reader.

Weather.com enables you to use one of three readers. Both My Yahoo! and Bloglines are based on RSS. The XML reader is based on *Atom*, which is a pair of related protocols that enable access to feeds written in the XML.

- XML reader—Recall that XML stands for Extensible Markup Language and is a markup language developed to enable the description of data for the purpose of sharing the data over many devices.

- *My Yahoo!* reader—My Yahoo! is a Web-based service from Yahoo! that provides access to RSS content as well as other features, such as e-mail. You can sign up at *http://e.my.yahoo.com/config/my_init?.intl=us&.partner=my&.from=i.*

- **Bloglines** reader—Bloglines is a Web-based service that enables you to subscribe to RSS feeds as well as create blogs. You can sign up for an account at *http://www.bloglines.com.*

Figure 6.6

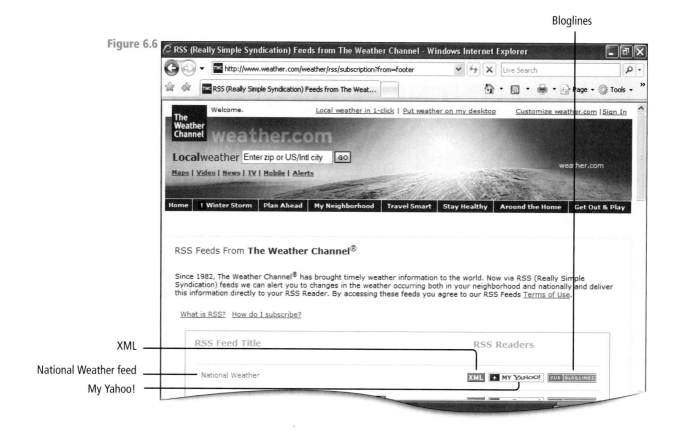

3 In the **Address bar**, click one time to select the existing text, and then type **http://www.yahoo.com** and press Enter to display the **Yahoo!** home page. In the upper left corner, locate and click the **My Yahoo!** link. Compare your screen with Figure 6.7.

The My Yahoo! Web page displays. My Yahoo! is a service of Yahoo! that functions as a ***portal*** that enables you to customize the content displayed at your My Yahoo! Web page. Recall that a portal is a Web page that contains interesting content, frequently used links, and services such as current and breaking news, e-mail access, and search capabilities. Because My Yahoo! is customized, you must first sign in to access the content and services.

Figure 6.7

My Yahoo! URL

My Yahoo! Sign In

Content choices

4 At the top of the **My Yahoo!** Web page, click the **Sign In** link to display the Web page where you sign into Yahoo!. If necessary, in the **Security Alert** dialog box, click **OK**.

Alert!

Do you already have a Yahoo! user ID?

If you have created a Yahoo! user ID for any of the Yahoo! services, you can use the same user ID and password for My Yahoo! Recall that earlier in the book, you created a Yahoo! user ID so that you could use the Yahoo! e-mail service. You can use that Yahoo! user ID for this activity.

5 In the **Sign in to Yahoo!** Web page, click into the **Yahoo! ID** text box and then type the Yahoo! user ID that you established for your Yahoo! e-mail account. Then click in the **Password** text box and type your password. Click the **Sign In** button. Then, in the **Security Alert** dialog box, click **Yes**.

Your My Yahoo! Web page displays with the basic categories of content. This includes a Yahoo! Search text box, the news headlines, and the weather.

6 At the top of the **My Yahoo!** Web page, locate the statement that welcomes your user ID, the **Sign Out** link, and the **My Account** link. Then locate the **Add Content**, **Change Layout**, and **Change Colors** links. Compare your screen with Figure 6.8.

The Sign Out link should be used when you are done with your activities at My Yahoo! to prevent anyone else using the same computer from accessing your Yahoo! account. The My Account link should be used when you want to set or change any of your Yahoo! account information or preferences.

The Add Content link displays a Web page that enables you to find and add content to your My Yahoo! Web page. The Change Layout link displays a Web page that enables you determine the location and the order in which the content is displayed on your My Yahoo! Web page. The Change Colors link enables you to select a customized theme and color palette for your My Yahoo! Web page.

Figure 6.8

User ID

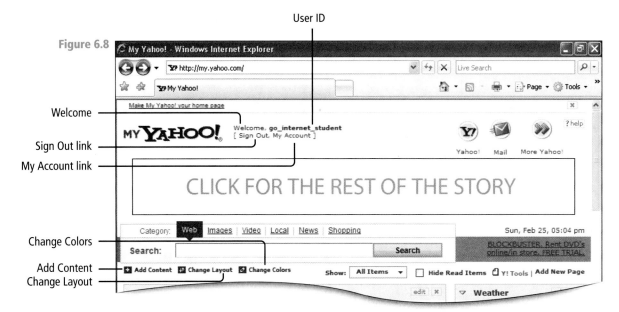

Welcome

Sign Out link

My Account link

Change Colors

Add Content
Change Layout

7 In the browser window, click the **New Tab** button. When the new tab displays, in the **Address bar**, click one time to select the text, type **http://www.weather.com** and then press Enter.

The Weather.com home page displays in the new tab. You visited this Web site already in this activity. Recall that you can easily navigate between tabs by clicking each tab.

8 In the **Weather.com** home page, scroll down and locate the **RSS Feeds** link. Click the **RSS Feeds** link. Compare your screen with Figure 6.9.

The RSS Feeds From The Weather Channel Web page displays. You can add the National Weather as content to your My Yahoo! Web page by clicking one of the RSS readers located at this Web page.

Figure 6.9

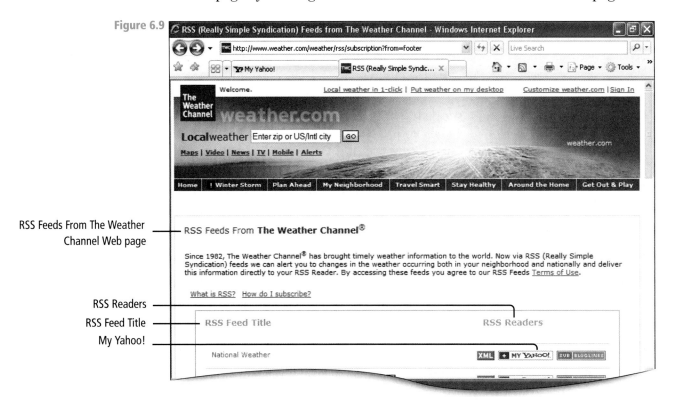

RSS Feeds From The Weather Channel Web page

RSS Readers

RSS Feed Title

My Yahoo!

9 On the right side of the Web page, click the **My Yahoo!** reader that corresponds to the National Weather feed title to display a Web page where you can add the Weather Channel National Weather Outlook to your My Yahoo! Web page. Click the **Add To My Yahoo!** button. Compare your screen with Figure 6.10.

A Web page displays to confirm that the source—The Weather Channel National Weather Outlook—has been added to My Yahoo! Web page. Links are provided to enable you to go back to the previous Web page or go to your My Yahoo! Web page.

Figure 6.10

Go to My Yahoo! link

The Weather Channel: National Weather Outlook

10 In the upper right corner, click the **Go to My Yahoo!** link to display your **My Yahoo!** Web page. Scroll down the page and notice that The Weather Channel: National Weather Outlook has been added as content. Compare your screen with Figure 6.11.

Figure 6.11

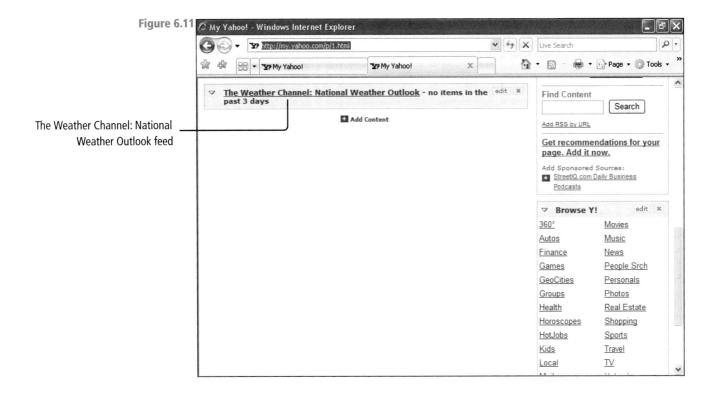

The Weather Channel: National Weather Outlook feed

11 Using the storage location—your hard drive, USB flash drive, or other storage location—add the footer **6B_Feed_Firstname_Lastname** to the **My Yahoo!** Web page. Save the Web page to the **Chapter_6_Resources** folder with the name **6B_Feed_Firstname_Lastname**

12 Check your *Chapter Assignment Sheet* or *Course Syllabus* or consult your instructor to determine if you are to submit your assignments by printing on paper or electronically by using your college's course information management system. Print the Web page and submit it as instructed.

13 In the new tab, click the **Close Tab** button ☒ to close the second tab. In the upper left of your **My Yahoo!** Web page, click the **Sign Out** link to sign out of My Yahoo!. Keep your browser open for the next activity.

Objective 6
Manage Travel Arrangements Online

RSS feeds are an example of push technology where you are automatically notified of updated Web content. But content can also be accessed by using **pull technology**. The term pull technology is used when you actively seek out new information from Web sites. For example, if you pull the most recent blogs, you visit each blogging site and look for updates at the Web site. Another example of using pull technology is searching for maps and directions for finding businesses in your local area or anywhere in the world.

Activity 6.7 Searching for Maps and Travel Directions to Businesses

Gerard Kim, Media Specialist for the University Medical Center, feels it would be helpful for patients if they could locate maps and travel directions online. Many patients must travel from surrounding cities or from a distance for treatment. Families of patients need to be able to find the University Medical Center so that they can make travel plans when visiting patients. In this activity, you show Gerard how to find maps and travel directions online.

1 If necessary, **Start** 🔲start Internet Explorer and **Maximize** 🔲 the window. In the **Address bar**, click one time to select the existing text, and then type **http://www.google.com** and press Enter. As an alternative, click the Favorites Center button ☆ and locate and click the Google Web site link.

The Google Web page displays.

2 In the middle of the **Google** Web page, locate and click the **Maps** link to display the **Google Maps** Web page. Compare your screen with Figure 6.12.

Google Maps is a service of Google that provides search capability for locating maps and finding directions through your computer or mobile phone. Google Maps provides three options: *Search the map*, *Find businesses*, or *Get directions*. To use Google Maps, simply type a business keyword and zip code, and then click the Search Maps button.

Google provides another mapping service in a three dimensional format called *Google Earth*. The service uses satellite images, maps, and the Google search engine to zoom in from sky level down to street level as if you are flying overhead in an airplane. To use Google Earth you must download a software program onto your computer. There is a free version of Google Earth that may be used only for personal use. Versions with more advanced features are available for a fee and may be used commercially.

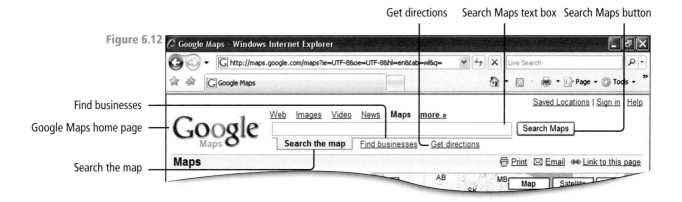

Figure 6.12

3 In the **Search the map** text box, type **University Medical Center Florida** and then click the **Search Maps** button to display the search results. Notice that you can print, e-mail, or link to the search results Web page. You can view the maps either as a traditional map, as a

Satellite view, or a Hybrid that combines both traditional and satellite views. The Traffic view enables you to zoom in to view traffic conditions for a specific area of the map. Compare your screen with Figure 6.13. Then click each view of the map.

The addresses of several medical centers that are associated with universities are marked with letters and displayed along the left side of the search results page. A map with lettered markers corresponding to the list is displayed on the right side of the screen. If you do not see the results you were expecting, you can modify your search.

Figure 6.13

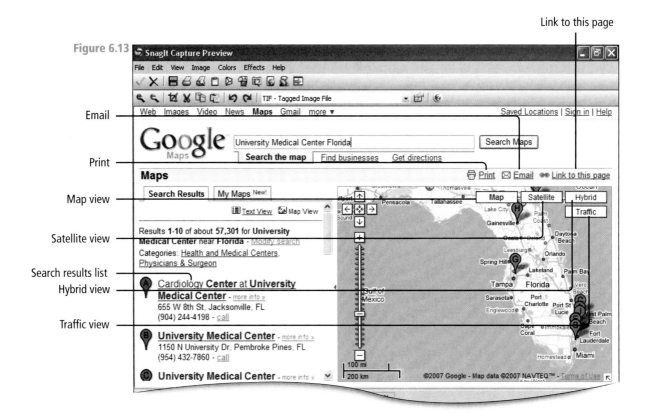

4. On the left side of the screen, locate and click the **Modify search** link to display options for modifying your search. Notice you can get a map of the location specified in the search. You can also find businesses matching the current location specified within the map view. In addition, text boxes are provided so that you can modify the location and find businesses matching or near a new location that you specify. Compare your screen with Figure 6.14.

Figure 6.14

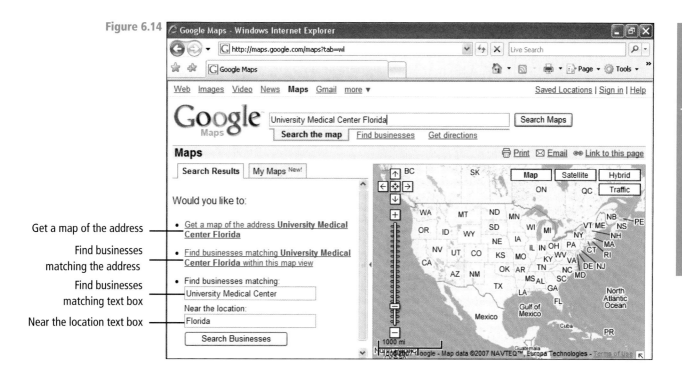

Get a map of the address

Find businesses matching the address

Find businesses matching text box

Near the location text box

5 In the browser window, click the **Back** button. On the map, click the first visible lettered marker.

A balloon providing specific information such as street address, phone number, and Web site URL—if available—displays over the map. The balloon also provides links to get directions to or from a certain location and the medical center. An option to send it to your phone is available. A Close button enables you to close the balloon.

6 In the balloon, find the section labeled **Get directions** and click the link. In the **Start address** text box that displays, type your school's street name, city, and state. Compare your screen with Figure 6.15, and then click the **Go** button to the immediate right of the text box.

After several seconds, a new Web page displays showing directions and a map. The start address, the end address, the distance, and the amount of time needed to make the trip are listed at the top of the page. Along the left side you also find numbered directions. Each number is a link that when clicked displays a detailed street map corresponding to that part of the trip within a balloon superimposed over the map.

Figure 6.15

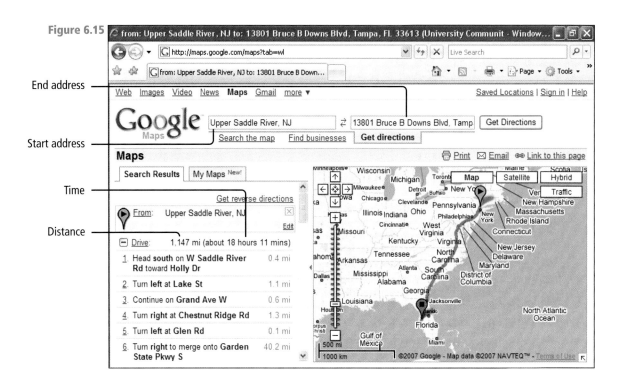

End address

Start address

Time

Distance

7 On the left side of the Web page, click the last numbered direction to display a balloon—pop-up—containing a small detailed map. Notice the location. Then, in the upper right corner of the balloon, click the **Close** button. Then click directly into the map and drag your mouse upward to display the lower portion of the Florida peninsula.

Google Maps features a dynamic interactive map that responds to your mouse movements. Many mapping Web sites must re-draw the map each time you try to move around it. This feature found at Google Maps simulates having the map in your hands and being able to look at another section of the map.

8 In the upper right of the screen, locate and click the **Print** link.

A printer-friendly version of the travel directions displays in a second browser window. This version of the directions is formatted to fit 8 ½-by-11 paper. You can print or save this Web page.

9 Using the storage location—your hard drive, USB flash drive, or other storage location—add a footer **6B_Map_Firstname_Lastname** to the **Google Maps** Web page. Then save the Web page to the **Chapter_6_Resources** folder with the name **6B_Map_Firstname_Lastname**

10 Check your *Chapter Assignment Sheet* or *Course Syllabus* or consult your instructor to determine if you are to submit your assignments by printing on paper or electronically by using your college's course information management system. Print the Web page and submit it as instructed.

11 Keep your browser open for the next activity.

Activity 6.8 Exploring Travel Arrangement Sites

The University Medical Center has patients from all parts of the United States. The families of these patients often need to stay for an extended period of time and need accommodations at a local hotel. In this activity, you show Gerard Kim, Media Specialist for the University Medical Center, how to compare sites offering flight and hotel bookings online so that he can share this information with patients and their families.

1 If necessary, **Start** start Internet Explorer and **Maximize** the window. In the **Address bar**, click one time to select the existing text, type **http://www.travelocity.com** and then press Enter.

The Travelocity home page displays. Travelocity offers vacation packages, flights, hotel reservations, car rentals, train tickets, and cruises packages. Travelocity offers last-minute packages and special pricing on some trips.

2 Add the **Travelocity** Web site to your **Favorites** folder created for this chapter. On the left side of the Web page, click the **Flight+Hotel** button. In the **From** text box, type the name of your city. As an alternative, type the city closest to you that has an airport. In the **To** text box, type **Tampa**.

3 In the section labeled **Depart**, click the small calendar icon to display a pop-up calendar. Click the last Saturday of the current month.

The pop-up calendar closes and the date is displayed on the Web page.

4 In the section labeled **Return**, click the small calendar icon to display a pop-up calendar. Click the first Saturday of the following month to add that date to the Web page. From the menu labeled *Rooms*, click the down arrow, and then click **1**. From the menu labeled *Adult*, click the down arrow, and then click **2**. Compare your screen with Figure 6.16. Click the **Search Now** button.

A Web page displays letting you know that Travelocity is searching for your trip. After several choices are located, a Web page displays with the search results.

Internet | chapter 6

Figure 6.16

Flight + Hotel
To
From
Depart
Calendar icon
Return

Adult menu

Search Now button

5 At the top of the search results page, notice the flight information. Compare your screen with Figure 6.17.

The airline, the dates, the times, and flight numbers are displayed. You can change the flight if this one is not suitable.

Change Flight

Figure 6.17

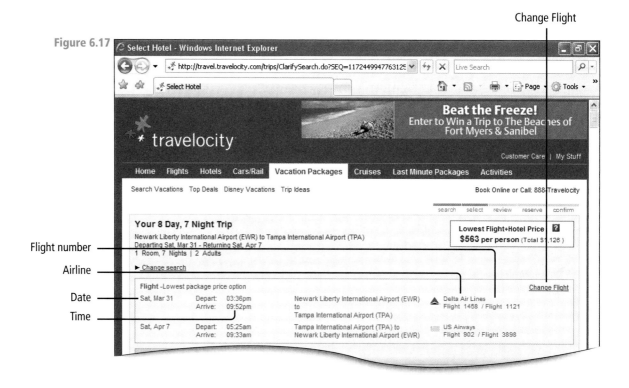

Flight number
Airline
Date
Time

6 Scroll down the search results page and notice that several hotel choices are available. On the right side, notice the price for each hotel displayed. Click the **Select** button for the first hotel.

7 Scroll down to the bottom of the Web page and click the **Select This Hotel** button.

The Customize Your Trip Web page displays. On this page you should carefully review the selection and change either flight or hotel arrangements if necessary. You may also customize your trip with a rental car or other transportation or by adding various activities or services.

8 At the bottom of the **Customize Your Trip** Web page, click the **Continue** button. In the **Security Alert** dialog box, click **OK**. In the **Security Information** dialog box, click **Yes**.

If all arrangements are satisfactory, the next step is to log in if you are a member of Travelocity or become a member of Travelocity. After membership is determined, payment by credit card is collected. Do not go any further for this activity.

Alert!

Are you registered?

You must register with Travelocity and other travel arrangement sites before actually booking a flight or finalizing trip and hotel arrangements. You must provide a credit card number to confirm your trip. You are not expected to confirm your trip for this activity.

9 Scroll back to the top of the Web page. Using the storage location—your hard drive, USB flash drive, or other storage location—and folder created for this chapter, add the footer **6B_Travel_Firstname_ Lastname** to the **Review and Continue** Web page. Then save the Web page to the **Chapter_6_Resources** folder with the name **6B_Travel_ Firstname_Lastname**

10 Check your *Chapter Assignment Sheet* or *Course Syllabus* or consult your instructor to determine if you are to submit your assignments by printing on paper or electronically by using your college's course information management system. Print the Web page and submit it as instructed.

11 **Close** ☒ the **Internet Explorer** window.

End **You have completed Project 6B**

Project 6C Finding Informational Resources on the Web

In Objectives 7 and 8, you will explore several types of informational resources on the Web. These resources include people and address search tools. You will also investigate resources for legal information and educational opportunities on the Web.

Objective 7
Find People Using Online Resources

How can the Web be used to find people? Whether you need to locate an old friend whom you've lost touch with, a high school classmate, or distant family members, the World Wide Web enables you to easily find contact information for people.

You can use a search engine to find out information about a person by simply using that person's name as the keyword query. If that person posts to a blog, USENET newsgroup, forum, or other public discussion group, or if that person has appeared as a point of content in a Web site or created a Web site, the name may be returned as part of a search results list.

You can also locate people using Web sites developed especially for this purpose. Specialized directories provide information such as an e-mail address, street address, or phone number for almost anyone you want to locate. This type of online directory is developed from existing print white or yellow page directories. Other sources of public information may also be used to create databases for these types of Web sites. Typically, cell phone numbers are not included, but some directories may include unlisted numbers.

What is reverse lookup? Typically, sites where you can locate people by name also offer a *reverse lookup* service. Reverse lookup enables you to type in a phone number or an e-mail address in order to retrieve the name of the person associated with that information. In addition, some sites provide *only* reverse lookup services. This can be useful when you have a phone number or e-mail address but are unsure of the person's correct name.

What are commonly used Web sites for locating people? The table in Figure 6.18 shows the names and URLs of several Web sites where you can look up information about people. The Web sites are used like a paper-based telephone directory where you provide a name and an address, and a phone number is returned. A few of the Web sites provide information only about their own subscribers or people who have registered at the Web site. An example is AOL White Pages.

People Search Web Sites and Their URLs

Web Site	URL
AOL White Pages	*http://site.aol.com/netfind/whitepages.adp*
AnyWho	*http://www.anywho.com*
Bigfoot	*http://search.bigfoot.com/en/index.jsp*
FamilySearch	*http://www.familysearch.org*
InfoSpace	*http://www.infospace.com*
Lycos WhoWhere	*http://www.whowhere.lycos.com*
PeopleFinders	*http://www.peoplefinders.com*
ReverseRecords.org	*http://reverserecords.org*
SuperPages	*http://www.superpages.com*
Switchboard	*http://www.switchboard.com*
The National Archives	*http://www.archives.gov/genealogy*
WhitePages	*http://www.whitepages.com*
Yahoo! People Search	*http://people.yahoo.com*

Figure 6.18

Are there any fees for using these Web sites? A lot of information can be located for free using any of the specialized directories because the information is considered public information. A few sites offer information for free after you register at the Web site. You may also have to consent to having your information included as part of the records at that Web site before you will be allowed use of the information. For example, you can locate a classmate for free using Classmates.com after you register at the Web site.

Which sites charge a fee for finding people? Some directories provide more information by combining public information with other sources. These types of searches combine public information with civil records, school records, military records, criminal records, or government information and may be used as background checks. Typically, you must pay for the more in-depth searches. Figure 6.19 shows the names and URLs for some of these Web sites.

In-Depth People Search Web Sites and Their URLs

Web Site	URL
Abika	*http://www.abika.com*
ChoiceTrust	*http://www.choicetrust.com*
Docusearch	*http://www.docusearch.com*
FBI State Sex Offender Registry	*http://www.fbi.gov/hq/cid/cac/states.htm*
Intelius	*http://www.intelius.com*
US Search	*http://www.ussearch.com*

Figure 6.19

What are the drawbacks of these types of Web sites?   There are several Web sites where you can search for people. Although all of the information is considered public information, the ease in locating it and the ability to compile data from multiple resources causes some concerns with privacy. Some people feel these types of Web sites make too much personal information available. For this reason, some of the Web sites allow you to ***opt-out*** of the directory. To opt-out means that you do not want to participate or be included in the company's or organization's database of records. When you opt-out, your information is hidden or deleted.

Objective 8
Locate Legal Information and Educational Opportunities

The World Wide Web enables anyone to search for information in the privacy of their own surroundings. Keeping up with new legislation or researching other types of legal information can now be easily obtained without having to pay fees up front. In addition, many people are able to enroll in online programs to continue or upgrade their education. Or they may pursue a topic of interest or upgrade skills for their own personal enjoyment.

Legal Information

How do I find information about current legislation?   *THOMAS* is a database that is part of the Library of Congress. It was created in response to a directive made by Congress to make federal legislative information available to the public. THOMAS provides a rich search tool that allows you to locate bills, resolutions, and other activities that take place in Congress. It also enables you to search the Congressional record, determine schedules and calendars, and find committee information, presidential nominations, treaties, and government resources.

The Library of Congress has other related resources such as the Law Library and an online exhibit covering lawmaking and documents from the Continental Congress and Constitutional Convention. The Library of Congress has a collection of ***webcasts*** on law-related topics and other topics. A webcast is a recorded audio and video presentation stored on a Web server and replayed from a Web site.

Where do I go to find legal information?   Many Web sites are available that provide free access to legal information and downloadable legal forms such as wills. Some of the sites provide news about recent legal decisions; other Web sites provide access to specific laws or other legal information. The Web sites listed in Figure 6.20 provide information relevant to both the general public and to the practicing attorney.

Alert!

Have you taken legal advice from an online resource?
Getting legal information should not be confused with getting legal advice. It is always a good idea to consult with an attorney in matters of law.

Web Sites Offering Legal Information and Their URLs

Web Site	URL
American Bar Association	*http://www.abanet.org*
FindLaw	*http://www.findlaw.com*
Law.com	*http://law.com*
LawDepot.com	*http://www.lawdepot.com*
LegalZoom	*http://www.legalzoom.com*
LexisNexis	*http://www.lexisnexis.com*
Nolo	*http://www.nolo.com*
THOMAS	*http://thomas.loc.gov*

Figure 6.20

Educational Opportunities

What is distance learning? *Distance learning* is a term used in the field of education to describe learning opportunities that use technology to replace physical classrooms. Distance learning is also referred to as *online learning*. Distance learning provides many students educational opportunities that may not be available in a classroom. Distance learning provides the advantage of flexibility in arranging study time.

Many colleges and universities offer courses in an online format along with courses scheduled in a classroom. Some institutions offer entire degrees online while others offer just a few courses online. Some courses combine classroom time with some portion of the course work completed in the online format. This is called *hybrid learning*.

Who participates in distance learning programs? Students who are eligible for high school can participate in online learning. Home-schooled students, students in rural communities, or other high school students are able to enrich their studies by taking online courses offered at other high schools or through *virtual high schools*. A virtual high school is a school that offers a full catalog of courses where the courses are completed entirely online. The courses are likely to be developed by a number of participating high schools or may be offered through a for-profit educational institution.

Both college-age students and working adults participate in distance learning programs. Students can complete college-level course work and non-credit courses. Employee training and professional development are also offered online. Some employers offer time off from work duties and provide computer equipment in order to permit their employees to complete training modules onsite during work hours.

What types of skills and equipment are needed to take an online course? To participate in an online course, you need dependable access to a computer with an Internet connection. Having a DSL, cable, or another fast connection rather than a dial-up connection is an advantage. During an online class, a student can expect to exchange e-mail, participate in a discussion board, chat, or instant messages with the instructor and other students.

Typically, a student will read materials both in online format and from a textbook. They may hear a webcast, or view videos. In addition, a student may use a microphone and Web cam to participate in a video conference with the instructor and classmates.

What are the disadvantages of online learning? While distance learning offers convenience and flexibility, students enrolled in online courses must be motivated to complete the course work. Typically, there is a schedule to follow with due dates and exams given at specific points during the course just like a traditional face-to-face learning environment. The student's ability to manage time well is extremely important for successfully completing an online course. Other important points include:

- Careful reading and following instructions—Instructors spend a lot of time developing course materials and making sure the materials work together to help students work through information and develop it into knowledge.

- Clear communication by both student and instructor—Because the student and instructor are not in the same room, it much more difficult to assess whether or not a student understands the materials. Therefore, a student must be able to communicate clearly and not be afraid to ask questions. The instructor must also be a good communicator and responsive to the student's inquiries.

- The instructor and student are not online at the same time—Because online students work on the course materials at a time that is convenient to them, it is not always possible for the instructor to be online at the same time. Typically, an online instructor will set a specific time or day for office hours where students can be certain to contact the instructor. The office hours are handled by using instant messages, chat, telephone, or actual time in an office.

- Be aware of hardware and software requirements—Some courses may require special software in order to complete the course work. Typically, these requirements are listed as part of the course description or in the course syllabus.

What other ways can the Web support education? Numerous Web sites exist that provide learning opportunities such as learning standards, lesson plans, tutorials, or courses for learners of all ages. Because these resources are on the World Wide Web, students from around the world can use them. Some of the Web sites, such as **Internet2**, offer opportunity for collaborating with other students. Internet2 is a consortium of education and research leaders brought together by extremely fast network solutions for the purpose of collaboration and learning. A sampling of educational sites is listed in Figure 6.21.

Educational Web Sites

Web Site	URL
Global SchoolNet Foundation	*http://www.globalschoolnet.org/index.html*
Internet2	*http://www.internet2.edu*
Journey North	*http://journeynorth.org*
TERC	*http://www.terc.edu*
UC Berkeley Extension Online	*http://learn.berkeley.edu*

Figure 6.21

What is OpenCourseWare? *Massachusetts Institute of Technology*, or *MIT*, has developed a system of free courses available online as part of the university's mission. MIT is a prestigious university that primarily focuses on instruction in science and technology. The system is known as *MIT OpenCourseWare*, or *MIT OCW*. Anyone in the world may use this free, high-quality set of instructional materials for self-taught instruction. You do not need to apply to the university or register for the class, but you will not have access to faculty.

Other universities around the world have created similar OCW projects. China, France, Japan, and Vietnam offer courses online in a variety of topics. In addition, a few more universities in the United States have started similar projects. The table in Figure 6.22 shows some of these universities.

Participants in the MIT OCW

Participating School	URL
Carnegie Mellon OpenLearning Initiative	*http://www.cmu.edu/oli*
China Quality OpenCourseWare	*http://www.core.org.cn/cn/jpkc/index_en.html*
FETP OpenCourseWare	*http://ocw.fetp.edu.vn/home.cfm*
Japan OCW Consortium	*http://www.jocw.jp*
JHSPH OpenCourseWare	*http://ocw.jhsph.edu*
MIT OpenCourseWare	*http://ocw.mit.edu*
ParisTech "Graduate School"	*http://graduateschool.paristech.org*
Tufts OpenCourseWare	*http://ocw.tufts.edu*
Utah State University OpenCourseWare	*http://ocw.usu.edu/Index/ECIndex_view*

Figure 6.22

End You have completed Project 6C

Online Quiz

Project 6C

Take the online self-study quiz for this chapter:

1. Go to **www.prenhall.com/go** and select the textbook *GO!* **with the Internet**.

2. Select **chapter 6**.

3. Select **Self-Study Quiz Project 6C**.

Project 6D Locating Entertainment Sites

The World Wide Web provides entertainment for millions of users. With Web sites developed on nearly every topic imaginable, everyone can find something of interest. In Objectives 9 through 11, you will identify award-winning Web sites and you will compare gaming sites and multimedia resources.

Objective 9
Identify Award-Winning Web Sites and Portals

With so many Web sites available, it is easy to overlook some of the most interesting or helpful sites. Portals and recommendations of award-winning sites can help you focus your browsing activities.

Award-Winning Web Sites

Where can I find interesting Web sites?   Because there are so many types of Web sites, trying to get a lot of viewers to visit one can be a challenge. Web designers, developers, and programmers spend a lot of time creating Web sites that serve a purpose: communicate a message, entertain, or sell a product.

Certain organizations, such as the Webby Awards, ask for nominations of outstanding Web sites. These organizations evaluate the design and honor the best Web sites with awards. After a Web site has achieved an award, it typically advertises the achievement on the Web site. Earning this type of award helps to build recognition and traffic for the Web site. Web users are more likely to trust sites that have earned awards. Figure 6.23 shows the Webby Awards Web site.

URL

Figure 6.23

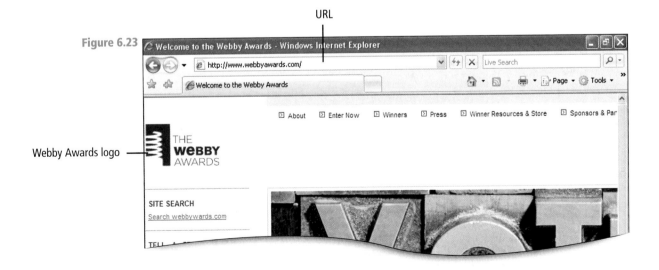

Webby Awards logo

Many people find new sites they enjoy by reviewing the award sites. Other times you hear about Web sites from friends or by using a portal to locate interesting Web sites. Figure 6.24 provides the URLs for some resources for locating outstanding Web sites.

Resources For Locating Outstanding Web Sites

Web Site	URL
Cool Site of the Day	http://www.coolsiteoftheday.com
Interactive Media Awards	http://www.interactivemediaawards.com
refdesk.com	http://www.refdesk.com/textcool.html
The Internet Tourbus	http://www.internettourbus.com
The Webby Awards	http://www.webbyawards.com
Web100.com	http://www.web100.com
Yahooligans	http://yahooligans.yahoo.com

Figure 6.24

Portals

How can I use a portal?   Several portals exist that provide hours of top-notch entertainment value and information for Web users. Because portals contain interesting content, frequently used links, and services, many people like to set their browser's default home page to a portal. Then when they start their Web browsers they quickly get to the content that they want to see.

Some portals allow you to customize the layout or content in your portal. Others simply provide plenty of links to a variety of interests. For example, About.com keeps a constant set of resources created by guides who thoroughly know their subject areas. Figure 6.25 shows the About.com Web site. The table in Figure 6.26 describes some popular portals.

Figure 6.25

Popular Portals

Portal	URL	Description
About.com	*http://about.com*	Practical advice on everyday topics provided by accomplished freelancers who are experts in their fields.
AOL	*http://www.aol.com*	A wide range of content and search tools provided by a name familiar as one of the first ISPs.
Craig's List	*http://sfbay.craigslist.org*	A text-based listing of links to commonly sought information customized for local communities.
Excite	*http://www.excite.com*	Customized portal content with membership available provided by one of the first search sites on the Web.
iVillage	*http://www.ivillage.com*	A wide variety of topics of special interest to women.
MSN	*http://www.msn.com*	Customized portal sponsored by Microsoft.
My Yahoo!	*http://www.yahoo.com*	Customized content sponsored by Yahoo!
Netscape	*http://www.netscape.com*	All content is voted on by the users of the portal provided by a name familiar as one of the first browsers.
USA.gov	*http://www.USA.gov*	The official portal for the U.S. government.

Figure 6.26

Objective 10
Compare Gaming Sites

How has online gaming evolved?   Early games from the 1980s were single-player games. *Multi-User Dungeon* games, or a **MUD**, combine role-playing with chat rooms. These games are text-based; you type in commands that control the characters within a fantasy or science fiction scenario. *Dungeons & Dragons* is a popular MUD.

MUD Object Oriented games, or a **MOO**, are similar to MUDs because they are text-based and allow multiple players. The difference is that MOOs enable players to write programming to create new rooms or object within the scenario. MOOs are sometime used in distance learning programs.

Multi-User Shared Hack games, or a ***MUSH***, are played in a text-based environment among multiple players. Typically these games are used for role-playing. Any player can create a character, extend the existing world, and define the behaviors of the objects.

The next big step in gaming came with ***first-person shooting games***. These games use graphics instead of text. The onscreen view is shown from the viewpoint of the main character of the game. ***Real-time strategy games*** enable each player to play continuously and not take turns. Typically, these games are military-themed.

How are games played on the World Wide Web? Web-based games use lots of graphics and scripts. Some Web-based games are for single players. Players compete by seeing who has the highest score. Other Web-based games involve multiple players spread across many countries. These games are referred to as ***Massively Multiplayer Online Games***, or a ***MMOG***. The scenario of these games continues whether players are online or not and they are never finished. A popular Web-based MMOG is *RuneScape*. Figure 6.27 shows the *RuneScape* Web site. The table in Figure 6.28 summarizes these online games.

URL   *RuneScape* logo

Figure 6.27

Online Games

Name	Acronym	Description
First-person shooting game		Graphically oriented, role-playing game viewed from the main character's perspective.
Massively Multiplayer Online Games	MMOG	Web-based played among several players but not necessarily at the same time.
MUD Object Oriented	MOO	Text-based game played among several players who can create new programs.
Multi-User Dungeon	MUD	Text-based, role-playing game played individually.
Multi-User Shared Hack	MUSH	Text-based, role-playing game played among several players.
Real-time strategy game		Graphically oriented, role-playing game where players play continuously and do not take turns.

Figure 6.28

What other kinds of games are available online? Playing games is a big part of online entertainment. From Solitaire to multiplayer online games, it seems almost everyone can find a game online to play. The newest games provide both visual effects and mental challenges for the players.

Games can be categorized into broad categories such as arcade, board, or card games. Other categories include word games, multiplayer games, video games, skill games, children's games, educational games, or puzzles. Figure 6.29 shows the Yahoo! Games Web site where you can choose from several games categories.

Figure 6.29

Skill games

Video games

Multiplayer games

Arcade games

Board games

Card games

Puzzle games

Word games

Objective 11
Explore Multimedia Resources

What is a multimedia Web site? A *multimedia Web site* uses some combination of pictures, animations, audio, video, and virtual reality within a Web site. Multimedia adds richness and interest to Web sites. It may be used to convey ideas, instruction, or preserve historical moments.

You can enjoy thousands of radio stations with music streamed to your computer. *Streaming* is a method of delivering digital content to a computer so that the content plays as soon as it is received by the computer.

What do I need to use a multimedia Web site? When a Web page has a multimedia file included as content, the browser is able to handle the multimedia by using *plug-ins* or *scripts*. Recall that a plug-in is a small software program developed to work within a Web browser to execute proprietary file types that the browser can't interpret. Scripts are coded instructions embedded within a program or file to allow customization or add interactivity to a Web page. To play multimedia, your computer must have certain plug-ins installed or the browser must be configured to allow scripts to run. Your computer also needs certain hardware such as speakers, a sound card, and a video card in order to be considered a multimedia-capable computer.

How do plug-ins work? Multimedia file types require the appropriate plug-ins. When a multimedia file is located by the browser as part of a Web site, the plug-in will automatically start and the multimedia plays within the browser window.

Certain Web sites have an embedded script that can detect whether you have the right plug-ins needed to play the multimedia file. If the script finds that your computer does not have the correct plug-ins, a link to another Web site where you can download the correct plug-ins will display.

To see what plug-ins are currently on your computer, check your browser's menu bar. Using Internet Explorer 7, you must look under the Tools menu, and the Internet Options command and then Manage Add-ons. It is easy to download plug-ins and install them on your computer. Typically, the plug-in download contains a wizard to help you. After responding to the questions in the wizard, the plug-in self-installs. The table in Figure 6.30 shows several Web sites where you can locate and download plug-ins.

Where To Get Plug-ins

Plug-in	URL
Add-ons for Internet Explorer	*http://www.windowsmarketplace.com/category.aspx?bcatid5834&tabid51&dl51*
Download.com	*http://www.download.com/Utilities-Plug-Ins/3150-2169_4-0.html*
Firefox Add-ons	*https://addons.mozilla.org/firefox/plugins*
Plugin.com	*http://www.plugin.com/*
Tucows	*http://www.tucows.com*

Figure 6.30

How does the browser know which plug-in to use for each file type?
Windows Media Player is the default multimedia player for computers using the Windows operating system. Computers with the Macintosh operating system typically use Apple's QuickTime as the default multimedia player. Both players feature a *console* to play, pause, stop, and control the volume. A console is a pop-up window that enables you to control the playing of multimedia by clicking buttons or dragging sliders across the console. Figure 6.31 shows a console being used to play multimedia.

Figure 6.31

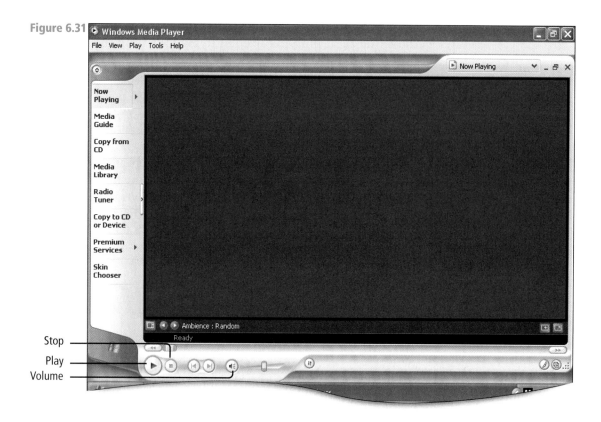

Stop
Play
Volume

Although Windows Media Player is the default player for a computer with the Windows operating system, you can set a different multimedia player as the default instead. You use Windows Explorer to view or change the file extensions that are associated with each program or plug-in installed on your computer. For example, if your browser encounters a **WAV** file at a Web site, it will automatically use Windows Media Player to play that file. A WAV file is a standard type of audio file developed by Microsoft. However, if you prefer to use another plug-in such as RealPlayer, you can change the association. Then next time the browser finds a WAV file, it will use RealPlayer to play the file instead of Windows Media Player.

What Web sites use multimedia?   You may already know of several favorite Web sites that use multimedia content. The table in Figure 6.32 shows several Web sites that use multimedia.

Web Sites That Use Multimedia

Web Site	URL
AOL Music	*http://music.aol.com*
American Memory	*http://memory.loc.gov/ammem/index.html*
Comedy Central	*http://www.comedycentral.com*
Disney Online	*http://disney.go.com*
Flickr	*http://www.flickr.com*
Internet Movie Database	*http://www.imdb.com*
iStockphoto	*http://www.istockphoto.com/index.php*
Louvre	*http://www.louvre.fr*
MTV	*http://www.mtv.com*
NASA	*http://www.nasa.gov/home*
National Geographic	*http://www.nationalgeographic.com*
NPR	*http://www.npr.org*
YouTube	*http://www.youtube.com*

Figure 6.32

How can I locate multimedia files? You can easily search for multimedia files using a search engine such as Google, AltaVista, Dogpile, or Yahoo!. All have a special tabbed area for locating multimedia files such audio or video files.

In addition, several specialized search sites have developed that search only for multimedia content. For example, both Podscope and the Podcasting Station allow you to search only for podcasts or vodcasts.

End You have completed Project 6D ────────────

Online Quiz

Project 6D

Take the online self-study quiz for this chapter:

1. Go to **www.prenhall.com/go** and select the textbook *GO!* **with the Internet**.

2. Select **chapter 6**.

3. Select **Self-Study Quiz Project 6D**.

Assessments

Summary

In this chapter, you have accessed special-interest Web sites and other helpful resources using several search techniques. You located health information using a directory and a search engine. You refined your search with advanced search techniques. Then you compared these search techniques to determine the credibility and usefulness of the Web sites. You compared push and pull technology for locating information online. You located Web sites that constantly update their content and use feeds to notify you of the updates. You installed a feed on your computer. You searched for maps and travel directions for businesses. You explored a travel arrangement Web site. You examined how to locate people, legal information, and educational opportunities. You identified award-winning Web sites, portals, online gaming sites, and multimedia resources.

Key Terms

Atom 351	**Massively Multiplayer Online Games (MMOG)** 374	**Portal** 352
Bloglines 352		**Push technology** 350
Console 377	**Multi-User Dungeon (MUD)** 373	**Pull technology** 356
Distance learning 367		**Real-time strategy game** 374
Extensible Markup Language (XML) 348	**Multimedia Web site** 376	
	Multi-User Shared Hack (MUSH) 374	**Reverse lookup** 364
First-person shooting game 374	**My Yahoo!** 351	**RSS feed** 348
Google Earth 357	**National Oceanic and Atmospheric Administration (NOAA)** 349	**RSS reader** 350
Google Maps 357		**Script** 376
Hybrid learning 367		**Streaming** 376
Internet2 368		**THOMAS** 366
Massachusetts Institute of Technology (MIT) 369	**National Weather Service (NWS)** 349	**Virtual high school** ..367
	Online learning 367	**Vodcast** 350
	Opt-out 366	**WAV** 378
MIT OpenCourseWare (MIT OCW) 369	**Plug-in** 376	**Weather.com** 351
MUD Object Oriented (MOO) 373	**Podcast** 350	**Webcast** 366

Assessments

Matching

Match each term in the second column with its correct definition in the first column by writing the letter of the term on the blank line in front of the correct definition.

_____ **1.** An individual Web document in the XML format that contains content such as news, weather, or blog posts.

_____ **2.** A Web-based service from Yahoo! that provides access to RSS content among other features.

_____ **3.** A technology that works on the World Wide Web where users are provided with new and updated information either automatically or at specified intervals.

_____ **4.** An organization that provides the information that television and private meteorological companies use to prepare the forecasts.

_____ **5.** A government organization that is part of the U.S. Department of Commerce that conducts research and provides recommendations on climates, oceans, fisheries, air quality, and weather.

_____ **6.** A software program or Web-based service that provides access to RSS feeds.

_____ **7.** The download of MP3 audio files from the World Wide Web to MP3-compatible computers or portable audio players using RSS technology.

_____ **8.** A Web site that provides several categories for health-related topics reviewed and organized by a staff of professional editors.

_____ **9.** A Web-based service that allows you to create blogs as well as subscribe to RSS feeds.

_____ **10.** A markup language developed to allow the description of data for the purpose of sharing the data over many devices.

_____ **11.** A service of Google that provides search capability for locating maps and finding directions through either your computer or mobile phone.

_____ **12.** A pair of related protocols that allow access to feeds written in the XML.

_____ **13.** The download of video files from the World Wide Web to compatible computers or portable video players using RSS technology.

A Atom

B Bloglines

C Google Maps

D My Yahoo!

E NOAA

F NWS

G Podcast

H Portal

I Pull technology

J Push technology

K RSS feed

L RSS reader

M Vodcast

N XML

O Yahoo! Health Directory

(Continued)

Assessments

——— **14.** A Web page that contains interesting content, frequently used links, and services such as current and breaking news, e-mail access, and search capabilities.

——— **15.** A technology that works on the World Wide Web where users actively seek out new information from Web sites.

Assessments

Fill in the Blank

Write the correct answer in the space provided.

1. A common way to keep up with the constant change of content on the Web is by using _____.

2. RSS feeds are considered a form of _____.

3. You can locate information about university medical centers, such as name and location, by using _____.

4. When evaluating a Web site, looking for obvious misinformation or biased statements helps you determine the _____.

5. Determining the authority, affiliation, or credentials helps you to determine the credibility of the Web site and its _____

6. Government Web sites can be identified by the top-level domain, _____.

7. XML stands for _____.

8. To use an RSS feed you need a(n) _____.

9. You can use search engine filters to help you find Web sites with *.gov* as the _____.

10. A pair of related protocols that allow access to feeds written in XML is called _____.

11. A well-known weather-related television resource that also has a Web site is named _____.

12. You can book vacation packages, flights, and hotel reservations at Web sites such as _____.

13. Once you have a Yahoo! user ID, you can use it at _____ service.

14. Searching for maps and directions on the Web is an example of _____.

15. A service uses satellite images, maps and the Google search engine to allow zooming in from sky level down to street level as if you were flying overhead in an airplane is called _____.

Assessments

Internet

Rubric

Projects 6A and 6B in the front portion of this chapter, and Projects 6E through 6K that follow have no specific correct result; your result will depend on your approach to the information provided. Make Professional Quality your goal. Use the following scoring rubric to guide you in how to approach the search problem and then to evaluate how well your approach solves the search problem.

The *criteria*—Internet Mastery, Content, Format and Layout of Search Results, and Process—represent the knowledge and skills you have gained that you can apply to solving the search problem. The *levels of performance*—Professional Quality, Approaching Professional Quality, or Needs Quality Improvements—help you and your instructor evaluate your result.

	Your completed project is of Professional Quality if you:	Your completed project is Approaching Professional Quality if you:	Your completed project Needs Quality Improvement if you:
1–Internet Mastery	Choose and apply the most appropriate search skills, tools, and features and identify efficient methods to conduct the search and locate valid results.	Choose and apply some appropriate search skills, tools, and features, but not in the most efficient manner.	Choose inappropriate search skills, tools, or features, or are inefficient in locating valid results.
2–Content	Conduct a search that is clear and well organized, contains results that are accurate, appropriate to the audience and purpose, and are complete.	Conduct a search in which some results are unclear, poorly organized, inconsistent, or incomplete. Misjudge the needs of the audience.	Conduct a search that is unclear, incomplete, or poorly organized, containing some inaccurate or inappropriate content.
3–Format and Layout of Search Results	Format and arrange all search results to communicate information and ideas, clarify function, illustrate relationships, and indicate relative importance.	Apply appropriate format and layout features to some search results, but not others. Overuse search techniques, causing minor distraction.	Apply format and layout that does not communicate the search results clearly. Do not use format and layout features to clarify function, illustrate relationships, or indicate relative importance. Use available search techniques excessively, causing distraction.
4–Process	Use an organized approach that integrates planning, development, self-assessment, revision, and reflection.	Demonstrate an organized approach in some areas, but not others; or, use an insufficient process of organization throughout.	Do not use an organized approach to solve the problem.

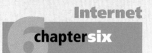

Assessments

Mastering the Internet

Internet
chapter six

Project 6E—Finding Gaming Sites

Objectives: 1. *Perform a Directory Search and Evaluate a Special-Interest Web Site;* **10.** *Compare Gaming Sites.*

Ricardo Teixeira, Media Specialist for the University Medical Center, is helping to develop a new Web site for the Center. Part of the Web site is intended to help pediatric patients recover from long illnesses. In this Assessment, you will help Ricardo locate online games that might be suitable for the patients. You will locate online gaming sites that are appropriate for children.

For Project 6E, you will need the following file:

Web page printout

You will save your file as
6E_Games_Firstname_Lastname

1. **Start** Internet Explorer and **Maximize** the window. In the **Address bar**, click one time to select the existing text, type **http://dmoz.org** and then press Enter. The **Open Directory Project** Web page displays. Open Directory Project is an easy-to-use directory search site. You can use the home page as a directory search engine or you can perform keyword queries.

2. Near the middle of the screen, locate and click the **Kids and Teens** link. Near the middle of the Web page that displays, locate and click the **Games** link. Several broad categories display. Locate and click the **Online** link. At the top of the Web page, notice the breadcrumb trail for navigating through the directory.

3. Scroll down the Web page and review the categories and the Web sites listed. Click the **Arcade** link. Evaluate the types of sites listed. Notice the names of the sites, the intended audience, and the names of the games that can be played at each site.

4. In the breadcrumb trail, click the **Online** link to return to the **Online** Web page. Then near the top of that Web page, click the **Collections** link. Scroll down the Web page. Evaluate the types of sites listed. Notice the names of the sites, the intended audience, and the names of the games that can be played at each site.

5. In the breadcrumb trail, click the **Online** link. Between the two sub-categories that you visited—Arcade and Collections—determine which is more appropriate to recommend for the **University Medical Center** Web site. Return to that sub-category Web page.

(Project 6E–Finding Gaming Sites continues on the next page)

Assessments

(Project 6E–Finding Gaming Sites continued)

6. Add the **footer 6E_Games_Firstname_Lastname** to the sub-category Web page, and then save the Web page as **6E_Games_Firstname_Lastname** in the folder you created for this course.

7. Check your *Chapter Assignment Sheet* or *Course Syllabus* or consult your instructor to determine whether you are to submit your assignments by printing on paper or electronically by using your college's course information management system. To submit the document electronically, follow the instructions provided by your instructor.

8. **Close** the **Internet Explorer** window.

End **You have completed Project 6E**

Assessments

Mastering the Internet

Project 6F—Finding Zip Codes

Objectives: 2. *Perform a Search for Special-Interest Web Sites Using a Search Engine and an Advanced Search;* **6.** *Manage Travel Arrangements Online.*

Ms. Anh Dinh, the Administrative Assistant at University Medical Center, is working on a mass mailing to announce successful clinical trial results to physicians and clinics across the U.S. She does not want to miss any geographic areas. In this Assessment, you will help Anh locate a map that details all of the U.S. Postal zip codes.

For Project 6F, you will need the following file:

Web page printout

You will save your file as
6F_Zip_Codes_Firstname_Lastname

1. **Start** Internet Explorer and **Maximize** the window. In the **Address bar**, click one time to select the existing text, and then type **http://www.google.com** Press [Enter]. The **Google** Web page displays. Formulate a keyword query such as **Digital Zip Code Maps**, and then type it into the **search** text box. Press [Enter]. Look at the results of the search.

2. In the **search results** list, scroll down and click the first hit that is not a sponsored site. Notice the URL, the name of the site, the date stamp, and the copyright notice. Locate where you can search for a zip code and test it with your own zip code.

3. Add the **footer 6F_Zip_Codes_Firstname_Lastname** and then save the Web page as **6F_Zip_Codes_Firstname_Lastname**

4. Check your *Chapter Assignment Sheet* or *Course Syllabus* or consult your instructor to determine whether you are to submit your assignments by printing on paper or electronically by using your college's course information management system. To submit the document electronically, follow the instructions provided by your instructor.

5. **Close** the **Internet Explorer** window.

End **You have completed Project 6F** ───────────

Assessments

Mastering the Internet

Project 6G — Accessing Recipes Online

Objective: 2. *Perform a Search for Special-Interest Web Sites Using a Search Engine and an Advanced Search.*

The Assistant Director of the University Medical Center, Telma Leong, has just returned from a conference on diets and their effects on common major health disorders. She would like to promote healthy eating but knows that patients often have a hard time finding recipes that contain the best food choices. In this Assessment, you will locate a recipe Web site that uses advanced search tools to match recipes with ingredients.

For Project 6G, you will need the following file:

Web page printout

You will save your file as
6G_Recipes_Firstname_Lastname

1. **Start** Internet Explorer and **Maximize** the window. In the **Address bar**, click one time to select the existing text, type **http://allrecipes.com** and then press Enter. The **All Recipes** Web page displays. Scroll down the Web page and notice there are several ways to locate recipes of all types.

2. At the top of the Web page, click the **More Searches** button. Click the **Ingredient Search** command. In the **Ingredient Search** Web page that displays, type in the **Ingredients I want** text boxes, three ingredients that you want and in the **Ingredients I don't want** text box, type in one ingredient. Click the **Search In** menu, and then click an appropriate category. Then click the **Go** button. If a *We couldn't find any results* message displays, review the suggestions for modifying your search.

3. After a search results list displays, scroll down the list and click one of the recipe links. The recipe displays. Read the review, the ingredient list, and the directions. Locate and click the **Print Full Page** link to display the recipe as a full page.

4. Add the **footer 6G_Recipes_Firstname_Lastname** and then save the Web page as **6G_Recipes_Firstname_Lastname**

5. Check your *Chapter Assignment Sheet* or *Course Syllabus* or consult your instructor to determine whether you are to submit your assignments by printing on paper or electronically by using your college's course information management system. To submit the document electronically, follow the instructions provided by your instructor.

6. **Close** the **Internet Explorer** window.

End **You have completed Project 6G**

Mastering the Internet

Project 6H — Accessing Weather Videos Online

Objectives: 4. *Access Weather Information Online;* **11.** *Explore Multimedia Resources.*

Rachel Foster, Web Content Manager for the University Medical Center, wants to include some multimedia at the new University Medical Center Web site. She feels weather-related multimedia would be especially beneficial for patients. In this Assessment, you show a Web site to Rachel that patients will find interesting and helpful.

For Project 6H, you will need the following file:

Web page printout

You will save your file as
6H_Weather_Firstname_Lastname

1. **Start** Internet Explorer and **Maximize** the window. In the **Address bar**, click one time to select the existing text, and then type **http://home. accuweather.com/index.asp?partner=accuweather** Press Enter. The **AccuWeather** Web page displays. Scroll down the Web page and notice how multimedia—animation, video, and audio—is used at this Web site.

2. Locate the **America's Wittiest Weatherman** section. Click the **Press to hear Elliot Abrams** button. If your computer has the necessary hardware, you will hear a brief audio file play.

3. Scroll to return to the top of the **AccuWeather** home page and locate the section labeled **Latest National News**. Under the heading *Related Links*, click the **Video** link. A pop-up window displays that contains a video player, a console, and links to several categories of video clips. Locate and click the **Sports** link. A brief video displays in the pop-up. Use the **Volume** control in the console to adjust the volume. In the upper right corner of the pop-up, click the **Close** button to close the Video Player and return to the **AccuWeather** home page.

4. Add the **footer 6H_Weather_Firstname_Lastname** and then save the Web page as **6H_Weather_Firstname_Lastname**

5. Check your *Chapter Assignment Sheet* or *Course Syllabus* or consult your instructor to determine whether you are to submit your assignments by printing on paper or electronically by using your college's course information management system. To submit the document electronically, follow the instructions provided by your instructor.

6. **Close** the **Internet Explorer** window.

End You have completed Project 6H ————

Assessments

Project 6I — Adding an RSS Feed

Objectives: 5. *Install a Feed On Your Computer;* **8.** *Locate Legal Information and Educational Opportunities;* **9.** *Identify Award-Winning Web Sites and Portals.*

Mike Martinez, Director of Public Affairs, has a busy schedule but still needs to be aware of the most recent education news. He wants to help the University Medical Center maintain its reputation as a leader of university medical centers. In this Assessment, you show Mike where he can get a feed to help him stay informed of recent education news stories.

For Project 6I, you will need the following file:

Web page printout

You will save your file as
6I_Feed_Firstname_Lastname

1. **Start** Internet Explorer and **Maximize** the window. In the **Address bar**, click one time to select the existing text, and then type **http://www.washingtonpost.com/** and then [Enter]. The **Washington Post** Web page displays. The Washington Post is a highly-respected news Web site.

2. Scroll to the bottom of the page and click the **RSS** link. The **RSS Feeds** Web page displays. Click the **Education** link, and then on the Web page that displays next, click the **XML Education** link. The **washingtonpost.com Education** Web page displays. Click the **Subscribe to this feed** link.

3. In the **Internet Explorer Subscribe to this feed** dialog box that displays, click the **Subscribe** button. The feed will be added to your Favorites Center.

4. When the feed has been added and displays on washingtonpost.com Education Web page, use the techniques you have practiced to add the **footer 6I_Feed_Firstname_Lastname** Then save the Web page as **6I_Feed_Firstname_Lastname**

5. Check your *Chapter Assignment Sheet* or *Course Syllabus* or consult your instructor to determine whether you are to submit your assignments by printing on paper or electronically by using your college's course information management system. To submit the document electronically, follow the instructions provided by your instructor.

6. **Close** the **Internet Explorer** window.

End **You have completed Project 6I**

Assessments

Internet

GO! Search

Project 6J—Finding an Attorney in Your Area

Objectives: 7. *Find People Using Online Resources;* **8.** *Locate Legal Information and Educational Opportunities.*

For Project 6J, you will need the following file:

New blank Notepad document

You will save your file as
6J_Attorney_Firstname_Lastname

Mike Martinez, Director of Public Affairs, wants to make sure the University Medical Center has access to more legal counsel. A recent surge in medical malpractice and unresolved insurance claims keeps the current legal staff on overtime. Sometimes the types of issues brought up in the legal cases are beyond the scope of the attorneys on staff. Mike is looking for an attorney with extensive background in the most recent court rulings involving medical malpractice and insurance claims. Using the techniques you have practiced, locate three attorneys: one in your zip code, one who specializes in medical malpractice, and one who specializes in insurance claims.

When you have found all three attorneys, use Notepad to write a brief paragraph detailing the attorneys' names, their addresses, and areas of specialization. Then state what Web site(s) you used to locate them. Provide the name of the Web site(s) and the URL(s). Save your file as **6J_Attorney_Firstname_Lastname** Submit it to your instructor as directed.

 End **You have completed Project 6J**

Assessments

Internet
chaptersix   *GO!* Search

Project 6K—Planning a Trip to Disney World

Objectives: 6. *Manage Travel Arrangements Online;* **11.** *Explore Multimedia Resources.*

For Project 6K, you will need the following file:

Web page printout

You will save your file as
6K_Disney_Firstname_Lastname

The Assistant Director for the University Medical Center, Telma Leong, is trying to develop a new brochure to give to the families of terminally ill young children. The University Medical Center has an endowment that provides funding to support trips for a family of four for four days to the Walt Disney World Resort. Many of these children have never been there and a short trip is a good way to relieve the family stress while caring for these children. Using what you have learned in the chapter and the Web site at **http://disneyworld.disney.go.com** plan a trip for one of these families. Go as far as you can in the booking process without actually submitting credit card information to confirm the trip. Save the Web page **6K_Disney_Firstname_Lastname** Submit it to your instructor as directed.

End **You have completed Project 6K** _____

Glossary

Access point See Hotspot.

Accessibility compliance An initiative to provide features in order to accommodate people with visual or physical disabilities so that they can access the Internet with modifications to the browser or Web sites.

Acronym A series of letters that stand for the first letter of words in a phrase.

Active X A technology that works within Web pages to display animation, multimedia, and interactive objects.

Add-ons A browser feature that enables you to personalize your browsing experience in the areas of security, timesaving features, offline browsing, and entertainment.

Address bar The toolbar in Internet Explorer into which individuals type the address of a specific Web site that they want to display.

Address book A feature that stores the names and e-mail addresses of your friends, colleagues, or other contacts you would like to communicate with using e-mail.

Administrative address A mailing list address that is reserved for use for sending commands such as *Subscribe* and *Unsubscribe* to the mailing list.

Advanced Research Projects Agency (ARPA) The U.S. Department of Defense agency developed to promote scientific research and technological development in order to help the United States gain a leading edge in the race in science and technology among the world's developed nations.

Advanced search A search engine feature providing options for refining a keyword query by specifying additional criteria for returned search results.

Adware A software program that collects information about your preferences by tracking your browsing habits and in response, displays advertisements on your screen as pop-ups or as icons on your desktop.

Aggregator See Blog feed.

Anonymous FTP A Web site that permits you to log in and access files on a server without identifying yourself to the server with a user ID and password. Typically, an anonymous FTP site accepts the word *guest* or *anonymous* as the user ID and a password is unnecessary.

Anti-adware program A program that scans the hard drive or any other location you specify on your computer for known adware that may be on your computer. Once located, the program disables the adware.

Anti-spyware program A program that scans the hard drive or any other location you specify on your computer for known spyware that may be on your computer. Once located, the program disables the spyware.

Anti-virus program A program that scans the hard drive or any other location you specify on your computer for known viruses that may be on your computer. Once located, the program disables the virus.

Archive An electronic copy of a file that can be stored in a separate location and retrieved at a future date.

ARPA See Advanced Research Projects Agency.

ARPANET A large network developed by ARPA in the 1960s that allowed for sensitive governmental communications and the exchange of academic and scientific research without interruption in the event of a catastrophe.

Article The original message of a thread found in a newsgroup.

As Attachment An option to forward a message as a separate file that must be viewed as an attachment by the recipient.

As Inline Text An option to forward a message embedded into the message body.

Asynchronous communication Electronic communication in which the participants do not need to be online at the same time, and all participants can view the communication when they want to do so.

"At" sign (@) A character that is always part of an e-mail address and separates the user ID from the host name.

Atom A pair of related protocols that enable access to feeds written in the XML.

Attachment Additional files sent along with an e-mail message to support the meaning or subject matter of the e-mail.

Avatar A graphic used to represent a message board, instant message, or chat participant.

Back button A browser feature that moves you to the last Web page that you visited.

Bandwidth The transmission speed or transfer capacity of data on a network, measured in bits per second.

Bcc See Blind carbon copy.

Berners-Lee, Tim The scientist who proposed combining the use of the Internet with hypertext to create a tool for collaboration and data sharing that subsequently became the World Wide Web.

Big Eight The seven original top-level USENET hierarchies plus the category added in 1995, humanities.*

Big Seven The seven original top-level USENET hierarchies: comp.*, misc.*, news.*, rec.*, sci.*, soc.*, and talk.*.

Bit The smallest unit of data that can be used in computing or sent along a network.

Bits per second (bps) The unit of measure for bandwidth— the transmission speed or transfer capacity of data on a network.

File Transfer Protocol (FTP) A protocol that enables individuals to copy files from one computer to another on a network.

Filters An e-mail feature used to automatically sort your e-mail messages into folders as the messages arrive instead of placing them directly into in the Inbox by default.

Firewall A software program that is used to protect your computer from outside threats by blocking direct communication with the Internet.

First-person shooting game A graphically oriented game where the view on the screen is shown from the viewpoint of the main character of the game.

Flame An abusive or insulting message sent to someone on a mailing list, listserv, or in a chat room.

Folder An e-mail feature used to collect, organize, and store your e-mail.

Font A certain named style of text that represents qualities of size, spacing, and shape of letters.

Form data Anything that you have typed into the Address bar or on Web pages during a browsing.

Formatting toolbar A set of onscreen tools that enables you to customize the appearance of text.

Forum See Message board.

Forward An e-mail feature that sends a message you have received, modified, or left in its original form, to another recipient who is not the original sender.

Forward button A browser feature that moves you to the Web page you were viewing before you clicked the Back button.

Freeware Software programs that are made available to the user free of charge.

Frequently Asked Questions (FAQs) A list of commonly asked questions and the answers to those questions.

From line An e-mail component that indicates the name or user ID of the sender of the e-mail.

FrontPage A popular software program developed by Microsoft that is used to create Web pages.

FTP See File Transfer Protocol.

FTP client Software that lets you make a connection to an FTP site and then copy files to and from that site.

Full-text indexing A search engine's index created by spiders that search the entire file or document noting where the words are located within the file or document and how often they appear within the content of the Web page.

Go button A green arrow at the right end of the Address bar that appears as you type and will take you to the URL that is typed in the Address bar.

Google Earth A service that uses satellite images, maps, and the Google search engine to enable zooming in from the sky level down to the street level as if you were flying overhead in an airplane.

Google Maps A service of Google that provides search capability for locating maps and finding directions through your computer or mobile phone.

Groom To establish a level of trust and develop an increasingly exploitative relationship between a victim and a predator.

Hackers People with sophisticated computer skills who access networks and servers to steal data, examine code, or infect computer systems with malicious programs.

Help A feature that provides access to an index of answers to questions about using Internet Explorer, a tour of Internet Explorer, online support, and feedback options.

Hierarchy A topic category that provides the structure for a newsgroup name.

History A browser feature where a list is automatically generated for Web sites that have been visited during a browsing session.

Hit Each individual link in the search results list.

Hoax An e-mail making false statements or outrageous offers.

Home button A button that always returns you to the default home page that is set for the computer you are working on.

Home page The starting point or the first Web page displayed at a Web site.

Host computer A computer within an organization that has access to all other computers on the organization's network and provides services for those computers such as the storage of Web pages.

Host name The name of the server and the domain name of the organization where e-mail is received and stored.

Hosting provider An organization that provides server space for Web sites or blogs either free of charge or for a monthly fee.

Hotspot A Wi-Fi connection point consisting of a small box that is hardwired to the Internet and is commonly found in airports, coffee shops, hotels, and libraries.

HTML See Hypertext Markup Language.

HTTP See Hypertext Transfer Protocol.

Hybrid learning Courses combining classroom time with some portion of the course work completed in the online format.

Hyperlink See Hypertext link.

Hypertext Text linked together in a way that lets people browse through related topics in a nonlinear web of associations.

Hypertext link A connection often represented by blue underlined text or blue bordered images in a Web page. When clicked, the visitor is transferred to another part of the Web page, another part of the Web site, or to a new Web site.

Hypertext Markup Language (HTML) A language that uses tags to mark a Web page's text and graphics. The tags indicate how a Web browser should display these elements.

Hypertext Transfer Protocol (HTTP) The protocol used to carry the request from the Web browser on the client computer to the server computer, and then to transport copies of files from the server computer back to the client computer for display by the browser.

ICANN See Internet Corporation for Assigned Names and Numbers.

IE See Internet Explorer.

IM See Instant messaging.

IM client A program installed on your computer that enables you to send and receive messages instantly.

IMAP See Internet Message Access Protocol.

Inbox The default folder in an e-mail system where incoming messages are placed.

Index An enormous database, used in a search engine, that stores references to words found in documents and Web files located by the spider.

Instant messaging (IM) Interactive, text-based, synchronous discussions similar to chat, however, usually only two people are participating within one window.

Instant Search A search tool that allows you to locate Web sites, images, and maps on the Internet from the toolbar of the Internet Explorer window.

Internal search engine A search engine that indexes only a particular Web site in order to create a search results list that contains only results from that Web site.

Internet A worldwide system of networked computers that use a common set of rules enabling collaboration, communication, and commerce.

Internet Corporation for Assigned Names and Numbers (ICANN) The organization that oversees the registration of new domain names and administers IP addresses on the Internet.

Internet Explorer A browser developed by Microsoft that is designed to work with the Windows operating system.

Internet Message Access Protocol (IMAP) The protocol that enables the e-mail client to read and manage e-mail messages using the user's computer but the messages remain stored on the server.

Internet Protocol address A number that uniquely identifies each computer connected to the Internet to other computers connected to the Internet for the purpose of communication and the transfer of data packets.

Internet Relay Chat (IRC) The first system developed to enable multiple individuals to participate in text-based, real-time conversations over the Internet.

Internet Service Provider (ISP) A company or organization that provides access to the Internet.

Internet telephony (Voice over Internet Protocol or VoIP) The transmission of voice communication over the Internet by using packet switching and TCP/IP.

Internet2 A consortium of education and research leaders brought together by extremely fast network solutions for the purpose of collaboration and learning.

Invisible Web (Deep Web) Documents and files stored on Web servers or in electronic databases that are not accessible using directories and search engines typically used when searching the World Wide Web.

IP address See Internet Protocol address.

IPng See IPv6.

IPv4 standard The current standard for the Internet Protocol, under which the mathematical possibilities for IP addresses have almost been reached due to the explosive growth of the Internet.

IPv6 A new standard for the Internet Protocol, also referred to as IPng (an acronym for Internet Protocol next generation), that allows for the future growth of the Internet.

IRC See Internet Relay Chat.

ISP See Internet Service Provider.

Keyword query A word or phrase that represents the subject you want to find out about and is used to begin a search.

LAN See Local area network.

Link See Hypertext link.

Link Select pointer The mouse pointer view that displays as a pointing hand as you point to a link.

List address A mailing list address used for posting messages and replying to messages on a mailing list.

List server The server where the mailing list manager software is installed.

Listserv (Mailing list) A subscription-based list of several names and e-mail addresses combined under one e-mail address generally managed by software and used for the discussion of specific topic areas.

LISTSERV A program that is commonly used to manage mailing lists.

Local area network (LAN) A group of computers and devices forming a network and located in a limited area connected so that any computer or device can communicate with any other computer or device on that network.

Lurk When you receive and read posts, but you do not reply to any of them.

Mail header An e-mail component located at the top of the e-mail message and contains information about the message, such as the sender's e-mail address, the recipient's e-mail address, and the subject.

Mail server A large computer that receives, stores, and sends e-mail messages.

Mailing list See Listserv.

Mailing list manager A software program installed on a server that handles accepting messages and posting them on the list.

Majordomo A program that is commonly used to manage mailing lists.

Malware A software program that invades computers and networks for the purpose of disruption or destruction of the network or data.

Massachusetts Institute of Technology (MIT) A prestigious university that primarily focuses its instruction in science and technology.

Massively Multiplayer Online Game (MMOG) A Web-based game involving multiple players spread across many countries.

Privacy Your ability to determine which personal information, such as your email messages and stored files, is shared and for what purpose.

Privacy policies Policies that inform you of how any information about you gathered at a Web site may be used or shared with other parties.

Private key An encryption tool that is used to decode the data after it is transmitted over the Internet.

Protocol A common set of rules for how computers communicate and exchange information.

Proximity How near each word in the query appears on the Web page in relation to the other words of the query.

Public key An encryption tool that is used to code the data before sending it over the Internet.

Publish To make available after writing.

Pull technology A technology that works on the World Wide Web where users actively seek out new information from Web sites.

Push technology A technology that works on the World Wide Web where users are provided with new and updated information either automatically or at specified intervals.

Quick Tabs An Internet Explorer feature that only displays when multiple tabs are open and permits navigation among open tabs.

Rankings The algorithms used to retrieve and list words from the search engine's index.

Really Simple Syndication (RSS) A system developed to automatically alert subscribers of updates made to sites such as blogs, news, weather, or sports sites.

Real-time communication See Synchronous communication.

Real-time strategy game A graphically-oriented game in which each player can play continuously and not take turns.

Relevance How closely the search results relate to your keyword query.

Reply Your electronic response to an e-mail message that enables you to send the original e-mail and additional information or comments back to the sender.

Reply To Everyone An e-mail feature that sends your reply message to the sender of the message and all of the recipients of the original message.

Reply To Sender An e-mail feature that sends your reply only to the sender of the original message.

Restore Down button A Windows feature that, when clicked, makes the window smaller and enables you to move the Internet Explorer window.

Reverse lookup A service that enables you to type in a phone number or an e-mail address, and then the name of the person associated with that information is returned.

RSS See Really Simple Syndication.

RSS feed An individual Web document in the XML format that contains content such as news, weather, or blog posts.

RSS reader A software program or Web-based service that provides access to RSS feeds.

Sandbox A practice area where individuals new to wikis can practice making edits without damaging the real content of the wiki.

ScreenTip A Windows feature that temporarily displays a small box providing information about, or the name of, a screen element as you hold the mouse pointer over buttons or images in Internet Explorer or other Web browsers.

Script Coded instructions embedded within a program to enable customization or add interactivity to a Web page.

Scroll bars A vertical and/or horizontal bar located on the edge of the browser window enables you to move the content so that the hidden parts of the Web page come into view.

Search engine A computer program used to locate files, documents, and Web pages containing specific keyword queries or natural language queries.

Search engine software A program that compares the keyword or natural language query to the words and references stored in the index and then generates the search results list that displays in the browser window.

Search filter Techniques used to limit the search results to specific criteria, such as format of the results.

Search results list The list of Web pages containing the query and displayed as links that are located by any given search engine.

Secure Sockets Layer (SSL) A protocol that uses encryption during the transmission of data over the Internet. SSL is used to protect data such as credit card numbers or other personal information being sent from Web sites.

Security The technologies involved with features keeping your data and computer free from unauthorized access.

Sent folder An e-mail folder that stores a copy of all of the e-mail messages that you send out.

Server A network-connected computer that stores files and has administrative software to control access to network resources.

Service pack Product updates and patches to solve software bugs and security issues available as downloads from a Web site or by installing from a CD.

Shouting Typing in all capital letters—the online equivalent of raising your voice.

Signature file A file that you create that contains your name and other information that can be automatically added to every e-mail you send.

Simple Mail Transfer Protocol (SMTP) The protocol that handles outgoing messages and routes them to their destination.

SMTP See Simple Mail Transfer Protocol.

Social networking Interaction with others conducted at Web sites providing opportunities to view or exchange e-mails, discussions threads, blog entries, photos, audio files, and videos with other participants.

Spam Unsolicited and unwanted e-mail sent to several recipients at once generally for the purpose of advertising.

Specialized database An electronic database that contains information and materials on a specific topic.

Spider (Crawler or Bot) A program that searches the Internet for new documents and Web files, and then catalogs the words found within the documents and files for use in a search engine.

Sponsored links See Sponsored sites.

Sponsored results See Sponsored sites.

Sponsored sites (Sponsored results or Sponsored links) Web sites that try to market themselves by paying search engine owners to be shown as a listing in search result lists.

Spyware A software program that invades your computer and gathers information about you by tracking your keystrokes and collecting a list of the Web sites that you visit.

SSL See Secure Sockets Layer.

Start button A Windows feature found in the lower left corner of the screen that, when clicked, causes the Start menu to display.

Start menu A Windows feature that provides access to all the programs and helpful features on your Windows computer through a series of commands.

Status bar A horizontal bar near the bottom of the browser window that provides information about the security of a site, information about a link's destination as you roll over a link, or information about any submenu command.

Stop words Short words connecting the more important words of a natural language query and having little impact on the meaning.

Streaming A method of delivering digital content to a computer so that the content plays as soon as it is received by the computer.

Style sheet A set of rules for how to format fonts, characters, and page layout within an HTML document.

Subject catalog See Directory.

Subject line An e-mail component created by the sender and summarizing in a couple of words the main idea of the e-mail message.

Submenu A detailed list of commands, displayed after clicking a command, which enables you to perform several tasks to enhance your browsing experience.

Subscription fee A fee charged by ISPs for Internet access for a specified period of time.

Surf See Browse.

Synchronous communication (Real-time communication) A form of electronic communication in which two or more participants are online at the same time and are communicating with each other.

Synonym Words that mean nearly the same thing.

Syntax The order followed when writing the parts of a Web address or code.

Tab An area of the browser window that displays the name of the Web site and also enables navigation between Web sites.

Tabbed browsing A feature that enables visitors to open multiple Web pages within the same browser window.

Tags Categories for the organization of blog topics that are added to the blog when the blog is written.

Taskbar A part of the Windows operating system that displays buttons for all open programs and files.

TCP/IP See Transmission Control Protocol/Internet Protocol.

Telnet A protocol that enables you to access a remote computer to complete tasks as if you were sitting at the keyboard of that computer.

Template A predesigned document that can be added to or modified for use in a blog, Web page, or word-processed document.

Temporary Internet files A browser feature where copies of Web pages, images, and media that are saved for faster viewing.

Text shortcut A series of letters that sound like the word they stand for.

The Net See Internet.

The Web See World Wide Web.

THOMAS A part of the Library of Congress created in response to a directive made by Congress to make federal legislative information available to the public.

Thread An article and all of the posts that follows along a specific topic in a newsgroup.

Thumbnail A graphic depicting a miniature version of each open Web page that can be used for navigation.

TILE.NET A well-respected search tool used for locating Internet references for newsletters, discussion lists, USENET newsgroups, vendors for computer products, Internet Service Providers, and Web design companies.

Timestamp An expression of time—hour or day—to indicate the most recent update for a blog or a Web site.

Title bar A blue, horizontal bar at the top of the browser window that identifies the application and displays the name of the active Web page.

TLD See Top-level domain.

To line An e-mail component that provides the name and e-mail address of the recipient or recipients of the e-mail message.

Toolbar An area of a software program's interface that provides text or buttons which, when clicked, enable you to perform certain commands and tasks within that software program.

Tools button A button that enables you to perform several commands that are frequently used while browsing the Web such as those related to safe browsing strategies, the display of toolbars within the browser interface, and setting browsing preferences.

Index

A

Abika Web site, 365
About.com Web site, 180
acceptable use policies, 352
access points, 13
accessibility compliance, 69
accounts
    blogs, 281–284
    e-mail signup, 207–213
acronyms, 42, 243, 308
Active X, 123
Add a Favorite dialog box, 91
Add to Favorites button, 78
Add to Favorites command, 78
add-ons, 110
Add-Ons for Internet Explorer Web site, 377
Address bars, 6, 75, 82
    browsing Web, 87–88
    Web searches, 152–155
Address Book button, 218
address books, e-mail, 240
administrative addresses,mailing lists, 249
Advanced Research Projects Agency (ARPA),
    36–37
advanced searches, 150
    World Wide Web
        Boolean operators, 166–169
        invisible web resources, 173–179
        news and opinion resources, 169–173
adware, 122
.aero domain, 31
aggregators (blog feed), 278
Alltheweb Web site, 183
AltaVista Web site, 183
alternate e-mail addresses, 213
American Bar Association Web site, 367
American Memory Web site, 379
anonymous FTP sites, 311
anti-adware, 122
Anti-Phishing Working Group Web site, 121
anti-spyware, 122
anti-virus programs, 122
AnyWho Web site, 365
AOL Mail Web site, 239
AOL Music Web site, 379
AOL White Pages Web site, 365
archives, 294
ARPA (Advanced Research Projects Agency),
    36–37
ARPANET, 36–37
articles (newsgroups), 291
Ask the Experts Web page, 158
Ask.com Web site, 183
associative indexing, 37
asynchronous communications, 41,
    208, 291

Atlanta-Fulton Public Library link, 162
attachments, e-mail, 222–228
avatars, 306
award-winning Web sites, 371–372

B

Back button, 11, 75, 82
bandwidth, 11
Berners-Lee,Sir Tim, 38–40
Big Eight, 293
Big Seven (USENET hierarchies), 293
Bigfoot Web site, 365
bitmaps, 98
bits per second (bps), 33
.biz domain, 31
blind carbon copies, 215
blog feed (aggregators), 278
Bloglines, 352
blogosphere, 277
blogrolls, 276
blogs, 42–43
    creation, 273–290
        account setup, 281–284
        existing blogs, 274–280
        publishing posts, 284–290
    software programs, 281
.bmp file extension, 98
Boolean operators, 150, 166–169
bots, 147
bps (bits per second), 33
breadcrumb trails, 157
Broadband Services Offered category, 14
broadbands, 13
browsers, 4
    comparisons of popular, 108–115
    plug-ins, 107–108
browsing, 26
    WWW (World Wide Web)
        Address bar, 87–88
        default home page specification,
            83–85
        Favorites Center, 90–93
        History feature, 88–90
        Internet Explorer commands, 65–74
        links, 86–87
        plug-ins, 107–108
        privacy risks, 116–121
        safe strategies, 121–125
        toolbar commands, 74–82
bulletin boards, 305–307
Bush, Dr. Vannevar, 40
    hypertext, 37–38
    Memex machine, 38
business news resources, searching
    for, 172
byte, 33

C

cable connections, 12
cable TV, Internet connection methods, 33
cache, managing Web content, 102–104
calendaring, e-mail, 240
CamelCase, 304
CAPTCHA, 212, 283
carbon copies, e-mail, 215
CERN, 38
channel operators (IRC), 312
channels (IRC conversations), 311–312
Chat Rooms, 41
   privacy risks, 118–119
   protecting children, 119–120
Chats, 41, 43, 312–314
   clients, 313
   e-mail, 240
Check Mail button, 229
children, protecting in Chat Rooms,
   119–120
Children's Online Privacy Protection Act
   (COPPA), 119
ChoiceTrust Web site, 365
citizen journalism, 304
City of Desert Park Arizona, 62
   browsing World Wide Web, 63
     Address bar, 87–88
     default home page specification, 83–85
     Favorites Center, 90–93
     History feature, 88–90
     Internet Explorer commands, 65–74
     links, 86–87
     performing commands, 65–74
     plug-ins, 107–108
     popular browser comparison, 108–115
     toolbar commands, 74–82
   managing Web content with Internet Explorer
     clearing cache and cookies, 102–104
     desktop shortcuts, 100–101
     e-mailing Web pages and links, 98–99
     history, 104–106
     printing text and graphics, 94–96
     saving Web pages, 96–98
client-based e-mail systems, 237–238
clients, 27
   chat, 313
   FTP, 42
   server communication, 28
client-server architectures, 27
Close buttons, 64, 82
closed lists, 248
Clusty Web site, 181
CNET Web site, 252
collaboration, World Wide Web, 271–335
   blog creation, 273–290
   newsgroups, 291–301
   synchronous communication tools, 311–317
   tools, 317
   Web-based communication tools, 302–310
.com domain, 31
Comedy Central Web site, 379

commands
   IRC, 312
   mailing lists, 251
communication tools
   blogs, 273–290
   synchronous, 311–317
     chat, 312–314
     Internet telephony, 314–315
     IRC, 311–312
     video conferencing, 316–317
     VoIP, 314–315
   Web-based, 302–310
     bulletin boards, 305–307
     instant messaging, 307–310
     message boards, 305–307
     Vlogs, 304–305
     Web-based forums, 305–307
     Wikis, 302–304
communications
   e-mail
     creating messages, 214–218
     receiving and replying, 222–228
     signature files, 218–221
     Web-based account signup, 207–213
   Internet use, 41–42
   remote, 42
connections, Internet
   dial-up, 8, 33
   common terms, 25–26
   hardware and software requirements, 32–33
   methods, 33
   Web site requests, 27–32
   wireless options, 34–35
consoles, 377
contact lists, 308
context-sensitive menus, 72
cookies, 73, 102–104
Cool Site of the Day Web site, 372
.coop domain, 31
COPPA (Children's Online Privacy Protection
   Act), 119, 305
copyright notices, 186
Craig's List Web site, 373
crawlers, 147
Create a Folder dialog box, 91
customer support
   Firefox, 112
   Internet Explorer, 110
   Netscape Browser, 111
   Opera, 113
   Safari, 114
customization
   Firefox, 112
   Internet Explorer, 110
   Netscape Browser, 111
   Opera, 113
   Safari, 114

D

Dam, Dr. Andries van, 38, 40
dashboards, 284

databases, specialized advanced searches, 173–179
date stamps, 186
dedicated services, 8
Deep Web, 173
default home pages, 5
The Definitive ISP Buyer's Guide, 6
Deja News, 294
Delete Browsing History dialog box, 102–104
Delete Cookies button, 103
demodulators, 8
desktop shortcuts, Web pages, 100–101
DHTML (Dynamic HTML), 112
dialer programs, 122
dial-up Internet connections, 8, 33
Digital Subscriber Lines (DSL), 12, 33
direct satellite system (DSS), 13–14, 33
directories, 18, 149
   locating health information resources, 340–342
   popular search sites, 180
   search site, 180–181
Disney Online Web site, 379
distance learning, 367
Docusearch Web site, 365
Dogpile Web site, 181
domain names, 31–32
dotted quads, 30
Download.com Web site, 377
downloads, 26, 108
Dreamweaver, 29
drilling down, 157
DSL (Digital Subscriber Lines), 12, 33
DSS (direct satellite system), 13–14, 33
Dynamic HTML (DHTML), 12
dynamically generated results, 163

E

Edit command (Menu Bar Internet Explorer), 66
.edu domain, 31
educational resources, 367–369
El Cuero Specialty Wares, e-mail messages
   creating basic, 214–218
   deleting from account, 235–236
   folders and filers, 230–234
   printing, 228–230
   receiving and replying, 222–228
   signature files, 218–221
   Web-based account signup, 207–213
electronic mail. *See* e-mail
Electronic Privacy Information Center Web site, 121
e-mail, 41, 43
   addresses, 209
   comparing systems
     client-based, 237–238
     features, 240
     protocols, 240–241
     web-based, 238–240
   deleting from account, 235–236

Firefox, 112
folders and filers, 230–234
Internet Explorer, 109
mailing lists, 247–248
   commands, 251
   locating, 248–249
   subscribing and unsubscribing, 249–251
messages
   creating basic, 214–218
   signature files, 218–221
minimizeing nuisances, 244–246
netiquette
   acronyms, 243
   expressing emotion, 242–243
   guidelines, 242
   text shortcuts, 244
Netscape Browser, 111
newsletters, 252–253
Opera, 113
printing messages, 228–230
privacy, 120–121
receiving and replying, 222
   checking e-mail, 223–225
   forward and reply features, 225–228
Safari, 113
Web-based account signup, 207–213
emoticons, 42, 242–243, 308
encryption, 124–125
Englebert, Doug, 38, 40
Excite Web site, 373
expert resources
   document comparing, 160–161
   locating on Web, 157–160
eXtensible Markup Language (XML), 348, 351

F

FamilySearch Web site, 365
FAQs (Frequently Asked Questions), 110
Fastmail Web site, 239
Favorites Center
   browsing World Wide Web, 90–93
   button, 77
   Internet Explorer, 71–74, 82
Favorites command (Menu Bar Internet Explorer), 66
FBI State Sex Offender Registry Web site, 365
Federal Consumer Information Center Consumer Action Web site, 121
Federal Trade Commission Complaint Form Web site, 120
feeds, computer installation, 350–356
Feeds button, 76, 82
File command (Menu Bar Internet Explorer), 66
File Transfer Protocol. *See* FTP
file types, searches, 150
files, 27, 42–43
filters, e-mail, 230–234
Find dialog box, 68
FindLaw Web site, 367
Firefox Add-ons Web site, 377
Firefox features, 112

firewalls, 123
first-person shooting games, 374
Flickr Web site, 379
folders, e-mail, 230–234
Formatting toolbar, 287
form data, 102
forums, 305–307
Forward button, 11, 74–75, 82
forwarding e-mail, 225–228
freeware, 109
Frequently Asked Questions (FAQs), 110
FrontPage, 29
FTP (File Transfer Protocol)
    anonymous sites, 311
    clients, 42–43
full-text indexing, 184

G

Galaxy Web site, 180
gaming sites, 373–376
GetNetWise Web site, 120
GIF (Graphics Interchange Format), 98
.gif file extension, 98
Gigablast Web site, 183
Gmail Web site, 239
Go button, 83
Google
    archives, 294
    blog search, 275
    finding news, 169–170
    Web site, 183
Google Earth, 357
Google Maps, 357
.gov domain, 31
graphics
    printing Web content, 94–96
    Web file types, 98
Graphics Interchange Format (GIF), 98
Greater Atlanta Job Fair
    advanced Web searches
      Boolean operators, 166–169
      invisible web resources, 173–179
      news and opinion resources, 169–173
    Web searches, 144–145
      Address bar searches, 152–155
      formulating keyword queries, 146–152
      Instant Search feature, 156–157
      locate expert resources, 157–161
      locating online scholarly resources, 161–165
green arrow button, 88
grooming, 118

H

hackers, 121
hardware, Internet connection requirements,
    32–33
health information Web sites
    accessing resources, 339
      directory searches, 340–342
      special interest searches, 342–346
    comparing special interest sites, 346–347

Help command (Menu Bar Internet
    Explorer), 66
history
    Internet
      early history summary, 36–37
      hypertext features, 38–40
      key developers, 37–38
      popular uses, 40–43
    Internet Explorer, 73
History button, 78, 88
History feature, browsing World Wide Web,
    88–90
hoax e-mail, 245
Home button, 76, 82
home pages, 6, 83–85
host computers, 6
host names, 209
hosting providers, 281
hotspots, 13
HTML (Hypertext Markup Language), 26,
    29–30
HTTP (Hypertext Transfer Protocol), 28, 241
hybrid learning, 367
hyperlinks, 25
hypertext
    documents, 25
    links, 25
    origins, 37
    unique features, 38–40
Hypertext Editing System, 38
Hypertext Markup Language (HTML), 26,
    29–30
Hypertext Transfer Protocol (HTTP), 28, 241

I

ICANN (Internet Corporation for Assigned Names
    and Numbers), 31
    registering domain names, 32
IM (Instant Messaging), 42–43, 307–310
    clients, 307
    e-mail, 240
IMAP (Internet Message Access Protocol), 241
Import and Export command, 78
indexes, 147
.info domain, 31
InfoSpace Web site, 365
InfoWorld Web site, 252
instant messaging. *See* IM
Instant Search feature, 82, 156–157
.int domain, 31
Intelius Web site, 365
Interactive Media Awards Web site, 372
Internet, 1–2
    connecting to
      common terms, 25–26
      hardware and software requirements,
        32–33
      methods, 33
      Web site requests, 27–32
      wireless options, 34–35
    history
      early history summary, 36–37

hypertext features, *38–40*
key developers, *37–38*
popular uses, *40–43*
ISP (Internet Service Provider), 3
   compiling information from Web, *15–17*
   locating one in local area, *4–8*
   refining searches, *9–14*
researching history of
   browse directory for information, *18–23*
   events and technologies affecting development,
    23–24
telephony, *314–315*
**Internet Corporation for Assigned Names and
  Numbers (ICANN), 31–32**
Internet Explorer, 4, 6
  browsing World Wide Web
   performing commands, 65–74
   toolbar commands, 74–82
  changing default search engine, 153
  features, 82, 109–111
  managing Web content
   clearing cache and cookies, 102–104
   desktop shortcuts, 100–101
   history, 104–106
   printing text and graphics, 94–96
   saving Web pages, 96–98
  passwords, 300
**Internet Message Access Protocol (IMAP),
  241**
Internet Movie Database Web site, 379
Internet Options dialog box, 73, 84
Internet Protocol, 30
Internet Relay Chat (IRC), 311–312
Internet Service Provider. *See* **ISP**
The Internet Tourbus Web site, 372
Internet2, 368
invisible text, 288
**Invisible Web, advanced searches,
  173–179**
IP addresses, 30–31
IPng standards, 30
IPv4 standards, 30
IPv6 standards, 30
IRC (Internet Relay Chat), 311–312
ISPs (Internet Service Provider)
  compiling information from Web,
   15–17
  local area provider, 4–8
  locating, 3
  refining searches, 9–14
iStockphoto Web site, 379
iVillage Web site, 373
Ixquick Web site, 181

J

**Joint Photographic Experts Group
  (JPEG), 98**
**JPEG (Joint Photographic Experts
  Group), 98**
.jpeg file extension, 98
.jpg file extension, 98
JupiterMedia Newsletters Web site, 252

K

keyword queries, formulating
  comparing search engines, 151–152
  developing queries, 146–147
  identifying search engines, 147–151
keywords, 18

L

Lake Michigan City College, 2
  ISP (Internet Service Provider), 3
   compiling information from Web, 15–17
   locating one in local area, 4–8
   refining searches, 9–14
  researching history of Internet
   browse directory for information, 18–23
   *events and technologies affecting development,
    23–24*
LAN (local area network), 32
Law.com Web site, 367
LawDepot.com Web site, 367
**legal information, online resources,
  366–367**
LegalZoom Web site, 367
LexisNexis Web site, 367
Librarians' Internet Index
  searching for Internet history, 18–23
  Web site, 180
library catalogs, locating online, 161–165
Library of Congress Web site, 163
Libweb home page, 162
Link Select pointers, 86
link select pointers, 26
links, 25
  browsing World Wide Web, 86–87
  opening in new browser window, 159
list addresses, mailing lists, 249
LISTSERV, 247
listservs, 41, 43, 247
Live Search, 76
local area network (LAN), 32
LookSmart Web site, 180
Louvre Web site, 379
lurking (chat), 314
Lycos Mail Web site, 239
Lycos Web site, 183
Lycos WhoWhere Web site, 365

M

mail headers, 214
mail servers, 222
Mail.com Web site, 239
mailing lists, 41, 247–248
  commands, 251
  locating, 248–249
  managers, 247
  subscribing and unsubscribing,
   249–251
Majordomo, 247
malware, 121
Mamma Web site, 181
MarketResearch Newsletter Web site, 252

Massively Multiplayer Online Games (MMOG), 374
Maximize button, 5, 16, 65
MediaFinder Web site, 252
Memex, 37
menu bars, 64–68
   hiding, 66
   Internet Explorer, 82
message boards, 305–307
messages
   bodies, 214
   e-mail
      creating basic, 214–218
      deleting from account, 235–236
      printing, 228–230
      signature files, 218–221
MetaCrawler Web site, 181
meta-search engines, 149, 181–182
metatags, 184
Microsoft Dreamweaver, 29
Microsoft FrontPage, 29
Microsoft Outlook, 237
.mil domain, 31
military, Internet use, 36–37
MILNET, 36–37
MIME (Multipurpose Internet Mail Extensions), 241
Minimize button, 64, 82
MIT OpenCourseWare (MIT OCW), 369
MMOG (Massively Multiplayer Online Games), 374
modems, 8
moderated lists, 248
moderated newsgroups, 299
moderators, 299
modulators/demodulators, 8
MOO games, 373
MSN Hotmail Web site, 239
MSN Web site, 183
MSNBC Newsletters Web site, 252
MTV Web site, 379
MUD games, 373
MUD Object Oriented games, 373
multimedia resources, 376–379
Multipurpose Internet Mail Extensions (MIME), 241
Multi-User Dungeon games, 373
Multi-User Shared Hack games, 374
.museum domain, 31
MUSH games, 374
My Yahoo! reader, 351

N

.name domain, 31
name resolutions, 30, 241
NASA Web site, 379
The National Archives Web site, 365
National Center for Missing and Exploited Children Web site, 120
National Geographic Web site, 379
natural language queries. See keyword queries
Nelson, Ted, 38, 40

Net. See Internet
.net domain, 31
Net Family News Web site, 120
netiquette, e-mail
   acronyms, 243
   expressing emotion, 242–243
   guidelines, 242
   shortcuts, 244
Netscape Browser, features, 111–112
Netscape Web site, 373
NetSmartz Workshop Web site, 120
network etiquette. See netiquette
newbies (chat), 314
news resources
   Advanced Search features, 170–171
   business news searches, 172
   comparison document, 173
   finding at Google, 169–170
news servers, 296
newsfeeds, 296
newsgroups, 41, 291–301
   moderated, 299
   threads, 291, 296–301
   unmoderated, 299
   USENET, 291–294
   Web-based, 294–296
Newsletter Access Directory Web site, 252
newsletters, e-mail, 252–253
newsreaders, 41, 297
NLS (oNLine System), 38
NOAA NWS, 349
nodes, 30
Nolo Web site, 367
Notepad, 15
NPR Web site, 172, 379
NSFNET, 37

O

offline, 94
OnGuard Online Web site, 121
oNLine System (NLS), 38
Open Directory Project Web site, 180
open lists, 248
open sources, 112, 304
OpenCourseWare, 369
Opera features, 113
opinion resources
   Advanced Search features, 170–171
   business news searches, 172
   comparison document, 173
   finding at Google, 169–170
.org domain, 31
Organize Favorites command, 78
Organize Favorites dialog box, 92
Outlook, 237
Outlook Express, 237
overlaps, 183

P

packet switching, 36–37
Page button, 77, 82

Page Setup dialog box, 16
pages, 6
passwords
    e-mail, 210
    Internet Explorer, 300
    verification, 213
paths, 20, 75
PDF files, 163
PeopleFinders Web site, 365
permalinks (blogs), 276
pharming, 121
phishing, 120, 246
photo sharing, e-mail, 240
PHP files, 163
pinned panels, 77
Plugin.com Web site, 377
plug-ins, 107–108, 376
PNG (Portable Network Graphics), 98
.png file extension, 98
podcasts, 169, 350
POP3 (Post Office Protocol 3), 241
pop-ups, 72, 288
Portable Network Graphics (PNG), 98
portals, 83, 372–373
Post Office Protocol 3 (POP3), 241
postings, 247, 275
primary sources, 185
Print button, 76, 82
Print dialog box, 95
Print Preview dialog box, 67, 155
printer-friendly versions, 229
privacy
    policies, 116
    World Wide Web security risks, 116–117
        Chat Rooms, 118–119
        e-mail, 120–121
        protecting children, 119–120
Privacy Rights Clearinghouse Web site, 120
private keys, 125
.pro domain, 31
Proteus Internet Search Web site, 181
protocols, 28, 240–241
providers, VoIP, 315
proximity, 166
public keys, 124
Public Libraries link, 162
pull technologies, 356
push and pull content, resources
    feed installation, 350–356
    travel arrangement management,
        356–363
    weather information online, 348–350
push technologies, 350

Q

queries, developing, 146–147
Quick Tabs button, 80

R

rankings, 184
Really Simple Syndication. *See* RSS

real-time communications, 41
real-time strategy games, 374
refdesk.com Web site, 372
Refine Your Search boxes, 9
Refresh button, 74, 75, 82
relevance sorts, 170
remote communications, 42
resources
    award-winning Web sites, 371–372
    comparing special interest Web sites, 346–347
    educational opportunities, 367–369
    gaming sites, 373–376
    health information Web site, 339
        directory searches, 340–342
        special interest search, 342–346
    legal information, 366–367
    locating on Web
        document comparing, 160–161
        expert resources, 157–160
    multimedia, 376–379
    news and opinions
        Advanced Search features, 170–171
        business news searches, 172
        comparison document, 173
        finding at Google, 169–170
    online people locators, 364–366
    portals, 372–373
    push and pull content
        feed installation, 350–356
        travel arrangement management, 356–363
        weather information online, 348–350
    Wikis, 303
Restore Down button, 5, 64–65, 82
reverse lookups, 364
ReverseRecords.org Web site, 365
REVIEW listname command, 251
RSS (Really Simple Syndication), 76,
    277–278
    feeds, 348
    Firefox, 112
    installing feeds, 350–356
    Internet Explorer, 110
    Netscape Browser, 111
    news resources, 169
    Opera, 113
    Safari, 114

S

Safari features, 113–114
sandbox (wikis), 304
Save Picture dialog box, 97
Save Webpage dialog box, 96
scholarly resources, locating online,
    161–165
screen displays, 274
ScreenTips, 75, 287
scripts, 376
scroll bars, 86
Search button, 77
search engines, 18, 147
    blog location, 274–279
    changing default, 153

comparison, 151–152
identifying, 147–151
mailing lists, 247
operation, 183–185
search filters, 150
Search.com Web site, 181
searches
    advanced (*See* advanced searches)
    evaluating results, 185–188
    Firefox, 112
    Internet Explorer, 110
    Netscape Browser, 111
    Opera, 113
    popular directories, 180
    results checklists, 187–188
    Safari, 113
    World Wide Web, 144–145
        Address bar searches, 152–155
        developing strategy guidelines, 183–188
        expert resources, 157–161
        formulating keyword queries, 146–152
        Instant Search feature, 156–157
        locating online scholarly resources,
            161–165
        tools, 180–182
Secure Sockets Layer (SSL), 124–125
security
    Firefox, 112
    Internet Explorer, 110
    Netscape Browser, 111
    Opera, 113
    Safari, 114
    World Wide Web risks
        browsing strategies, 121–125
        Chat Rooms, 118–119
        e-mail, 120–121
        privacy, 116–117
        protecting children, 119–120
servers, 27–28
services packs, 110
SET listname conceal command, 251
SET listname digest command, 251
SET listname noconceal command, 251
settings, changing defaults, 155
shortcuts, e-mail netiquette, 244
shouting, netiquette, 242
signature files, e-mail messages, 218–221
SIGNOFF listname command, 251
SMTP (Simple Mail Transfer Protocol), e-mail, 241
social networking, 118
software
    blogs, 281
    Internet connection requirements, 32–33
    search engine, 147
    video conferencing, 316
Southland Gardens, World Wide Web collaboration, 271–335
    blog creation, 273–290
    newsgroups, 291–301
    synchronous communication tools, 311–317
    Web-based communication tools, 302–310

spam, e-mail, 244–245
special interest Web sites, 342
    Advanced Searches, 344–345
    search engine site comparisons,
        343–344
specialized databases, advanced searches, 173–179
spider, 147
sponsored links, 148
sponsored results, 148
sponsored sites, 148
spyware, 122
SSL (Secure Sockets Layer), 124–125
Start button, 4, 15
Start menu, 4
Status bars, 69, 82
Staysafe.org Web site, 121
Stop buttons, 75, 82
stop words, 156
streaming, 376
style sheets, 110
subject catalogs, 157
Subject lines, e-mail, 216
submenus, 65
SUBSCRIBE listname command, 251
subscribing, mailing lists, 249–251
SuperPages Web site, 365
surfing, 26
SurfWax, Inc. Web site, 181
Switchboard Web site, 365
synchronous communications, 41
    tools, 311–317
        chat, 312–314
        Internet telephony, 314–315
        IRC, 311–312
        video conferencing, 316–317
        VoIP, 314–315
synonyms, 146
syntax, 20

T

tabbed browsing, 22, 79–82
    Firefox, 112
    Internet Explorer, 110
    Netscape Browser, 111
    Opera, 113
    Safari, 114
Tabs, Internet Explorer, 82
tags, 278
Taskbars, 4, 82
TCP/IP (Transmission Control Protocol/Internet Protocol), 28
Telnet, 42–43
templates, 284
temporary Internet files, 73, 104
Temporary Internet Files and History Settings dialog box, 105
text
    customizing, Internet Explorer, 69–71
    printing Web content, 94–96
text shortcuts, e-mail netiquette, 244

THOMAS, 366–367
threads, newsgroups, 291, 296–301
thumbnails, 80
timestamped posts (blogs), 275
Title bars, Internet Explorer, 82
TLD (top level domain), 19, 275
toolbars, 64
   Formatting, 287
   hiding, 68–69
   Internet Explorer commands, 74–82
tools
   collaborative, 317
   Web searches, 180–182
Tools button, 65, 82
Tools command (Menu Bar Internet Explorer), 66
top level domain (TLD), 19, 275
trackback feature (blog), 276
transferring files, 42–43
Transmission Control Protocol/Internet Protocol (TCP/IP), 28
transmission media, 33
travel arrangement management, 356
   maps and directions, 357–360
   site exploration, 361–363
Trojan horse, 122
Tucows Web site, 377

U

Uniform Resource Locator. *See* URL
University Medical Center
   push and pull content
      feed installation, 350–356
      travel arrangement management, 356–363
      weather information online, 348–350
   resources
      comparing special interest Web sites, 346–347
      searching health information, 339–346
unmoderated lists, 248
unmoderated newsgroups, 299
UNSUBSCRIBE listname command, 251
unsubscribing, mailing lists, 249–251
urban legends, e-mail, 245
URL (Uniform Resource Locator), 6
   IP address comparison, 30
   locating numeric IP address, 30–31
   Web site requests, 27
US Search Web site, 365
USA.gov Web site, 373
Use current button, 84
Use default button, 84
USENET Newsgroup, 36–37, 43, 291–294
user IDs, e-mail, 209

V

video conferencing, 316–317
video logs (vlogs), 304–305
View command (Menu Bar Internet Explorer), 66
virtual high schools, 367
virtual libraries, 18
viruses, 122, 246

vloggers, 304
vlogosphere, 304
vlogs (video logs), 304–305
vodcasts, 350
voice messaging, e-mail, 240
Voice over Internet Protocol (VoIP), 314–315
VoIP (Voice over Internet Protocol), 314–315

W

W3C, 39
WAV files, 378
weather information online, 348–350
Web, 25
Web browsers, 4
Web cams, 309
Web logs. *See* blogs
Web pages, 6
   format, 29–30
   printing text and graphics, 94–96
   saving, 96–98
   viewing, 26
Web servers, 6
Web sites, 6. *See also* individual named Web sites
   award-winning, 371–372
   requesting URLs, 27
Web-based communication tools, 302–310
   bulletin boards, 305–307
   instant messaging, 307–310
   message boards, 305–307
   Vlogs, 304–305
   Web-based forums, 305–307
   Wikis, 302–304
web-based e-mail systems, 238–240
Web-based forums, 305–307
Web-based newsgroups, 294–296
The Webby Awards Web site, 372
webcasts, 366
Web100.com Web site, 372
whiteboard features (IM clients), 309
WhitePages Web site, 365
Wi-Fi (wireless fidelity), 13
   Internet connection
      methods, 33
      options, 34–35
wikiengines, 304
Wikipedia, 303
Wikis, 302–304
WikiWord, 304
wildcard characters, 168
wireless fidelity. *See* Wi-Fi
Wisenut Web site, 183
wizards, plug-in installation, 108
World Wide Web. *See* WWW
World Wide Web Consortium, 39
worms, 122
WWW (World Wide Web), 25, 62
   advanced searches
      Boolean operators, 166–169
      invisible web resources, 173–179
      news and opinion resources, 169–173

browsing, 63
  Address bar, 87–88
  default home page specification, 83–85
  Favorites Center, 90–93
  History feature, 88–90
  Internet Explorer commands, 65–74
  links, 86–87
  plug-ins, 107–108
  popular browser comparison, 108–115
  safe strategies, 121–125
  toolbar commands, 74–82
collaboration, 271–335
  blog creation, 273–290
  newsgroups, 291–301
  synchronous communication tools, 311–317
  Web-based communication tools, 302–310
defined, 43
managing content with Internet Explorer
  clearing cache and cookies, 102–104
  desktop shortcuts, 100–101
  e-mailing Web pages and links, 98–99
  history, 104–106
  printing text and graphics, 94–96
  saving Web pages, 96–98
searching, 144–145

  Address bar searches, 152–155
  developing strategy guidelines, 183–188
  formulating keyword queries, 146–152
  Instant Search feature, 156–157
  locate expert resources, 157–161
  locating online scholarly resources, 161–165
  tools, 180–182
security risks
  Chat Rooms, 118–119
  e-mail, 120–121
  privacy, 116–117
  protecting children, 119–120
WWW Virtual Library Web site, 167

X

Xanadu project, 38
XML (Extensible Markup Language), 348, 351

Y

Yahoo! Mail Web site, 239
Yahoo! People Search Web site, 365
Yahoo! Web site, 180
Yahooligans Web site, 372
YouTube Web site, 379